Contemporary Research and Practices for Promoting Financial Literacy and Sustainability

Lan Sun
Central Queensland University, Australia

IGI Global
PUBLISHER of TIMELY KNOWLEDGE

Published in the United States of America by
IGI Global
Business Science Reference (an imprint of IGI Global)
701 E. Chocolate Avenue
Hershey PA, USA 17033
Tel: 717-533-8845
Fax: 717-533-8661
E-mail: cust@igi-global.com
Web site: http://www.igi-global.com

Library of Congress Cataloging-in-Publication Data

Names: Sun, Lan, 1972- editor.
Title: Contemporary research and practices for promoting financial literacy and sustainability / edited by Lan Sun.
Description: Hershey, PA : Business Science Reference, [2024] | Includes bibliographical references and index. | Summary: "This book intends to collect a comprehensive list of research topics in the contemporary finance research"-- Provided by publisher.
Identifiers: LCCN 2023058658 (print) | LCCN 2023058659 (ebook) | ISBN 9798369308639 (hardcover) | ISBN 9798369308646 (ebook)
Subjects: LCSH: Finance--Research. | Finance--Study and teaching.
Classification: LCC HG152 .C67 2024 (print) | LCC HG152 (ebook) | DDC 332.072--dc23/eng/20240126
LC record available at https://lccn.loc.gov/2023058658
LC ebook record available at https://lccn.loc.gov/2023058659

British Cataloguing in Publication Data
A Cataloguing in Publication record for this book is available from the British Library.

Advances in Finance, Accounting, and Economics (AFAE) Book Series

Ahmed Driouchi
Al Akhawayn University, Morocco

ISSN:2327-5677
EISSN:2327-5685

MISSION

In our changing economic and business environment, it is important to consider the financial changes occurring internationally as well as within individual organizations and business environments. Understanding these changes as well as the factors that influence them is crucial in preparing for our financial future and ensuring economic sustainability and growth.

The **Advances in Finance, Accounting, and Economics (AFAE)** book series aims to publish comprehensive and informative titles in all areas of economics and economic theory, finance, and accounting to assist in advancing the available knowledge and providing for further research development in these dynamic fields.

Coverage

- Health Economics
- Economics of Risks, Uncertainty, Ambiguity, and Insurance
- Managerial Accounting
- Taxes
- E-Accounting
- Stock Market
- Field Research
- Statistical Analysis
- Applied Finance
- Finance

IGI Global is currently accepting manuscripts for publication within this series. To submit a proposal for a volume in this series, please contact our Acquisition Editors at Acquisitions@igi-global.com or visit: http://www.igi-global.com/publish/.

The (ISSN) is published by IGI Global, 701 E. Chocolate Avenue, Hershey, PA 17033-1240, USA, www.igi-global.com. This series is composed of titles available for purchase individually; each title is edited to be contextually exclusive from any other title within the series. For pricing and ordering information please visit http://www.igi-global.com/book-series/advances-finance-accounting-economics/73685. Postmaster: Send all address changes to above address.

Titles in this Series

For a list of additional titles in this series, please visit: www.igi-global.com/book-series

Risks and Challenges of AI-Driven Finance Bias, Ethics, and Security
Siraj Kariyilaparambu Kunjumuhammed (Modern College of Business and Science, Oman) Hisham Madi (Modern College of Business and Science, Oman) and Mahmoud Abouraia (Modern College of Business and Science, Oman)
Business Science Reference • copyright 2024 • 391pp • H/C (ISBN: 9798369321850) • US $335.00 (our price)

Global Developments in Central Bank Digital Currency
Peterson K. Ozili (Central Bank of Nigeria, Nigeria)
Business Science Reference • copyright 2024 • 307pp • H/C (ISBN: 9798369355886) • US $295.00 (our price)

Integrating RegTech Solutions for Industry 4.0
Swati Gupta (Universal AI University, India) Smita Gupta (Galgotias University, India) and Badri Narayanan Gopalakrishnan (University of Washington, USA)
Business Science Reference • copyright 2024 • 339pp • H/C (ISBN: 9798369333228) • US $235.00 (our price)

Safeguarding Financial Data in the Digital Age
Farah Naz (Department of Accounting and Finance, Kinnaird College for Women, Pakistan) and Sitara Karim (Department of Economics and Finance, Sunway University, Malaysia)
Business Science Reference • copyright 2024 • 331pp • H/C (ISBN: 9798369336335) • US $255.00 (our price)

Decentralized Finance and Tokenization in FinTech
Luan Vardari (University "Ukshin Hoti" Prizren, Kosovo) and Isuf Qabrati (University "Ukshin Hoti" Prizren, Kosovo)
Business Science Reference • copyright 2024 • 392pp • H/C (ISBN: 9798369333464) • US $275.00 (our price)

IGI Global
PUBLISHER of TIMELY KNOWLEDGE

701 East Chocolate Avenue, Hershey, PA 17033, USA
Tel: 717-533-8845 x100 • Fax: 717-533-8661
E-Mail: cust@igi-global.com • www.igi-global.com

Table of Contents

Detailed Table of Contents

to extensively explore household financial vulnerability, including its determinants, theoretical frameworks, assessment methodologies, and strategies for mitigation.

This chapter will examine the value of accounting for sustainability, as well as how its implementation supports sustainability and financial literacy in modern business operations. In order to increase transparency and accountability, the chapter will explore the crucial components of assessing sustainability and the necessity of related financial reporting disclosures. Businesses have become more aware of the importance of incorporating sustainability into their accounting procedures because of an increased emphasis on aspects relating to the environmental, social, and governance (ESG). This chapter intends to shed light on how businesses can track their sustainability performance and inform stakeholders of important information. By promoting financial literacy and sustainable practices, the chapter will help achieve the book's main goal of increasing knowledge regarding the dynamic relationship between sustainability and business today.

Water is one of the planet's essential and extensively used resource. However, it is predicted that around 3.2 billion people will face severe water shortages by 2030. Hence, there is an urgent need to expand water utilities, water infrastructure, and water treatment plants to maximally protect water resources. Investment in water is essential for supporting this cause, and private funding is a way to meet the financial needs of the water industry. This study examines returns and volatility of four water exchange-traded funds (ETFs). Using the GARCH, EGARCH, and TGARCH models, this study shows the existence of persistence of volatility among the four water ETFs at the 1% level. The analyses and results of this study show important implications for investors and stakeholders, enabling them to make appropriate decisions.

In a complex financial world, lack of awareness complicates money management and savings. Emphasizing financial literacy is vital for informed decision-making. This study explores global financial illiteracy, advocating international initiatives. In India, it assesses disparities and government activities and reviews tax-saving and mobile banking. Gaps include limited studies on Indian households, necessitating gender-specific analyses and research on education's impact. The methodology outlines justification, operational definitions, and data collection techniques. With ANOVA and descriptive statistics on 285 respondents, the study reveals demographic analysis, indicating higher financial literacy with age and a gender gap. Education positively correlates with financial literacy. Recommendations include interventions like financial seminars, collaboration with regulators, and destigmatizing money talks at home to enhance financial literacy and bridge gaps.

The dependence on digital financial technologies influences financial behaviors among people. This systematic review aims to identify and understand the variables interplay between digital financial literacy and financial behavior. The systematic literature review uses the PRISMA systematic review guidelines to identify and screen the literature. The results show there is a positive significant relation between digital financial literacy and financial behaviors. It was found that there are minimal studies on the variables interplaying between digital financial literacy and financial behavior. The interplaying variables identified are financial self-efficacy, financial confidence, self-control, financial autonomy, financial capability, psychological biases and digital, financial socialization, and socio-economic and demographic factors. This review develops a framework for future exploration explaining the relationship between digital financial literacy and financial behavior identifying financial wellbeing as the outcome.

Green finance is increasing its awareness and impact slowly but steadily across the globe. As it is envisioned, green financing is a regulated, organized, and well-coordinated financial activity with fine-tuned products and services, viz., loans, debt mechanisms, and investments, that's been designed to guarantee a healthier environmental result. It is expected that the green bond market possibly will be worth $2.36 trillion by 2023. To explore the receptivity of green financing and to understand its adoption among different countries, qualitative research was proposed with the support of interpretive philosophy. The green finance initiative scenarios from two countries were gathered through systematic literature review, case studies, and content analysis. Data extracted from the literature is analysed with proper coding and categorisation. The observations associated with two countries' analyses, viz., UK and India, clearly indicate that green financing is undeniably a vital approach that enables the shift to sustainable economic growth.

Financial technology (FinTech) has revolutionized the financial services industry, leading to the emergence of various financial innovations. Among these innovations, embedded finance has gained prominence as it integrates financial services into non-financial products and platforms. Additionally, the integration of artificial intelligence (AI) into financial processes has transformed how firms manage their financing and investment activities. This chapter provides an in-depth analysis of embedded finance and AI's impact on firm financing and investment strategies through case studies, highlighting the opportunities and challenges presented by these financial innovations.

The chapter aims to investigate the sustainable and social impacts of micro Fintech in Indonesia. To achieve the research goal, the chapter utilized the case of Amartha Micro Fintech firm based in Indonesia. Data were collected from the annual Amartha's social accountability/sustainability reports between 2016 and 2022. The chapter employed both descriptive and SWOT analyses to evaluate the sustainable impacts of Fintech in terms of social services, financial models, empowerment of women entrepreneurs, environmental awareness campaign, as well collaboration with external partners. The results of findings revealed substantial sustainable impacts of Amartha Fintech, particularly in providing social impact services such as health and education and the empowerment of women micro entrepreneurs. In addition, it has pushed its frontier in collaborating with external partners and donors in both domestic and international spheres. However, the SWOT analysis showed that the firm needs to integrate a green digital innovation framework into its business model.

Preface

Finance is about wealth accumulation and allocation of capital in an efficient manner. The changing in global economy, the advances in technology and financial innovations have reshaped the role of finance in many ways as we have observed today. The development of electronic trading platforms, digital currencies, and financial technologies have transformed the financial service business models. Fintech companies, embedded finance, sustainable finance and investment, green bonds and social bonds have emerged, offering innovative products that are changing the face as well as the purpose of finance. Finance education should be current and remain relevant to the changing of economy. Finance education should be also informative regarding finance history. The goal of finance teaching is to improve our financial literacy with a deeper understanding of the theoretical concepts and practical applications of finance through learning from the history and the emerging trends.

This book provides an avenue for the academic researchers and expert writers in the field of accounting and finance to contribute their cutting-edge scientific works to advance the fast-evolving financial markets. The introduction chapter provides an overall view for this book, that is, improving financial literacy through learning from the history and the emerging trends of finance research. Chapter 1 explores household financial vulnerability including its determinants, theoretical frameworks, assessment methodologies, and strategies for mitigation. Chapter 2 evaluates accounting sustainability from the perspective of accounting measurements and financial reporting disclosure, the purpose is to enhance the understanding of firm's sustainability performance and ensure that shareholders and stakeholders are well informed. Chapter 3 examines returns and volatility of water exchange-traded funds (ETFs), this chapter calls for investment in the water industry and private funding paves the way to meet the financial needs of the sector. Chapter 4 presents to us an in-depth investigation of financial literacy levels in Indian Households and Chapter 5 provides a systematic review for digital financial literacy and financial behaviours. Chapter 6 explores green finance initiatives scenarios from two countries that were gathered through systematic literature review, case studies, and content analysis. Chapter 7 reviews the initiatives and strategies for sustainable green finance with a comparative study between UK and India. The book concludes with two chapters in the field of FinTech, Chapter 8 reviews financial innovations in FinTech, suggesting the power of embedded finance and AI in firm financing and investment strategies; and Chapter 9 reports micro-Fintech practices in Indonesia and its impacts on sustainability.

This book intends to bridge the gap between academia and practice. It also offers accounting and finance graduates an opportunity to explore some of the 'hot topics' that the accounting and finance profession is more likely to encounter but are not necessarily addressed in standard textbooks. The book audience is composed of academics, researchers, industry practitioners, financial planners, consultants/advisors, accountants, auditors, economists, managers, decision makers, regulators concerned with the accounting and finance practices, and students in pursuing the accounting and finance degrees. The objective is to ensure that future accountants and finance practitioners are aware of the key issues in accounting and finance, and they are equipped with a solid understanding of the phenomenon that have re-shaped the financial landscape.

Lan Sun
Central Queensland University, Australia

Introduction

1. LEARNING FINANCE FROM THE HISTORY

At the end of World War II, the United States controlled two thirds of the world's gold and they insisted to create the Bretton Woods system (Ghizoni, 2013). The Bretton Woods system essentially is a system of fixed exchange rates, where the U.S. dollar's value was fixed against gold and other currencies would 'peg' the U.S. dollar. The system did not allow the capital to flow freely from one country to the another. Until 1971, in order to solve the problem of trade deficit and a costly war in Vietnam, Richard Nixon suspended dollar's convertibility into gold and put an end to the Bretton Woods system (Kenen, 2008). The exchange rate system then gradually moved to the float exchange rate, which completely changed the world in the way that a company could purchase materials or sell products in the currency other than its home currency. This also creates room for foreign exchange hedging. In 1972, a former lawyer and also the chairman of the Chicago Mercantile Exchange (CME), Leo Melamed, saw the business opportunity and he launched currency futures on the CME. This is the world's first financial futures exchange, under Melamed's leadership CME created US Treasury Bills futures in 1976, Eurodollars futures in 1981, and stock index futures in 1982. Leo Melamed is regarded as a pioneer of financial futures (Loo, 2014).

Options were known in the ancient history. The concept of trading an option date back to at least 350 B.C. Aristotle in his famous book *Politics* told the story about how a philosopher and mathematician made a fortune through using options to gain the right to use olive presses in a harvest (Aristotle, 1984). Some merchants in the Middle Ages of Mediterranean developed a similar instrument called credit contracts, where the seller of the contract agreed to buy cargo if the ship did not come back on time (Poitras, 2009). In 1973, Fischer Black and Myron Scholes from the University of Chicago developed a model for calculating the theoretical estimate of an option's price. At the same time, Robert Merton published a study and mathematically established the Black-Scholes model. The Chicago Board Options Exchange was then set up as a forum for trading options and the Black-Scholes model was widely applied in pricing options. Later, this model changed the landscape for options valuation and Myron Scholes and Robert Merton were awarded Nobel Prize in Economics in 1997.

The concept of swap is no more complicated than two parties swapping things. If one party has apples and another party has oranges, they both need the other's commodity, what they can do is to swap. In the 1970s, the idea of financial swap originated in the UK. The British government introduced a policy of taxing foreign exchange transactions that involved the British pounds, this policy made outflow of capital more expensive restricting the capital to leave the country and thereby increasing its domestic investment. To avoid such taxes, companies used back-to-back loans which were considered as an original swap (Hodgson, 2009). For example, one company located in the UK and the other located in the US. Two companies could swap loans denominated in their respective home currencies. This process allowed both companies to have access to the foreign capital market and avoid paying any foreign currency taxes.

In 1981, the first formalized currency swap was written in London between the World Bank and IBM. It allowed the World Bank to obtain Swiss Francs and German Marks to finance its operations in Switzerland and West Germany; and on the other side, IBM had borrowed large amounts of those currencies but needed US dollars. In 1981 the interest rate in the US was 17% as a result of the tight monetary policy to fight for inflation, while the interest rate was only 8% in Switzerland and 12% in West Germany (Park, 1984). Salomon Brothers suggested the idea of swap - that the World Bank swapped its dollars for the IBM's francs and marks. So, the World Bank swapped its dollar payment obligation to IBM in exchange for IBM's debt in Swiss franc and deutsche mark. This is also known as the first interest rate swap (Park, 1984). The standard '*vanilla*' interest rate swap often works between two parties holding fixed and variable interest rates debt obligations respectively. The party with fixed rate debt tends to worry about interest rate will decrease; while the party with variable rate debt normally is concerned that the interest rate will go high. Therefore, depending on the projection of whether interest rate will go high or low, the two parties maybe want to change their risk exposure and willing to swap the debt obligation and the interest payment. After the first swap showed to the world, now the market for swap grew to trillions of dollars. A recent development is credit-default swap (CDS) where investors can simply separate the interest rate risk from default risk.

In the 18th century BC, gold is regarded as wealth and currency. In Egypt and Mesopotamia, gold is deposited in temples for safe keeping. In Babylon at the time of Hammurabi, there are records that the priests of the temple lent gold to people in need. This is the earliest loans, and the concept of banking was born (Mesopotamian Economy and Money, from Facts and Details September 2018). Banking practices became more sophisticated in Greece - taking deposits and making loans, undertaking currency transactions and changing one currency to another, testing coins for weight and purity. By the 2nd century AD, Rome regularized the banking practices of Greece. The word 'bank' is rooted in the Latin meaning 'bench' - where money lenders used to hang out in Roman forum. The debt needed to be registered with public notaries, once the lump sum was paid off to a bank the debt could be officially retired (Woytek, 2014). But the banking business became less flourish after the collapse of the Roman empire and usury was seen morally offensive when the Christian church was hostile towards the charging of interest.

Another financial concept originated from the Ancient Romans is 'stock exchange' involving people met outdoors in the Roman Forum at the Temple of Castor to buy and sell shares. The shares in Latin were called '*partes*' and the companies were called '*publicani*'. The Roman corporations always had trade with the government, for example they would feed horses for the army. Sometimes they fed geese, the geese were hallowed in Ancient Rome because once they warned of an invasion by cackling. They started to talk about share prices in the Roman forum at the temple, which is the earliest version stock exchange (Strangio, 2022). After the fall of the Roman Empire, the stock exchange disappears. It was such a long gap until English stock exchange was born. In 1602 the Dutch East India Trading Company was formed. The company was a 'joint stock' company that a number of merchants and investors jointed owned the company and shared the profit and risk of the operation.

By the end of the 17th century there were at least 100 companies selling stocks in London. In 1571, Queen Elizabeth I opened the first English stock exchange - the Royal Exchange (Smith, 1929). However, stockbrokers were banned from entering the Royal Exchange because they were too rowdy. They had to operate in the streets and turned to local coffee shops. Trading stocks in coffee house was a big thing in the late 1600s. The coffee houses often employed boys to wait near London's docks where thousands of ships were coming and going, once they heard any news happened to the vessels they ran quickly to the coffee houses. Then they would report to the houses and the news would be displayed on a board behind the bar. Stock prices fluctuated according to the news that received - if sailors returned with packed boat the price would up; while the price would down if the ship loss of cargoes.

Jonathan's Coffee House in Change Alley, near the Bank of England's office, was the most popular one among those coffee shops. Jonthan's Coffee House was opened by Jonathan Miles in 1680 and in 1698 the meetings of stockbrokers became more organised. John Castaing was a broker who spent a lot of time at Jonathan's and he took the initiative and began to post stock prices, commodity prices and exchange rates on the wall. Sooner he printed the sheet with list of prices and news on every Tuesday and Friday as *'The Course of Exchange'* (Neal, 1982). The stockbrokers also used auctions to carry out their transactions, known as 'by the inch of candle auction' as it only lasted for as long as a candle would burn. This is the earliest evidence of organised stock exchange. Surprisingly, the famous London Stock Exchange grew out of Jonathan's Coffee House. The stockbrokers continued to meet at Jonathan's Coffee House to buy and sell for many years until 1773 when 150 brokers decided to start a more official exchange (Stott, 1973). They moved into a new building in Sweeting's Alley which had a formal dealing room on the ground floor and a coffee room upstairs to keep their tradition. The new place they called it 'the Stock Exchange'. Initially brokers only needed to pay an entrance fee to trade in the Stock Exchange, but in 1801 a formal annual membership fee was introduced. Since then, a regulated exchange - the London Stock Exchange was born. The financial innovation of stock exchange was suggested as a turning point in finance history and has shaped the financial institutions today.

2. THE EFFICIENT MARKET HYPOTHESIS AS A FOUNDATIONAL THEORY IN FINANCE

There are many theories in finance. The classical efficient market hypothesis serves as the foundation for the fields of asset pricing, corporate finance, financial derivatives and the like. The efficient market hypothesis (EMH) suggests that at any given time period, stock prices fully, immediately reflect all relevant available information, no one can easily 'time' the market for excess risk-adjust return over long term.

Samuelson (1965) suggested that asset price in an efficient market should fluctuate randomly through time because of the unanticipated information. Fama (1970) started to use the term EMH in his study '*Efficient Capital Markets*'. This study argued it is impossible for an individual to beat the market consistently in an active market because the stock price already reflected all available information. He further demonstrated that market could be efficient at three forms - weak, sem-istrong and strong, based on what information was reflected in prices. Fama (1976) showed that stock price evolves as a random walk with drift. The drift parameter is the mean value of returns (or asset's expected rate of return). Statistically, he suggested that stock returns just fluctuate randomly around their mean value. An investor attempting to predict today's price cannot do any better than use yesterday's price. Today's price differs from yesterday's in a way that is defined by an error term which is an unpredictable shock from new information. Beechey et al. (2000) summarized the previous evidence and concluded that on balance the hypothesis of 'stock price follows a random walk' was at least approximately true, and thus no one could predict future returns by analyzing past stocks price. They further argued that stock returns were partially predictable, both in the short term and long term. Efficiency was documented in various markets: the New York Stock Exchange (Schwert, 1977); the treasury bill market (Roll, 1970); the auction market (Stein, 1977); and the derivative market (Larson, 1964; Mandelbrot, 1964).

In practice, however, many active portfolio managers are trying to beat the market and earn a high return. A well-known case would be Warren Buffett, who have beaten the market by investing in undervalued stocks. The debate therefore raised - if market is efficient, investors will be better off by holding an index fund since none of the active founds will constantly outperform the market; but why active managers still beat the market? Grinblatt and Titman (1992) studied the persistence of mutual funds' performance and documented that mutual fund managers can earn excess returns after controlling for firm size, dividend yield, interest rate, beta, past returns and skewness. Finnerty (1976) studied 30,000 individual insider transactions between January 1969 and December 1972 and suggested that insiders are able to beat the market. Roll (1983), Haugen and Lakonishok (1988) revealed a systematic difference in returns by months. They all found stock market anomalies, which challenge the orthodox theory of efficient market hypothesis.

Whether fundamental analysis or technical tool can be constantly used to predict future return? Does stock price follow a 'random walk'? These questions remain unresolved. To date, random walks have been increasingly tested in the worldwide markets, including the United Kingdom (Poon, 1996); Spain (Regúlez and Zarraga 2002); the Czech Republic (Hajek 2002); Korea (Ayadi and Pyun, 1994; Ryoo and Smith 2002); China (Lee et al. 2001); Hong Kong (Cheung and Coutts 2001).

3. THE EMERGENCE OF SUSTAINABLE INVESTING

Sustainable investing, also known as impact investing or social responsible investment, is a style of investing that considers both financial returns and environmental, social and corporate governance (ESG) objectives (Sun and Small, 2022). The essence of sustainable investing is about long-term impact, not short-term performance. It aims to produce competitive financial performance on an ongoing basis. It also aims to help companies to establish a more stakeholder-centric model of corporate behaviour in a long term.

Sustainable investing has ancient origins. In 1139, the Catholic Church imposed a universal prohibition on usury (Lewison, 1999). Islamic investors also avoid investing in interest-based financial institutions based on the teaching of the Koran. The investment screens have evolved over time and broadly can be classified into negative screens and positive screens. The first generation and the most basic impact investing strategies is negative screens which can be applied to an asset pool such as the S&P 500 stocks. A typical negative screen excludes tobacco, alcohol, gambling, weapons, nuclear power industries, or companies with poor performance in labour relations and environment protection. The second generation of impact investing is mostly based on positive screens. A positive screen will select companies with a good track record in corporate governance, labour relations, renewable energy usage, and the promotion of cultural diversity. Then there is the third generation of impact investing, which is known as the approach of 'sustainability' or 'triple bottom line' integrating both negative and positive screens with the economic, environmental and social criteria (i.e. profit, planet and people). The fourth generation is the ethical funds, which combines the third-generation sustainable investing approach with shareholder activism and commitment on environmental issues, global labour standards and employment conditions etc.

Sustainable investing is becoming a phenomenon - not only policymakers, corporates and institutional investors show the interest, individual investors also start to incorporate respective sustainability ratings in investment decisions. For example, investors tend to prefer mutual funds with high sustainability ratings in ESG criteria and those more 'sustainable' mutual funds attract high net inflows in investment (Hartzmark and Sussman, 2019). Most sustainable funds focus on using ESG metrics to evaluate companies. Sustainable investors are not only interested in financial returns but also in achieving positive environmental and societal impact. The sustainable funds help the investors to achieve goals by identifying companies with lower ESG risks or has embed sustainability into their business model.

The growing interest in sustainable investing has led to the development of evaluation matrix on how well companies has performed on ESG pillars. In 2016, MorningStar launched a MorningStar Sustainability Rating. The purpose is to classify funds with ESG scores relative to their MorningStar peers. Morningstar first published sustainability ratings in March of 2016. There were 20,000 mutual funds, representing a market value of $8 trillion dollars, were ranked and given a rating between one to five globes (Morningstar, 2020). To judge a fund's financial profile, investors can start own research from the website like Morningstar and see how the fund performed over various time periods such as three-, five- and ten-years relative to peers.

4. UNDERSTANDING THE FINANCIAL VULNERABILITY

Financial vulnerability can be viewed as the risk of exposure to potential unfavourable financial event. A better understanding of financial vulnerability will improve households' financial management and reduce poverty. Financial distress is more likely to occur among the low wealth asset households, especially if they are facing large financial liabilities.

Swain and Floro (2007) define financial vulnerability as household's ability to cope with risk, shocks, and their attitude towards risks. Jappelli et al. (2013) conceptualise financial vulnerability as an inability to repay financial debt. Lewis and AV Lewis (2014) describe financial vulnerability as the vulnerable conditions that exclude and marginalise individuals from participating in economic, social and cultural activities (Lewis and AV Lewis, 2014). Anderloni et al. (2012) consider households as financial vulnerable if there is over commitment to excess indebtedness, or other financial instabilities, such as the inability to handle utility bills, rental payment and other daily expenses. Households who have experienced unemployed and received low income are regarded as financially vulnerable. Low income and unemployed working status are found to be significantly associated with financial vulnerability, that is, households with low incomes and employment tend to show greater difficulty in paying their living expenses (Al-Mamun and Mazumder, 2015; Rodrigo, 2016; Yusof et al., 2015).

Studies from Austria, Italy, and UK tend to view financial vulnerability as income poverty (Albacete & Lindner, 2013; Guarcello et.al, 2010; Lewis & AV Lewis, 2014). Vulnerable households with poverty possess insufficient financial resources for coping with unexpected crises. While in Ireland, Murphy and Scott (2014) view financial vulnerability as asset poverty. In their study, financial vulnerability is measured by housing crash, economic crisis and austerity conditions and they find that financial vulnerable households are more likely from the areas with an over housing supply. Al-Mamun and Mazumder (2015) find that financial vulnerable households tend to show lower liquid assets and higher leverage in balance sheet. In Australia, Schofield et al. (2010) survey 8,864 people between age 45 to 64 and find that financial vulnerable individuals possess characteristics of low wealth asset, who have retired earlier with health conditions, and who have inability to cope financial distress. In their study, financial vulnerability is measured by amount of wealth accumulation and income predictor.

In Malaysia, the Poverty Line Income (PLI) is used to assess the households' poverty status. Households' Poverty Line Income is measured based on the households' minimum requirement on the basis necessities, which is the standards set by the Department of Social Welfare. A few studies' findings revealed further that Malaysia urban households are financially vulnerable as compared with households in rural area (Yusof, Rokis & Jusof, 2015). Malaysia urban households with more than a fifth of the members are financially vulnerable; urban households are not able to survive for at least three month if their income is cut off. One of the core reasons of high poverty rate among urban households is due to the cumulative growth of urbanization, that the level of urbanization was 34.2% in 1980 and reached 71% in 2010 (Yusof, Rokis & Jusof, 2015).

Financial vulnerability increases with the decrease in welfare. As insufficient financial security and disability in providing adequate post-retirement income are suggested to be the factors contributing to high financial vulnerability (Lin and Grace, 2007; Rodrigo, 2016). Financial vulnerability of households increases the level of poverty. The previous literature shows a strong relationship between financial vulnerability and poverty (Al-Mamun and Mazumder, 2015; Lewis & AV Lewis, 2014). People are said to be in poverty if there is inadequate income and resources to provide them a living standard which is acceptable by the society (European Commission, 2004). As a solution, finance and economic programs should assist households to manage their finance effectively. The government should protect households and help them to be in a better financial position against any form of external shocks. The programme should look into how to increase households' income, ability to cope with external shocks, credit rationing, and how to reduce financial vulnerability.

5. THE RISE OF ESG ETFS

Exchange-traded funds (ETFs) are investment vehicles the pool stocks, bonds, commodities, derivatives or a combination of securities together. If investors purchase ETF shares, they do not directly buy the underlying assets, instead investors will get a slice of the entire portfolio in just one transaction. ETFs trade like a stock, investors can buy and sell on the stock exchange. ETFs usually track the performance of an index and thus are considered as passive funds. Due to the convenience, the number of ETFs and the value of fund assets have risen dramatically - from 2005 to 2019, the number of ETFs increased from 453 to 6,658, representing an annual growth rate of 19.6 per cent; the total value of fund assets has increased from $418 billion to $5,436 billion, which is more than tenfold (UNCTAD, 2020). In 2019, the U.S. has the most developed ETF market, with 30 per cent of all ETFs worldwide and the total value of ETF assets under management accounting for 71 per cent of the global market.

Figure 1. Number of ETFs worldwide and assets under management (AUM), 2005 – 2019 (billions of dollars)

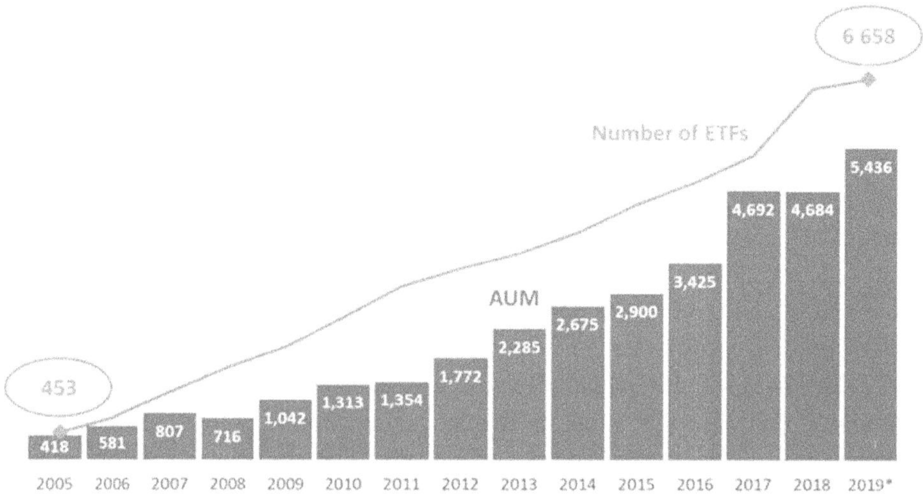

Source: UNCTAD (2020)

ESG ETFs are the exchange-traded funds based on corporate environmental, social and governance (ESG) profile. The funds use the ESG credentials in portfolio selection and asset management. The number of ESG ETFs has jumped from 39 in 2009 to 221 in 2019, the growth is accelerated particularly after 2015 with a net increase of 153 ESG ETFs in less than four years. The total value of ETF assets under management has grown from $6 billion in 2015 to $25 billion in 2019. The total value of ESG ETFs is highly concentrated in Europe and the U.S. with a total value of 56 per cent for Europe and 41 per cent for the U.S. in 2019. Despite being the world's largest ETF market, the U.S. ESG ETFs growth lags behind Europe. A few big players are leading the ESG ETFs market. For example, MSCI is the leading provider with 122 ESG ETFs that track an MSCI sustainability index. MSCI accounts for 55 per cent of the ESG ETFs around the world and UBS and iShares capture 46 per cent.

Figure 2. Number of ESG ETFs by the top 7 index providers and ETF providers

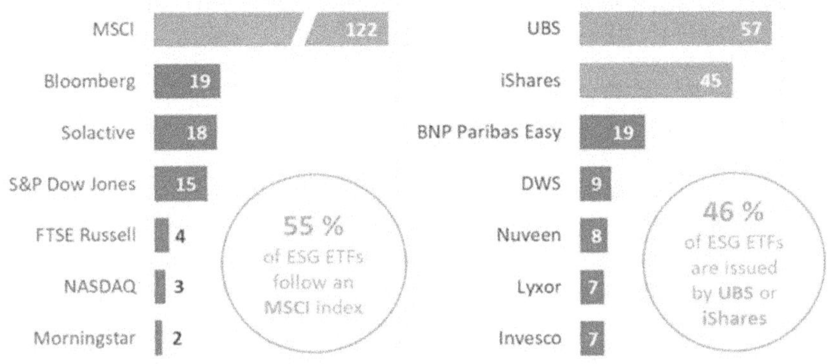

Source: UNCTAD (2020)

6. ESG, ETFS, SDGS, AND SUSTAINABILITY LINKAGE

Many countries have enacted regulations to foster sustainable investment practices and Europe has been the main driver for ESG ETFs growth. The EU introduced the Sustainable Finance Action Plan in May 2018 to promote investments in sustainable development. The Sustainable Finance Action Plan proposes stringent disclosure of ESG risks from both providers and investors. Providers must outline all ESG risks for the financial products they offer; and investors must integrate ESG risks in their decision making. Under the proposal, all financial firms that are involved in assets management and investment for their clients will have to inform the European Commission of how their practices are impacting the planet and local environment. These rules require greater disclosure on sustainable investments, sustainability risks and imposes mandatory climate-related reporting (EU, 2019). The regulation has not only improved the transparency in the sustainability disclosure, but also forced many investors to pay closer attention to the topic of sustainability when they are making investment decisions. The proposal also intends to provide a clear definition of ESG and if providers want to label products as environmentally sustainable, then what are the common metrics should be used in classification of the financial products.

Introduced in 2006, the United Nations Principles for Responsible Investment (UN PRI) currently has over 1,000 signatories, including asset owners, investment managers, and professional service partners, who seek to integrate ESG factors into investment practice (UNCTAD, 2014). To act on climate change, worldwide leaders signed Paris Agreement and also agreed on the United Nations Sustainable

Development Goals (SDGs) in 2015. To achieve the United Nations Sustainable Development Goals (SDGs), there is a need for $2.5 trillion a year investment in developing countries' infrastructure, agriculture, energy and public services for a period from 2015 to 2030 (UNCTAD, 2014).

Figure 3. SDG coverage by ESG ETFs

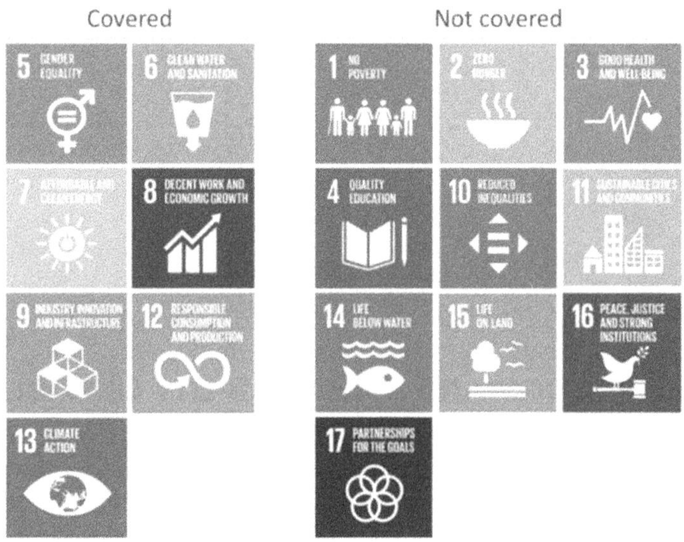

Source: UNCTAD (2020)

The agreement also requires a transition to green and sustainable financial markets through the promotion of green financial products and the greening of mainstream financial markets. The 17 UN Sustainable Development Goals (SDGs) provide a useful framework to guide sustainable investing. One potential investment vehicle is ESG ETFs. ESG ETFs adopt a thematic strategy target specific SDGs - climate action (SDG 13), gender equality (SDG 5), affordable and clean energy (SDG 7), industry, innovation and infrastructure (SDG 9), decent work and economic growth (SDG 8), responsible consumption and production (SDG 12), clean water and sanitation (SDG 6). Almost 90% of themed ESG ETFs follow 3 of the 17 SDGs. The other 10 SDGs, No Poverty (SDG 1), Zero Hunger (SDG 2), Good Health and Well Being (SDG 3) and Quality Education (SDG 4) are not covered by ESG ETFs. While ESG metrics can assist investors to identify good investments from a risk and return perspective, the SDG provides a broader framework that allows investors to assess the impact from investing.

REFERENCES

Al-Mamun, A., & Mazumder, M. N. H. (2015). Impact of Microcredit on Income, Poverty, and Economic Vulnerability in Peninsular Malaysia. *Development in Practice*, 25(3), 333–346. 10.1080/09614524.2015.1019339

Albacete, N., & Lindner, P. (2013). Household Vulnerability in Austria–A Microeconomic Analysis based on the Household Finance and consumption survey. *Financial Stability Report*, *25*, 57-73.

Anderloni, L., Bacchiocchi, E., & Vandone, D. (2012). Household Financial Vulnerability: An Empirical Analysis. *Research in Economics*, 66(3), 284–296. 10.1016/j.rie.2012.03.001

Aristotle, . (1984). *The politics. Translated and with an introduction, notes and glossary by Carnes Lord.* University of Chicago Press.

Ayadi, O. F., & Pyun, C. S. (1994). An Application of Variance Ratio Tests to the Korean Securities Market. *Journal of Banking & Finance*, 18(4), 643–658. 10.1016/0378-4266(94)00012-3

Beechey, M., Gruen, D., & Vickery, J. (2000). *The Efficient Market Hypothesis: A Survey, Economic Research Department.* Reserve Bank of Australia, Research Discussion Paper 2000-01.

Cheung, K. C., & Coutts, J. A. (2001). A Note on Weak Form Market Efficiency in Security Prices: Evidence from the Hong Kong Stock Exchange. *Applied Economics Letters*, 8(6), 407–410. 10.1080/135048501750237865

EU. (2019). Unsubstantiated or Misleading Claims about Sustainability Characteristics and Benefits of an Investment Product. Press Release, 7 March 2019. Brussels.

European Commission. (2004). Joint Report on Social Inclusion. Employment and Social Affairs. Social Security and Social Inclusion, European Commission, Directorate-General for Employment and Social Affairs, Unit E.2, Brussels. Available at:_https://ec.europa.eu/employment_social/social_inclusion/docs/final_joint_inclusion_report_2003_en.pdf

Facts and Details. (2018). Mesopotamian Economy and Money. https://factsanddetails.com/world/cat56/sub363/item1514.html

Fama, E. (1970). Efficient Capital Markets: A Review of Theory and Empirical Work. *The Journal of Finance*, 25(2), 383–417. 10.2307/2325486

Fama, E. (1976). *Foundations of Finance.* Basic Books.

Finnerty, J. E. (1976). Insiders and Market Efficiency. *The Journal of Finance*, 31(4), 1141–1148. 10.1111/j.1540-6261.1976.tb01965.x

Ghizoni, S.K. (2013). *Creation of the Bretton Woods System*. Federal Reserve History.

Grinblatt, M., & Titman, S. (1992). The Persistence of Mutual Fund Performance. *The Journal of Finance*, 47(5), 1977–1984. 10.1111/j.1540-6261.1992.tb04692.x

Guarcello, L., Mealli, F., & Rosati, F. C. (2010). Household Vulnerability and Child Labor: The Effect of Shocks, Credit Rationing, and Insurance. *Journal of Population Economics*, 23(1), 169–198. 10.1007/s00148-008-0233-4

Hajek, J. (2002). Weak-form Efficiency in the Czech Equity Market. *Politicka Ekonomie*, 50(3), 377–389.

Hartzmark, S. M., & Sussman, A. B. (2019). Do investors value sustainability? A natural experiment examining ranking and fund flows. *The Journal of Finance*, 74(6), 2789–2837. 10.1111/jofi.12841

Haugen, R., & Lakonishok, J. (1988). *The Incredible January Effect*. Dow Jones-Irwin.

Hodgson, R. (2009). The Birth of the Swap. *Financial Analysts Journal*, 65(3), 32–35. 10.2469/faj.v65.n3.4

Jappelli, T., Pagano, M., & Di Maggio, M. (2013). Households' Indebtedness and Financial Fragility. *Journal of Financial Management. Markets and Institutions*, 1(1), 23–46.

Kenen, P. B. (2008). Bretton Woods System. In *The New Palgrave Dictionary of Economics*. Palgrave Macmillan. 10.1057/978-1-349-95121-5_2669-1

Larson, A. B. (1964). Measurement of a Random Process in Futures Prices. In Cootner, J. (Ed.), *The Random Character of Stock Market Prices* (pp. 219–230). MIT Press.

Lee, C. F., Chen, G. M., & Rui, O. M. (2001). Stock Returns and Volatility on China's Stock Markets. *Journal of Financial Research*, 24(4), 523–543. 10.1111/j.1475-6803.2001.tb00829.x

Lewis, & , & Lewis, . (2014). Processes of Vulnerability in England? Place, Poverty and Susceptibility. *Disaster Prevention and Management*, 23(5), 586–609. 10.1108/DPM-03-2014-0044

Lewison, M. (1999). Conflicts of Interest? The Ethics of Usury. *Journal of Business Ethics*, 22(4), 327–339. 10.1023/A:1006164904326

Lin, Y., & Grace, M. F. (2007). Household Life Cycle Protection: Life Insurance Holdings, Financial Vulnerability, and Portfolio Implications. *The Journal of Risk and Insurance*, 74(1), 141–173. 10.1111/j.1539-6975.2007.00205.x

Loo, J. (2014). Leo Melamed: The Market Maker. Chicago Daily Law Bulletin. https://www.chicagolawbulletin.com/archives/2014/09/09/leo-melamed-profile-9-9-14

Mandelbrot, B. (1964). The Variation of Certain Speculative Prices. In Cootner, J. (Ed.), *The Random Character of Stock Market Prices* (pp. 307–332). MIT Press.

Morningstar. (2020). The Morningstar Sustainability Rating Methodology. Available at: https://www.morningstar.com/content/dam/marketing/shared/Company/Trends/Sustainability/Detail/Documents/SustainabilityRatingMethodology2019.pdf

Murphy, E., & Scott, M. (2014). Household Vulnerability in Rural Areas: Results of an Index Applied during a Housing Crash, Economic Crisis and under Austerity Conditions. *Geoforum*, 51, 75–86. 10.1016/j.geoforum.2013.10.001

Neal, L. (1982). Efficient Markets in the Eighteenth Century? Stock Exchanges in Amsterdam and London. *Business and Economic History*, 11, 81–101.

Park, Y. S. (1984). Currency Swaps as a Long-Term International Financing Technique. *Journal of International Business Studies*, 15(3), 47–54. 10.1057/palgrave.jibs.8490494

Poitras, G. (2009). The Early History of Option Contracts. In Hafner, W., & Zimmermann, H. (Eds.), *Vinzenz Bronzin's Option Pricing Models*. Springer. 10.1007/978-3-540-85711-2_24

Poon, S. H. (1996). Persistence and Mean Reversion in UK Stock Returns. *European Financial Management*, 2(2), 169–196. 10.1111/j.1468-036X.1996.tb00037.x

Regúlez, M., & Zarraga, A. (2002). Common Features between Stock returns and Trading Volume. *Applied Financial Economics*, 12(12), 885–893. 10.1080/09603100110053317

Rodrigo, S. K. (2016). Working for Welfare: Inequality and Shared Vulnerability among the Malaysian Middle Classes. *Malaysian Journal of Economic Studies*, 53(1), 9.

Roll, R. (1970). *The Behaviour of Interests Rates*. Basic Books.

Roll, R. (1983). On Computing Mean Returns and the Small Firm Premium. *Journal of Financial Economics*, 12(3), 371–386. 10.1016/0304-405X(83)90055-7

Ryoo, H. J., & Smith, G. (2002). Korean Stock Prices under Price Limits: Variance Ratio Tests of Random Walks. *Applied Financial Economics*, 12(8), 545–553. 10.1080/09603100010015789

Samuelson, P. A. (1965). Proof That Properly Anticipated Prices Fluctuate Randomly. *Industrial Management Review*, 6(2), 41–49.

Schofield, D. J., Percival, R., Passey, M. E., Shrestha, R. N., Callander, E. J., & Kelly, S. J. (2010). The Financial Vulnerability of Individuals with Diabetes. *The British Journal of Diabetes & Vascular Disease*, 10(6), 300–304. 10.1177/1474651410385864

Schwert, W. (1977). Stock Exchange Seats as Capital Assets. *Journal of Financial Economics*, 4(1), 51–78. 10.1016/0304-405X(77)90036-8

Smith, C. F. (1929). The Early History of the London Stock Exchange. *The American Economic Review*, 19(2), 206–216.

Stein, J. P. (1977). The Monetary Appreciation of Paintings. *Journal of Political Economy*, 85(5), 1021–1036. 10.1086/260619

Stott, J. R. (1973). The Stock Exchange. In *Basic Commerce for First Examinations*. Palgrave. 10.1007/978-1-349-81561-6_20

Strangio, D. (2022). The Roman Stock Exchange between the 19th and 20th Centuries, A History of the Italian Stock Market. In Coffman, D. M., Moore, T. K., Allen, M., & Reinert, S. (Eds.), *Palgrave Studies in the History of Finance*. Springer Nature.

Sun, L., & Small, G. (2022). Has Sustainable Investing Made an Impact in the Period of COVID-19? Evidence from Australian Exchange Traded Funds. *Journal of Sustainable Finance & Investment*, 12(1), 251–273. 10.1080/20430795.2021.1977577

Swain, R. B., & Floro, M. (2007). *Effect of Microfinance on Vulnerability, Poverty and Risk in Low Income Households*. Department of Economics, Uppsala University.

UNCTAD. (2014). *World Investment Report: Investing in the SDGs: An Action Plan*. United Nations.

UNCTAD. (2020). Leveraging the Potential of ESG ETFs for Sustainable Development. UNCTAD.

Woytek, B. E. (2014). Monetary Innovation in Ancient Rome: The Republic and Its Legacy. In Bernholz, P., & Vaubel, R. (Eds.), *Explaining Monetary and Financial Innovation. Financial and Monetary Policy Studies* (Vol. 39). Springer. 10.1007/978-3-319-06109-2_8

Yusof, S. A., Rokis, R. A., & Jusoh, W. J. W. (2015). Financial Fragility of Urban Households in Malaysia. *Jurnal Ekonomi Malaysia*, 49(1), 15–24. 10.17576/JEM-2015-4901-02

Chapter 1
Role of the Financial System for Sustainable Development:
Evidence From OECD Countries

Ecenur Ugurlu Yildirim
https://orcid.org/0000-0001-6465-4781
Social Sciences University of Ankara, Turkey

ABSTRACT

The challenges posed by industrialization and resource depletion complicate achieving sustainable development, necessitating judicious resource utilization. This study explores how capital allocation, via market mechanisms or financial institutions, impacted sustainable development from 2001 to 2019 in OECD countries using dynamic panel data techniques. Sustainable development, responding to resource depletion, seeks responsible resource management for collective human benefit. Research on financial systems' impact on economic growth reveals contrasting views, emphasizing banks' risk management and markets' efficiency. This study uncovers short-term positive effects of a bank-based system and long-term benefits of a market-based one on sustainable development, emphasizing the nuanced interplay of information asymmetry, innovation, and financing decisions. This research, pioneering in underscoring financial structure's significance in sustainable development, implies policymakers must choose financial systems carefully for sustainable growth.

DOI: 10.4018/979-8-3693-0863-9.ch001

1. INTRODUCTION AND LITERATURE REVIEW

Sustainable development, which encompasses economic, sociological, and environmental factors, is the optimal approach for countries aiming to maximize well-being within the constraints of limited resources (Ulucak et al., 2020). However, as industrialization and resource depletion increase, achieving sustainable development becomes more challenging, despite the goal of minimizing environmental pollution (Rehman et al., 2021). The prudent utilization of resources is crucial for attaining sustainable development. In this context, the allocation of capital by investors and corporations can occur through either market mechanisms or banks, and these two components of the financial system may prioritize resource distribution differently. This study focuses on examining the influence of the financial system on promoting sustainable development in OECD countries from 2001 to 2019, employing dynamic panel data techniques. Notably, this study represents the first attempt to investigate the significance of financial structure on sustainable development.

Over two decades ago, the Brundtland Commission, in its influential publication "Our Common Future", introduced and explained the concept of sustainable development (Barkemeyer et al., 2011; WCED, 1987). The concept of sustainable development emerged as a response to the depletion of natural resources and the need to manage them responsibly for the benefit of humanity (Ramachandran, 2000). In the realm of the real economy, financial development has the potential to impact climate change through various channels (Chang et al., 2019). On one hand, financial development can stimulate economic growth, leading to increased energy use and carbon emissions (Shahbaz et al., 2013). It can also drive consumer credit and consumption of polluting goods, further exacerbating carbon emissions (Dong et al., 2021; Xu et al., 2022). On the other hand, some studies suggest that financial development can facilitate investments in low-carbon technologies, resulting in reduced emissions (Chang, 2015; Yang and Tang, 2021). A robust financial system can provide funding for renewable technologies at favorable rates, promoting investment and meeting energy demands (Aluko and Obalade, 2020). Additionally, financial development can support technology advancements through green finance, contributing to emissions reduction (Churchill et al., 2019).

The categorization of financial systems into market-based or bank-based depends on whether banks or financial markets are utilized by investors and corporations to acquire capital (Ugurlu-Yildirim and Ordu-Akkaya, 2022). Each classification has its own advantages and limitations (Uzunkaya, 2012). Extensive research has been conducted to examine the impact of different financial systems on economic growth and compare the benefits and drawbacks of market-based and bank-based systems. Proponents of the bank-based theory highlight the crucial role of banks in economic growth, as they excel in handling moral hazards and exhibit superior performance in environments with imperfect contract implementation (Goldsmith, 1969; Stulz, 2000). They argue that bank-based systems outperform market-based systems, particularly in the early stages of economic development, due to banks' ability to identify sound investments and effectively mobilize savings (Stiglitz, 1985). Banks, through their long-term relationships with businesses and selective information disclosure, help mitigate issues related to information asymmetry (Boot et al., 1993). In contrast, proponents of the market-based theory assert that market-based systems are superior, as they are better equipped to address problems arising from inadequate information, allocate capital efficiently, and provide risk management tools (Allen and Gale, 1999). However, other research suggests that these two systems are not necessarily competitors but rather complementary to each other (Levine, 2002; Arize et al., 2018).

However, the understanding of the role of financial systems in sustainable development is still limited. In recent years, sustainable investing has successfully captured the interest of global investors. Also known as impact investing or socially responsible investment, sustainable investing is an investment approach that takes into account both financial returns and objectives related to environmental, social, and corporate governance (ESG). The environmental aspect focuses on carbon fuels, the social aspect includes considerations such as workplace diversity and avoidance of tobacco or weapons production, while governance pertains to shareholder democracy (Sun and Small, 2021). Financial institutions hold significant importance as they contribute to global economic development and overall societal well-being (Jones et al., 2017). Furthermore, they indirectly contribute to environmental protection by supporting environmentally conscious firms through their lending practices (Chatzitheodorou et al., 2021). The 2021 United Nations Climate Change Conference held in Glasgow identified finance and the utilization of financial strategies for sustainable development as primary themes. The conference emphasized the mobilization of public and private sector finance to support global net-zero emissions, reinforcing market resilience through climate change mitigation and adaptation measures (Kuo et al., 2023; United Nations, 2021). In the 2022 United Nations Climate Change Conference, banks faced increased pressure to address climate change (Kuo et al., 2023). Recognizing the crucial role of the business community in sustainable development, banking institutions have started incorporating sustainable criteria into their lending processes to manage risks associated with lending decisions. Increasing stakeholder demand for sustainability-related information, the aftermath of the financial crisis, and the financial sector's role in sustainable development have motivated many banking institutions to disclose their sustainability practices. Research findings indicate that the banking sector prioritizes Sustainable Development Goals (SDGs) that promote economic growth, decent work, fairness, and transparent processes across all levels (Sardianou et al., 2021). Investors prioritize sustainability by investing in companies excelling in environmental, social, and governance (ESG) aspects, aligning with the view that capitalism can drive a shift towards sustainability (UN Global Compact, 2004; Fernando, 2003). Scholtens (2006) characterizes finance as both the lubricant of the economy and a catalyst for corporate social responsibility, establishing links between finance and sustainability. The financial sector, acting as an intermediary, plays a vital role in allocating capital for climate mitigation, enabling investments in renewable energy and efficient technologies (Kuo et al., 2023; Richardson, 2009; Labatt & White, 2007). Sustainability finance within the banking sector provides valuable evidence for identifying investment opportunities by screening and rating information for businesses. It is crucial to address information asymmetry between the banking sector and firms regarding their environmental performance. Banking institutions bear indirect responsibility for their decisions to lend to unsustainable firms and projects (Chatzitheodorou et al., 2021). While financial institutions do not directly impact the environment, they can promote environmentally favorable activities, such as green procurement or green building, and facilitate climate-related financial products (Kuo et al., 2023).

The financial sector holds the potential to introduce loan products conducive to fostering sustainable production and consumption. Notably, these may include financial instruments tailored for renewable energy projects, provision of low-interest loans to bolster corporate sustainability endeavors, and the facilitation of specialized loans targeting green entrepreneurs (Gupta, 2015). Empirical evidence suggests that the provision of "green credit" serves as a catalyst for enterprises to embrace environmentally conscious practices, with a strategic aim to enhance both environmental performance and creditworthiness, thereby facilitating improved access to financial institutions (Aizawa and Yang, 2010). Moreover, scholarly investigations underscore the intricate influences shaping the adoption of environmentally friendly lending practices, wherein global institutional dynamics, national factors, and informal channels collectively contribute to shaping financial institutions' approaches (Falcone et al., 2018).

Furthermore, the paradigm of sustainable development offers a distinctive avenue for banking institutions to actively contribute to overarching sustainability goals. This involvement may manifest through the adoption of multifaceted practices, including the incorporation of environmental management systems and the initiation of Corporate Social Responsibility (CSR) projects (Gangi et al., 2019). Of particular significance is the role of stakeholders in exerting pressure on banking institutions to integrate specific CSR and sustainability programs, thereby enhancing institutional reputation and conferring a competitive advantage (Rebai et al., 2016). These strategic initiatives not only serve to bolster reputation but also contribute to operational efficiencies, thereby aligning with broader sustainability objectives. However, empirical studies do not reach a consensus on whether being a sustainable firm actually improves a company's profitability. Some studies show that investors are gaining positive returns from investing in sustainable firms, mutual funds, and ETFs (Moskowitz, 1972; Bragdon and Marlin, 1972; Roberts, 1992). On the other hand, the opposing viewpoint suggests that sustainable funds are not performing better than conventional funds. This argument claims that a strong preference for sustainability is evident only among a small proportion of investors, while the majority don't inherently value sustainability (Berk and Green, 2004). Studies by Hong and Kacperczyk (2009) and Geczy et al. (2003) even suggest that ESG screening might have a negative impact on investment performance (Sun and Small, 2021).

The distinct and influential role of financial institutions stems from their mediation in investment and financing activities (Aras et al., 2018). To shed light on the relationship between financial development and carbon emissions, Yuan et al. (2022) employ cross-province data from China between 2000 and 2019 and utilize the decoupling model. The study reveals that the establishment of a bank-based financial sector contributed to emissions reduction during the global recession. However, after the financial crisis, the decoupling of financial development from emissions was facilitated by the development of a market-based financial sector. This can be attributed to technological advancements in the stock market that helped reduce emissions, while the expansion of capital-labor inputs resulting from bank loans hindered the decoupling process. Nevertheless, the existing literature is limited in terms of understanding the influences of financial systems on sustainable development. This paper aims to address this gap by examining whether a market-based or bank-based financial system is superior in promoting sustainable development in OECD countries.

The subsequent sections of this study are organized as follows. Section 2 presents the data utilized, while Section 3 outlines the methodology adopted in this chapter. The empirical results are then elaborated upon in Section 4. Lastly, Section 5 serves as the conclusion of the paper.

2. DATA

This study examines annual data from 2001 to 2019 for 30 OECD countries, excluding Luxembourg, Denmark, Finland, and Sweden due to data unavailability.

To assess sustainable development, the study employs natural logarithmic values of the Sustainable Development Index (LNSDI). The SDI is an extension of the Human Development Index (HDI) and captures the ecological effectiveness of human growth within Earth's limits. The LNSDI calculates each country's ecological overshoot by comparing its consumption-based CO2 emissions and material footprint with the fair shares of planetary boundaries. It incorporates factors such as life expectancy, education, and income to measure a country's human development score. Countries that achieve high levels of human development while remaining within or close to the planetary boundaries are considered the most developed in this context.

The financial structure variable is constructed based on the methodology proposed by Beck and Levine (2002). It utilizes the first principal component of two variables that gauge the activity and size of banks and markets. The activity component is computed using the logarithm of the value traded to bank credit ratio, representing the proportion of stock exchange activity to Gross Domestic Product (GDP). The size component is determined by the logarithm of the market capitalization to bank credit ratio, which reflects the relative size of the market compared to bank credit. An increase in this variable, FS, indicates a transition towards a more market-based economy. Figure 1 illustrates the average values of financial structure variables for each country throughout the sample period. As depicted in Figure 1, 15 of the sample countries, including Austria, Costa Rica, Czechia, Germany, Greece, Hungary, Ireland, Italy, Korea, New Zealand, Norway, Portugal, Slovak Republic, Slovenia, and Spain, exhibit a predominance of bank-based financial systems. On the other hand, Australia, Belgium, Canada, Chile, Colombia, France, Israel, Japan, Mexico, Netherlands, Poland, Switzerland, Turkey, the United Kingdom, and the United States lean more towards market-based financial systems. Among the sample countries, Costa Rica has the most bank-based system, while the United States has the most market-based system.

Figure 1. Financial structure (Author calculations)

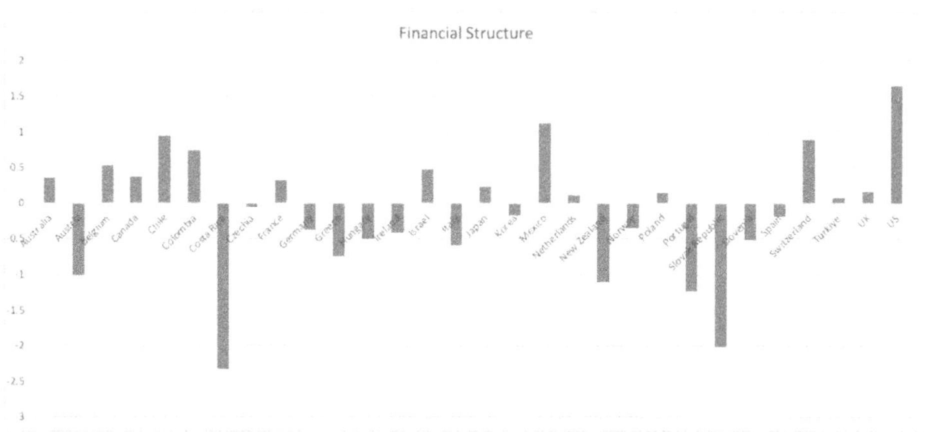

Control variables consistent with existing literature include the natural logarithmic values of Gross Domestic Per Capita (LNGDPPC) and CO_2 emissions (LNCO2).

The data for all variables, except the Sustainable Development Index (SDR), are sourced from the World Bank's World Development Indicators. The SDR data is obtained from the sustainabledevelopmentindex.org website. Descriptive statistics for each variable are presented in Table 1. The number of observations ranges from 491 to 570, depending on data availability. Notably, the average value of the financial structure measure for countries is negative, indicating a predominantly bank-based system, as shown in Table 1.

Table 1. Descriptive statistics

EV	Mean	Std. Dev.	Min	Max	Skewness	Kurtosis	Observations
SDR	23.583	8.160	6.080	45.940	0.002	2.892	570
GDPPC	31432.150	19846.300	2305.083	102913.500	0.871	3.743	570
CO_2	7.920	3.902	1.337	20.172	0.906	3.926	570
FS	-0.082	1.020	-3.023	6.923	0.224	7.097	491

Notes: SDR, GDPPC, CO_2, and FS indicate Sustainable Development Index, GDP per capita, CO_2 emissions, and financial structure index, respectively.

3. METHODOLOGY

This paper predominantly employs dynamic panel data models, specifically relying on the mean group (MG) estimator, pooled mean group estimator (PMG), and dynamic fixed effects (DFE), due to their inherent advantages. A salient advantage, as expounded by Pesaran et al. (1999), lies in the consistent estimation facilitated by the panel autoregressive distributed lag (ARDL) methodology. This method ensures robust estimations, irrespective of the variables' stationarity characteristics—whether they are stationary at levels, integrated of order 1, or a combination of both. An additional merit of the panel ARDL models is their capacity to facilitate the interpretation of short- and long-run causality, even in the absence of cointegration. Moreover, by judiciously determining the lag lengths of variables, this method effectively addresses the challenge posed by endogenous regressors. Lastly, in the event of employing logarithmic values for variables, the long-run coefficients derived from this method furnish elasticity estimates, further contributing to the methodological richness of the approach (Pesaran et al., 1999).

In the preliminary phase of the analysis, we evaluate the integration levels by employing panel unit-root tests, such as the Im-Pesaran-Shin (IPS) and Fisher-type tests. In accordance with the guidelines provided by Pesaran et al. (1999), it is imperative for variables to exhibit an integration order lower than two to render them suitable for inclusion in panel autoregressive distributed lag (ARDL) models. Panel unit-root tests confer a distinct advantage over individual time-series tests by amalgamating information from both cross-sectional and time-series data, as asserted by Breitung (2000) and Hadri (2000). The rejection of the null hypothesis in these tests signifies the stationarity of the variable at the panel level, as elucidated by Im et al. (2003).

Once the stationarity levels of each variable have been identified, the panel autoregressive distributed lag (ARDL) models are examined. The ARDL specifications for the models analyzed in this paper are demonstrated in Equation (1);

$$LNSDI_{it} = \sum_{j=1}^{p} \beta_{ij} LNSDI_{i,t-j} + \sum_{j=0}^{q} \gamma_{1ij} LNFS_{i,t-j} + \sum_{j=0}^{q} \gamma_{2ij} LNGDPPC_{i,t-j} + \sum_{j=0}^{q} \gamma_{3ij} LNCO2_{i,t-j} + \mu_i + \varepsilon_{it}$$

where 'p' represents the order of the dependent variable, and 'q' represents the order of the explanatory variables. The coefficients of the dependent and independent variables are denoted as β and γ, respectively. The country and year are represented by 'i' and 't'.

Furthermore, Equation (2) demonstrates the error-correction form of Equations (1) after reparameterization;

$$SDI_{it} = \theta_i(LNSDI_{i,t-1} - \vartheta_i X_{it}) + \sum_{j=1}^{p} \beta_{ij} \Delta LNSDI_{i,t-j} + \sum_{j=0}^{q} \gamma_{1ij} \Delta LNFS_{i,t-j} + \sum_{j=0}^{q} \gamma_{2ij} \Delta LNGDPPC_{i,t-j} + \sum_{j=0}^{q} \gamma_{3ij} \Delta LNCO2_{i,t-j} +$$

In this equation, β and γ represent the short-term coefficients of the lagged dependent and explanatory variables, respectively. As the coefficients of the first-differenced variables indicate the short-run impacts, the short-run period in this study is defined as one year. The long-term coefficient is denoted as ϑ, while the speed of adjustment of the dependent variable towards the long-term equilibrium following a change in the explanatory variables (X_s) is demonstrated by θ. $\theta_i<0$ ensures the existence of a long-run relationship.

This study employs three prominent methodologies—specifically, the mean group (MG), pooled mean group (PMG), and dynamic fixed effects (DFE)—for the estimation of dynamic heterogeneous models, as elucidated earlier. The PMG model accommodates country-specific variations in short-term coefficients, whereas the MG model allows for alterations in both long-term and short-term slopes across countries. Consequently, the MG estimator of the error-correction representation within the autoregressive distributed lag (ARDL) model is deemed appropriate for panels characterized by heterogeneity across groups, while the reliability of the PMG estimator is contingent upon the assumption of homogeneity in long-run slopes (Pesaran and Smith, 1995; Pesaran et al., 1999). Conversely, the DFE estimator permits intercept variations across countries while maintaining fixed slopes. To ascertain the validity of pooling long-term coefficients, the Hausman test for long-run homogeneity of parameters is employed. The non-rejection of the null hypothesis concerning homogeneity in long-run coefficients signifies the suitability of applying the PMG estimator (Pesaran et al., 1999). The empirical findings derived from these analyses will be expounded upon in the ensuing section.

4. EMPIRICAL RESULTS

In the initial stage of the analysis, panel unit-root tests are executed to evaluate the stationarity characteristics of the variables. This step is pivotal in determining the appropriate application of panel autoregressive distributed lag (ARDL) models, which are designed to accommodate variables with varying levels of integration, including levels, I(1), or a combination thereof. The Fisher-type and Im-Pesaran-Shin panel unit-root tests are employed, and the outcomes are presented in Table 2. The results indicate that all variables, with the exception of LNCO2, exhibit stationarity. Conversely, LNCO2 is identified as being integrated of order 1. Given that all variables in this model manifest either order 0 or 1 integration, the utilization of panel ARDL models is deemed apt for the analysis, as explicated by Pesaran et al. (1999).

Table 2. Unit-root test results

	Fisher Type			IPS	
	Statistics	**p-value**		**Statistics**	**p-value**
Panel A: Levels					
LNSDR	-5.407	0.000		-6.106	0.000
LNGDPPC	-7.268	0.000		-7.459	0.000
LNCO2	5.854	1.000		5.785	1.000
FS	-4.369	0.000		-4.076	0.000
Panel B: First-Differences					
LNSDR	-10.285	0.000		-11.598	0.000
LNGDPPC	-7.888	0.000		-7.899	0.000
LNCO2	-13.504	0.000		-15.419	0.000
FS	-13.560	0.000		-15.114	0.000

Notes: LNSDR, LNGDPPC, $LNCO_2$ and FS indicate the log value of the Sustainable Development Index, log value of the GDP per capita, log value of the CO_2 emissions, and financial structure index, respectively. IPS stands for the Im-Pesaran-Shin unit-root test. Panel A illustrates the outcomes of panel unit-root tests conducted on the variables at their original levels. Panel B displays the results of panel unit-root tests conducted on the first differences of the variables.

Table 3 presents the findings of the analysis, which explores the impact of the financial structure on sustainable development. Initially, the equations are estimated using three different estimators: MG, PMG, and DFE. To determine the most suitable estimator, a Hausman test is conducted. The results indicate that the null hypothesis of coefficient homogeneity in the long run cannot be rejected when comparing the MG and PMG estimators. However, the null hypothesis is rejected when comparing the PMG and DFE estimators. Therefore, it can be concluded that the DFE estimator is the most efficient for this model. Consequently, the discussion will focus exclusively on the results obtained from the DFE model.

Table 3 depicts that in the short run, the impact of FS on sustainable development is significant and negative, which indicates that having a more bank-based system enhances sustainable development. This finding complements Schumpeter (1912) that posits effectively operating financial institutions play a pivotal role in fostering technological innovation through the identification and financial support of entrepreneurs deemed most likely to achieve successful innovative endeavors. Furthermore, this discovery indirectly backs Kuo et al.'s (2023) assertion that financial institutions can improve their sustainability performance by focusing resources on sustainable areas, beginning with corporate governance. Moreover, the findings of this paper are in line with Greenwood and Jovanovic (1990) and King and Levine (1993) that demonstrate financial intermediaries possess the potential to elevate the pace of technological innovation by discerning and supporting entrepreneurs most likely to successfully introduce novel goods and production processes. Therefore, having a bank-based financial system has a positive impact on sustainable growth in the short-run.

However, in the long-run, the coefficient of FS is positive and significant at 1 percent. As an increase in the FS implies having a more market-based financial system, this finding suggests that having a market-based financial structure has a significant positive impact on sustainable development. This finding is in line with Allen and Gale (1999) that contend in the realm of emerging technologies, investors are prone to harbor diverse opinions stemming from disparities in prior beliefs rather than variations in information. Financial markets exhibit the capability to facilitate funding even in the presence of substantial diversity of opinion among investors. In contrast, intermediated finance involves entrusting the financing decision to a manager who bears the costs requisite for opinion formation. This arrangement introduces an agency problem, given that the manager may not share the same prior beliefs as the investor. The analysis posits that systems grounded in market mechanisms are more conducive to innovation compared to those reliant on banking structures. Consequently, the role of markets assumes heightened significance in the phase of economic growth at the technological frontier (Allen and Gale, 1999; Allen and Oura, 2004). Furthermore, this discovery indirectly reinforces the findings of Clarkson et al. (2008), which argue that companies succeeding in environmental practices are more transparent in channels where they have control over what to disclose. This aligns with the predictions of the voluntary disclosure theory based on economics. Companies excelling in environmental practices, driven by proactive environmental strategies, seek to communicate their approach to investors and others by voluntarily providing more environmental information. Essentially, their goal is to disclose their performance level, something not readily observable by investors and others, by directly sharing information that is challenging for less environmentally-friendly companies to replicate. Moreover, given the information asymmetry between borrowers and lenders, as elucidated by Stiglitz and Weiss (1981), the latter are predisposed to exhibit bias towards projects employing conventional methodologies. In the short-run, as financial intermediaries help to reduce information asymmetry, having bank-based financial system fosters sustainable development. In the long-run, with an increase in the information level of the participants, having market-based system enhances sustainable development by allocating capital to more innovative projects (see Goldstein, 2001).

Finally, Table 3 also shows the impact of economic growth on sustainable development. GDP is incapable of gauging environmental degradation, as observed by Aşıcı (2013), and it is incompetent in measuring social well-being (Gaspar et al., 2017; Li and Fang, 2014; Costanza et al., 2009). The findings of this paper indicate that economic growth has a significant positive impact on sustainable development both in the long and the short-run. So, although economic growth and sustainable development have different characteristics, an increase in economic growth enhances sustainable development.

Table 3. ARDL estimation results (Dependent variable: LNSDR)

EV	MG Estimates				PMG Estimates				DFE Estimates			
		Standard Error				Standard Error				Standard Error		
Panel A: Long-run												
	4.460	1.289	3.46		3.243	0.545	5.95		2.995	0.807	3.71	
LNCO2	8.739	4.494	1.94		6.876	1.437	4.78		9.140	1.859	4.92	
FS	3.809	1.444	2.64		3.230	0.377	8.55		2.119	0.504	4.20	
Panel B: Short-Run												
	0.018	0.087	0.20		0.195	0.075	2.60		0.124	0.023	5.31	
	0.086	0.081	1.06		0.121	0.052	2.34		0.148	0.050	2.95	
ΔFS	-0.041	0.012	-3.39		-0.021	0.006	-3.40		-0.007	0.004	-1.88	
Constant	-1.777	0.818	-2.17		-0.253	0.037	-6.81		-2.244	0.097	-2.53	
ECT	-0.04	0.006	-6.26		-0.012	0.002	-7.11		-0.010	0.001	-9.10	
	Housman Test Result (MG-PMG)						Housman Test Result (DFE-PMG)					
	0.77 (0.856)						85.70 (0.000)					

Notes: LNSDR, LNGDPPC, $LNCO_2$ and FS indicate the log value of the Sustainable Development Index, log value of the GDP per capita, log value of the CO_2 emissions, and financial structure index, respectively. EV stands for explanatory variables. MG, PMG, and DFE represent mean-group, pooled mean-group, and dynamic fixed effect estimators, respectively. The significance levels for the Hausman-test results are indicated in parentheses.

5. CONCLUSION

The escalating forces of industrialization and resource depletion pose formidable challenges to achieving sustainable development, despite the overarching goal of curtailing environmental pollution (Rehman et al., 2021). Essential to this pursuit is the judicious utilization of resources, prompting an examination in this study of how capital allocation, executed through either market mechanisms or banking institutions, may divergently influence sustainable development. Uniquely, this study spans the years 2001 to 2019 in OECD countries, deploying dynamic panel data techniques to explore the hitherto unexplored interplay between financial structures and sustainable development.

Emerging as a response to depleting natural resources, the concept of sustainable development aims to responsibly manage resources for the collective benefit of humanity (Ramachandran, 2000). In the realm of the real economy, financial development emerges as a pivotal force with the potential to impact climate change through diverse channels (Chang et al., 2019). The intricate dynamics underscore the role of a robust financial system in promoting sustainable technology advancements, with financial institutions offering funding for renewable technologies and championing green finance to contribute to emissions reduction (Aluko and Obalade, 2020; Churchill et al., 2019). Extensive research has scrutinized the impact of the financial systems on economic growth, with proponents of the bank-based theory underscoring the role of banks in effective risk management and superior performance. In contrast, advocates of the market-based theory argue for the efficiency of markets in allocating capital and providing risk management tools. The limited understanding of financial systems' role in sustainable development prompts a focus on their significance, not only in contributing to economic development but also in indirectly supporting environmental preservation through lending practices (Jones et al., 2017; Chatzitheodorou et al., 2021).

In addressing the dearth of understanding, this study's empirical findings are presented, revealing distinctive short-term and long-term impacts of financial systems on sustainable development. In the short run, a more bank-based system is associated with significant positive effects on sustainable development, aligning with Schumpeter's (1912) notion of financial institutions fostering innovation. Conversely, in the long run, a market-based financial structure exhibits a significant positive impact on sustainable development, echoing arguments by Allen and Gale (1999) regarding markets' efficacy in handling diverse opinions and facilitating funding. The intricate interplay between information asymmetry, innovation, and financing decisions is explored, shedding light on the evolving role of markets and banking structures in promoting sustainable development (Yuan et al., 2022; Allen and Gale, 1999). The findings highlight the nuanced nature of financial systems' influence, emphasizing the imperative of considering both short-term and long-term dynamics in fostering sustainable development.

To the best of our knowledge, our research marks the inaugural attempt to underscore the significance of financial structure in sustainable development. From a sustainable growth-oriented perspective, the long-term superiority of the market-based system over the bank-based one becomes apparent. Consequently, this investigation holds implications for policymakers as they navigate decisions on which financial system to endorse to enhance growth in a sustainable way.

REFERENCES

Aizawa, M., & Yang, C. (2010). Green credit, green stimulus, green revolution? China's mobilization of banks for environmental cleanup. *Journal of Environment & Development*, 19, 119–144.

Allen, F., & Gale, D. (1999). *Comparing Financial Systems*. MIT Press.

Allen, F., & Oura, H. (2004). Sustained Economic Growth and the Financial System. *Monetary and Economic Studies*, 22, 95–119.

Aluko, O. A., & Obalade, A. A. (2020). Financial development and environmental quality in sub-Saharan Africa: Is there a technology effect? *The Science of the Total Environment*, 747, 141515.32795805

Aras, G., Tezcan, N., & Furtuna, O. K. (2018). Multidimensional comprehensive corporate sustainability performance evaluation model: Evidence from an emerging market banking sector. *Journal of Cleaner Production*, 185, 600–609.

Arize, A., Kalu, E. U., & Nkwor, N. N. (2018). Banks versus markets: Do they compete, complement or co-evolve in the Nigerian financial system? An ARDL approach. *Research in International Business and Finance*, 45, 427–434.

Aşıcı, A. A. (2013). Economic growth and its impact on environment: A panel data analysis. *Ecological Indicators*, 24, 324–333.

Barkemeyer, R., Holt, D., Preuss, L., & Tsang, S. (2011). What happened to the 'development' in sustainable development? Business guidelines two decades after Brundtland. *Sustainable Development*, 22, 15–32.

Beck, T., & Levine, R. (2002). Industry growth and capital allocation: Does having a market-or bank- based system matter? *Journal of Financial Economics*, 64, 147–180.

Berk, J. B., & Green, R. C. (2004). Mutual Fund Flows and Performance in Rational Markets. *Journal of Political Economy*, 112, 1269–1295.

Boot, A. W., Greenbaum, S. I., & Thakor, A. V. (1993). Reputation and discretion in financial contracting. *The American Economic Review*, 83, 1165–1183.

Bragdon, J., & Marlin, J. (1972). Is Pollution Profitable? *Risk Management*, 19, 9–18.

Breitung, J. (2000). The local power of some unit root tests for panel data. *Advances in Econometrics*, 15, 161–178.

Chang, K., Zeng, Y., Wang, W., & Wu, X. (2019). The effects of credit policy and financial constraints on tangible and research and development investment: Firm-level evidence from China's renewable energy industry. *Energy Policy*, 130, 438–447.

Chang, S. C. (2015). Effects of financial developments and income on energy consumption. *International Review of Economics & Finance*, 35, 28–44.

Chatzitheodorou, K., Tsalis, A. T., Tsagarakis, K. P., Grigoroudis, E., & Nikolaou, I. (2021). A new practical methodology for the banking sector to assess corporate sustainability risks with an application in the energy sector. *Sustainable Production and Consumption*, 27, 1473–1487.

Churchill, S. A., Inekwe, J., Smyth, R., & Zhang, X. (2019). R&D intensity and carbon emissions in the G7: 1870–2014. *Energy Economics*, 80, 30–37.

Clarkson, P. M., Li, Y., Richardson, G. D., & Vasvari, F. P. (2008). Revisiting the relation between environmental performance and environmental disclosure: An empirical analysis. *Accounting, Organizations and Society*, 33, 303–327.

Costanza, R., Hart, M., Posner, S., & Talberth, J. (2009). Beyond GDP: The need for new measures of progress. *Pardee Papers*, 39(0109), 970401.

Dong, Y., Ma, S., Zhang, B., Wang, W., & Pacheco, J. (2021). Financial incentives to poor countries promote net emissions reductions in multilateral climate agreements. *One Earth*, 4, 1141–1149.

Falcone, P. M. (2018). Green investment strategies and bank-firm relationship: A firm-level analysis. *Economic Bulletin*, 38, 2225–2239.

Fernando, J. L. (2003). *Rethinking Sustainable Development.* SAGE Publications.

Gangi, F., Meles, A., D'Angelo, E., & Daniele, L. M. (2019). Sustainable development and corporate governance in the financial system: Are environmentally friendly banks less risky? *Corporate Social Responsibility and Environmental Management*, 26, 529–547.

Gaspara, J. S., Marquesb, A. C., & Fuinhas, J. A. (2017). The traditional energy-growth nexus: A comparison between sustainable development and economic growth approaches. *Ecological Indicators*, 75, 286–296.

Geczy, C., Stambaugh, R., & Levin, D. (2003). *Investing in Socially Responsible Mutual Funds*. Working Paper, University of Pennsylvania.

Goldsmith, R. W. (1969). *Financial structure and development.* Yale University Press.

Goldstein, D. (2001). Financial sector reform and sustainable development: The case of Costa Rica. *Ecological Economics*, 37, 199–215.

Greenwood, J., & Jovanovic, B. (1990). Financial Development, Growth, and the Distribution of Income. *Journal of Political Economy*, 98, 1076–1107.

Gupta, J. (2015). Role of Green Banking in Environment Sustainability- A study of selected Commercial Banks in Himachal Pradesh. *International Journal of Multidisciplinary Research and Development*, 2, 349–353.

Hadri, K. (2000). Testing for stationarity in heterogeneous panel data. *Econometrics Journal. Revue Economique et Sociale*, 3, 148–161.

Hong, H., & Kacperczyk, M. (2009). The Price of Sin: The Effects of Social Norms on Markets. *Journal of Financial Economics*, 93, 15–36.

Im, K. S., Pesaran, M. H., & Shin, Y. (2003). Testing for unit roots in heterogeneous panels. *Journal of Econometrics*, 115, 53–74.

Jones, P., Hillier, D., & Comfort, D. (2017). The sustainable development goals and the financial services industry. *Athens Journal of Business and Economics*, 3, 37–50.

King, R., & Levine, R. (1993). Finance, Entrepreneurship and Economic Development. *Journal of Monetary Economics*, 32, 513–542.

Kuo, Y. C., Huang, Y. H., Sun, L., Small, G., & Lin, S. J. (2023). Identifying key factors of sustainability practice in financial institutions based on decision-making trial and evaluation laboratory method. *Asian Review of Accounting*, 31, 661–679.

Labatt, S., & White, R. (2007). *Carbon Finance: The Financial Implications of Climate Change*. John Wiley.

Levine, R. (2002). Bank-based or market-based financial systems: Which is better? *Journal of Financial Intermediation*, 11, 398–428.

Li, G., & Fang, C. (2014). Global mapping and estimation of ecosystem services values and gross domestic product: A spatially explicit integration of national green GDP accounting. *Ecological Indicators*, 46, 293–314.

Moskowitz, M. (1972). Choosing Socially Responsible Stocks. *Business and Society Review*, 1, 71–75.

Pesaran, M. H., Shin, Y., & Smith, R. (1999). Pooled mean group estimation of dynamic heterogeneous panels. *Journal of the American Statistical Association*, 94, 621–634.

Pesaran, M. H., & Smith, R. (1995). Estimating long-run relationships from dynamic heterogeneous panels. *Journal of Econometrics*, 68, 79–113.

Ramachandran, N. (2000). *Monitoring Sustainability: Indices and Techniques of Analysis*. Concept Publishing Company.

Rebai, S., Azaiez, M. N., & Saidane, D. (2016). A multi-attribute utility model for generating a sustainability index in the banking sector. *Journal of Cleaner Production*, 113, 835–849.

Rehman, A., Ma, H., Ahmad, M., Irfan, M., Traore, O., & Chandio, A. A. (2021). Towards environmental Sustainability: Devolving the influence of carbon dioxide emission to population growth, climate change, Forestry, livestock and crops production in Pakistan. *Ecological Indicators*, 125, 107460.

Richardson, B. (2009). Climate finance and its governance: Moving to a low carbon economy through socially responsible financing? *The International and Comparative Law Quarterly*, 58, 597–626.

Roberts, R. W. (1992). Determinants of Corporate Social Responsibility Disclosure. *Accounting, Organizations and Society*, 17, 595–612.

Sardianoua, E., Stauropouloub, A., Evangelinosc, K., & Nikolaou, I. (2021). A materiality analysis framework to assess sustainable development goals of banking sector through sustainability reports. *Sustainable Production and Consumption*, 27, 1775–1793.

Scholtens, B. (2006). Finance as a driver of corporate social responsibility. *Journal of Business Ethics*, 68, 19–33.

Schumpeter, J. (1934). *Theorie der Wirtschaftlichen Entwicklung (The Theory of Economic Development)* (Opie, R., Trans.). Harvard University Press.

Shahbaz, M., Hye, Q. M. A., Tiwari, A. K., & Leitao, N. C. (2013). Economic growth, energy consumption, financial development, international trade and CO_2 emissions in Indonesia. *Renewable & Sustainable Energy Reviews*, 25, 109–121.

Stiglitz, J., & Weiss, A. (1981). Credit rationing in markets with imperfect information. *The American Economic Review*, 71, 393–410.

Stiglitz, J. E. (1985). Credit markets and the control of capital. *Journal of Money, Credit and Banking*, 17, 133–152.

Stulz, R. M. (2000). Financial structure, corporate finance and economic growth. *International Review of Finance*, 1, 11–38.

Sun, L., & Small, G. (2021). Has sustainable investing made an impact in the period of COVID-19?: Evidence from Australian exchange traded funds. *Journal of Sustainable Finance & Investment*, 12, 251–273.

Ugurlu-Yildirim, E., & Ordu-Akkaya, B. M. (2022). Does the impact of geopolitical risk reduce with the financial structure of an economy? A perspective from market vs. bank-based emerging economies. *Eurasian Economic Review*, 12, 681–703.

Ulucak, R., & Danish, K. Y. (2020). An assessment of the environmental sustainability corridor: Investigating the non-linear effects of environmental taxation on CO_2 emissions. *Sustainable Development*, 28, 1010–1018.

United Nations. (2004). The Global Compact Leaders Summit. Author.

United Nations. (2021). Climate Change Conference (COP26) Glasgow: Mobilise finance. Available at https://ukcop26.org/cop26-goals/finance/

Uzunkaya, M. (2012). Economic performance in bank-based and market-based financial systems: Do non-financial institutions matter? *Journal of Applied Finance and Banking*, 2, 159–176.

WCED. (Ed.). (1987). *Our Common Future: The World Commission on Environment and Development*. Oxford University Press.

Xu, D., Sheraz, M., Hassan, A., Sinha, A., & Ullah, S. (2022). Financial development, renewable energy and CO_2 emission in G7 countries: New evidence from non-linear and asymmetric analysis. *Energy Economics*, 109, 105994.

Yang, X., & Tang, X. (2021). Does financial structure affect CO_2 emissions? Evidence from G20 countries. *Finance Research Letters*, 41, 101791.

Yuan, R., Liao, H., & Wang, J. (2022). A nexus study of carbon emissions and financial development in China using the decoupling analysis. *Environmental Science and Pollution Research International*, 29, 88224–88239.35831650

KEY TERMS AND DEFINITIONS

Climate Change: Climate change refers to long-term alterations in precipitation, temperature, and other atmospheric circumstances, mainly driven by human activities such as deforestation, burning fossil fuels, and industrial processes.

CO2 Emission: CO2 emissions refer to the discharge of carbon dioxide into the atmosphere, mainly resulting from human activities like burning fossil fuels and industrial operations, and play a major role in global warming and climate change.

Financial System: Financial systems are the structures within an economy that enable the movement of funds between savers and borrowers, including both bank-based systems, where banks primarily handle the allocation of capital, and market-based systems, where financial markets like stock and bond markets are key in directing funds.

Panel ARDL: Panel ARDL (Auto-Regressive Distributed Lag) methodology is a statistical approach for examining the dynamic relationship between variables in panel data, accommodating various lags and capturing both short-term and long-term impacts across different cross-sectional units over time.

Sustainable Development: Sustainable development involves fulfilling current needs while ensuring that future generations can also meet theirs, by harmonizing economic growth, social equity, and environmental conservation.

Chapter 2
The Path to Resilience:
Exploring Household Financial Vulnerability

Diya Susan Biju
Christ University, India

Veerta Tantia
https://orcid.org/0000-0002-8487-5175
Christ University, India

ABSTRACT

Household financial vulnerability represents a significant financial challenge, predominantly impacting low and middle-income households when faced with sudden changes in income or expenses. At the household level, this vulnerability might arise as short-term liquidity issues or long-term solvency concerns. While household debt is a primary factor contributing to this vulnerability, elements like financial capability and the use of digital payments also play roles. The repercussions of household financial vulnerability encompass financial stress and potential bankruptcy, underscoring the critical need to comprehend its dynamics. Thus, this chapter aims to extensively explore household financial vulnerability, including its determinants, theoretical frameworks, assessment methodologies, and strategies for mitigation.

INTRODUCTION

Household financial vulnerability persists when there is inadequate management of monetary resources. The global health crisis and the economic downturn have increased household financial vulnerability (Kukk, 2016; Yazdanparast & Alhenawi, 2022). The aforementioned statement can be supported by the events

DOI: 10.4018/979-8-3693-0863-9.ch002

during the economic recession of 2008. The recession was precipitated by concerns surrounding residential property and the repayment of mortgage loans (Yilmazer et al., 2015). A key contributor to this problem might be a lack of comprehension regarding household financial vulnerability.

During the economic downturn of 2007-2008, it initially drew attention due to soaring unemployment rates, making it challenging for individuals to repay loans (Pissarides, 2013). Risk or uncertainty exposes numerous households to vulnerability, indicating their lack of preparedness (Ampudia et al., 2016). Debt, widely regarded as the primary factor influencing household financial vulnerability, has seen a notable rise relative to disposable income across several nations in the aftermath of the global pandemic and accompanying economic downturn (Leclaire, 2023). This demonstrates the extent to which households are facing financial difficulties. The debt-to-income ratio also helps gauge whether a household can pay off debts (JOHNSON & LI, 2010; K. T. Kim et al., 2017). The absence of insurance policies has also put households in a very vulnerable situation. Furthermore, it has been noted in numerous countries that households heavily depend on informal sources that charge high rates for financial support. Therefore, the issue of household financial vulnerability has attracted significant attention from governments and researchers worldwide.

A financially vulnerable household finds it difficult to meet its daily expenses or adapt to fluctuations in income or expenditure (K. N. Singh & Malik, 2022). An income shock refers to job loss, while an expenditure shock can pertain to an unforeseen medical expense (L. Sun et al., 2022). Generally, households often resort to debt to compensate for this deficit, exacerbating their financial vulnerability (Anderloni et al., 2012a). However, additional fundamental elements, such as the incapacity to dine out or embark on a brief vacation, contribute to a household's vulnerability. The susceptibility to financial adversities depends on the household income level (Hamilton et al., 2019).

Therefore, understanding the vulnerability of households to financial challenges is of paramount significance, as it not only enhances the resilience of households but also has implications for the overall economy of a nation. One notable observation regarding household financial vulnerability is its impact not only during times of crisis but also in periods of economic stability within a nation (Alhenawi & Yazdanparast, 2022). Developing nations such as India are characterized by a significant proportion of their population belonging to low-income and middle-income families, which bear the most significant burden of economic challenges (Kharas, 2010). Low-income households encounter challenges in meeting their basic needs due to unemployment or reliance on seasonal employment (Janssens et al., 2021). This phenomenon is classified as a financial vulnerability for these households. Middle-income households may become susceptible to financial vulnerability due to an unexpected increase or decrease in income, so they'll have to make financial compromises. Therefore, there exists variation in financial susceptibility among different nations and income categories (Van Nguyen et al., 2022). The preservation of households in the face of various shocks relies heavily on the financial sustainability of these households. Hence, this book chapter aims to analyze the notion of household financial vulnerability thoroughly. The comprehensive analysis encompasses factors contributing to vulnerability at micro and macro levels, its repercussions, varied measurement methodologies, and potential mitigation strategies.

Household Financial Vulnerability

Household financial vulnerability is a term that is often used interchangeably with financial distress, fragility, and debt burden (Daud et al., 2019). While it is true that not all households are inherently financially vulnerable, it is crucial to recognize that any change or risk has the potential to trigger vulnerability across all households. Previous scholarly works have concentrated on debt as the primary factor contributing to a household's financial vulnerability (Leclaire, 2023; Worthington, 2006).

Debt is widely acknowledged as a significant determinant of households' financial fragility. However, it is crucial to recognize that there are additional factors that contribute to their decision to incur debt. Certain households tend to be short-sighted (Loibl, 2017). They exhaust their monthly income without setting up sufficient savings to address unforeseen circumstances. Some households may attempt to emulate the lifestyle of others to cultivate a particular societal image (Copur et al., 2014). Therefore, numerous variables beyond purely financial factors can impact a household's financial stability.

The financial vulnerability experienced by households can manifest as both a short-term and long-term problem. The short-term financial vulnerability might pose challenges in meeting the ends meet. This scenario predominantly aligns with a household characterized by low income. However, it is essential to note that this may not always be true. Middle-income households may experience short-term financial vulnerability when they encounter unexpected changes in income or sudden expenditure shocks (Christen & Morgan, 2005). The primary distinguishing feature of this phenomenon is its inherent constraint on liquidity (Cunha et al., 2011). However, middle-income households may find it less challenging to achieve financial stability by reducing discretionary spending, such as dining out or engaging in leisure travel. These households may feel overwhelmed and emotionally tricky; nevertheless, their ability to meet their fundamental requirements remains unaffected. Individual and governmental interventions can address and mitigate short-term financial vulnerability (Buckland & Spotton Visano, 2022a). Nevertheless, households may encounter challenges when confronted with long-term financial vulnerability. If a household's accumulated savings surpass their expenditures throughout their lifetime, they will encounter long-term financial vulnerability. The disparity in long-term financial vulnerability is also evident between middle-income and low-income households. Middle-income households may encounter difficulties meeting their loan obligations and EMIs, necessitating significant adjustments such as downsizing their residence or selling their vehicle. Nevertheless, low-income households may encounter challenges acquiring essentials such as food, water, and other necessities. A circumstance may arise wherein these households are compelled to sell their residence and experience homelessness (Heckman & Hanna, 2015).

What might pose a vulnerability to a middle-income household could represent a luxury for a low-income household. Financial vulnerability, hence, refers to the condition in which a household cannot cope with unexpected changes in income or expenses (Anderloni et al., 2012b). The crux lies in a household's capacity to manage and adapt to these unforeseen disruptions effectively. If a household can navigate such circumstances by relying on any source of income, it can be inferred that they do not possess financial vulnerability.

THEORETICAL FRAMEWORK

1. Life Cycle Theory and Household Financial Vulnerability

The life cycle theory holds substantial importance in understanding household income dynamics. It delves into the financial behaviors of households across different life phases, shedding light on potential vulnerabilities that may emerge. According to the theoretical framework posited, households consistently exhibit a propensity to uphold a stable level of consumption for their lifespan (Baek & Hong, 2004). Although households desire a seamless consumption experience, their income exhibits irregularity. Therefore, households resort to borrowing to address the fluctuations and stabilize their consumption patterns (Eika et al., 2020). The primary reason for this early debt accumulation is often linked to impulsive buying behavior. Subsequently, when households progress through their lifespan and see an increase in income, they repay their financial obligations. The debt is usually entirely settled by the end of their lifespan (Ando & Modigliani, 1963). However, the schedule for repaying the loan does not exhibit a flawless, regular, and smooth pattern.

Households saving behavior is contingent upon their income level since it determines whether they will engage in saving or refrain from doing so to sustain their current level of consumption (Shefrin & Thaler, 1988). Their income level can also fluctuate due to losing their job or significant investment loss, which affects their consumption level and can lead a household into financial vulnerability. Access to comprehensive data on debt, spending habits, and financial prospects empowers households to manage their financial affairs autonomously (Seymour & Peterman, 2018). However, possessing decision-making skills does not guarantee financial resilience; it can also render households vulnerable to economic fluctuations. Thus, understanding these financial dynamics and their implications allows households to navigate potential vulnerabilities and reinforce their financial stability.

It is common for young households to engage in borrowing activities and repay their debts later in life (Gamble et al., 2019). Per the life cycle hypothesis, it is established that every household borrows at least once over its lifespan. Each household will project or forecast their future income by considering their present income and educational qualifications (Massenot & Pettinicchi, 2019). Financial vulnerability arises if initial expectations are unmet, causing projected income levels to fall short (Bayer et al., 2019). Any unforeseen event causing financial strain can exacerbate vulnerability, impacting the household's overall financial stability.

Throughout different life cycle stages, households face financial fluctuations, leading to either saving or dissaving (consumption). Multiple factors influence households' financial decision-making processes, including age, number of children, and behavioral tendencies (Brounen et al., 2016). Based on the life cycle hypothesis, households engage in consumption, savings, and borrowing activities intending to repay loans, maintain stable consumption patterns, and accumulate sufficient savings to meet the specific needs associated with different life stages (Feiveson & Sabelhaus, 2019). However, this phenomenon is only observed in theoretical contexts; in practical applications, it stays rooted in idealism. Financial decisions and unexpected events at various times might render households susceptible to financial vulnerability.

2. Structuration Theory and Household Financial Vulnerability

Anthony Giddens introduced the theory of structuration. It is a sociological theory that clarifies how agency (action) and structure are related. Social structures are institutions, conventions, regulations, and practices that influence a household's behavior (action) (Farrall, 2021). Government policies, employment prospects, recessions, inflation, and central bank rules can also impact a household's financial well-being (Stones, 2005).

The theory's recursive nature denotes that actions result from existing structures and contribute to their formation (Mead & Neves, 2018). Institutions, laws, policies, and the labor market shape the household's financial environment, capturing the crux of structuration theory (Ge et al., 2021; Jiang et al., 2022). Consequently, households make financial assessments based on this established social framework. For instance, Canada's housing crisis exerts a tangible impact on household financial capacities and decisions, potentially leading to a state of financial vulnerability for affected households (V. Singh, 2022).

As previously noted, sudden fluctuations in income and expenses can leave a household susceptible to financial vulnerability. Yet, societal structures, such as financial institutions, influence a household's readiness to handle unforeseen circumstances (C. Yu et al., 2022). These institutions often serve as sources of debt to mitigate unexpected financial disruptions. Debt management depends on various factors, including borrowing terms, availability, and interest rates (Abd Samad et al., 2020).

Moreover, government policies are pivotal in shaping households' vulnerability levels. Tax policies (Choi & Shin, 2023), housing regulations (Winkler, 2017), healthcare provisions (Mazumder & Miller, 2016), and educational initiatives influence a household's financial stability. Social norms also substantially shape the dynamics in a household.

Social structures exert major influence over a household's financial decisions, while parallelly, the actions of households affect their internal dynamics. For example, investors have an increasing demand for sustainability; many companies are trying to create sustainable investment opportunities (Camilleri, 2017). This interaction results in the creation of various innovative financial instruments.

Social structures are important in making a household financially resilient or vulnerable. The long-term consequences depend upon the strategies adopted by the household to address this vulnerability. The degree to which household members are influenced by their past experiences managing financial matters and future financial goals is also a very important factor (Buckland & Spotton Visano, 2022b). The application of structuration theory aids in grasping the dynamic interaction between structure and agency, revealing their impact on a household's resilience or susceptibility. This theoretical framework offers insights into the multifaceted elements affecting a household's financial vulnerability, aiding in a comprehensive understanding of this intricate phenomenon.

3. Social Capital and Household Financial Vulnerability

Financial vulnerability is a multifaceted issue that affects households across various income groups. Social capital is considered to be one of the contributing variables (Biju & Tantia, 2023). The concept under consideration pertains to the social dynamics encompassing exchanges, networks, and relationships within and outside households (Johnson, 2016).

Establishing robust connections and close-knit connections can yield financial advantages for households. Within these tightly-knit and cohesive social groups, those who constitute them include immediate family members and intimate friends.

They will have developed trust and mutual support (Son & Feng, 2019). A broad social network can prove advantageous during periods of financial instability. Many individuals will be available to offer financial aid (Rani et al., 2021). Therefore, social capital has the potential to serve as a protective mechanism against financial adversity.

Households that maintain such a social network have enhanced well-being and success. Providing diverse financial resources and knowledge enables households to strengthen their ability to navigate financial challenges effectively (Berry & Welsh, 2010). Households, hence, acquire knowledge about investing, employment prospects, and financial management. Along with the aforementioned connections, the formal institution can also be categorized as social capital. The concept being discussed resembles the propositions put forth by the structuration theory. The concept of structuration theory examines the influence of formal institutions on the behaviors shown within a household. In social capital, the primary focus revolves around establishing and maintaining interpersonal connections (Field, 2016). Establishing connections with formal agencies and enterprises might greatly value households. Implementing this measure can mitigate the likelihood of joblessness and establish a consistent source of financial support within the household.

Familial solid bonds and a wide range of social ties can mitigate household financial vulnerability (Coleman, 1988). Households characterized by a wide range of social capital exhibit enhanced financial resilience. Establishing trust and inclusion within these groups is paramount to fully leveraging the benefits of social capital. In short, acquiring social capital can enhance a household's financial resilience and stability and, in turn, reduce household financial vulnerability.

4. Behavioral Finance and Household Financial Vulnerability

The decisions and actions made by households have the potential to render them either vulnerable or resilient. These decisions and choices are not made rationally. The cognitive abilities and decision-making capabilities of households are influenced by the knowledge, evidence, and education at their disposal and psychological factors (Sabri et al., 2020). Households frequently exhibit suboptimal financial decision-making because they disregard unfavorable and unpleasant information. For instance, households that frequently encounter unforeseen medical costs could have potentially mitigated such expenses by seeking medical attention in the initial stages of the illness. This could have allowed them to provide sufficient time for organizing such expenditures or establishing financial plans (Hoffmann & McNair, 2019).

Their financial behavior determines the money management approach adopted by households. Behavioral finance postulates various characteristics of human behavior (DeBondt et al., 2010). Engaging in various financial behaviors such as financial planning, budgeting, and borrowing promptly, which exceeds one's financial capacity in terms of spending, can contribute to a household's exposure to financial vulnerability (Alp & Seven, 2019).

The amalgamation of household finance and psychology offers valuable insights into the underlying motivations behind households' investment decisions, debt acquisition, spending patterns, and investment behaviors (Muradoglu & Harvey, 2012). What factors contribute to specific households' propensity to assume higher risk levels? Psychological bias is evident in this particular setting. Households frequently exhibit a heightened emotional response to losses compared to the emotional satisfaction derived from gains (Nofsinger, 2012). This engenders a heightened sense of caution and a more risk-averse attitude among households. Simultaneously, specific households tend to have overconfident bias (Warmath et al., 2019). These financial behaviors can potentially render a household prone to adverse financial circumstances.

Behavioral finance provides insights into why specific households have difficulties saving (Dolan et al., 2012; Morris et al., 2022). Households frequently defer actions or decisions due to hyperbolic discounting, a cognitive bias characterized by a preference for instant gratification over fulfilling long-term objectives (Eisenhauer & Ventura, 2006). Therefore, all households must seize the chance to engage in investment and savings activities to secure their future financial well-being.

As with saving, spending patterns also are determined by behavioral factors. Cognitive bias plays a huge part in this context. Households often characterize their spending behavior to meet their preconceived notions (Bahaddin et al., 2019). Additionally, when a household's primary source of income increases, their spending also increases, which hinders their ability to save. Many households do not see mindful spending, which can lead them to experience household financial vulnerability. Herding behavior and confirmation bias can make households invest, leading to suboptimal portfolio construction. Investing sound financially is paramount for households (Din et al., 2021). Behavioral finance also sheds light on debt management in households. Overconfidence bias that they can pay off their debt and prioritizing current consumption over debt reduction can make a household vulnerable (Warmath et al., 2019).

Household financial decisions are made due to various psychological attributes. Understanding this household-level behavior is important to comprehend the reasons for being financially vulnerable and to mitigate the same.

FACTORS AFFECTING HOUSEHOLD FINANCIAL VULNERABILITY

Micro Factors

Micro factors are the various factors that households can control. They can significantly impact the financial stability of households. Understanding these factors is of utmost importance to navigating through the complex financial landscape of households.

1. Socio-Demographic Characteristics

Socio-demographic variables, such as age, gender, ethnicity, education, income, marital status, and household size, significantly affect a household's vulnerability to financial fragility (Lusardi et al., 2018; Sullivan & Meschede, 2016). Several factors contribute to the capacity of households to tolerate various shocks.

Income disparities emerge as a pivotal factor among various considerations. As previously said, there exists a disparity in household financial vulnerability between middle-income and low-income households, with some experiencing a surplus of financial resources (Salisbury et al., 2023). In contrast, others face insufficiencies in their financial situation. Deciding households' savings capacity and debt repayment capability depends on their income. Many households, particularly those with modest incomes, frequently encounter challenges when saving money. Despite possessing financial literacy and being aware of the various financial prospects available, those with low income may see a reduction in their ability to accumulate funds. Low-income households are prone to financial vulnerabilities due to their limited capacity to cope with unexpected expenses or a sudden decrease in income (French & McKillop, 2016). Income variations not only pose challenges in securing debt but also exacerbate affordability concerns, further impacting the financial stability of households.

A positive association exists between household members' education level and financial well-being (Ali et al., 2020). The many socio-demographic parameters exhibit interdependence. Acquiring a quality education can elevate a household's income, thus influencing their vulnerability to financial insecurity. Hence, education is a defining element in determining a household's financial vulnerability.

Age is also a significant determinant of financial vulnerability. Households may encounter challenges throughout certain phases, while others may experience a state of abundance, as previously discussed in the life cycle theory within the theoretical framework (Kureishi et al., 2021). Early adulthood can provide households with financial challenges due to college loan obligations and the availability of entry-level employment opportunities (J. Kim & Chatterjee, 2021; Richardson et al., 2017). Subsequently, more familial obligations arise concurrently with attaining a more favorable employment position. Effectively handling these tasks necessitates implementing robust financial planning and management strategies. Later, there are periods characterized by high incomes, a tendency towards stability, and reduced expenditure in retirement(Bonekamp & van Soest, 2022). The comprehension of the many obstacles and prospects encountered throughout different phases of life has a pivotal role in determining the financial vulnerability of a household.

Gender also has a significant impact in this context. The global rise in female-headed households highlights the persistent gender-based income disparity. Gender-based income discrepancies persist, resulting in women earning a lower salary than their male colleagues (Cutillo & Centra, 2017). Consequently, households may encounter financial vulnerability due to their constrained ability to accumulate savings and engage in investment activities. In addition to their professional obligations, women globally also bear the burden of unpaid care work. Including these supplementary duties diminishes their effectively compensated working hours, impacting their financial stability (Long, 2018).

Ethnicity and race also significantly contribute to household financial vulnerability across nations. Ethnic minorities have historically found difficulty dealing with limited financial resources, opportunities, and high fixed expenses. The financial resilience among Black and Hispanic families in the United States has always dealt with this kind of difficulty. They find it challenging to generate emergency funds to address unforeseen financial responsibilities. These groups' income, savings, debt, and investment influence their perceived inadequacy in handling unexpected expenses (Lusardi et al., 2023). Worldwide, ethnic minorities face different obstacles, heightening their financial vulnerability. Socio-demographic factors, like age, income, gender, ethnicity, and race, greatly influence a household's susceptibility to financial insecurity.

2. Financial Capability

The term "financial capability" includes financial skills, behavior, inclusion, and literacy. These attributes hold similar importance in mitigating household financial vulnerability. An individual who exhibits all of the above is deemed financially capable. Financial literacy is merely one aspect of financial capability. The importance of financial literacy cannot be emphasized enough, as it helps households make informed financial choices. Despite the advancement in financial literacy across many nations, low-income households in developing and underdeveloped nations continue to face challenges (Van Nguyen et al., 2022). Many research studies have established a correlation between less financial literacy and increased financial vulnerability within households (Babiarz & Robb, 2014; French & McKillop, 2016). Households who know about budgeting, saving, investing, and debt management display more informed decision-making. These households have greater budgeting capabilities, reducing the probability of extreme spending and falling into a cycle of indebtedness (Sabri et al., 2020). Financial inclusion is equally important. Affordable financial services are of utmost importance, as they help facilitate effective money management and promote savings, potentially alleviating vulnerability (Morgan & Long, 2020). These attributes hold similar importance in mitigating household financial vulnerability.

Decreased household financial vulnerability is not solely linked to financial literacy, as it also depends upon opportunities for households to take action. Knowing a financial product or service is inadequate; households must take action on the financial opportunities provided by these products or services to gain financial advantages (M. S. Sherraden & Ansong, 2016). To address the financial vulnerability, households must have adequate financial capabilities. The capacity for taking action can be noticed in different forms. Opening a savings account can be the first action that is taken by households. Studies have shown that households participating in saving activities showcase positive financial behavior (Brounen et al., 2016). Adequate financial resources allow a household to allocate funds towards emergency savings. Furthermore, it was demonstrated that households with ample financial resources could allocate funds toward unforeseen expenses.

Therefore, financial capability plays a very important role in decreasing household financial vulnerability by providing households with the tools and skills to manage the complexities of personal finance efficiently (Fernández-López et al., 2023; S. Sun et al., 2022). Households can reduce financial difficulties and risks by improving their financial knowledge, skills, and behavior, which is by improving their financial capability. A household becomes financially capable by lowering the financial vulnerability of their household through financial literacy, financial inclusion, positive financial behaviour, and financial skill development

3. Financial Socialization

The process of financial socialization significantly influences the level of financial vulnerability households suffer. This pertains to how household members acquire knowledge and demonstrate behavior associated with financial matters. An individual's upbringing and societal factors can impact a household's financial choices and decisions (Zhao & Zhang, 2020). Money management strategies are mainly learned and perceived during the formative years. For example, many parents give their children an allowance from an early age to teach them financial management skills. Lack of access to basic financial education might pose a difficulty for households in effectively managing unexpected financial crises, thus making them vulnerable to financial insecurity.

Another important aspect of financial socialization is fostering habits that promote higher savings and discourage debt accumulation. Fostering a culture that promotes excessive spending or unsustainable borrowing practices can worsen household financial vulnerability (Sohn et al., 2012). Skills like financial planning and budgeting are developed through diverse socialization agents.

Parents and guardians are important financial role models who majorly affect children's financial perspectives and behaviors (LeBaron et al., 2018). Furthermore, a household's lack of access to financial services and products can influence an individual's capacity to make well-informed financial decisions. A setting that promotes financial literacy, prudent money management, and savings practices can help reduce household financial vulnerability (Anthony et al., 2021). On the other hand, the lack of these factors could contribute to increased household financial vulnerability. Hence, financial socialization plays a pivotal role in promoting responsible financial behaviors and reducing the vulnerability of households to financial instability.

4. Digitalized Payments

The universal adoption of digitalized payments has seen a notable surge, especially after the COVID-19 pandemic. The ease and convenience of these products or services have led to a considerable rise in their usage. The development of payment technologies is set to bring about a substantial change in the financial behavior of households. As these technologies continue to advance, households will certainly adapt their financial behavior to align with the new opportunities and conveniences they offer (Khando et al., 2022). With the surge in the usage of digital payment methods such as mobile wallets, contactless cards, and online banking, the design of financial transactions is also swiftly changing (Mützel, 2021). This change not only affects the way households pay for goods and services; it also affects the way they manage their finances and make financial decisions. Households experience a new degree of convenience due to the rise in the usage of digitalized payments. With just a few taps on a smartphone, households can make purchases without the difficulty of carrying cash or a physical card (Malik & Annuar, 2021). This simplicity of payment may come with its share of problems. One of the possible drawbacks of digitalized payment methods is the inclination to make impulsive purchase decisions (Hellemans et al., 2023). Conventional payment methods, such as cash or physical cards, give individuals a physical representation of their money. They can physically see the amount of cash in their wallet or the number of cards they possess. This visual reminder can act as a prevention to overspending. On the other hand, digital payment methods frequently detach individuals from the physical aspect of money (Khando et al., 2022).

In the current digital era, the ease of making payments through platforms like Google Pay and Apple Pay has grown in popularity. Nevertheless, it is important to consider the degree of transparency these digitalized payment methods offer in contrast to conventional cash transactions. One of the main benefits of using cash is its transparency (Ha et al., 2021). The transaction is simple and easy to understand when you purchase with physical currency. You hand over the cash and receive your change (if applicable), and both parties involved in the transaction clearly understand the exchange. Households using more transparent payment methods, such as cash, experience a phenomenon known as the “pain of paying” (Ofer, 1996). This concept refers to individuals' psychological unease or reluctance when they make cash payments. The study suggests that the pain of paying is intensified when people can physically see and feel the money leaving their hands. Transactions with cash provide a physical reminder that they are spending, increasing people’s awareness of the expense and possibly leading to an increased sense of loss. Conversely, though, when using less transparent payment methods like credit cards or digital wallets, the pain of paying is often lessened (George & Krishnan, 2022). These methods create a psychological distance between the consumer and the act of spending money, as there is no physical exchange. The increasing prevalence of digitalized payment methods in our daily lives has the potential to desensitize individuals to overspending. These associated risks exacerbate a household's financial vulnerability, making them precarious. In today's digital age, it is essential to balance the advantages of digital payments and the potential risks they pose (H.-C. Yu et al., 2002). This balance is crucial to protect households from heightened financial vulnerability in an ever-evolving digital landscape. As technology continues to advance, digital payments have become increasingly prevalent. The aforementioned risks can exacerbate a household's financial vulnerability. Ensuring the appropriate equilibrium between the advantages of digital payments and the mitigation of accompanying dangers is paramount to protect households from a heightened financial vulnerability within an ever more digitalized environment.

MACRO FACTORS

Macro factors are those factors that are not in households' control. It includes economic factors like inflation, unemployment, interest rates, government policies, and climate change.

1. Economic Conditions

Recent economic situations have impacted households globally, including inflation, unemployment, and fluctuating interest rates. The escalating food, petrol, and energy costs have imposed significant financial strain on people (Ansah et al., 2021). Numerous nations are using diverse monetary strategies to address the issue of inflation; hence, acquiring debt is a formidable task. In addition to this, inflation affects the purchasing power of households. The possible impact on low-income households could be quite large. Inflation generally gives rise to financial insecurity (Ghosh et al., 2021). It is an unpredicted situation that a household has not made preparations for. This challenges households in calculating expenses and carrying out future financial planning. The impact of inflation on households' financial instability is extensive and complex (Kaplan & Schulhofer-Wohl, 2017). The negative impact of inflation on buying capacity, the challenges it poses for savings and investment, debt, and its uncertainty all contribute to the increased financial vulnerability that households experience.

Like inflation, unemployment is also a prevalent economic phenomenon that impacts households' financial situations. This situation is marked by uncertainty and significantly alters and may even put a stop to households' main source of income, making them ill-prepared to bear the consequences (Giustozzi, 2023). The unanticipated loss of income can affect households' capacity to fulfill their everyday expenses, satisfy mortgage and EMIs, and pay their healthcare expenditures. The possible consequences of unemployment include an adverse impact on households' savings and the likelihood of them relying on debt to sustain their financial stability (Bayer et al., 2019). Unemployment engenders a cascading effect, leading to diminished expenditure and exerting more influence on the economic growth of a nation.

In addition to inflation and unemployment, a nation's interest rates significantly affect households' financial vulnerability ("Portugal," 2023). Every household creates a projection and a financial plan for allocating their income, encompassing savings and debt settlement. Therefore, it may be inferred that interest rates directly impact households. An increase in the interest rate will result in a corresponding rise in the cost of living, impacting the planned budget of households, particularly those with limited flexibility. Fluctuations in interest rates significantly influence household spending, affecting households' overall financial well-being and vulnerability.

A country's economic situation heavily influences households' financial stability, encompassing inflation, unemployment, interest rates, GDP, and government policies.

2. Climate Change

Climate change can potentially induce adverse environmental consequences and significantly impact households' financial health (Churchill et al., 2023). While the effect may not be felt uniformly across all households, primarily agricultural households bear the brunt of the consequences (Yang et al., 2022). The susceptibility of households is influenced by both temperature and precipitation. Like the sudden pandemic, climate change also impacts households, particularly those with limited financial means, as they lack the necessary economic resources to endure unpredictable circumstances. The impact of climate change on households in Tanzania was observed to manifest in the form of heightened unemployment rates and increased levels of insecurity (Van Aelst & Holvoet, 2018).

The financial strength of households is unfavorably affected by climate change, mainly owing to air pollution, natural calamities, and disasters (Faiella et al., 2022). The potential repercussions of climate change on the well-being of household members can greatly impact their financial vulnerability (Selvaraj et al., 2022). Research has established that the decline in health harms the financial strength of households. Household income is reduced due to medical expenses and reduced efficiency associated with health-related problems. In addition to the unfavorable impact on health, the negative effects on household assets also become evident. Climate alterations of this nature result in financial institutions' reluctance to provide credit. This phenomenon is mostly seen in underdeveloped countries.

The monetary impacts of climate change are extensive, encompassing several aspects such as property destruction, heightened insurance expenses, healthcare expenditures, fluctuations in food prices, elevated energy costs, and employment volatility (Jalal et al., 2021). Like climate change, unforeseen events or emergencies can affect households' financial vulnerability.

APPROACHES FOR EVALUATING THE SUSCEPTIBILITY OF HOUSEHOLDS TO FINANCIAL VULNERABILITY

Before delving into the intricacies of household financial vulnerability from a technical standpoint, it is essential to acknowledge that two distinct methods exist to measure this phenomenon. There are two measures: objective and subjective (Fernández-López et al., 2023). Historically, the literature primarily relied on objective metrics. Objective measures encompass quantifiable variables that can be expressed in monetary terms. The components enclosed within this category are debt levels, savings, overall expenses, investments, assets, liabilities, etc. Subjective measures examine a household's perception and comprehension of financial challenges, encompassing debt repayment and fulfilling daily necessities.

Diverse methodologies exist for assessing the degree of household financial vulnerability across distinct nations. A financial vulnerability index is commonly developed to quantify household financial vulnerability (HFV) (Anderloni et al., 2012b). An index is a comprehensive measure that utilizes several items to gather data on a particular construct. The utilization of an index is seen as superior to that of a scale due to its ability to provide scores at both individual and aggregate levels (Wu, 2022). When constructing an index, researchers can adopt either subjective or objective methodologies. The assessment of households' financial vulnerability is contingent upon using an accurate technique, which entails an evaluation of the household's financial status. Conversely, when employing a subjective methodology, evaluation is conducted based on expectations, emotions, or individual impressions. Principal component analysis (PCA) is used as a statistical technique to construct an index (Greenacre et al., 2022). In addition to this, the application of machine learning technology can also be employed for the evaluation of household financial vulnerability. Clustering methods are used to partition observations into distinct homogeneous subgroups (Azzopardi et al., 2019).

Ways for Overcoming Household Financial Vulnerability

The limitations of households to save, invest, and borrow within their means often lead to such financial vulnerability. Although certain households can bypass such circumstances, low-income households frequently struggle to deal with them. Racism and gender often determine the opportunities that households receive. This criterion can hinder households seeking a job and might face limited support. Hence, it can be difficult for households to obtain financial services and products. For instance, an indigenous grandfather and granddaughter tried to create a bank account in Canada but were stopped. It would not have happened if the family had been white (BBC, 2020).

The fundamental step in averting household vulnerability is ensuring adequate financial knowledge. This literacy is very important for households to tolerate sudden shifts in income or expenses (Sconti, 2022). Understanding savings, budgeting, and borrowing allows households to make well-versed financial choices. Early integration of financial education into school curricula, a step many nations take, is very important (Cordero et al., 2022; DREVER et al., 2015; Erner et al., 2016). However, mere financial literacy in an imbalanced society is not enough. Policymakers must actively participate with low-income households to formulate policies focusing on their needs. Therefore, apart from teaching financial literacy, household voices need to be heard, and current financial institutions should assess and craft appropriate policy interventions to enhance households' resilience and eliminate vulnerability.

Another important facet to focus on involves ensuring greater access to financial products and services for households worldwide. Merely having a bank account isn't enough. Financial institutions must design their offerings to prioritize convenience and accessibility purposefully (Swamy, 2018). Across various regions globally, rural areas still grapple with limited access to diverse banking services. It's imperative to ensure that households have access to and find ease and convenience in utilizing financial products and services. This access is pivotal in enabling households to navigate and withstand unexpected financial disruptions effectively.

In addition to financial literacy and inclusion challenges, reliance on seasonal or temporary work often heightens household financial vulnerability. Job security and scarcity is a very big problem. Japan's lifetime employment system can be adopted across countries to ensure job security. Once a person joins a company, they get to work till their pension. They receive job stability even though it is a very traditional model in which they must pledge loyalty. Hence, they are more ready for an income or an expenditure shock due to a stable source of income. Job scarcity presents a significant obstacle, with unemployment significantly impacting a household's resilience. The availability of employment isn't within the control of households; instead, it's contingent upon a country's governmental employment policies. Targeting low-income communities for economic development strategies can create jobs in those areas (Meltzer & Ghorbani, 2017). However, the feasibility of such plans ultimately rests on the government's capacity and commitment to implementing them.

Managing debt is also crucial to prevent households from entering a cycle of indebtedness. Encouraging responsible borrowing and spending is key to ensuring households don't accumulate excessive debt (Sussman & O'Brien, 2016). Countries like the UK, Canada, and Australia provide free healthcare to their citizens. Hence, they do not have to face many financial difficulties if they face a sudden medical expense. At the same time, households in India, China, and Brazil do not have such medical services provided to them free of cost. Hence, if unprepared, the households in these countries will be vulnerable if a medical expense comes in. Overcoming financial vulnerability at the household level, a joint effort involving government policies, community programs, financial institutions, and individual commitment is very important. Early integration of financial education into school curricula, designing financial products to prioritize convenience and accessibility, a good government policy towards employment, and developing rural areas are some of the policies that can be adopted.

CONCLUSION

Household financial vulnerability is a complex issue. Households experience such financial vulnerability when they experience either an income or an expenditure shock. Although both

low- and middle-income households can experience this vulnerability, it might vary. Apart from income, a household's financial vulnerability can manifest as long-term and short-term. Socio-demographic factors like age, gender, ethnicity, education, income, and household size strongly influence a household's financial vulnerability. Besides this, financial literacy, socialization, and digital payments can heighten or alleviate a household's susceptibility to financial vulnerability. Macro factors like economic conditions and climate change, beyond a household's control, also affect their financial well-being.

After all, the financial vulnerability of households is a situation of possibility; it can or cannot happen. All one can do is grasp the past vulnerability situations of households to devise strategies and mitigate measures to overcome them in the near future. It can create financial stress in households and also health problems. Policy implications like providing early financial literacy and ensuring financial access aim to bolster household resilience against such shocks. While these policies and strategies might not entirely wipe out financial vulnerability, they can be small steps toward the bigger goal of ensuring financial sustainability for households.

REFERENCES

Abd Samad, K., Mohd Daud, S. N., & Mohd Dali, N. R. S. (2020). Determinants of household debt in emerging economies: A macro panel analysis. *Cogent Business & Management*, 7(1), 1831765. 10.1080/23311975.2020.1831765

Alhenawi, Y., & Yazdanparast, A. (2022). Households' intentions under financial vulnerability conditions: Is it likely for the COVID-19 pandemic to leave a permanent scar? *International Journal of Bank Marketing*, 40(3), 425–457. 10.1108/IJBM-05-2021-0200

Ali, L., Khan, M. K. N., & Ahmad, H. (2020). Education of the Head and Financial Vulnerability of Households: Evidence from a Household's Survey Data in Pakistan. *Social Indicators Research*, 147(2), 439–463. 10.1007/s11205-019-02164-2

Alp, E., & Seven, Ü. (2019). The dynamics of household final consumption: The role of wealth channel. *Central Bank Review*, 19(1), 21–32. 10.1016/j.cbrev.2019.03.002

Ampudia, M., van Vlokhoven, H., & Żochowski, D. (2016). Financial fragility of euro area households. *Journal of Financial Stability*, 27, 250–262. 10.1016/j.jfs.2016.02.003

Anderloni, L., Bacchiocchi, E., & Vandone, D. (2012). Household financial vulnerability: An empirical analysis. *Research in Economics*, 66(3), 284–296. 10.1016/j.rie.2012.03.001

Ando, A., & Modigliani, F. (1963). The "Life Cycle" Hypothesis of Saving: Aggregate Implications and Tests. *The American Economic Review*, 53(1), 55–84.

Ansah, I. G. K., Gardebroek, C., & Ihle, R. (2021). Shock interactions, coping strategy choices and household food security. *Climate and Development*, 13(5), 414–426. 10.1080/17565529.2020.1785832

Anthony, M., Sabri, M. F., Wijekoon, R., Abdul Rahim, H., & Abdullah, H., Othman, M. A., & Md. Yusoff, I. S. (2021). The Influence of Financial Socialization, Financial Behavior, Locus of Control and Financial Stress on Young Adults' Financial Vulnerability. *International Journal of Academic Research in Business & Social Sciences*, 11(19). Advance online publication. 10.6007/IJARBSS/v11-i19/11738

Azzopardi, D., Fareed, F., Lenain, P., & Sutherland, D. (2019). Assessing Household Financial Vulnerability: Empirical evidence from the U.S. using machine learning. In *OECD Economic Survey of the United States: Key Research Findings* (pp. 121–142). OECD.

Babiarz, P., & Robb, C. A. (2014). Financial Literacy and Emergency Saving. *Journal of Family and Economic Issues*, 35(1), 40–50. 10.1007/s10834-013-9369-9

Baek, E., & Hong, G.-S. (2004). Effects of Family Life-Cycle Stages on Consumer Debts. *Journal of Family and Economic Issues*, 25(3), 359–385. 10.1023/B:-JEEI.0000039946.59422.5f

Bahaddin, B., Weinberg, S., Luna-Reyes, L. F., & Andersen, D. (2019). Building a bridge to behavioral economics: Countervailing cognitive biases in lifetime saving decisions. *System Dynamics Review*, 35(3), 187–207. 10.1002/sdr.1631

Bayer, C., Luetticke, R., Pham-Dao, L., & Tjaden, V. (2019). Precautionary Savings, Illiquid Assets, and the Aggregate Consequences of Shocks to Household Income Risk. *Econometrica*, 87(1), 255–290. 10.3982/ECTA13601

BBC. (2020, February 9). *Indigenous man and girl handcuffed for opening bank account*. BBC.

Berry, H. L., & Welsh, J. A. (2010). Social capital and health in Australia: An overview from the household, income and labour dynamics in Australia survey. *Social Science & Medicine*, 70(4), 588–596. 10.1016/j.socscimed.2009.10.01219931236

Biju, D. S., & Tantia, V. (2023). Social capital in the form of self-help groups in India: A powerful resilient solution to reduce household financial vulnerability. *Social Work with Groups*, 1–14. 10.1080/01609513.2023.2257754

Bonekamp, J., & van Soest, A. (2022). Evidence of behavioural life-cycle features in spending patterns after retirement. *The Journal of the Economics of Ageing*, 23, 100408. 10.1016/j.jeoa.2022.100408

Brounen, D., Koedijk, K. G., & Pownall, R. A. J. (2016). Household financial planning and savings behavior. *Journal of International Money and Finance*, 69, 95–107. 10.1016/j.jimonfin.2016.06.011

Buckland, J., & Spotton Visano, B. (2022). *Financial Vulnerability in Canada*. Springer International Publishing. 10.1007/978-3-030-92581-9

Camilleri, M. A. (2017). Socially Responsible and Sustainable Investing. In *Corporate Sustainability, Social Responsibility and Environmental Management* (pp. 61–77). Springer International Publishing. 10.1007/978-3-319-46849-5_4

Choi, S., & Shin, J. (2023). Household indebtedness and the macroeconomic effects of tax changes. *Journal of Economic Behavior & Organization*, 209, 22–52. 10.1016/j.jebo.2023.02.022

Christen, M., & Morgan, R. M. (2005). Keeping Up With the Joneses: Analyzing the Effect of Income Inequality on Consumer Borrowing. *Quantitative Marketing and Economics*, 3(2), 145–173. 10.1007/s11129-005-0351-1

Churchill, A. S., Trinh, T.-A., & Danquah, M. (2023). *Temperature, climate change, and household financial behaviour*. Academic Press.

Cifuentes, R., Margaretic, P., & Saavedra, T. (2020). Measuring households' financial vulnerabilities from consumer debt: Evidence from Chile. *Emerging Markets Review*, 43, 100677. 10.1016/j.ememar.2020.100677

Coleman, J. S. (1988). Social Capital in the Creation of Human Capital. *American Journal of Sociology*, 94, S95–S120. 10.1086/228943

Copur, Z., Gutter, M. S., & Erkal, S. (2014). Behavioral Approach to Financial Distress and Health. In *Globalization of Financial Institutions* (pp. 217–233). Springer International Publishing. 10.1007/978-3-319-01125-7_16

Cordero, J. M., Gil-Izquierdo, M., & Pedraja-Chaparro, F. (2022). Financial education and student financial literacy: A cross-country analysis using PISA 2012 data. *The Social Science Journal*, 59(1), 15–33. 10.1016/j.soscij.2019.07.011

Cunha, M. R., Lambrecht, B. M., & Pawlina, G. (2011). Household Liquidity and Incremental Financing Decisions: Theory and Evidence. *Journal of Business Finance & Accounting*, 38(7–8), 1016–1052. 10.1111/j.1468-5957.2011.02248.x

Cutillo, A., & Centra, M. (2017). Gender-Based Occupational Choices and Family Responsibilities: The Gender Wage Gap in Italy. *Feminist Economics*, 23(4), 1–31. 10.1080/13545701.2017.1285041

Daud, S. N. M., Marzuki, A., Ahmad, N., & Kefeli, Z. (2019). Financial Vulnerability and Its Determinants: Survey Evidence from Malaysian Households. *Emerging Markets Finance & Trade*, 55(9), 1991–2003. 10.1080/1540496X.2018.1511421

DeBondt, W., Forbes, W., Hamalainen, P., & Gulnur Muradoglu, Y. (2010). What can behavioural finance teach us about finance? *Qualitative Research in Financial Markets*, 2(1), 29–36. 10.1108/17554171011042371

Din, S. M. U., Mehmood, S. K., Shahzad, A., Ahmad, I., Davidyants, A., & Abu-Rumman, A. (2021). The Impact of Behavioral Biases on Herding Behavior of Investors in Islamic Financial Products. *Frontiers in Psychology*, 11, 600570. Advance online publication. 10.3389/fpsyg.2020.60057033613358

Dolan, P., Elliott, A., Metcalfe, R., & Vlaev, I. (2012). Influencing Financial Behavior: From Changing Minds to Changing Contexts. *Journal of Behavioral Finance*, 13(2), 126–142. 10.1080/15427560.2012.680995

Drever, A., Odders-White, E., Kalish, C. W., Else-Quest, N. M., Hoagland, E. M., & Nelms, E. N. (2015). Foundations of Financial Well-Being: Insights into the Role of Executive Function, Financial Socialization, and Experience-Based Learning in Childhood and Youth. *The Journal of Consumer Affairs*, 49(1), 13–38. 10.1111/joca.12068

Eika, L., Mogstad, M., & Vestad, O. L. (2020). What can we learn about household consumption expenditure from data on income and assets? *Journal of Public Economics*, 189, 104163. 10.1016/j.jpubeco.2020.104163

Eisenhauer, J. G., & Ventura, L. (2006). The prevalence of hyperbolic discounting: Some European evidence. *Applied Economics*, 38(11), 1223–1234. 10.1080/00036840500392391

Erner, C., Goedde-Menke, M., & Oberste, M. (2016). Financial literacy of high school students: Evidence from Germany. *The Journal of Economic Education*, 47(2), 95–105. 10.1080/00220485.2016.1146102

Faiella, I., Lavecchia, L., Michelangeli, V., & Mistretta, A. (2022). A climate stress test on the financial vulnerability of Italian households and firms. *Journal of Policy Modeling*, 44(2), 396–417. 10.1016/j.jpolmod.2021.11.001

Farrall, S. (2021). *Where Have All the People Gone? Theories of Structuration.* Practice and Agency. 10.1007/978-3-030-74830-2_6

Feiveson, L., & Sabelhaus, J. (2019). Lifecycle Patterns of Saving and Wealth Accumulation. *Finance and Economics Discussion Series, 2019*(10). 10.17016/FEDS.2019.010

Fernández-López, S., Álvarez-Espiño, M., Castro-González, S., & Rey-Ares, L. (2023). Financial capability and households' financial vulnerability: Evidence for the Spanish case. *Managerial Finance*, 49(4), 679–702. 10.1108/MF-02-2022-0086

Field, J. (2016). *Social Capital.* Routledge. 10.4324/9780203794623

French, D., & McKillop, D. (2016). Financial literacy and over-indebtedness in low-income households. *International Review of Financial Analysis*, 48, 1–11. 10.1016/j.irfa.2016.08.004

Gamble, A., Gärling, T., & Michaelsen, P. (2019). Young Adults' Consumption Desires, Feelings of Financial Scarcity and Borrowing. In *Indebtedness in Early Adulthood* (pp. 89–108). Springer International Publishing. 10.1007/978-3-030-13996-4_5

Ge, Y., Chen, H., Zou, L., & Zhou, Z. (2021). Political Background and Household Financial Asset Allocation in China. *Emerging Markets Finance & Trade*, 57(4), 1232–1246. 10.1080/1540496X.2020.1865147

George, N. L., & Krishnan, M. R. (2022). Pain of Paying and Different Payment Paradigms. In *New Innovations in Economics, Business and Management Vol. 4* (pp. 161–167). Book Publisher International (a part of SCIENCEDOMAIN International). 10.9734/bpi/niebm/v4/15522D

Ghosh, T., Sahu, S., & Chattopadhyay, S. (2021). Inflation expectations of households in India: Role of oil prices, economic policy uncertainty, and spillover of global financial uncertainty. *Bulletin of Economic Research*, 73(2), 230–251. 10.1111/boer.12244

Giustozzi, C. (2023). Unemployment and Social Integration: Analysing the Impact of Financial Strain, Social Roles, and Identity. *KZfSS Kölner Zeitschrift Für Soziologie Und Sozialpsychologie*. 10.1007/s11577-023-00893-4

Greenacre, M., Groenen, P. J. F., Hastie, T., D'Enza, A. I., Markos, A., & Tuzhilina, E. (2022). Principal component analysis. *Nature Reviews. Methods Primers*, 2(1), 100. 10.1038/s43586-022-00184-w

Ha, X. S., Le, T. H., Phan, T. T., Nguyen, H. H. D., Vo, H. K., & Duong-Trung, N. (2021). *Scrutinizing Trust and Transparency in Cash on Delivery Systems*. 10.1007/978-3-030-68851-6_15

Hamilton, R. W., Mittal, C., Shah, A., Thompson, D. V., & Griskevicius, V. (2019). How Financial Constraints Influence Consumer Behavior: An Integrative Framework. *Journal of Consumer Psychology*, 29(2), 285–305. 10.1002/jcpy.1074

Heckman, S. J., & Hanna, S. D. (2015). Individual and Institutional Factors Related to Low-Income Household Saving Behavior. *Financial Counseling and Planning*, 26(2), 187–199. 10.1891/1052-3073.26.2.187

Hellemans, J., Willems, K., & Brengman, M. (2023). Covid-19 and mobile payment in Belgium: Closing the digital divide or just for the young, social, and impulsive? *Electronic Commerce Research*, 23(3), 1539–1564. 10.1007/s10660-022-09655-4

Hoffmann, A. O. I., & McNair, S. J. (2019). How Does Consumers' Financial Vulnerability Relate to Positive and Negative Financial Outcomes? The Mediating Role of Individual Psychological Characteristics. *The Journal of Consumer Affairs*, 53(4), 1630–1673. 10.1111/joca.12233

Iacoviello, M. (2008). Household Debt and Income Inequality, 1963–2003. *Journal of Money, Credit and Banking*, 40(5), 929–965. 10.1111/j.1538-4616.2008.00142.x

Jalal, M., Khan, M. A., Hossain, M. E., Yedla, S., & Alam, G. M. M. (2021). Does climate change stimulate household vulnerability and income diversity? Evidence from southern coastal region of Bangladesh. *Heliyon*, 7(9), e07990. 10.1016/j.heliyon.2021.e0799034585010

Janssens, W., Pradhan, M., de Groot, R., Sidze, E., Donfouet, H. P. P., & Abajobir, A. (2021). The short-term economic effects of COVID-19 on low-income households in rural Kenya: An analysis using weekly financial household data. *World Development*, 138, 105280. 10.1016/j.worlddev.2020.105280

Jiang, M., Sun, R., & Zhang, B. (2022). Social networks and household financial decisions: Evidence from China. *Journal of Applied Econometrics*, 25(1), 58–92. 10.1080/15140326.2021.2007725

Johnson, K. W., & Li, G. (2010). The Debt-Payment-to-Income Ratio as an Indicator of Borrowing Constraints: Evidence from Two Household Surveys. *Journal of Money, Credit and Banking*, 42(7), 1373–1390. 10.1111/j.1538-4616.2010.00345.x

Johnson, L. (2016). *What Is Social Capital?*10.1007/978-3-319-33264-2_4

Kaplan, G., & Schulhofer-Wohl, S. (2017). Inflation at the household level. *Journal of Monetary Economics*, 91, 19–38. 10.1016/j.jmoneco.2017.08.002

Khando, K., Islam, M. S., & Gao, S. (2022). The Emerging Technologies of Digital Payments and Associated Challenges: A Systematic Literature Review. *Future Internet*, 15(1), 21. 10.3390/fi15010021

Kharas, H. (2010). *The Emerging Middle Class in Developing Countries*. Academic Press.

Kim, J., & Chatterjee, S. (2021). Financial Debt and Mental Health of Young Adults. *Journal of Financial Counseling and Planning*. 10.1891/JFCP-18-00048

Kim, K. T., Wilmarth, M. J., & Henager, R. (2017). Poverty Levels and Debt Indicators Among Low-Income Households Before and After the Great Recession. *Financial Counseling and Planning*, 28(2), 196–212. 10.1891/1052-3073.28.2.196

Kukk, M. (2016). How did household indebtedness hamper consumption during the recession? Evidence from micro data. *Journal of Comparative Economics*, 44(3), 764–786. 10.1016/j.jce.2015.07.004

Kureishi, W., Paule-Paludkiewicz, H., Tsujiyama, H., & Wakabayashi, M. (2021). Time preferences over the life cycle and household saving puzzles. *Journal of Monetary Economics*, 124, 123–139. 10.1016/j.jmoneco.2021.10.004

LeBaron, A. B., Hill, E. J., Rosa, C. M., & Marks, L. D. (2018). Whats and Hows of Family Financial Socialization: Retrospective Reports of Emerging Adults, Parents, and Grandparents. *Family Relations*, 67(4), 497–509. 10.1111/fare.12335

Leclaire, J. (2023). Does Household Debt Matter to Financial Fragility? *Review of Political Economy*, 35(2), 434–453. 10.1080/09538259.2021.1945192

Loibl, C. (2017). Living in Poverty: Understanding the Financial Behaviour of Vulnerable Groups. In *Economic Psychology* (pp. 421–434). Wiley. 10.1002/9781118926352.ch26

Long, M. G. (2018). Pushed into the Red? Female-headed Households and the Pre-crisis Credit Expansion. *The Forum for Social Economics*, 47(2), 224–236. 10.1080/07360932.2018.1451762

Lusardi, A., Mitchell, O. S., & Oggero, N. (2018). The Changing Face of Debt and Financial Fragility at Older Ages. *AEA Papers and Proceedings. American Economic Association*, 108, 407–411. 10.1257/pandp.20181117

Lusardi, A., Mitchell, O. S., Sconti, A., & Sticha, A. (2023). *Understanding Financial Vulnerability Among Asians*. Blacks, and Hispanics in the United States.

Malik, A. N. A., & Annuar, S. N. S. (2021). *The Effect of Perceived Usefulness, Perceived Ease of Use, Reward, and Perceived Risk toward E-Wallet Usage Intention*. 10.1007/978-3-030-65147-3_8

Massenot, B., & Pettinicchi, Y. (2019). Can households see into the future? Survey evidence from the Netherlands. *Journal of Economic Behavior & Organization*, 164, 77–90. 10.1016/j.jebo.2019.05.021

Mazumder, B., & Miller, S. (2016). The Effects of the Massachusetts Health Reform on Household Financial Distress. *American Economic Journal. Economic Policy*, 8(3), 284–313. 10.1257/pol.20150045

Mead, G., & Neves, B. B. (2018). Recursive approaches to technology adoption, families, and the life course: actor network theory and strong structuration theory. In *Connecting Families?* (pp. 41–58). Policy Press. 10.2307/j.ctv2867xm.9

Meltzer, R., & Ghorbani, P. (2017). Does gentrification increase employment opportunities in low-income neighborhoods? *Regional Science and Urban Economics*, 66, 52–73. 10.1016/j.regsciurbeco.2017.06.002

Morgan, P. J., & Long, T. Q. (2020). Financial literacy, financial inclusion, and savings behavior in Laos. *Journal of Asian Economics*, 68, 101197. 10.1016/j.asieco.2020.101197

Morris, T., Maillet, S., & Koffi, V. (2022). Financial knowledge, financial confidence and learning capacity on financial behavior: A Canadian study. *Cogent Social Sciences*, 8(1), 1996919. Advance online publication. 10.1080/23311886.2021.1996919

Muradoglu, G., & Harvey, N. (2012). Behavioural finance: The role of psychological factors in financial decisions. *Review of Behavioral Finance*, 4(2), 68–80. 10.1108/19405971211284862

Mützel, S. (2021). Unlocking the payment experience: Future imaginaries in the case of digital payments. *New Media & Society*, 23(2), 284–301. 10.1177/1461444820929317

Noerhidajati, S., Purwoko, A. B., Werdaningtyas, H., Kamil, A. I., & Dartanto, T. (2021). Household financial vulnerability in Indonesia: Measurement and determinants. *Economic Modelling*, 96, 433–444. 10.1016/j.econmod.2020.03.02832836621

Nofsinger, J. R. (2012). Household behavior and boom/bust cycles. *Journal of Financial Stability*, 8(3), 161–173. 10.1016/j.jfs.2011.05.004

Ofer, Z. (1996). *The pain of paying*. Carnegie Mellon University.

Pissarides, C. A. (2013). Unemployment in the Great Recession. *Economica*, 80(319), 385–403. 10.1111/ecca.12026

Platt, H., & Platt, M. (2008). Financial Distress Comparison Across Three Global Regions. *Journal of Risk and Financial Management*, 1(1), 129–162. 10.3390/jrfm1010129

Pollin, R. (1988). The growth of U.S. household debt: Demand-side influences. *Journal of Macroeconomics*, 10(2), 231–248. 10.1016/0164-0704(88)90060-2

Portugal. (2023). *IMF Staff Country Reports, 2023*(219), 1. 10.5089/9798400246104.002

Rani, A., Quddoos, A., Yaseen, M. R., Tabassum, S., & Asif, A. (2021). The Impact of Social Capital on Household Well-being in Pakistan. *Social Indicators Research*, 158(3), 927–946. 10.1007/s11205-021-02717-434456449

Richardson, T., Elliott, P., Roberts, R., & Jansen, M. (2017). A Longitudinal Study of Financial Difficulties and Mental Health in a National Sample of British Undergraduate Students. *Community Mental Health Journal*, 53(3), 344–352. 10.1007/s10597-016-0052-027473685

Sabri, M. F., Abd Rahim, H., Wijekoon, R., Zakaria, N. F., Magli, A. S., & Reza, T. S. (2020). The Mediating Effect of Money Attitude on Association Between Financial Literacy, Financial Behaviour, and Financial Vulnerability. *International Journal of Academic Research in Business & Social Sciences*, 10(15). Advance online publication. 10.6007/IJARBSS/v10-i15/8254

Salisbury, L. C., Nenkov, G. Y., Blanchard, S. J., Hill, R. P., Brown, A. L., & Martin, K. D. (2023). Beyond Income: Dynamic Consumer Financial Vulnerability. *Journal of Marketing*, 87(5), 657–678. 10.1177/00222429221150910

Sconti, A. (2022). Having Trouble Making Ends Meet? Financial Literacy Makes the Difference. *Italian Economic Journal*. 10.1007/s40797-022-00212-4

Selvaraj, J. J., Guerrero, D., Cifuentes-Ossa, M. A., & Guzmán Alvis, Á. I. (2022). The economic vulnerability of fishing households to climate change in the south Pacific region of Colombia. *Heliyon*, 8(5), e09425. 10.1016/j.heliyon.2022.e0942535620620

Seymour, G., & Peterman, A. (2018). Context and measurement: An analysis of the relationship between intrahousehold decision making and autonomy. *World Development*, 111, 97–112. 10.1016/j.worlddev.2018.06.027

Shefrin, H. M., & Thaler, R. H. (1988). The Behavioral Life-Cycle Hypothesis. *Economic Inquiry*, 26(4), 609–643. 10.1111/j.1465-7295.1988.tb01520.x

Sherraden, M. (2013). Building Blocks of Financial Capability. In *Financial Capability and Asset Development* (pp. 3–43). Oxford University Press. 10.1093/acprof:oso/9780199755950.003.0012

Sherraden, M. S., & Ansong, D. (2016). Financial Literacy to Financial Capability: Building Financial Stability and Security. In *International Handbook of Financial Literacy* (pp. 83–96). Springer Singapore. 10.1007/978-981-10-0360-8_7

Singh, K. N., & Malik, S. (2022). An empirical analysis on household financial vulnerability in India: Exploring the role of financial knowledge, impulsivity and money management skills. *Managerial Finance*, 48(9/10), 1391–1412. 10.1108/MF-08-2021-0386

Singh, V. (2022). Dynamics of affordability and immigration in the Canadian housing market. *International Journal of Housing Markets and Analysis*, 15(3), 709–732. 10.1108/IJHMA-04-2021-0037

Sohn, S., Joo, S., Grable, J. E., Lee, S., & Kim, M. (2012). Adolescents' financial literacy: The role of financial socialization agents, financial experiences, and money attitudes in shaping financial literacy among South Korean youth. *Journal of Adolescence*, 35(4), 969–980. 10.1016/j.adolescence.2012.02.00222418452

Son, J., & Feng, Q. (2019). In Social Capital We Trust? *Social Indicators Research*, 144(1), 167–189. 10.1007/s11205-018-2026-9

Stones, R. (2005). *Structuration Theory*. Macmillan Education UK. 10.1007/978-0-230-21364-7

Sullivan, L., & Meschede, T. (2016). Race, Gender, and Senior Economic Well-Being: How Financial Vulnerability Over the Life Course Shapes Retirement for Older Women of Color. *The Public Policy and Aging Report*, 26(2), 58–62. 10.1093/ppar/prw001

Sun, L., Small, G., Huang, Y.-H., & Ger, T.-B. (2022). Financial Shocks, Financial Stress and Financial Resilience of Australian Households during COVID-19. *Sustainability (Basel)*, 14(7), 3736. 10.3390/su14073736

Sun, S., Chen, Y.-C., Ansong, D., Huang, J., & Sherraden, M. S. (2022). Household Financial Capability and Economic Hardship: An Empirical Examination of the Financial Capability Framework. *Journal of Family and Economic Issues*, 43(4), 716–729. 10.1007/s10834-022-09816-535095251

Sussman, A. B., & O'Brien, R. L. (2016). Knowing When to Spend: Unintended Financial Consequences of Earmarking to Encourage Savings. *JMR, Journal of Marketing Research*, 53(5), 790–803. 10.1509/jmr.14.0455

Swamy, V. (2018). Financial Inclusion And The Resilience Of Poor Households. *Journal of Developing Areas*, 53(4). Advance online publication. 10.1353/jda.2018.0079

Van Aelst, K., & Holvoet, N. (2018). Climate change adaptation in the Morogoro Region of Tanzania: Women's decision-making participation in small-scale farm households. *Climate and Development*, 10(6), 495–508. 10.1080/17565529.2017.1318745

Van Nguyen, H., Ha, G. H., Nguyen, D. N., Doan, A. H., & Phan, H. T. (2022). Understanding financial literacy and associated factors among adult population in a low-middle income country. *Heliyon*, 8(6), e09638. 10.1016/j.heliyon.2022.e0963835677404

Warmath, D., Piehlmaier, D., & Robb, C. (2019). The impact of shared financial decision making on overconfidence for married adults. *Financial Planning Review*, 2(1), e1032. Advance online publication. 10.1002/cfp2.1032

Winkler, S. (2017). Housing, Finance, Policy and the Wider Economy. *Journal of Management and Sustainability*, 7(2), 45. 10.5539/jms.v7n2p45

Worthington, A. C. (2006). Debt as a source of financial stress in Australian households. *International Journal of Consumer Studies*, 30(1), 2–15. 10.1111/j.1470-6431.2005.00420.x

Wu, H.-S. (2022). Constructing Indices and Scales. In *CFDR Workshop Series*. Bowling Green State University.

Xiao, J. J., Huang, J., Goyal, K., & Kumar, S. (2022). Financial capability: A systematic conceptual review, extension and synthesis. *International Journal of Bank Marketing*, 40(7), 1680–1717. 10.1108/IJBM-05-2022-0185

Yang, S., Zou, K., Lei, T., Ni, Z., & Yang, J. (2022). Climate Change and Farmers' Household Financial Vulnerability: Evidence From China. *Frontiers in Environmental Science*, 10, 908428. Advance online publication. 10.3389/fenvs.2022.908428

Yazdanparast, A., & Alhenawi, Y. (2022). Impact of COVID-19 pandemic on household financial decisions: A consumer vulnerability perspective. *Journal of Consumer Behaviour*, 21(4), 806–827. 10.1002/cb.203837519436

Yilmazer, T., Babiarz, P., & Liu, F. (2015). The impact of diminished housing wealth on health in the United States: Evidence from the Great Recession. *Social Science & Medicine*, 130, 234–241. 10.1016/j.socscimed.2015.02.02825728483

Yu, C., Jia, N., Li, W., & Wu, R. (2022). Digital inclusive finance and rural consumption structure – evidence from Peking University digital inclusive financial index and China household finance survey. *China Agricultural Economic Review*, 14(1), 165–183. 10.1108/CAER-10-2020-0255

Yu, H.-C., Hsi, K.-H., & Kuo, P.-J. (2002). Electronic payment systems: An analysis and comparison of types. *Technology in Society*, 24(3), 331–347. 10.1016/S0160-791X(02)00012-X

Zhao, H., & Zhang, L. (2020). Talking money at home: The value of family financial socialization. *International Journal of Bank Marketing*, 38(7), 1617–1634. 10.1108/IJBM-04-2020-0174

KEY TERMS AND DEFINITIONS

Expenditure Shock: Expenditure shock is when someone encounters a sudden expenditure for which they are unprepared. It can be a sudden medical expense, major repair, etc. (K. N. Singh & Malik, 2022).

Financial Capability: Financial capability is an individual's ability to grab financial opportunities through financial products or services. They should be able to understand these financial products and services, be financially included, and exhibit their financial skills and behavior. An individual who exhibits all these qualities is said to be financially capable (M. Sherraden, 2013; Xiao et al., 2022).

Financial Socialization: Financial socialization is a process through which individuals acquire financial knowledge, skills, and behavior in a social setting. This social setting can be friends, family, and teachers. These socialization agents shape their financial behavior s(LeBaron et al., 2018; Zhao & Zhang, 2020).

Household Financial Vulnerability: Households are deemed to be financially vulnerable if they are not able to meet their day-to-day expenses or if they cannot withstand a sudden income or an expenditure shock (Anderloni et al., 2012b).

Income Shock: Income shock occurs when someone loses their main source of income. It can happen due to one losing their job, business not doing well, or encountering an investment loss (K. N. Singh & Malik, 2022).

Objective Approach of Household Financial Vulnerability: The objective approach measures household financial vulnerability using quantitative measures like debt level, expenses, investment, income and asset level (Noerhidajati et al., 2021).

Subjective Approach of Household Financial Vulnerability: Subjective approach captures the perceptions and feelings of households. It measures the household's perception of meeting their needs and debt on time and whether they are financially capable enough to withstand a sudden income or an expenditure shock (Noerhidajati et al., 2021).

Chapter 3
Accounting for Sustainability:
The Measurements and Financial Reporting Disclosure

Siriyama Kanthi Herath
https://orcid.org/0000-0002-6443-9739
Clark Atlanta University, USA

Laksitha Maheshi Herath
New York University, USA

ABSTRACT

This chapter will examine the value of accounting for sustainability, as well as how its implementation supports sustainability and financial literacy in modern business operations. In order to increase transparency and accountability, the chapter will explore the crucial components of assessing sustainability and the necessity of related financial reporting disclosures. Businesses have become more aware of the importance of incorporating sustainability into their accounting procedures because of an increased emphasis on aspects relating to the environmental, social, and governance (ESG). This chapter intends to shed light on how businesses can track their sustainability performance and inform stakeholders of important information. By promoting financial literacy and sustainable practices, the chapter will help achieve the book's main goal of increasing knowledge regarding the dynamic relationship between sustainability and business today.

DOI: 10.4018/979-8-3693-0863-9.ch003

1. INTRODUCTION

The foundation for the chapter will be established in the introduction, which provides a comprehensive framework and highlights the growing importance of sustainability in contemporary corporate settings. Sustainability is defined as a *requirement of our generation to manage the resource base such that the average quality of life* that we ensure ourselves can potentially be shared by all future generations (Asheim, 1994, p. 1). The quality of life is what shapes the conditions in which a person lives. It goes beyond just physical things. Sustainability means, among other things, being able to thrive amid obstacles over long periods while keeping the social, economic, and ecological domains in an at least equitable state. It is an open initiative that emphasizes seeing how the environment, people, and finances are related. It is not only about saving resources for our future generations but also about making compelling changes in the way we live today -- changes that benefit nature and people on this planet.

Stakeholder theory is the foundation of sustainable development efforts since it sheds light on the importance of managing relationships among organizations and their stakeholders for beneficial gains. Traditionally, a business's success is measured only by how happy and rich it makes its shareholders (Clarkson, 1995). But now, managers do not just have to focus on making shareholders better off at the expense of other important people involved, as they are in charge of fulfilling the duties of the company to all its stakeholders (Clarkson, 1995). The main idea of thinking about stakeholders is to make the company last, as Freeman says it is getting a business to reach its goals (1984).

Sustainability is consistent with the theory of stakeholders and highlights the importance of establishing relationships, optimizing the value chain, and acknowledging interconnections (Sheehy, 2005). Both learning systems underscore the value of critical thinking skills, enabling corporations to enhance their business appeal by focusing on goals and objectives (Radin, 2007). In the last few years, many important events and ideas have caused an unexpected growth in stakeholders' attention to sustainable development (Barkemeyer et al., 2014). Now, most people and leaders support sustainable development. It might be the common way to talk about nature for almost everyone in these discussions (Jacobs, 1999). Sustainability practices have become an essential aspect of business operations as the world battles with major environmental problems and raises public awareness of them. This section will show how sustainability considerations are crucial to long-term viability and business prosperity today more than ever. Even though financial literacy is important, there is a bigger need to emphasize educating the public on how they can better contribute to sustainability goals. Both topics have unique challenges and requirements, and a specialized approach is needed to completely understand them.

First, we will discuss the effects of sustainability practices on understanding finances. Knowing financial results is more than just understanding financial reports. It now means learning things about balance, like how it can impact the world. This is because firms realize they need to care about nature and the community when making money choices. When we mix our understanding of money with care for the earth and all living things, we can make choices that are good for both business and helping people live healthy lives. Accounting, or business talk, plays a key role in accurately keeping track of and making sense of sustainability data. It also provides correct information to other people in businesses. The main goal is to show how accountants can completely check a company's sustainability results by filling the gap between money and non-money details.

We want to say how much caring for our environment and keeping the world safe matters. It supports the idea of considering all types of information, including both monetary and non-monetary. This helps us to truly understand the worth of a company and its effects on nature and people. In today's world, how long resources last is very important. It goes beyond the usual ways of doing things and living. In simple words, sustainability is about maintaining equilibrium by protecting the environment. This also means treating everyone fairly and ensuring financial stability. Ensuring sustainability is important because of the impacts of weather change, running out of resources, and inequality in employment and communities. Ignoring these important factors can threaten the well-being of future generations. Also, it might affect businesses through violations of regulations, harming their reputation.

Sustainability is becoming more popular, but it faces some challenges. They are mostly about measuring and informing people about what is happening in this area. It is hard to measure how much sustainability we have. This is because the environment, people, and profits are all connected in complicated ways. Sometimes, metrics and indicators keep changing, leading to challenges in reporting or comparing them with other groups. Also, the area of showing information has problems with clarity of responsibility. In these areas, companies could make their green actions seem bigger or better than they are. It is very important to fix these measuring and telling problems. This will help create trust, allow people to make decisions with knowledge, and work toward a long-lasting future.

In the next sections of this chapter, we will talk more about how adding sustainability to accounting increases financial understanding and creates a positive outlook. We will also share new ideas for businesses that use environmentally friendly practices to make them last longer.

2. UNDERSTANDING SUSTAINABILITY MEASUREMENTS

In its landmark publication 'Our Common Future', the World Commission on Environment and Development defined sustainable development as "development that meets the needs of the present without compromising the ability of future generations to meet their own needs" (1987, p. 8). The word "sustainable development" includes two main ideas. First, it highlights the important needs of poor people in our world. Second, it recognizes the rules set by technology and society on how much the environment can handle current needs and future demands (Dennis, 2020). In the private sector, sustainability is often put into practice through a series of reports about being sustainable. These are based on three main areas - social well-being, financial gains, and environmental healthiness. The Global Reporting Initiative (GRI) has become the most important set of standards for this kind of reporting (Barkemeyer et al, 2014). The GRI Guidelines follow some established standards and guidelines (GRI, 2021; GRI, 2016). These include being open, including everyone, and checking records to make sure they all match up properly and completely fit in context with sustainable stewardship. These principles aim to ensure that sustainability reports:

> *Show a balanced picture of how well the economy, environment, and society are doing;*
> *Allow comparisons both over time and between different things, and*
> *Truly deal with things that are important to the people involved* (Clarkson et al., 2008).

The GRI reveals that when companies use its rules, they show how their actions affect the triple bottom line; environment, society, and economy, and they can have good or bad effects (Manes-Rossi et al., 2018). When talking about longevity, it is important to measure how a company can affect the environment and its people using ESG (environmental, social, and governance) factors. According to many studies (Bassen and Kovacs, 2008; Tarmuji et al., 2016; Yoon et al., 2018; La Torre et al., 2018), ESG is a plan for sustainability. This means that decisions are made using different non-financial factors. Sustainable reports help businesses show how they are being responsible for society. They help improve communication with stakeholders by showing more openness and responsibility for non-monetary information (Patten & Zhao, 2014). ESG information helps businesses and individuals make environmentally friendly decisions. It covers topics like the environment, social concerns, and good leadership. Understanding the factors, mainly leadership, that drive the successful conservation of natural resources in certain communities is vital (Adams et al., 2011). Pollution, saving wild animals and plants, the 'greenhouse effect', and] waste disposal is some of the many environmental problems.

Also, using naturally available energy sources like power instead of harmful coal helps keep our planet cleaner. It is also important not to use more power than we need for living, ensuring the quality of life, diversity, and fairness in our community, including equal treatment of employees (Al-Qudah et al., 2021; Sultana et al., 2018; Xie et al., 2019). People often miss the possible trade-offs between nature and the financial growth or expansion of their businesses. Some businesses believe it is important to be sustainable to achieve lasting improvements. Therefore, some groups state they care about the environment or are getting better at it. However, some may hide real issues and still damage the environment while maintaining social unfairness (Barkemeyer et al., 2014). In recent times, the creation and use of GRI rules have changed non-financial disclosures from happening occasionally to regular efforts. These now include things like assessing risks, identifying chances, ways to stop corruption or deceitful practices in business, and managing how companies are governed (Manes-Rossi et al., 2018; Patten et al., 2015; Milne & Gray, 2007).

We will explore how businesses can track and measure their actions for sustainability. This includes reporting systems that keep shareholders informed on how they are doing to be more environmentally friendly (Figure 1). Amid a growing understanding of human impact on the planet and stakeholder pressures, there is a growing agreement that every company must aim to be environmentally friendly (Deloitte, 2021).

Figure 1. Understanding sustainability measurements

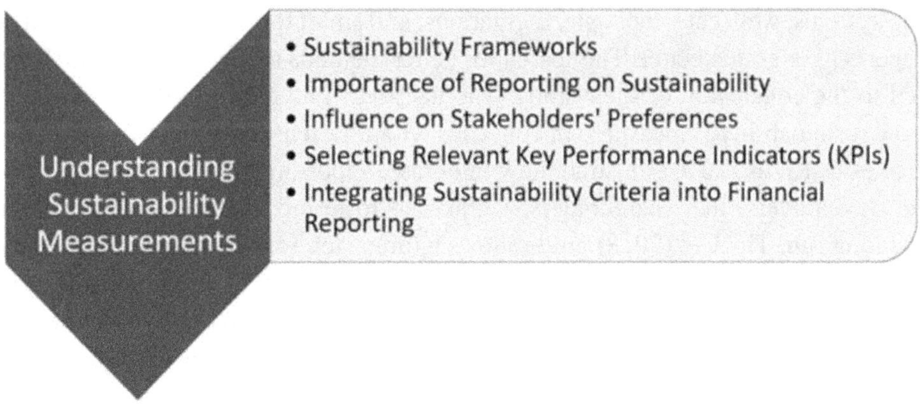

2.1 Sustainability Frameworks

One way many people share information about sustainability is through the Global Reporting Initiative (GRI). The Sustainability Accounting Standards Board (SASB), just like the GRI, provides standards for different areas of sustainability. These rules change how information is reported to match the special features of different business areas. Because they deal with ESG issues that can impact a company's financial position (FP), the Sustainability Accounting Standards are very important for stakeholders to assess an organization's sustainability. Fatihudin and Mochklas (2018) point out that financial performance is a way to measure how well a company manages its finances, and this includes aspects like having enough cash, doing operations efficiently, and using advantages smartly during a specific period.

2.2 Importance of Reporting on Sustainability

Sustainability reporting is no longer just a hobby; it has become an important part of company honesty and clear communication. Stakeholders like customers, workers, and investors also care about a company's ways of staying green. They consider these things when making decisions. Businesses can gain the trust of important stakeholders and build strong connections with them by sharing clear information about their efforts to be sustainable. Lai and Stacchezzini examined carefully how businesses and experts are having a hard time because of recent changes in regulations for disclosing sustainability measures (2021). Their study shows that big systems, well-known people, regulations, and smart tools used as sustainability reports have gotten better. The search for better methods to report on sustainability led to the conclusion of their study. The next part provides real-life evidence of how sustainability is measured in countries with different regulations and systems. Eccles & Krzus (2010) illustrate how integrated reporting helps the company and its stakeholders, like shareholders, while also fostering a sustainable society in the long run. The UN (2018) guide shows a three-step way to mix the Sustainable Development Goals (SDGs) into business and reporting. It helps companies show how they are affecting the SDGs and what stakeholders need to know. It follows UN rules for business dealing with human rights issues, along with GRI standards, too.

Measuring sustainability and using it to make rules or set up regulatory institutions vary in different countries based on their social and economic backgrounds, cultures, and environments. Here is a brief overview, incorporating empirical evidence from various institutional settings (WEO, 2023).

Advanced Economies (e.g., USA, European Union)

Empirical Evidence: The EU's Sustainability Action Plan and the US Environmental Protection Agency often show reports about greenhouse gas levels, lost animal life numbers, and usage of natural resources.

Institutional Setting: These countries usually have strong government groups, like the EPA or the European Environment Agency. They gather and study information about sustainability measures. They also have strong schools and research centers that help with these numbers.

Emerging Economies (e.g., Brazil, India)

Empirical Evidence: The Environmental Performance Index (EPI) ranks countries based on their performance measures in areas like health protection and environmental well-being. Countries like Brazil are reviewed based on how much their forests change. Meanwhile, India's score is inspected using air quality measures.

Institutional Setting: Newly affluent countries often struggle to balance their fast-growing economies with sustainability. Their institutional systems might still be growing, but there is more focus on making special environmental groups and working together with global organizations to get information and help.

Developing Countries (e.g., Sub-Saharan Africa, Southeast Asia)

Empirical Evidence: The United Nations Sustainable Development Goals (SDGs) give a worldwide plan, and many poor countries do voluntary national reviews (VNRs) to show their progress on these targets. For example, countries in sub-Saharan Africa might work on water and toilets (SDG 6) because there is not enough clean water.

Institutional Setting: These countries may have a young system, but they know that sustainability is important. Many people depend on support from other countries and work with large groups like the World Bank and UN agencies. They use this support to get better at what they do and collect important information.

Island Nations (e.g., Maldives, Pacific Islands)

Empirical Evidence: These countries have special problems, like increasing ocean levels. These often include special research projects that study the effects of climate change, how coral reefs decline, and ocean acidification.

Institutional Setting: Because they are vulnerable, several countries on islands have formed special groups for dealing with climate change. They also take part in worldwide meetings like the Conference of Parties (COP) to express their worries and ask for help.

The way we measure if something is sustainable can change depending on the ability, focus, and issues of an organization. Even though large countries may have many data points and set rules, smaller ones are now including ways to be kinder to the Earth in their plans for establishing laws. This is because it is important to them at home, and they promise it to other countries too.

2.3 Influence on Stakeholders' Preferences

Incorporating sustainability reporting into financial disclosures can significantly influence stakeholders' preferences and decisions. People who put money into companies are getting more worried about problems like pollution and unfair treatment of people. They start to realize that these may stop a company from making lots of profit in the future, so they care more now than before. So, they are more likely to put money in firms with good plans for sustainability initiatives and a commitment to being responsible business owners. People are beginning to care more about companies that do good things for others and the environment. This shows how important it is to provide reports on sustainability in all aspects of life. Broadstock et al. (2020) explained that often, investors think about ESG results when guessing how well a stock will do in the future or lower risk from it. Kaur & Lodhia (2018) point out that people need to take part in making plans, setting goals about staying green, and checking how well they are doing. They further believe we should review reports to see if their actions are protecting the Earth. Governments and stock markets should make sure that all public companies reveal their goals for being green as well as records they can prove are accurate (KPMG, 2020).

2.4 Selecting Relevant Key Performance Indicators (KPIs)

To measure how resilient a group is, we must choose the best Key Performance Indicators (KPIs). These measures help us see if our efforts to be green are getting better and giving good results. Businesses can get better and make clear goals for being nice to nature if they do the right things. Examples of sustainability KPIs include:

Carbon Emissions: Tracking how we use water, so this asset does not get wasted.

Worker Diversity: Helping different people and understanding the diverse nature of jobs to make a more equal place.

Volunteerism: Promoting staff involvement in helping others and giving to charity.

Governance Procedures: Checking if good business rules make companies act right and be responsible.

2.5 Integrating Sustainability Criteria Into Financial Reporting

To make sure everyone knows how well an organization is doing, rules about being sustainable should be mixed with financial reporting. By combining important ESG information with financial information, businesses can show they care about being green and point out how these steps line up with their overall plan for making cash. Lourenço et al., (2012) point out that using green methods helps businesses stand out better than their rivals in the business world. According to a study by Albuquerque et al., (2019), this change increases productivity and efficiency while also reducing risks from big problems.

Businesses need to measure and share their actions towards sustainability. Of the three main parts of sustainable development - economic, ecological, and social—the social aspect often remains the most ambiguous and least clearly defined in sustainable efforts (Vifell & Soneryd, 2012). Choosing agreed methods to protect the environment, picking important measures, and adding them to financial reports all help make a company's journey towards being eco-friendly clearer and more trustworthy. As stakeholders need companies to reveal how green and good they are, making sure businesses inspect their effects becomes a big deal for being successful in the future. It is hard to measure sustainability. We need many tests to identify all its components. A common method to identify how sustainable a business is to use rules about the environment, people, and leadership (ESG).

Environmental Metrics: These show how good a business is at protecting the environment. Common measures are what we do with our carbon footprint, water use, how to deal with trash, and energy usage. Groups like CDP (previously called the Carbon Disclosure Project) and SASB (Sustainability Accounting Standards Board) provided detailed information on steps to keep the environment safe.

Advantages: Environmental ratings measure how much a company harms the environment. They let people who invest in it or work with it know if they truly care about being friendly to Earth.
Disadvantages: These measures can sometimes be too big, possibly making complex natural problems easier than they are.

Social Metrics: They review how a company affects society. They look at things like work practices, the rights of people, involvement with the community, and diversity. Groups like the Global Reporting Initiative (GRI) and MSCI ESG Research provide information on how well companies do socially.

Advantages: Social measures focus on the people's side, making sure businesses think about their wider effects on society. This promotes more welcoming and responsible ways of doing business.
Disadvantages: It can be hard to set social measures that work everywhere because of culture, location, and job-related differences.

Governance Metrics: These evaluate how good a company's rules and actions are. They review things like who is on the board, pay for bosses, the rights of shareholders, and business in the right way. Firms such as Institutional Shareholder Services (ISS) and the Council of Institutional Investors (CII) focus on assessing how well companies' leaders are doing.

Advantages: Measurement of governance shows the value of clear and honest decision-making, helping to build trust among investors and partners.
Disadvantages: Governance measures are very important, but sometimes it is easier to count them compared with environmental and social factors. This could make some aspects seem more significant than others.

While the ESG system gives a complete picture of sustainability, each part has its advantages and disadvantages. The people who provide these numbers are very important, but we always have to change and improve them because sustainability changes all the time.

3. FINANCIAL REPORTING AND DISCLOSURE FOR SUSTAINABILITY

Businesses can use a variety of financial reporting disclosures to demonstrate their commitment to environmental, social, and governance (ESG) principles while achieving sustainable goals. The reason for providing information about sustainability in financial statements is so people can see how a company will do over time and if it is strong enough. This section examines why it is important to do that (Figure 2).

Figure 2. Financial reporting disclosure for sustainability

Financial Reporting Disclosure for Sustainability

- The Influence of International Financial Reporting Standards (IFRS) Foundation
- The Need for Uniform Disclosure Methods
- Benefits of Open Sustainability
- Impact of Regulations on Sustainability Reporting Practices
- Leveraging Sustainability Reporting for Strategic Advantage
- Integrating Financial and Sustainability Reporting

The Influence of the International Financial Reporting Standards (IFRS) Foundation: The International Financial Reporting Standards (IFRS) Foundation and other known bodies are helping create worldwide rules for money reporting. The IFRS Foundation is always searching for ways to incorporate sustainability into financial reporting rules as it becomes more well-known. We have learned a lot about the importance of reporting on sustainability due to larger financial issues.

The Need for Uniform Disclosure Methods: As companies reporting on their sustainability efforts gets more complicated, there's a growing need for standard ways to show information (IFRS, 2021b). This helps make clear comparisons between different firms possible. By having businesses tell important ESG information often, it makes rules for talking about how green a company is the same. This helps people and those who give money to check out each business's effect on our planet.

Benefits of Open Sustainability: Making transparent sustainability known is very important for getting trust from stakeholders. By giving a full look at how well an organization is doing on issues related to the environment, society, and governance practices, companies show they care about responsible operations that are good for the earth. Sharing information with stakeholders increases cooperation and shows a company's commitment to openness and good business practices. Showing how your company is sustainable can bring in good people who care about society and the environment. They use these facts when deciding to invest money. These investors look for businesses with good green practices. They think that putting money into those companies can help change society and the environment positively. Businesses can get money from good-hearted investors who agree with their goals to be more eco-friendly. This makes it easier for these companies to grow and thrive while also protecting our environment.

Impact of Regulations on Sustainability Reporting Practices: Many countries have begun to require businesses of certain types to give information on how they're being sustainable. This is because ESG factors are very crucial when it comes to investing money and considering risks. These rules focus on the need for correct reporting about how sustainability is being done. These guidelines assist a business in showing they are beneficial for people and nature. It also makes sure they follow the law correctly.

Leveraging Sustainability Reporting for Strategic Advantage: Companies do not just follow rules in sustainability reporting; it can be an important tool for them. When businesses look at, show, and fix how they care for the environment, they can find ways to grow. They also protect themselves from danger and generate new ideas. They can work well with partners, become more known, and get opportunities to invest from big bosses who care about doing good things for the planet.

Integrating Financial and Sustainability Reporting: Talking about money and nature together helps businesses clearly show how they do all things well. Businesses can clearly show how using green ways saves their money. This makes it clear why it is important to do business responsibly and care for the planet. Telling the truth about money and sustainability in business is becoming very important. By being honest about their impact on the environment, social issues, and fair treatment of workers, companies can gain trust. This will help them find good investors who care about ethics. They will also meet new rules made by governments in areas like pollution or worker rights. By doing this, they are setting themselves up for success over the long term after taking these key factors. As more and more businesses become sustainable, financial reporting becomes very important. It helps to push good changes forward so that growth can be long-lasting, too. Adams (2017) examines how ESG (environmental, social, and governance) risk, business strategy execution, and corporate reporting are changing. The focus is on non-financial reports in this area.

4. CHALLENGES OF INTEGRATING SUSTAINABILITY INTO ACCOUNTING PRACTICES

Getting sustainability ideas into company business accounting can be tough, but it gives businesses a way to run fairly and openly. Talking about sustainability is still tricky, though. According to Herzig and Schaltegger (2006), these challenges are always changing, making the study of corporate management increasingly difficult. According to Bebbington & Larrinaga (2014), firms continue to experience problems and unpredictability because of changing managerial expectations and shifting market conditions. Cho et al. (2015) claimed reporting systems can have similar problems, as described by Higgins and Coffey (2016). De Micco et al., (2021) specifically address the more pervasive issue of difficulties with sustainability reporting. The study is based on the generally acknowledged accounting notion that it is important to consider a company's financial results and their impact on society and the environment in which it operates. The main challenges that companies face when integrating sustainability into their accounting are covered in this part (Figure 3).

Figure 3. Challenges of integrating sustainability into accounting practices

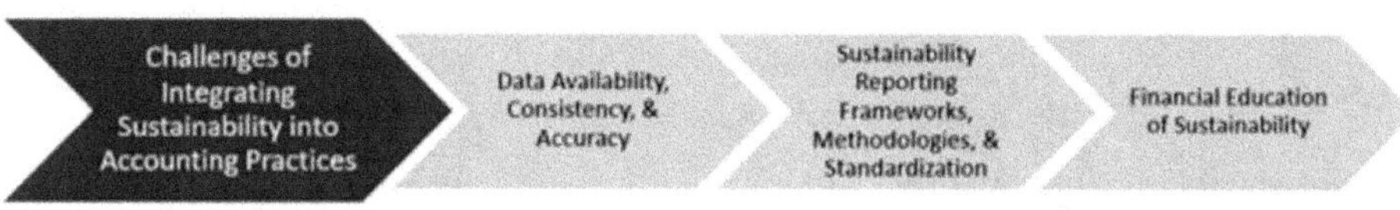

4.1 Data Availability, Consistency, and Accuracy

When incorporating sustainability into accounting practices, businesses must overcome several obstacles, such as data availability, consistency, and honesty. Collecting accurate and up-to-date statistics on sustainability criteria can be a rather challenging and long process. However, it is very difficult to establish a unified database for meaningful comparisons as various companies and organizations rely on numerous sources and methods of data collection.

Data availability is referred to as the fact that there are many issues of sustainability that have a lot of vital information about carbon emissions, water consumption and various waste management and social impact governing practices. Even though some organizations could have access to complete data, others might struggle because of a lack of funding, outdated data monitoring systems, or conflicting reporting guidelines.

Consistency in data refers to the dependability and homogeneity of sustainability information obtained throughout time and across several reporting periods. Inconsistent data could result from adjustments to the methods used to collect it, changes to the frequency of reporting, or differences in how the data were interpreted. Inconsistent data can lead to inaccurate assessments of an organization's sustainability performance, which also makes it more challenging to monitor progress and set reasonable goals.

Data accuracy is crucial for the viability of accounting systems. A lack of trust can be caused by faulty or inaccurate information, which can also affect sustainability reporting. Data-driven processes can produce poor outcomes because they rely on accurate information. A company's reputation and legal position might be damaged by inaccurate data. Organizations can use various strategies to address data availability, accuracy, and uniformity (Figure 4).

Figure 4. Strategies to address the issues of data availability, consistency, and accuracy

Gathering data on sustainability can be hard and take a long time. Organizations might find it hard to gather correct and important information, especially when they work in different countries or have complicated supply lines. To fix these problems, we could maybe make getting information the same in every case. Businesses need to deal with problems of getting data easily and correctly if they want their financial reporting to work well when bringing sustainability in. Groups can give a better and more complete picture of their sustainable actions by using special report platforms, using technology tools, and setting up strong check processes. Also, they work with other partners to solve these problems together. More clear and good data will help stakeholders make better decisions. This can lead us to a more sustainable future. These improvements will help in making decisions inside the company.

Leveraging Technology for Data Collection and Analysis: Two cutting-edge technologies that can significantly improve the collection and interpretation of sustainability data are data analytics and machine learning. Automated data collection methods can make the procedure go faster, reduce errors, and ensure the availability of real-time data. Trends, patterns, and anomalies can be discovered using data analytics to help with strategic planning and decision-making.

Establishing Robust processes for Data Validation: To make sure that sustainability numbers are accurate and reliable, we need to use strong methods for checking the data. Doing regular checks, getting the okay from others not in your company, and using famous reporting rules like GRI or SASB might be needed to finish this. It's key to make sure people involved in the process believe it is good. This makes reporting on sustainability truer and more accepted by others.

Collaborating with Supply Chain Partners and Industry Peers: Working with supply partners and others in the same field can make measuring performance better. Also, sharing data is easier this way. By working together, we can make data-gathering methods more standard. This helps to compare information in and out of businesses more easily. By working together, making reporting about sustainability better can lead to honesty and growth within a company.

Incorporating Sustainability Software and Reporting Platforms: Modern businesses need to use ways and tools for tracking sustainability in their work. These technologies make it easier to monitor how well the social, governance, and environmental parts are doing. They also help with managing data better. Support is given to openness by making sure that people involved are told about efforts for sustainability. These solutions make it easy to follow rules and manage the brand's image. In a world where being sustainable is becoming more important, using such programs should be an essential part of planning for success over the long term.

4.2 Sustainability Reporting Frameworks, Methodologies, and Standardization

To include sustainability in accounting rules, we must report on it correctly. It ensures that people can evaluate and see how good businesses are at being sustainable. This allows them to wisely compare various businesses or markets. When businesses and their partners similarly share sustainability information, they trust each other more. This happens because all businesses clearly and without any problems share this information. This discussion can be organized into three subsections.

Consistent Sustainability Reporting: To make sure that sustainability news is easy to understand and believable, we need strong ways of sharing it. Rules like the Global Reporting Initiative (GRI) or Sustainability Accounting Standards Board (SASB) assist with this task. These guides have easy steps and the required writing. They help businesses write their sustainability reports correctly by giving clear directions.

For example, GRI gives clear messages that discuss social issues like politics and the environment. Businesses can show how their actions affect people, the environment, and profits. Often, this helps stakeholders decide if a business is heading for lasting growth. Instead of making all-purpose rules, SASB makes special guidelines for each part. These adjustments make reporting needs fit for the special traits and major issues present in every business area.

By looking at how different companies in the same business act to help nature, people can do better and more modern studies.

Variability in Reporting Methodologies: Companies can use different reporting strategies, which may alter the scope, metrics, and limitations of their sustainability disclosures. As a result, stakeholders find it difficult to contrast corporate performance, which diminishes the importance of environmental reports.

Standardization of Reporting Frameworks: Supporting staff members' knowledge and skill expansion as they engage in sustainability reporting can be done on a budget. The skills needed to effectively manage sustainability data must be presented among employees if methods for data collection, analysis, and presentation are to be accurate and standardized.

4.3 Financial Education of Sustainability

Lack of awareness and education about financial literacy and sustainability can be an issue for many businesses. Similarly, training and capacity building can be challenging and intimidating for many employees. Some companies might not understand the need for routine reporting on sustainability, or might not have the skills and resources needed to put in place standardized reporting methods. Wider adoption may be promoted by raising understanding and informing people of the advantages of routine reporting.

Industry and the community need to work together to overcome these obstacles and establish standardized sustainability reporting. With the help of trade groups, environmental organizations, and rule makers, we can boost good methods for green accounting. They can also provide support for reporting that is sustainable.

Sharing thoughts and facts can create a setting where discussing sustainability is always getting better.

Businesses can talk to people who care about them and find out what they like or need. Groups can change their eco-friendly talks to work on specific issues and targets by asking for opinions from others. They should include people in the reporting steps too. This makes the information more important and helpful.

Regular reporting on sustainability is needed to use it well with accounting processes. Following good reporting rules like GRI and SASB makes the truth of sustainability reports better. It also helps them be fairer to compare with others. The business world might have to join forces and make synchronized efforts for similarity. Groups can make telling stories about green projects better as they help workers have a future that lasts a long time with health in mind. They could do this by changing things, understanding more, and bringing the people involved in decisions made together.

Helping workers learn more and get better at sustainability reporting is costly. Workers must have the skills and knowledge needed to properly manage sustainability information. This helps make sure the collection, analysis, and sharing of this data is correct and follows a set pattern.

Businesses can handle data problems well by using these solutions from analytics and AI. They should also work together to report on sustainability. These changes make it easier to handle data jobs. They provide important information for smart and eco-friendly business decisions. Businesses can make their sustainability reports better by being open and talking to people. This will eventually lead to good change that is friendly to the environment and responsible for our future world.

5. SOLUTIONS FOR DATA CHALLENGES

Businesses can use smart AI and data tools to make new solutions. These go beyond the problems of getting, correcting, and keeping information safe. Using this advanced technology can make dealing with tough nature information simpler and improve how we report on sustainability (Figure 5).

Figure 5. Solutions for data challenges

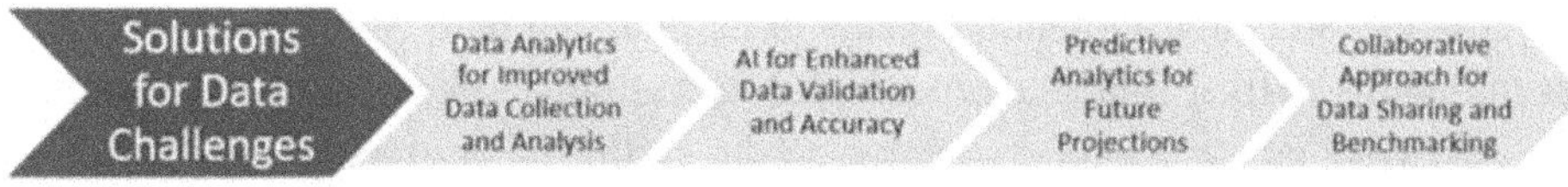

Data Analytics for Improved Data Collection and Analysis: Data analysis tools make the process of getting data from different places and systems faster by automating its collection. Automation lowers the chance of mistakes by people when getting data fast and efficiently. You can measure a company's sustainability work by looking at charts and graphs in the data. This is done using smart numbers and number-crunching methods.

AI for Enhanced Data Validation and Accuracy: Using artificial intelligence can greatly improve the accuracy and reliability of data. AI programs can check if data is right by comparing it to set rules and finding possible mistakes or differences that might be wrong. These companies can find and fix data problems before they hurt the reporting cycle by being green. This is because of how active they are at looking ahead to potential issues.

Predictive Analytics for Future Projections: Predictive analytics helps businesses guess future trends in sustainability and success. It uses old data and current actions to do this. By looking at old sustainability information and adding important outside things, companies can set realistic goals for being sustainable in the future.

Collaborative Approach for Data Sharing and Benchmarking: People involved, most others in the business world, and supply chain partners must be part of the talking process when using a team plan to keep everything going stronger. By including more people, groups can get a wider view of stability details and knowledge. This connection helps share facts, compare results, and share good practices, which boosts better reporting on sustainability in the business world.

They use digital reporting systems because they provide stronger places to store information for sustainability and help communication between many departments or interested people. These systems let people see data, making it easy for them to understand tough sustainability numbers. Digital reports make it easier for people involved to see and share information. This leads to more open reporting that others can trust.

6. THE AMAZING POSSIBILITIES OF SUSTAINABLE ACCOUNTING

Even though it's hard, using green accounting can make businesses stand out and do good things. A business can help people and the environment by including social, governance, and environmental aspects in its financial plan. When businesses add sustainability to their financial reports, they can attract customers who like products and services that are good for society and the earth. Using green accounting, companies can save money by eliminating waste and improving how they make things. It helps to find the problems in business too. Using sustainable practices makes a company's name better and brings in people who care about others and the environment. This helps make their finances stronger. Finally, green accounting gives companies a way to make the future more sustainable. It can be done in ways that are good for business, while taking care of people's and nature's well-being. Some of the many ways businesses can use good financial reporting practices to stand out and make positive changes are talked about below.

6.1 Attracting Ethical Consumers

Sustainable accounting gives businesses fz to attract customers who care about ethics. People want businesses that truly care about being green because they're starting to notice more problems with the environment and society. People who care about right shopping think of how buying things will change the community, nature, and future generations. By implementing sustainability into financial reporting, businesses may successfully inform consumers about their sustainability aims and results. The transparency with which a company shares sustainability data, such as greenhouse gas emissions, waste reduction, ethical sourcing, and involvement in the community, demonstrates its steadfast commitment to ethical business practices.

When individuals perceive a firm as socially and environmentally responsible, brand loyalty and customer loyalty may increase. Customers who uphold strong moral standards are more inclined to support and stick with companies that work to solve environmental and social problems.

According to moral uprightness, consumers can help your company surpass its competitors. Businesses that prioritize sustainability have an advantage over rivals that do not implement sustainable practices because sustainability is becoming a more significant predictor of customer demand. By embracing sustainable accounting, organizations can show their dedication to the environment and build credibility as brands that value both people and the environment. By marketing to moral consumers, businesses can strengthen their reputations and customer relationships. As a result, the community is motivated to grow, and the business benefits.

6.2 Increased Efficiency and Cost Savings

The two biggest benefits of using sustainable accounting are increased cost savings and improved production efficiency. Businesses can identify and solve operational inefficiencies, resulting in greater efficiency and resource-efficient operations, by integrating sustainability into financial reporting. Sustainable business methods push companies to use earth-friendly and resourceful practices in their daily work. Businesses can find places to use fewer resources and stop wasteful actions by doing careful checks about being sustainable. For example, sustainable accounting looks at ways to reduce the amount of energy, water, and raw materials that are wasted during production.

Companies that use resources smartly both help the environment and save a lot of money. Cutting down on energy use and trash can lead to cheaper power bills and running costs. Good management of resources also helps with better control over stock and lower costs for supplies. Sustainable bookkeeping supports the use of new and nature-friendly technologies. We could save money in the long run by using ways to cut down waste, managing our supplies sustainably, and making use of clean energy sources.

The whole company pushes for creativity and making things better all the time, using good money management. Businesses are told to look at new, green ways and tools that could increase output while lowering costs. This love for keeping things green may push us to do research and make new products that are helpful both for people and the environment.

Besides the clear money gains, green bookkeeping can increase work output and employee involvement. By giving people, a reason to do something, promoting good rules can make workers more eager and happier at their jobs. Workers will be more likely to look for and put into practice better ways of doing things if they think the company cares about being green.

Sustainable bookkeeping can make businesses better at making things and save money. Using resources well, using green technology, and encouraging creativity can help businesses do less harm to the environment while getting more money. Businesses that prioritize sustainability could grow more resilient and competitive, draw in investors and environmentally conscious clients, and pave the way for a prosperous and environmentally conscious future.

6.3 Access to Capital and Strengthening Brands

Important advantages of sustainable accounting include increased financial availability and the strengthening of a company's brand reputation. Investors and stakeholders are placing increased weight on governance, social, and environmental considerations when making decisions. An organization can promote itself as a forward-thinking, socially conscious institution and attract investors and stakeholders through the adoption of ethical business procedures and open reporting.

Sustainable accounting allows companies to prove their dedication to being green and fair in business. Companies can make investors trust them more by sharing information about how they care for the environment, people, and rules. They do this in their real places of work. So, more people who care a lot about sustainability might be interested in joining, too. Many more investors are searching for chances to combine their investments with what they believe in. Businesses can help investors understand their effects on society and nature by using green accounting. This lets them pick actions that match what's good for both people and the planet in a long-term way. So, companies that follow eco-friendly methods are more likely to get investors interested in making money and helping society at the same time.

Sustainable accounting makes a company's brand more well-respected. Businesses that care about being green are more likely to get the backing of customers who prioritize helping people and preserving nature. When companies share details about their green efforts and successes, people will be more loyal to the brand because they feel informed. Also, good word-of-mouth marketing can happen faster this way.

A good employer reputation that cares about sustainability and social responsibility can attract the best workers. In the work world now, firms that care about sustainability and social impact get more workers. The group may support good business behaviors and use the focus on public sharing of ESG details in green money matters to get more people to join.

By using good money management practices, companies can boost their name and get loans from banks that care a lot about doing right by people. Now, making things sustainable and reporting on progress has more honesty. Also, people who are involved in these matters pay better attention to them all. Businesses that follow good ways to help the environment can use these benefits to bring more people in as investors, keep customers happy, and give a nice name to their company. This will all help them do better and make money over time while caring about being green.

6.4 Resilience and Risk Management

Businesses can improve their risk management and be more sustainable by paying attention to environmental, social, and governance (ESG) problems using an account that is helpful for the Earth. Businesses can use ESG problems to assess their risks and create solid plans for these issues by incorporating sustainability into money-related operations. Business organizations can find and inspect issues with work tasks, stops in product flows, or changes to new rules using green financial reporting. They will also see how it affects their community's relationships and uses up resources like water or power. Businesses can create smart risk plans that fit their goals for staying green by finding and checking for these threats. A business can achieve its big goals and deal with surprise problems in a better way by understanding ESG risks. This also helps to handle them properly. Now, businesses must handle hard and quick-growing environmental problems. So being strong is important for them nowadays. Businesses can reduce the chance of harming their work, reputation, and profits by acting before problems happen.

Businesses can make operations better and save money by dealing with ESG issues. A business can make its carbon footprint smaller and be safer from changes in energy costs by putting money into things like wind or solar power. Getting things from dangerous places will be safer if we use good supply chain methods. This way, we can count on getting those items regularly and ethically.

Sustainable accounting also lets people talk about risk management methods with others, like investors, customers, and overseers. When people trust and believe in a company more, they are likely to support its green actions and choices about where to put their money. A proactive way of handling risk could help a company get more chances to grow in markets that are good for the environment. Companies that handle ESG risks well and show they are doing things for the environment sustainably will be better prepared to gain from people wanting eco-friendly or fair goods. This has become more important around the world.

Businesses that follow green accounting rules might be better at handling risks and bouncing back. By acting on ESG problems early, companies can keep their future goals safe. This also lets them fix weaknesses and grab chances for more environmentally friendly markets along the way. Sustainable accounting helps businesses make more informed choices, keep their money safe, and move forward for a brighter future with better care. It is very difficult to introduce the performance measures of nature and the environment into our accounting. Problems may include access to data, its stability and its accuracy. Nevertheless, the benefits that businesses can get from implementing sustainable accounting are huge and significant. As people from all over the world understand more and more that it is vital to preserve our planet and make something good of their lives, firms need to adopt green accounting. It is not just needed; it also gives them an advantage.

A big chance that comes with sustainable accounting is for companies to make themselves better at competing. If firms make their money plans green, they can match what more and more people who buy things or invest want. They care about social issues and our planet's health. This connection helps build trust in the brand and makes businesses stand out as market leaders. This draws customers who want to help companies that care about social good and are green-minded.

Sustainable accounting doesn't only draw in good-willed buyers. By finding and solving waste or inefficiency with green methods, companies can save money and have better production. Using less stuff and making things work better can help cut costs. This might mean more profit and good financial results.

In addition, good accounting practices sustainably offer businesses a chance to improve how others see their brand. Clear information about sustainability measures and advances makes stakeholders trust and believe more. As buyers get pickier, companies that focus on sustainability are seen as responsible and modern businesses. This helps them improve their brand image and what customers think about them.

More and more, people who invest money or have a share in companies are looking at businesses that show they care about being eco-friendly. Using green accounting and giving clear reports on your ESG work can bring in investors who care about society. These people want not only financial gains but also good effects for all others. This makes more people want to invest. This helps a company get money and make its finances stronger.

By using green financial rules, companies get quick gains. But they are also set up for success in a world that cares about people and nature. Beyond earning money, green accounting helps businesses do good for people and the environment. This promotes a company culture that cares about sustainability in responsible ways.

In short, when connecting sustainability to accounting methods, some problems can come up, like not having enough data or keeping it right. But the good results are worth it. Sustainable accounting gives businesses a chance to become more competitive, get good customers who care about ethics, save money on costs, and build up their brand name. It also helps them have better connections with the people they owe money or shares to. When businesses use honest accounting techniques, they can discover the path to a sustainable future. This helps them link their actions with those of good and careful people buying items or investing money. Agreeing with sustainability is more than just a good idea. It's also the right action, which can help create a better and safer world for future generations.

7. CASE STUDIES AND BEST PRACTICES IN SUSTAINABILITY ACCOUNTING AND DISCLOSURE

This time, we look at cool stories and great ways of doing things from many different businesses that have adopted good practices for making their money matter. Not only did they do this well, but they also made more profits from it. These examples show clearly that including sustainability in their main jobs produced good results and encouraged others to copy them.

One of these trips takes us to a famous worldwide company in the food and drink business. As customers wanted more openness and were worried about the environment, the company began switching to green actions. They made complicated systems to count waste, water use, and carbon emissions in their supply chain. They were aware of their power, so they could spot ways to get better and do things that would greatly decrease it. Furthermore, they saved lots of money and became better than others by managing things well. They also attract customers who like the environment, which is a fast-growing market for them.

Furthermore, we look at an already present factory company that has had growing demands from shareholders and overseers to follow eco-friendly ways. At first, it seemed hard to change, but the group worked on making everything they did more friendly to nature. They changed how they make things to reduce waste and dirt. At the same time, they tried harder to use energy efficiently. Through creative teamwork with nearby towns, they put in place social projects to better the lives of the places where their businesses were running. This change not only made their name better but also spread friendly feelings. It had a good effect on how happy and loyal the employees were to work there.

These examples, along with others in this part of the book, demonstrate how using green accounting and saying what we are doing can have a very good effect on things. They not only examined the ideas we discussed earlier, but also showed how useful they are for all people involved in making things more eco-friendly. These examples show that the sustainability journey is not only good for companies of all sizes and types, but it's also a smart choice. This involves better money results along with managing risks well. Plus, things like a stronger brand reputation make people more loyal customers too.

Unilever: Unilever Sustainable Living Plan (USLP) is a great example of how a company complies with sustainability (Uniliver, 2021). This plan was launched in 2010. Unilever has done better than others by seriously using green reporting and sharing methods in how they run their business. Unilever's big success comes from its strong goal to make the environment better. Understanding that something must be done about our environmental problems, the company has set up clear goals to lessen its harm to nature. At the same time, it hopes to improve how much good social effort is made. These goals help guide Unilever's path to a more eco-friendly and responsible future. They push them forward.

One of the key ways that Unilever shows it cares about openness and responsibility is by creating a yearly report on being eco-friendly. This big paper shows how the company is trying to be more sustainable. It talks about what they have done towards their goals and gives clear information on where it's worked well or if there are problems. Unilever shares its successes and problems with others, building trust. This makes people believe in the company. It helps to grow a sense of working together for sustainability goals shared by everyone.

At the heart of Unilever's efforts to do things in a good way is its special plan, called the Sustainable Living Plan. This big plan helps the company do things in a green way. It covers many actions and projects that fully tackle nature problems and social worries. Unilever's plan for being eco-friendly shows how they work with raw materials and save energy in manufacturing. Their steps help them reach their goal of living more sustainably.

The Sustainable Living Plan at Unilever is about more than just how they run their business. The company knows that real sustainability needs teamwork, so it often works together with partners, suppliers, and local groups. They help spread eco-friendly actions all over the whole work chain. Unilever helps charities by making good business decisions and supporting causes in the places where they work. This makes a good loop that helps more than just the business.

The Unilever Sustainable Living Plan is not only about what goes on inside the company. The company understands that teamwork is necessary for real, lasting success. So, it often works with partners and suppliers as well as community groups to share good ways of saving nature at its different levels in the value chain. Unilever helps promote good business practices with its partners and gives money to charities in the areas where it works. This creates more positive effects that reach beyond just their local area of influence!

Patagonia: Patagonia, a popular outdoor clothing manufacturer, puts love for the environment and its core values first. This shows that companies can take care of Earth while making big profits too (Patagonia, 2015). Patagonia's special business strategy, which is based on a strong feeling for doing what is right and taking care of others, made the company a leader in companies that look after nature (Matthews, 2021). The famous business that makes outdoor clothes and equipment has added caring for the environment to its bookkeeping methods. They also include it when they make decisions or create new products.

Patagonia's efforts to protect the environment are based on being responsible and honest. The business knows that it can't only measure its effect on society and the environment using money numbers. Patagonia does more than give complete, deep sustainability reports to people who matter. The data in these reports let readers know very well what the company does and its actions, which are more than just usual money details. This also shows us how it acts rightly or wrongly while doing business.

Patagonia is proud of showing its work to lessen harm to the environment and share actions for a better earth in these reports about sustainability. This is a great example of the company's clever use of old materials in its products. Patagonia is a good example of the circular economy because it focuses on using less new stuff and stopping trash from being thrown into landfills. It helps save resources, too. In these green reports, Patagonia likes to show how hard they are working on reducing their harm to nature and pushing forward with good ideas for the environment. This is a great example of the firm's creative use of old materials in its items. Patagonia is a good example of how the circular economy works. It focuses on using less new stuff and getting rid of more trash in landfills than is needed.

Patagonia's dedication to sustainability goes far beyond publishing. It actively incorporates those principles into its decision-making processes to ensure that moral and environmental concerns are at the forefront of establishing the company's strategy and future course. Every facet of Patagonia's commercial operations, from sourcing raw materials through product design and distribution, is permeated with a sense of its wider impact on the natural world and society.

The business is aware of its responsibilities to safeguard the environment and promote social justice, and that its decisions will have an ongoing impact. Patagonia's belief that ethical business practices may benefit society is supported by the fact that the corporation considers sustainability when making choices.

In addition to its area of influence, Patagonia's sustainability-focused strategy has a significant global impact. The company gains more customer trust and loyalty by being honest and forthcoming about its ecological policy, and it encourages other companies to do the same. The success of Patagonia is proof that a company can be profitable while also benefiting society and the natural world.

Because of its continued dedication to integrating sustainability into its decision-making procedures and financial reporting, Patagonia raises the bar for the commercial sector. Patagonia serves as an example of the value of open transparency and the beneficial effects of moral corporate behavior, inspiring and motivating individuals in the process. Others feel inspired to participate in the global movement for a just and sustainable future because of this.

IKEA: IKEA views sustainability as more than just a benefit; it infuses every facet of its supply chain operations and business processes (IKEA, 2021). Because it acknowledges the significance of solving environmental challenges and societal well-being, well-known global furniture retailer IKEA has made sustainability a priority in its pursuit of moral corporate conduct. IKEA's constant promise to care about the environment is built on its strict rules for measuring good actions. The company is aware that to manage its impact on nature properly, it needs to study and monitor key details about the resources used and emissions produced. To reach this goal, IKEA always gets and shares important information about how much water it uses. It also works on reducing waste and lowering the carbon emissions caused by its activities. IKEA uses these ideas to improve how they interact with nature over time.

IKEA is good at business because they include plans for being environmentally friendly in their financial reports. Rather than just focusing on money, the group uses many methods to measure things. This involves things like doing nice acts and looking after nature, together with handling money problems. IKEA's image as a business that values its staff and nature while also focusing on responsibility and honesty gets stronger from this true reporting.

IKEA's dedication to being green is more than just sharing its results. It directly affects how we handle the supply chain. The company works closely with its suppliers to make sure they use good and environmentally friendly methods to make things. This team effort aims to decrease damage caused by making and buying raw materials while maintaining good office actions and community values. IKEA has special programs that show its commitment to being eco-friendly. For example, the company is promoting ideas of a circular economy. IKEA wants people to use their things for a longer time, make less trash, and have more eco-friendly living. They do this by repurchasing furniture they made when they are done with it or recycling old pieces of Ikea furniture.

The total commitment of IKEA to sustainability has a big effect. The company affects positive change within its internal procedures and serves as an inspiring model for the industry and beyond by integrating sustainability into its fundamental operations. Because one of the most well-known companies in the world is pushing customers to make more morally informed purchases, customers actively support IKEA's activities.

Because of the company's dedication to sustainability, its brand value and reputation have grown. Due to its focus on environmental responsibility and moral business operations, IKEA has a loyal and moral customer base. More customers are drawn to brands with comparable principles.

IKEA is a great example of a company that places a high focus on sustainability in all facets of its operations. IKEA illustrates how businesses can have a beneficial impact on society and the natural world through morally sound activities, transparent reporting, and precise, sustainable accounting methods. By incorporating sustainability into its supply chain management and promoting circular economy ideas, the company acts as a catalyst for beneficial change within the industry and encourages customers and other businesses to join the journey towards a more sustainable and responsible future.

Natura &Co.: In 2020, Natura &Co launched a 10-year sustainable living plan, "Commitment to Life" (Natura &Co, 2021). It is their plan for ten years that will try to solve the problem of global warming and protect the Amazon Forest. They also promise fair opportunities for all people while trying to make better use of things without ruining Earth or restoring it bit by bit. In this part, we want to highlight the importance of taking care of our environment and safeguarding the Earth. The cosmetics and personal care product manufacturer Natura &Co. in Brazil have offered a great illustration of how sustainability and open reporting may be integrated to have a significant impact on the business environment. The company, a big supporter of good business actions, has made sure to include sustainability in everything it does each day.

The idea that money measures are not always good at showing if a business does well was the main part of Natura &Co. The company uses special reporting, saying they care about issues like effects on people and nature besides just making cash. Natura &Co. gives people who own part of the company a complete report on both its financial and non-financial results every year in their Integrated Report. The study also gives a deep look at how the business works and its impact on the overall community.

Their Integrated Report shows a lot of details about the company's good actions for people and nature. This means they are open about what they do. Natura &Co. truly cares about being good and doing right in business by telling everyone about its efforts to protect the environment. Natura &Co. shows it cares about people and nature by helping local community growth, implementing programs to save wildlife species diversity, and getting raw materials fairly. The company's open reporting rules have many benefits. Most importantly, it builds trust and belief among everyone involved - like customers, shareholders, employees, and rule-making groups. Natura &Co. creates an open and honest environment by clearly explaining its goals for sustainability to all parties involved and then ensuring everybody that these actions are happening through social responsibility.

Next, customers who value social responsibility have praised Natura &Co. for stressing sustainability a lot. People are starting to look for things and services from firms that agree with their beliefs as thoughtful buying grows. Natura &Co. has become well known for being a company that pushes good and environmentally friendly business practices. They help people learn what they need so they can make smart choices, too.

Because the group cares about being green, people who also like environmentally friendly ideas are interested in it. As more people care about sustainability in their money choices, Natura &Co. gets investors to help companies that want good things for the earth and society long-term along with making cash profits. The company's activities, as an important player in the cosmetics industry, have the potential to promote positive change in the sector and inspire other businesses to adopt equivalent transparent reporting practices and sustainability-focused business plans. Natura &Co.'s commitment to sustainability and open reporting is a fantastic illustration of how businesses may effectively integrate social and environmental responsibility into their core operations. Natura &Co. attracts customers and investors who value moral and ethical behavior by providing stakeholders with an in-depth understanding of the company's performance and sustainability initiatives. Natura &Co., a pioneer in the cosmetics sector, serves as a shining instance of how ethical company behavior may result in good change and direct the sector toward a more socially and environmentally conscious future.

Microsoft: Microsoft, a major participant in the technology industry and a pioneer in ethical business conduct, has set the bar for other businesses in the sector to match. The company's continued commitment to sustainability, accounting, and transparency has allowed it to make great progress in its struggle against climate change and environmental harm. The company's environmental journey is motivated by its ambitious goal of becoming carbon-negative by 2030. To accomplish this tough goal, they must significantly reduce their carbon emissions while aggressively increasing carbon extraction from the atmosphere. By making this courageous decision, Microsoft exhibits its strong sense of responsibility and commitment to addressing the urgent global challenge of managing climate change. By 2050, Microsoft wants to cancel out all the carbon dioxide emissions - from what they do directly or use in electricity since starting up back in 1975 (Microsoft (2023).

By publishing extensive annual environmental reports that outline its progress toward its sustainability goals, Microsoft actively encourages accountability and openness. Beyond generalizations, these reports provide great information about the company's environmental effects, energy-saving campaigns, and progress toward carbon neutrality. Microsoft promotes a culture of transparency by being open about company sustainability projects and problems. By doing this, it wins over stakeholders' trust and demonstrates its dedication to taking important, sustained action.

Microsoft is committed to sustainability in all areas of its operations, products, and services. To power its data centers and offices, the corporation makes significant investments in energy-efficient gadgets and renewable energy sources. By switching to more ecologically friendly energy sources, Microsoft lessens its environmental impact and sets an example for other businesses in the technology sector. Microsoft also makes use of its authority and reach to encourage its partners and suppliers to support sustainable business practices. Through the Supplier Code of Conduct and sustainability programs, the company increases the positive effects of its sustainability activities outside its operations by encouraging a shared commitment to social and environmental stewardship throughout its supply chain.

Microsoft enhances its standing as a market pioneer in sustainable practices by creating challenging sustainability goals and being open about its accomplishments. The company's unwavering commitment to combating climate change and promoting sustainability serves as an inspiration for others in the corporate world. Microsoft's proactive approach to sustainability displays that businesses can be powerful agents of positive change, leading the way in the global transition toward a more sustainable and resilient future.

In summary, Microsoft's remarkable attempts in sustainability accounting and disclosure demonstrates its leadership and dedication to addressing the critical challenges of climate change and environmental sustainability. Microsoft promises to cut its carbon footprint by 2030. It tells others what it is doing for the earth through clear updates, showing how setting big goals and acting in practical ways can make a difference. As the company goes on, it shows how to be good. This inspires tech companies and businesses in other areas too. They should all care about saving ways for future happiness by working together with these ideas equally.

The examples and good practices in this part give strong proof of how putting green accounting systems into businesses can create big changes. These examples show that being sustainable is not something extra, but it's now a big plan for businesses that want long-term success and good influence. These companies do not just think about making money and growing. They also care about helping make the world better for people and plants too! They use smart and careful ways to lessen their impact on nature, save natural things like trees or water, and help make society better. These actions match what many people around the world expect and help businesses be seen as forces of good. They are dedicated to making a real difference in our world.

One main advantage for companies that support sustainability is their power to get in touch with thoughtful buyers and responsible investors. People who buy things are getting more worried about how good or bad the businesses that make these goods behave. Listening to these groups' plans for making things last and telling the truth helps people who want to back companies that have the same ideas as they care about nature. This helps those businesses get trusted support from buyers.

Shareholders are starting to know that being green helps them last for a long time. This is just like what customers already understand. More and more people who care about ethics are looking to put their money into firms that focus strongly on helping the environment and society. By using practices that help the environment and telling investors about their eco-friendly actions, these companies become more interesting to people who want good environmental, social, and governance issues when they pick where to invest money.

Clear reporting is very important in building stakeholder trust. When companies show their plans for being green, how far they've come, and the problems they face, it shows a promise to be responsible. Openness helps build trust with customers and investors. Also, it encourages others, like workers, suppliers, and communities, to get involved in making things more environmentally friendly while working together on shared goals. Moreover, the examples given in this part show how important it is to make big goals for being sustainable. When companies aim high, they push themselves to come up with new ideas and keep getting better at being friendly to the environment and society. These big dreams make powerful changes. They encourage new ideas and push businesses to find fresh, healthy answers that help their work as well as the world they live in.

More groups should start using green accounting methods and learn from real-life examples. They help make a brighter future for everyone that lasts longer by saving the environment while doing well in business. When businesses all work together to keep things green and set it as a top goal, they become powerful leaders for good changes worldwide. The big change in sustainable actions isn't just for single businesses. It affects whole industries and sets a new normal for doing business in the 20th century.

The examples and good practices in this part show that sustainability is not just something we should do because it is right, but also helps businesses get ahead with long term sustainability (Tai & Chuang (2014). Businesses that use honest and clear bookkeeping practices are better off than their competition in the same industry. To make good changes and get honest investors and responsible customers, you need trust as a strong base. This plan should contain complete information shared, clear reporting, and tough environmental aims. If more people join us, a richer and more sustainable future for all can be possible.

8. CONCLUSION AND FUTURE RESEARCH DIRECTIONS

In the world of finance, good accounting maintains honesty and fairness in business. This part shows why accounting helps see how a company is doing, makes rules easier to make, and promotes kindness. It also speaks up for taking care of the environment. Businesses can gain trust, responsibility, and reliability by including information about protecting the environment in their financial reports. Also, give more details about how well they're doing all in all when it comes to being nice to nature.

The main ideas from the part about sustainability accounting are given in a section. This means learning about money and how it affects you, taking care of the environment, and using your cash carefully. The article highlights how important accounting systems are for a company to do well in its business and care about people and nature. Businesses can use their financial reports to show how well they're doing and make things equal. These reports should have sustainability in them, so people can easily understand and respect business needs.

This again shows how knowing about money is important for understanding big projects and their long-term effects. Stakeholders with money knowledge know about the good and bad things related to savings efforts. They are better at making smart choices due to this understanding. Groups can create a more sustainable future that follows the principles of doing good for people, the environment, and profits by helping to educate people about money matters. This part also stresses the importance of constant improvement and moving forward towards sustainable accounting. The section gives some ideas for more research that can help us learn and value green accounting methods even better. These suggestions for further study could help us better understand sustainable accounting practices and their effects.

Exploring the Impact of Sustainable Accounting on Financial Performance: Future research should look into the connection between green accounting practices and financial performance. Understanding how green projects change earnings, handle trouble, and save money can give leaders important knowledge. By counting the money effect of doing good things, companies can make better choices that meet their long-term goals for staying around.

Integrating ESG Factors into Investment Decision-Making: Investment decisions might include things like nature, people, and rules in the future. This could be a topic for study later on. You can see how important green accounting is to getting investors who care about society by looking at their use of sustainability data when planning investments.

Assessing the Effectiveness of Sustainability Reporting Frameworks: Studies looking at different ways to report on sustainability, like GRI, SASB, and integrated reporting (IFRS, 2021a), can measure how well they make things more responsible, comparable, and clear. By comparing different ways of reporting on sustainability, like GRI, SASB, and integrated reporting, we can see how effective they are in leading to responsibility, comparison between companies, and openness.

Examining the Impact of Regulatory Policies on Sustainable Accounting Practices: Analyzing the impact of regulatory requirements on organizations' sustainability disclosure and reporting practices can provide valuable insights into the role of government and policymakers in advancing sustainable accounting.

Investigating Stakeholder Perceptions of Sustainable Accounting Practices: Learning what people like customers, workers, and laws say about sustainability in accounting can guide the making of useful measures for helping with environmental matters.

Assessing the Non-Financial Benefits of Sustainable Accounting: Even though money matters a lot, good accounting can also provide many non-monetary benefits. We need to study these more. Research shows that using eco-friendly methods can make workers more interested, boost brand image, keep customers loyal, and improve relationships with shareholders. These hard-to-see benefits are important for making a company successful and strong.

Identifying Industry-Specific Sustainable Accounting Practices: Different industries have different needs and chances when it comes to being sustainable. Future studies can look into finding ways of being green in business that deal with the natural problems and human issues each one has. By making eco-friendly plans just for each kind of business, companies can do their best and help all parts of the industry get better.

Longitudinal Studies on Sustainable Accounting Performance: Doing long-term exams to watch how companies' green actions change over time can give useful knowledge about the lasting effects of keeping accounts in line with sustainability. Looking at changes and results over a period can show good plans that others might use. This helps businesses put sustainability deeply into their main work operations.

Investigating the Link Between Sustainable Accounting and Investor Decision-Making: We could study how investors see and use information about sustainability to make their investment choices. Understanding the link between environmentally friendly financial reports and investment choices can help in seeing what makes ethical investing work and how it affects businesses too.

Exploring the Role of Sustainable Accounting in Risk Management: Sustainable accounting can be very important for finding and handling risks related to ESG matters. More studies can look at how green money makes it easier to spot and handle risks, helping firms deal with potential problems while making things good for everyone.

In the last few years, there has been a strong drive to agree on ways and reporting rules for sharing environmental, social, and governance reports so that people get similar useful facts. Things done so far include creating worldwide groups and rules like the Sustainability Accounting Standards Board (SASB) and Task Force on Climate-related Financial Disclosures (TCFD). These have made guides that help companies show important ESG information. People are also starting to use worldwide reporting systems such as the Global Reporting Initiative (GRI) and Principles for Responsible Investment (PRI). This helps provide complete directions for ESG reports.

Even with these improvements, problems still exist. Still, there are not the same rules everywhere. This leads to differences in the way people report things across businesses and places around the world. Also, it's difficult to make rules that suit everyone because there are a lot of ESG issues. They don't work the same way for different companies, either. Also, lots of ESG reporting rules that businesses can pick to follow mean they are not all looked at the same way. This might result in not having enough information and power to inform people about how well a company is doing on matters such as the environment or worker rights. So, while significant advances have been made in terms of making ESG disclosures widespread, there is still a lot more to be done. This will help improve an accepted approach for all businesses to disclose meaningful ESG information consistently.

Finally, green accounting will deliver significant benefits that may ensure a more balanced and just global economy. By investigating the link between sustainability and financial reporting and considering how sustainable accounting impacts successful performance, we can find out a lot more about this relationship. Companies can lay the groundwork on which a healthy future is built through good financial reporting practices and educating people about finance. This will consider nature's needs, social responsibility, and business profits at the same time. By always looking for innovations and experiments, we can make the whole world a better place. They will focus on sustainable practices to help people now and in the future.

REFERENCES

Adams, C. A. (2017). Conceptualising the contemporary corporate value creation process. *Accounting, Auditing & Accountability Journal*, 30(4), 906–931. 10.1108/AAAJ-04-2016-2529

Adams, C. A., Heijltjes, M. G., Jack, G., Marjoribanks, T., & Powell, M. (2011). The development of leaders able to respond to climate change and sustainability challenges: The role of business schools. *Sustainability Accounting. Management and Policy Journal*, 2(1), 165–171. 10.1108/20408021111162191

Al-Qudah, A. A., Al-Okaily, M., & Alqudah, H. (2021). The relationship between social entrepreneurship and sustainable development from economic growth perspective: 15 'RCEP' countries. *Journal of Sustainable Finance & Investment*, 1(1), 1–18.

Albuquerque, R., Koskinen, Y., & Zhang, C. (2019). Corporate social responsibility and firm risk: Theory and empirical evidence. *Management Science*, 65(10), 4451–4469. 10.1287/mnsc.2018.3043

Asheim, G. B. (1994). Sustainability: Ethical foundations and economic properties. *Policy Research Working Paper Series, 1302*. The World Bank. https://documents1.worldbank.org/curated/en/605011468739497097/pdf/multi0page.pdf

Barkemeyer, R., Holt, D., Preuss, L., & Tsang, S. (2014). What happened to the development in 'sustainable development'? Business Guidelines Two Decades After Brundtland. *Sustainable Development (Bradford)*, 22(1), 15–32. 10.1002/sd.521

Bassen, A., & Kovacs, A. M. M. (2008). Environmental, social and governance key performance indicators from a capital market perspective. *Zeitschrift für Wirtschafts- und Unternehmensethik*, 9(2), 182–192. 10.5771/1439-880X-2008-2-182

Bebbington, J., & Larrinaga, C. (2014). Accounting and sustainable development: An exploration. *Accounting, Organizations and Society*, 39(6), 395–413. 10.1016/j.aos.2014.01.003

Broadstock, D. C., Chan, K., Cheng, L. T. W., & Wang, X. (2020). The role of ESG performance during times of financial crisis: Evidence from COVID-19 in China. *Finance Research Letters*, 38(1), 101716.32837385

Cho, C. H., Michelon, G., Patten, D. M., & Roberts, R. W. (2015). CSR disclosure: The more things change…? *Accounting, Auditing & Accountability Journal*, 28(1), 14–35. 10.1108/AAAJ-12-2013-1549

Clarkson, M. B. E. (1995). A Stakeholder Framework for Analyzing and Evaluating Corporate Social Performance. *Academy of Management Review*, 20(1), 92–117. 10.2307/258888

Clarkson, P. M., Li, Y., Richardson, G. D., & Vasvari, F. P. (2008). Revisiting the relation between environmental performance and environmental disclosure: An empirical analysis. *Accounting, Organizations and Society*, 33(4-5), 303–327. 10.1016/j.aos.2007.05.003

De Micco, P., Rinaldi, L., Vitale, G., Cupertino, S., & Maraghini, M. P. (2021). The challenges of sustainability reporting and their management: The case of Estra. *Meditari Accountancy Research*, 29(3), 430–448. 10.1108/MEDAR-09-2019-0555

Deloitte. (2021), Climate & sustainability. Retrieved from https://www2.deloitte.com/us/en/insights/focus/climate-and-sustainability.html

Dennis, O. (2020). Ethics of Posterity for Environmental Development of the Niger Delta. *GNOSI: An Interdisciplinary Journal of Human Theory and Praxis*, 3(3), 83–96.

Eccles, R. G., & Krzus, M. (2010). *One Report: Integrated Reporting for a Sustainable Strategy*. John Wiley & Sons.

Fatihudin, D., & Mochklas, M. (2018). How measuring financial performance. *International Journal of Civil Engineering and Technology*, 6(9), 553–557.

Freeman, R. E. (1984). *Strategic management: A stakeholder approach*. Pitman.

Global Reporting Initiative (GRI). (2016). GRI Standards: The World's Most Widely Used Sustainability Reporting Standards. Retrieved from https://www.globalreporting.org/standards/

Global Reporting Initiative (GRI). (2021). GRI Universal Standards. Retrieved from https://www.globalreporting.org/media/zauil2g3/public-faqs-universal-standards.pdf

Herzig, C., & Schaltegger, S. (2006). Corporate Sustainability Reporting. An Overview. In Schaltegger, S., Bennett, M., & Burritt, R. (Eds.), *Sustainability Accounting and Reporting* (Vol. 21). Springer. 10.1007/978-1-4020-4974-3_13

Higgins, C., & Coffey, B. (2016). Improving how sustainability reports drive change: A critical discourse analysis. *Journal of Cleaner Production*, 136, 18–29. 10.1016/j.jclepro.2016.01.101

IKEA. (2021). Sustainability Report FY21. Retrieved from https://about.ikea.com/en/newsroom/2022/01/17/sustainability-report-fy21-and-climate-report

International Financial Reporting (IFRS) Foundation. (2021a). Integrated Reporting Framework. Retrieved from https://www.integratedreporting.org/resource/international-ir-framework/

International Financial Reporting Standards (IFRS) Foundation. (2021b). Sustainability-related Reporting. Retrieved from https://www.ifrs.org/projects/completed-projects/2021/sustainability-reporting/

Jacobs, M. (1999). Sustainable development as a contested concept. In Dobson, A. (Ed.), *Fairness and Futurity* (pp. 21–45). Routledge. 10.1093/0198294891.003.0002

Kaur, A., & Lodhia, S. (2018). Stakeholder engagement in sustainability accounting and reporting: A study of Australian local councils. *Accounting, Auditing & Accountability Journal*, 31(1), 338–368. 10.1108/AAAJ-12-2014-1901

KPMG. (2020), The sustainable infrastructure opportunity. Retrieved from: https://kpmg.com/xx/en/home/insights/2020/06/covid-19-recovery.html

La Torre, M., Sabelfeld, S., Blomkvist, M., Tarquinio, L., & Dumay, J. (2018). Harmonising non-financial reporting regulation in Europe: Practical forces and projections for future research. *Meditari Accountancy Research*, 26(4), 598–621. 10.1108/MEDAR-02-2018-0290

Lai, A., & Stacchezzini, R. (2021). Organisational and professional challenges amid the evolution of sustainability reporting: A theoretical framework and an agenda for future research. *Meditari Accountancy Research*, 29(3), 405–429. 10.1108/MEDAR-02-2021-1199

Laine, M., Tregidga, H., & Unerman, J. (2021). *Sustainability Accounting and Accountability*. Routledge. 10.4324/9781003185611

Lourenço, I., Branco, M., Curto, J., & Eugénio, T. (2012). How does the market value corporate sustainability performance? *Journal of Business Ethics*, 108(4), 417–428. 10.1007/s10551-011-1102-8

Manes-Rossi, F., Tiron-Tudor, A., Nicolò, G., & Zanellato, G. (2018). Ensuring More Sustainable Reporting in Europe Using Non-Financial Disclosure—De Facto and De Jure Evidence. *Sustainability (Basel)*, 10(4), 1162. 10.3390/su10041162

Matthews, R. (2021). 10 Reasons Why Patagonia Is the World's Most Responsible Company. https://changeoracle.com/2021/09/10/10-reasons-why-patagonia-is-worlds-most/

Microsoft. (2023). Microsoft Carbon Removal Observations from our third year, Observations from our third year. https://query.prod.cms.rt.microsoft.com/cms/api/am/binary/RW16V26

Milne, M. J., & Gray, R. (2007). Future prospects for corporate sustainability reporting. *Sustainability Accounting. Management and Policy Journal*, 1, 184–207.

Natura &Co. (2021). Natura &Co gives first annual update on Commitment to Life 2030 Sustainability Vision. https://naturaeco.com/press-release/natura-co-gives-first-annual-update-on-commitment-to-life-2030-sustainability-vision/

Pantagonia. (2015). Environmental & Social Initiatives 2015. https://www.patagonia.com/on/demandware.static/Sites-patagonia-us-Site/Library-Sites-PatagoniaShared/en_US/PDF-US/patagonia-enviro-initiatives-2015.pdf

Patten, D. M., & Zhao, N. (2014). Standalone CSR reporting by U.S. retail companies. *Accounting Forum*, 38(2), 132–144. 10.1016/j.accfor.2014.01.002

Patten, M. D., Ren, Y., & Zhao, N. (2015). Standalone corporate social responsibility reporting in China: An exploratory analysis of its relation to legitimation. *Social and Environmental Accountability Journal*, 35(1), 17–31. 10.1080/0969160X.2015.1007467

Radin, T. J. (2007). Stakeholders and Sustainability: An Argument for Responsible Corporate Decision-Making. *William and Mary Environmental Law and Policy Review*, 31, 363. https://scholarship.law.wm.edu/wmelpr/vol31/iss2/4

Sheehy, B. (2005). Scrooge-The Reluctant Stakeholder: Theoretical Problems in the Shareholder-Stakeholder Debate. *University of Miami Business Law Review, 14*, 193. Retrieved from https://repository.law.miami.edu/umblr/vol14/iss1/6

Sultana, S., Zulkifli, N., & Zainal, D. (2018). Environmental, social and governance (ESG) and investment decision in Bangladesh. *Sustainability (Basel)*, 10(6), 1831. 10.3390/su10061831

Tai, F.-M., & Chuang, S.-H. (2014). Corporate Social Responsibility. *iBusiness, 6*(3), 13-19. 10.4236/ib.2014.63013

Tarmuji, I., Maelah, R., & Tarmuji, N. H. (2016). The impact of environmental, social and governance practices (ESG) on economic performance: Evidence from ESG score. *International Journal of Trade. Economics and Finance*, 7(3), 67–74.

Uniliver. (2021). Unilever Sustainable Living Plan 2010 to 2020 Summary of 10 years' progress. https://www.unilever.com/files/92ui5egz/production/16cb778e4d31b81509dc5937001559f1f5c863ab.pdf

United Nations Global Compact. (2018). Integrating the Sustainable Development Goals into Corporate Reporting: A Practical Guide. Retrieved from https://unglobalcompact.org/library/5628

Vifell, Å. C., & Soneryd, L. (2012). Organizing matters: How 'the social dimension' gets lost in sustainability projects. *Sustainable Development (Bradford)*, 20(1), 18–27. 10.1002/sd.461

World Commission on Environment and Development. (1987). Our Common Future (The Brundtland Report). In *Medicine and War (Vol. 4)*. 10.1080/07488008808408783

World Economic Outlook (WEO) Database. (2023). International Monetary Fund. Groups and Aggregates Information. https://www.imf.org/en/Publications/WEO/weo-database/2023/April/groups-and-aggregates

Xie, J., Nozawa, W., Yagi, M., Fujii, H., & Managi, S. (2019). Do environmental, social, and governance activities improve corporate financial performance? *Business Strategy and the Environment*, 28(2), 286–300. 10.1002/bse.2224

Yoon, B., Lee, J. H., & Byun, R. (2018). Does ESG performance enhance firm value? Evidence from Korea. *Sustainability (Basel)*, 10(10), 3635. Advance online publication. 10.3390/su10103635

ADDITIONAL READING

Bebbington, J., & Gray, R. (2001). An account of sustainability: Failure, success and reconceptualization. *Critical Perspectives on Accounting*, 2(5), 557–588. 10.1006/cpac.2000.0450

Carnegie, G. D. (2021). Accounting 101: Redefining accounting for tomorrow. *Accounting Education*, 31(6), 1–14.

Carnegie, G. D., Gomes, D., & McBride, K. (2023). COVID-19 and accounting as multidimensional technical, social and moral practice: A framework for future research. *Meditari Accountancy Research*, 31(1), 1–26. 10.1108/MEDAR-10-2022-1826

Castelo Branco, M. C., Gomes, D., & Martins, A. (2024). An institutionalist political-economy perspective on social and environmental accounting. *Meditari Accountancy Research*, 32(7), 35–55. 10.1108/MEDAR-12-2023-2248

Chiu, I. H. (2022). The EU sustainable finance agenda: Developing governance for double materiality in sustainability metrics. *European Business Organization Law Review*, 23(1), 87–123. 10.1007/s40804-021-00229-9

de Villiers, C., & Dimes, R. (2022). Critical analysis of the contribution of integrated reporting (IR) to sustainability. In Adams, C. A. (Ed.), *Handbook of Accounting and Sustainability* (pp. 210–213). Edward Elgar. 10.4337/9781800373518.00020

Lehner, O. M., & Harrer, T. (2019). Accounting for economic sustainability: Environmental, social and governance perspectives. *Journal of Applied Accounting Research*, 20(4), 365–371. 10.1108/JAAR-06-2019-0096

Lodhia, S. K., & Sharma, U. (2019). Sustainability accounting and reporting: Recent perspectives and an agenda for further research. *Pacific Accounting Review*, 31(3), 309–312. 10.1108/PAR-02-2019-121

KEY TERMS AND DEFINITIONS

Access to Capital and Strengthening Brands: The influence of eco-friendly bookkeeping on the improvement of financial success, a better reputation and socially responsible investors is huge.

Accounting: The language that has worked for business is clear communication, tracking the data and following up on results they can sustain.

Attracting Ethical Consumers: Determining a company's potential to attract ethically and environmentally conscious consumers based on the sustainability practices implemented in the business that may affect brand love.

Circular Economy: Addresses reuse, recycling and a change in product use to enable environmental sustainability.

Collaboration With Supply Chain Partners and Industry Peers: Highlights the advantages of collaboration, data standardization and information sharing with business partners.

Consistent Sustainability Reporting: The need to follow the standard reporting guidelines can be obtained by utilizing proven systems that ensure consistency in sustainability reports.

Data Availability, Consistency, and Accuracy: Aimed at solving the issues concerning the procurement, preservation and reliability of sustainability data.

Ethical and Moral Business Conduct: It is based on the positive behavior and right perceptions that lead a company to make good decisions, especially in terms of sustainability.

Financial Literacy: Interpreting financial documents and project ramifications that result from eco-friendly initiatives to ensure the welfare of the company, nature, and humanity.

Increased Efficiency and Cost Savings: Illustrates the impact of environmentally friendly accounting on preserving costs, increasing production or resolving operational problems.

Integration of Financial and Sustainability Reporting: However, it sheds light on the connection between financial success and environmental responsibility for a holistic assessment of an organization's performance.

International Financial Reporting Standards (IFRS) Foundation: Emphasizes the need for mentioning sustainability in the global financial reporting standards.

Investor Interest: Examines how the investors are affected by the firms' environmental performance because of their ESG concerns.

Key Performance Indicators (KPIs): The KPIs used to assess the success of a company's sustainability can be measured by various topics like water consumption and workforce diversity.

Lack of Awareness and Education: Conducting the company's growth analysis based on sustainability-related KPIs, including water consumption rates, personnel diversity and volunteer workforce contribution stages, as well as office processes.

Leveraging Technology for Data Collection and Analysis: Observing the way institutions use technology in the data collection, processing and analysis of sustainability.

Longitudinal Studies: To further embed the analysis of a company's long-term trends and outcomes in order to be able to track its sustainability practices throughout time.

Open Sustainability Reporting: Focuses on accurate environmental reporting that builds a fair and trustworthy relationship with the stakeholders.

Opportunities for Sustainable Accounting: Focuses on the benefits of a green accounting approach for firms that include significant savings and reputation.

Regulations on Sustainability Reporting: Recognizes this as a consequence of the limitations posed by the government on revelations regarding sustainability information.

Resilience and Risk Management: Involves the potential of ESG issues in developing resistance and risk management abilities into business practices.

Robust Processes for Data Validation: Provides robust methodologies for validating that the data is linked to the ESG themes and the environmental-social governance.

Stakeholder Engagement: It emphasizes the need to work together with customers, employees and shareholders in order to help move forward.

Standardization of Reporting Frameworks: Emphasizes the need to develop shared mechanisms for addressing sustainability challenges in a cohesive manner.

Strategic Use of Sustainability Reporting: This enables organizations to move beyond compliance and utilize the sustainability report as a mechanism for differentiation from environmentally conscious options.

Sustainability Accounting Systems: The tools employed by such a business can also be social and environmental activities.

Sustainability Frameworks: GRI and SASB standards reflect how such an organization indicates the environment that financial concerns must be placed within an environmental perspective.

Transparency and Accountability: It is characterized by truthful communication of a company's environmental activities and answering for its own impact.

Variability in Reporting Methodologies: They deal with many challenges that are associated with the different modes of information sharing, making it very impossible to judge the environmental efforts of the companies.

Chapter 4 Volatility Spillovers in Water Exchange-Traded Funds

Rajibur Reza
Griffith University, Australia

Gurudeo Anand Tularam
Griffith University, Australia

ABSTRACT

Water is one of the planet's essential and extensively used resource. However, it is predicted that around 3.2 billion people will face severe water shortages by 2030. Hence, there is an urgent need to expand water utilities, water infrastructure, and water treatment plants to maximally protect water resources. Investment in water is essential for supporting this cause, and private funding is a way to meet the financial needs of the water industry. This study examines returns and volatility of four water exchange-traded funds (ETFs). Using the GARCH, EGARCH, and TGARCH models, this study shows the existence of persistence of volatility among the four water ETFs at the 1% level. The analyses and results of this study show important implications for investors and stakeholders, enabling them to make appropriate decisions.

INTRODUCTION

Water is one of the planet's extensively used resources (FAO, 2017). Over the years, the problem of supply of potable drinking water has been growing around the world (Jin et al. 2015; Reza et al, 2021). The situation has become difficult due to lack of attention to this in research it seems. Only about 1% of the freshwater is

DOI: 10.4018/979-8-3693-0863-9.ch004

easily available for human consumption when statistics are analysed (Reza & Sun, 2023; Reza, 2017). The global human population has been increasing steadily, and it is predicted that the population may reach 8.6 billion by 2030 and between 9.5 and 13.3 billion in 2100 (FAO, 2017). In contrast, the world's population was around 2.5 billion in 1950 and 7.7 billion in 2019[1]. So, it has nearly tripled between 1950 and 2019. As the population has been growing rapidly water demand has increased in proportion with the water demand rising globally to around 2% annually[2]. The population and water demand growth has compounded the impact on water resources and indeed has led to scarcity (Tiwari et al.2023). The impact of climate change has also negatively affected the water-related infrastructures, products and services (Reza & Tularam, 2022). As a consequence, acute challenges relating to the water supply and water-related businesses may continue for some time (Roca et al., 2015; Tularam & Marchisella, 2014). Present statistics suggest that around 800 million people do not have access to clean water and 3.2 billion will face severe water shortage by 2030 due to the climate change related impacts[3]. Hence, there is an urgent need to expand water utilities, water infrastructure and water treatment plants to not only meet the growing demand and improve the living standards but also to allow water access to the most vulnerable in the developing world (Global Water and Development Report, 2020; Roca and Tularam, 2012).

In a water shortage scenario, the global water industry can play a significant role. However, this means we would need to improve the global water industry as a whole, requiring investment funds from both the government and private sectors. While governments can contribute to this in most instances, the sector is unable to make such significant investments from public funds; as such this contribution is mostly if not always insufficient (Chousa et al., 2020; Vandone et al., 2018). Thus, private sector investors need to play a major role in helping fund the necessary requirements. The investment from the private sector is vital to meet the financing demands of the water utilities. For these reasons, the issues related to risk and returns on water investments need further study and analysis. The findings of such studies will provide confidence in the industry and create opportunities for large amounts of private sector investment. Moreover, such information may help the public to better understand the risks and returns of their investments prompting them to participate in the development process and achieve self-gain in a "win-win" context. For these reasons, large increases in investments in the global water industry will be needed over the next few decades to address issues such as upgrading existing infrastructure and providing access for underserved communities.

The existing water industry allows investors to either invest indirectly via thematic water indices; namely, Dow Jones U.S. Water Index, ISE-B&S Water Index, NASDAQ Global Water Index, NASDAQ US Water Index; the MSCI ACWI Water Utilities Index, S-Network Global Water Index, S&P 1500 Water Utilities Index,

S&P Global Water Index and World Water Index that are water utilities, water treatments and water infrastructure (Díaz-Mendoza and Pardo, 2023; Reza et al.2021). Investors are further encouraged to participate in the Water ETFs that are focused on water and follow the behaviour of a water index (Vandone et al. 2018). In 2005 and 2007, two exchange-traded funds (ETFs) - Invesco Water Resources ETF and Invesco Global Water ETF were successively introduced to investors. Also, other ETFs are available to investors; for example, the First Trust ISE Water ETF and the Invesco S&P Global Water Index ETF. Importantly, water ETFs are considered a better option for investing in when using a single fund. Usually, water ETFs are shares of water companies that are involved in water infrastructure, water treatment, water purification and distribution. According to Tularam and Reza (2016), "Water EFTs are baskets of water-related shares aimed at replicating the performance of the water market..." (p. 2).

Not surprisingly, an important consideration in the share market investment industry is the aspect of investor risk and return. The same applies to the investment performance of water companies and market; with the concepts of regulatory risk, risk and returns being at the forefront. Therefore, several studies in this regard exist, as many researchers have conducted previous work focusing on various aspects of risks in the investment in water indices and water funds (see next section). While some have reported on price integration, portfolio diversification benefits, and returns and volatility, it seems that water investors do not appear to be well informed about the water ETFs' returns and volatilities related know-how. Hence, the objective of this study is to investigate returns and volatility of water ETFs to fill this gap in the literature. This study uses a large water database; particularly the period from July 2007 to July 2023; and this dataset will be analysed using some well accepted methods such as the generalized autoregressive conditional heteroskedasticity (GARCH), Exponential GARCH (EGARCH) and Threshold GARCH (TGARCH) approaches. The in-depth analzes, results and findings of this study therefore contribute to a better overall understanding of the volatility and leverage effects of water ETFs in the water industry; and that in turn will better guide investor decision-making.

LITERATURE REVIEW

In the finance literature, a large number of studies have investigated stock market volatility and returns, including asymmetric impact of news on volatility using established methods such as the GARCH, EGARCH, TGARCH and Multivariate GARCH models; focusing for example, on the US, European and Asian stock and bond markets (see, Engle, 2004; Vlady et al. 2008; Tularam et al. 2009; Chevalliera and Ielpo, 2013; Tsuji 2016; Jiang et al. 2018; Aliyev et al. 2020; Naimy et al. 2021;

Kalovwea et al., 2021; Wang et al 2022; Yadav et al.,2023; Chiu et al., 2024; Ma et al; 2024;Sahooa and Kumar, 2024; Vo, 2024). Recently, Yadav et al. (2023) study the volatility spillover on daily spot prices of energy commodities (CO2 emission, natural gas and crude oil) to the Shanghai Stock Exchange and European equity markets for the period of 2010-2022. Their results show that higher volatility and connectedness in the longer run. Moreover, they claim that natural gas contributes more significantly to the shocks, while crude oil is the primary recipient of these shocks through the network connection. More recently, Ma et al. (2024) examine the volatility spillover effects of regional carbon prices, gold prices, oil prices, natural gas prices, coal prices, and the Chicago Board Options Exchange Volatility Index (VIX) and the China stock market for the period of 2013 - 2023 using EGARCH model. They report that the volatility spillovers in regional carbon prices positively effects the China stock market. Similarly, Chiu et al. (2024) analyze the critical aspects of spillover and expiration effects, as well as volatility clustering and asymmetry at the Taiwan Futures Exchange for the period of May 18, 2017, to May 18, 2022 using a bivariate EGARCH model. They report that the regular trading session returns are lower volatility than the after-hours session. Further, Sahoo and Kumar (2024) investigate the volatility spillover among the sectors (financial services, auto, oil and gas, information technology, healthcare, and real estate) of India China, UK and US for the period of 2015 -2023 employing BEKK GARCH and GO-GARCH models. They found that the conditional volatility exists among each sector of own capital market of India China, UK and US. Similarly, Vo (2024) evaluates the market volatility across 13 (consumer discretionary, consumer staples, energy, financials, health care, industrials, information technology, materials, metals and mining, real estate investment trust (REIT), resources, telecom services, and utilities) Australian sectors for the period of 2010 to 2021 to identify the most vulnerable sectors using the ARMA-GARCH model. He points out that highest volatility spillovers from the Consumer Staples sector.

In the field of water finance and investment, various issues have been examined. in the private water industry (for example, Geman and Kanyinda 2007; Roca and Tularam 2012; Alvarez and Rodriguez 2015; Buckland et al. 2015; Jin et al. 2014; 2015, 2016 and 2019; Roca et al. 2015; Tularam and Reza 2016; Fiorelli and Mele 2017; Peri et al. 2017; Reza et al. 2017, 2018; 2021 and 2022; Roca et al., 2015; Vandone et al. 2018; Piñeiro-Chousa et al. 2020; Reza and Tularam, 2022; Samitas et al. 2022; Díaz-Mendoza and Pardo, 2023; Naeem et al.,2023; Tiwari et al.,2023). Unfortunately, despite its significance in water finance and investment, only a few studies have delved into the analysis of the returns and volatility of the water stocks, water indices and water funds using GARCH, AR-GARCH, GARCH, ARMA-GARCH, E-GARCH, multivariate GARCH and DCC-GARCH models. For instance, Peri et al. (2017), Reza et al. (2018) and (2022), and Reza and Tularam,

(2022) have applied GARCH, AR-GARCH, ARMA-GARCH, E-GARCH, multivariate GARCH and DCC-GARCH models in this area. Peri et al. (2017) conduct a study on volatility spillovers to examine the dynamic relationship between S&P global water index and S&P Agriculture-Livestock Index, and the S&P Energy Index for the period of 2001-2013 using Multivariate GARCH model. They claim that volatility spillovers are existed between these three water, energy, and food indices. Later, Reza et al. (2018) investigate the returns and volatility of the World Water index (WOWAX), S-Network Global Water Index, S&P Global Water Index and MSCI ACWI Water Utilities Index (MSCI ACWI), the Asia, Europe, Latin America and US water market indices, Pictet Global Water Fund and KBC Eco Water Fund in different (full, pre-GFC, GFC and post-GFC) periods using ARMA (1,1)-GARCH (1,1) and EGARCH (1, 1) models. They confirm that volatility and leverage spillovers emerge from these ten water assets during the full, pre-GFC, GFC and post-GFC periods. Recently, Reza et al. (2022) examine the dynamic relationships between the Chinese water indices and other four Asian water indices - Hong Kong, Japan, the Philippines and Singapore for the period 2005-2018 using the dynamic DCC-GARCH model. They report that volatility spillovers are existed among these five water indices. Moreover, they claim that there is a possibility of portfolio diversification benefits between pairs of these Asian water indices owing to the contrasting correlations. Further, Reza and Tularam, (2022) investigate the relationship between world water indices and water indices of different individual countries - China, Hong Kong, Singapore, Germany, France, the UK, Brazil, Chile, and the US for the period 2001-2020 using ordinary least square (OLS) and quantile regression models. Theu find that the indices of China, Hong Kong, Singapore, Germany, France, the UK, Brazil, Chile, and the US are positively related with world water indices. Their results show a high degree of persistency in the conditional volatility of stock returns for these water indices by using the ARMA (1,1)-GARCH (1,1) model.

A critical review reveals that only three studies (Tularam and Reza, 2016; Rompotis, 2016; Díaz-Mendoza and Pardo, 2023) have focused on water ETFs investments. Tularam and Reza (2016) examine the association between idiosyncratic risk and return among four water exchange-traded funds (namely PIO, PHO, FIW, and CGW). They claim that water ETFs exhibit lower idiosyncratic risk, impacting their returns across different regimes (Regime 1, Regime 2, and Regime 3). Further, their results confirm that most of the idiosyncratic risk of these ETFs transitions from low volatility (Regime 2) to relatively low volatility (Regimes 1 and 3). Also, Rompotis (2016) analyse the performance of the aforementioned four water ETFs, concluding that they demonstrate positive and normal performance, which may be appealing to socially responsible investors seeking above-average returns. More recently, Díaz-Mendoza and Pardo (2023) examine four water-related ETFs (PHO,

CGW, FIW and PIO) to evaluate their role in portfolio performance across six US and European stock, bonds, and volatility benchmarks. Their results indicate that water assets can be considered as hedges, diversifiers and/or safe-haven investments for equity, fixed-income and volatility indices respectively.

From the above literature review, it is evident that while the returns and volatility of stock and bond markets have been extensively examined, researchers have largely overlooked research on volatility spillovers in water investments. To the best of our knowledge, no studies have focused on returns and volatility in water ETFs using time-series analysis (such as GARCH, EGARCH and TGARCH models). Hence, this study seeks to address the gap in the literature; and in particular, the study will analyze the nature of persistence and asymmetric volatility of water ETFs using the GARCH, EGARCH and TGARCH models. In terms of the motivation of this study, none of researchers has focused on volatility spillovers on the water ETFs using the above models. Thus, this study holds significance for investors, particularly in understanding that water ETFs' stock returns exhibit volatility persistence and asymmetric effects, which may suggest potential spillovers from the water sector. Based on the above, we test two hypotheses in this paper; firstly

H_1. Stock returns are affected by volatility in the water ETFs; and the secondly:

H_2. The water ETFs exhibit asymmetric volatility.

Data

This study utilizes the four water ETFs - Invesco Water Resources ETF (PHO) based on the NASDAQ OMX US Water Index; Invesco Global Water ETF (PIO) based on the NASDAQ OMX Global Water Index, the First Trust ISE Water ETF (FIW) that is based on the ISE Clean Edge Water Index and the Invesco S&P Global Water Index ETF (CGW) based on the S&P Global Water Index. These water ETFs are based in the United States and in most instances, they invest at least 90% of their total assets in the common stocks of water companies. However, the investment "universe" of these Water ETFs is smaller than other types of ETFs. Table 1 presents the description of the four water ETFs.

Table 1. Description of the water ETFs

Water ETFs name	Fund Ticker	Launch Date	Benchmark Index
Invesco Water Resources ETF	PHO	December 06, 2005	NASDAQ OMX US Water Index
Invesco Global Water ETF	PIO	June 13, 2007	Nasdaq OMX Global Water Index

continued on following page

Table 1. Continued

Water ETFs name	Fund Ticker	Launch Date	Benchmark Index
First Trust ISE®Water ETF	FIW	May 08, 2007	ISE Clean Edge Water Index
Invesco S&P Global Water Index ETF	CGW	May 14, 2007	S&P Global Water Index

Sources[4], Sources[5], Sources[6] and Sources[7]

This study examines volatility spillovers in four water ETFs (namely, PHO, PIO, FIW and GGW) using the GARCH, EGARCH and TGARCH approaches. The monthly data are obtained from Bloomberg for the sample period: July 31, 2007 to July 31, 2023. Figure 1 shows the trend of prices for the four water ETFs prices over time. The monthly returns of water ETFs are transformed using the following formula: $R_t = \ln(Price_t/Price_{t-1}) \times 100$

Figure 1. Share price movement of four water ETFs, 2007-2023

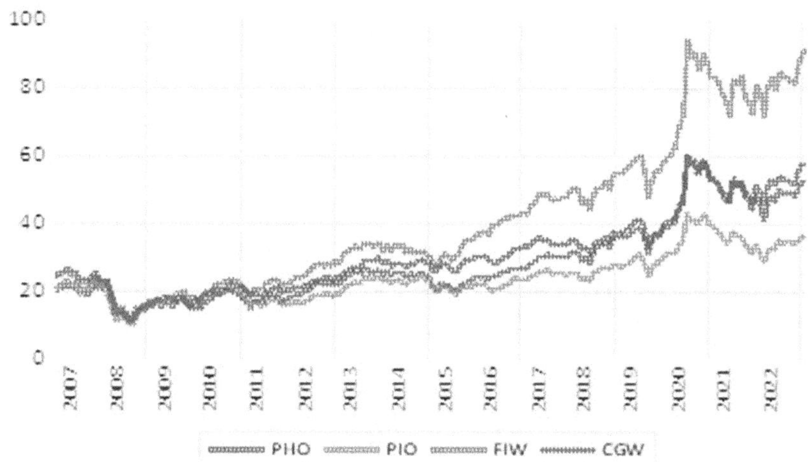

Data Source: Bloomberg

METHODOLOGY

GARCH Model

In 1986, the generalized autoregressive conditional heteroskedasticity (GARCH) model was introduced by Bollerslev. This study used the GARCH (p, q), model to estimate the mean (Equation 1) and variance-covariance (Equation 2) matrix of returns. The following two equations are generated from the GARCH model.

$$Y_t = \beta X_t' + \epsilon_t \tag{1}$$

$$\sigma_t^2 = \alpha + \gamma\epsilon_{t-1}^2 + \beta\sigma_{t-1}^2 \tag{2}$$

In Equation 1, Y_t is the dependent variable X_t''s are regressors and ϵ_t is the error term. In Equation 2, σ_t^2 is the conditional variance, γ and δ are the ARCH and GARCH respectively, and p and q are the lag order of the GARCH model.

EGARCH Model

Nelson introduced the exponential GARCH (EGARCH) model in 1991 in order to determine the asymmetric effects in time-series analysis. Usually, the EGARCH model allows asymmetric effects of the good news and bad news on conditional variances. This study uses the EGARCH (p, q) model as an exponential function when p=1 or 2, q=1or 2 which is:

$$\log(\sigma_t^2) = \omega + \alpha\left(\frac{\lfloor\varepsilon_{t-1}\rfloor}{\sqrt{\sigma_t^2 - 1}} - \sqrt{\frac{2}{\pi}}\right) + \gamma\frac{\varepsilon_{t-1}}{\sqrt{\sigma_t^2 - 1}} + \beta\log\left(\sigma_t^2 - 1\right) \tag{3}$$

where the asymmetric positive and negative shocks (ε_{t-1}) on conditional variance and $\frac{\varepsilon_{t-1}}{\sqrt{\sigma_t^2 - 1}} \sim N(0,1)$ are captured by the parameter γ. The negative coefficient of γ indicates that volatility rises more than the positive coefficient γ. The parameter γ (a negative sign) ensures that "bad news" that generates more volatility than good news. The coefficient of α captures the assembling effects of the volatility.

TGARCH Model

The asymmetric effect can be captured by E-GARCH (Nelson 1991) model. However, this model was criticised by Halkos and Sepetis (2007) due to its fixed relationship of different volatilities generated by positive and negative values. This study, therefore, applied the Threshold GARCH (TGARCH) model (Zakonian, 1994). The following TGARCH (1, 1) model (Poon and Granger, 2003) was applied using monthly stock returns.

Put in table: I have done this all the time you should also please all the time

$$\hbar_t = \omega + \alpha \varepsilon_{t-1}^2 + \delta I_{t-1} \varepsilon_{t-1}^2 + \beta \hbar_{t-1} \tag{4}$$

$$\text{where } I_{t-1} = \begin{cases} 1 \text{if} \varepsilon_{t-1} < 0 \\ 0 \text{if} \varepsilon_{t-1} \geq 0 \end{cases}$$

In Equation 4, the good news produces a positive ε_{t-1}, that only affects the α whereas the "bad news" give a negative ε_{t-1}, which impacts on both of the α and the δ. Hence, "bad news" produces higher volatility than good news (Bouchaud et al 2001).

EMPIRICAL RESULTS

Descriptive Statistics

Table 2 displays the descriptive statistics of four water ETFs. The results show that the mean returns are positive for the four water ETFs. FIW has the highest mean returns among them; whereas the lowest mean return is noted in PIO. The water ETFs with the highest standard deviation is PHO and the lowest standard division is noted in CGW. Figure 2 summarizes the results regarding mean and standard deviation.

Table 2. Descriptive statistics

Variables	Observations	Mean	Std. Dev.	Min	Max
PHO	193	0.536	6.147	-29.203	26.987
PIO	193	0.195	6.118	-31.015	21.830
FIW	193	0.760	6.008	-25.217	27.343
CGW	193	0.392	5.517	-22.523	25.890

Note: This table reports the descriptive statistics for four water ETFs: PHO, PIO, FIW and CGW.

Figure 2. Movements of mean and standard deviation

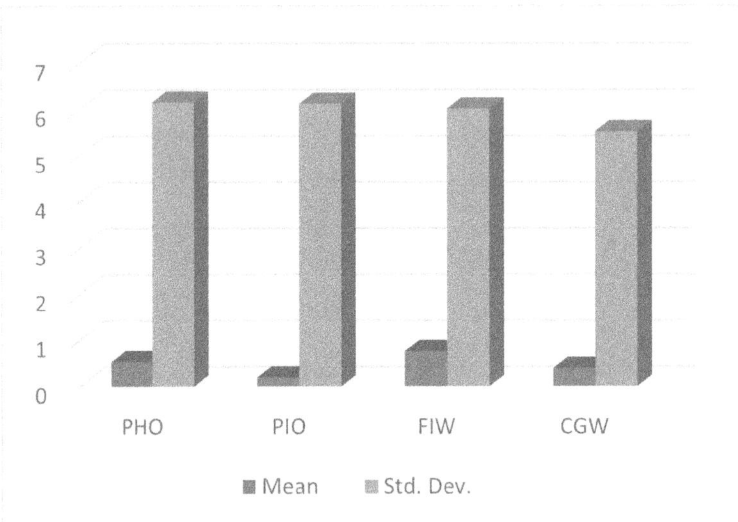

Data Source: Bloomberg

Correlation Analysis

Table 3 exhibits the Correlation matrix. The results show that the four water ETFs are positively correlated with each other. It is observed that PHO, PIO, FIW and CGW are highly correlated; indicating that these four water ETFs tends to move in the same direction. As the correlation is not low or negative, there is little scope for hedging in the water ETFs. This suggests that the water investors cannot get diversification benefits within a portfolio of investments or assets.

Table 3. Correlation matrix

Variables	PHO	PIO	FIW	CGW
PHO	1.000			
PIO	0.927	1.00		
FIW	0.976	0.902	1.000	
CGW	0.925	0.941	0.924	1.000

Note: This table reports the correlation results among four water ETFs: PHO, PIO, FIW and CGW.

GARCH Model

The GARCH model results are presented in Table 4. According to the minimum values of Akaike information criterion (AIS), the GARCH (2.2), GARCH (2.1), GARCH (1.1) models have been estimated to explain the volatility in the monthly returns for PHO, PIO, FIW and CGW. It is noted that the parameters $\gamma_1$and γ_2 describe news about volatility from the previous period, which is measured as the lag of the squared residuals from the mean equation. GARCH (2.2)'s parameter γ_1 of PHO, is positively significant at the 5% level. The GARCH (2.1) results show that the parameter γ_2 of PHO and FIW is positively significant at the 1% and 10% levels, respectively. The GARCH (1.1) results confirm that the parameter γ_1 of CGW has a positive significance at the 1% level. The GARCH (2.2) and GARCH (2.1) results show that only β_1 coefficients of PHO, PIO and FIW are positively significant at the 1% level in the monthly returns. However, β_1 coefficient of CGW is not significant. The GARCH (2.2) results show that β_2 coefficient of PHO is significant at the 1% level. Hence, based on the analyses, the GARCH (2.2) and GARCH (2.1) models have been estimated to explain the high volatility in the monthly returns except for CGW. Figure 3 presents the estimated volatility of monthly returns of the four water ETFs, which reveals more information regarding the volatility using GARCH model.

Table 4. GARCH model

	PHO GARCH (2,2)	PIO GARCH (2,1)	FIW GARCH (2,1)	CGW GARCH (1.1)
ω	0.045 (0.050)**	0.142 (0.150)	0.128 (0.050)	1.395 (0.000)***
γ_1	0.146 (0.054)**	- 0.061(0.002)***	-0.040 (0.410)	0.433 (0.000)***
γ_2	-0.095 (0.371)	0.199 (0.000)***	0.219 (0.009)***	-
β_1	1.615 (0.000)***	0.814 (0.000)***	0.738 (0.000)***	-0.020 (0.904)
β_2	-0.698 (0.000)***	-	-	-

Notes: *, ** and *** indicate significance at 10%, 5% and 1% levels, respectively.
We run the following model using monthly returns to find out the volatility spillovers in water ETFs.

$$Y_t = \beta X_t^{'} + \epsilon_t$$

$$\sigma_t^2 = \alpha + \gamma \epsilon_{t-1}^2 + \beta \sigma_{t-1}^2$$

wherre σ_t^2 is the conditional variance, γ and δ are the ARCH and GARCH respectively, and p and q are the lag order of the GARCH model.

Figure 3. Estimated volatility of GARCH model

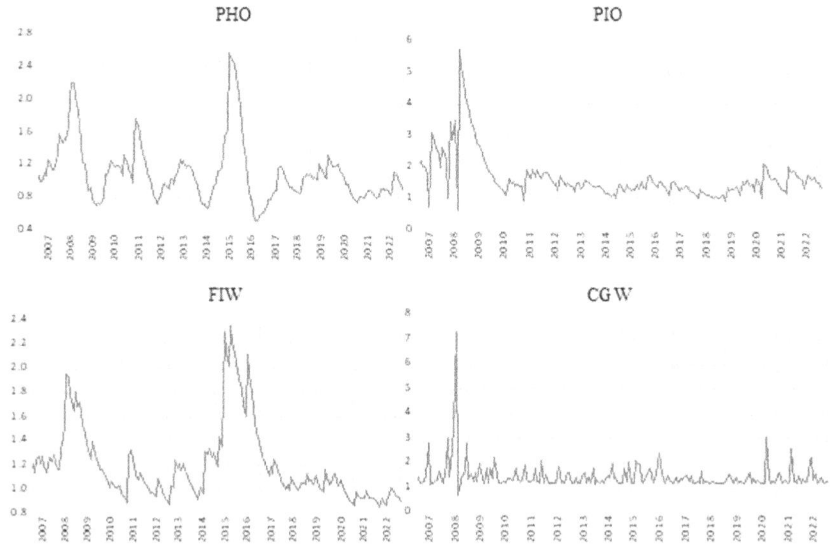

Data Source: Bloomberg

EGARCH Model

To understand the leverage impact on the volatility of water ETFs, the results for the EGARCH model are shown in Table 5. Based on the minimum AIC, the EGARCH (1, 2) model is selected for PHO and CGW, while the EGARCH (2, 1) is a better fit for PIO and FIW. The EGARCH (1, 2) results show that γ_1 does not have a significant leverage impact on the volatility of PHO; whereas γ_1 has a positive and significant asymmetric (leverage) effect on CGW at 1% level. Moreover, the EGARCH (2, 1) results show that γ_1 presents the positive leverage effect on the volatility of PIO at the 5% level of significance; whereas γ_1 has a negative impact on CGW at 5% level. It is noted that the parameter γ_2 does not present the asymmetric (leverage) effects of PIO, but the parameter γ_2 has significantly leverage impact on the volatility of FIW at the 1% level of significance. The parameter β_1 for the EGARCH (2, 1) model confirms that "bad news" generate volatility in FIW. This result appears to be in line with Reza et al. (2018). Figure 4 presents the estimated volatility of monthly returns of the four water ETFs, revealing more information regarding the asymmetric volatility using EGARCH model.

Table 5. EGARCH model

	PHO EGARCH (1,2)	PIO EGARCH (2,1)	FIW EGARCH (2,1)	CGW EGARCH (1,2)
ω	0.456 (0.072)	0.664 (0.000)	0.027 (0.431)	0.728 (0.013)
α_1	-0.006 (0.850)	0.303 (0.000)***	-0.037(0.788)	-0.332 (0.000)***
α_2	-	-0.522 (0.000)***	0.211(0.127)	-
γ_1	0.038 (0.399)	0.261 (0.041)**	- 0.887(0.000)***	0.636 (0.000)***
γ_2	-	-0.257 (0.100)	1.246 (0.000)***	-
β_1	-1.116 (0.000)***	0.240 (0.115)	0.870 (0.000)***	-0.166 (0.454)
β_2	-0.997 (0.000)***	-	-	0.049 (0.853)

Notes: *, ** and *** indicate significance at 10%, 5% and 1% levels, respectively.

We run the following model using monthly returns to understand leverage impact on the volatility of water ETFs.

$$\log(\sigma_t^2) = \omega + \alpha\left(\frac{\lfloor\varepsilon_{t-1}\rfloor}{\sqrt{\sigma_t^2 - 1}} - \sqrt{\tfrac{2}{\pi}}\right) + \gamma\frac{\varepsilon_{t-1}}{\sqrt{\sigma_t^2 - 1}} + \beta\log\left(\sigma_t^2 - 1\right)$$

where the asymmetric positive and negative shocks (ε_{t-1}) on conditional variance and $\frac{\varepsilon_{t-1}}{\sqrt{\sigma_t^2 - 1 \sim N,(0,1)}}$ are captured by the parameter γ. The negative coefficient of γ indicates that volatility rises more than the positive coefficient γ.

Figure 4. Estimated volatility of EGARCH model

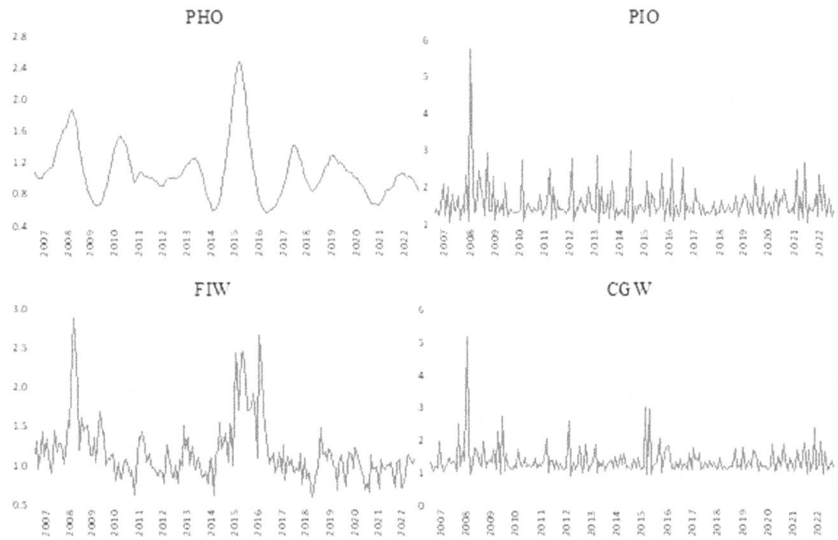

Data Source: Bloomberg

TGARCH Model

TGARCH (1. 1) model appears to be a better model for identifying the asymmetric effects in EGARCH modelling process. Based on the condition of minimum AIC, the TGARCH (1, 1) model is considered to be the best fit for PHO, PIO, FIW and CGW. The TGARCH (1. 1) results are presented in Table 6. The TGARCH (1.1) results show that the parameter δ of PHO, PIO and FIW are not significant. However, δ of CGW is significant at the 1% level. It is important to note that the TGARCH (1. 1) results confirm that β coefficients of PHO, PIO and FIW are positively significant, except in the case of CGW, at the 1% level. As the asymmetric effects of PHO, PIO and FIW are significant, these three water ETFs volatility respond to "good and bad news" more critically.

Table 6. TGARCH (1,1) model

	PHO	PIO	FIW	CGW
ω	0.208 (0.123)	0.045 (0.046)	0.108 (0.112)	1.343 (0.000)
α	0.355 (0.035)**	-0.0578 (0.429)	0.0726 (0.279)	0.810 (0.004)**

continued on following page

Table 6. Continued

	PHO	PIO	FIW	CGW
δ	-0.235 (0.311)	-0.057 (0.598)	0.079 (0.510)	-0.674 (0.027)
β	0.602 (0.000)***	1.555 (0.000)***	0.809 (0.000)***	-0.008 (0.961)

Notes: *, ** and *** indicate significance at 10%, 5% and 1% levels, respectively.

At the end of each month, we run the following TGARCH (1, 1) model (Poon & Granger, 2003) using monthly stock return.

$$\hbar_t = \omega + \alpha \varepsilon_{t-1}^2 + \delta I_{t-1} \varepsilon_{t-1}^2 + \beta \hbar_{t-1}$$

$$\text{where } I_{t-1} = \begin{cases} 1 \text{if} \varepsilon_{t-1} < 0 \\ 0 \text{if} \varepsilon_{t-1} \geq 0 \end{cases}$$

CONCLUSION

The objective of this study is to analyse the stock returns and volatility of the four water ETFs with the purpose of investigating general profitability of water-related investments using GARCH, EGARCH and TGARCH models for the period of July 2007-July 2023. In terms of correlation results analysis, we find that PHO, PIO, FIW and CGW are strongly correlated with each other. Thus, there is little possibility for international portfolio diversification, Hence, water investors could be deprived from the portfolio diversification benefits during the investment epochs.

The GARCH (2,2) and GARCH (2.1) models utilize data indicating a high level of volatility for PHO, PIO and FIW in relation to the monthly returns, except in the case of CGW. These results support the first hypothesis (H_1). The findings suggest that persistence and asymmetric (leverage) effects can be captured for PHO. PIO and FIW water ETFs by using the EGARCH (1.2) and EGARDCH (2,1) models, being the best fit for our data. The model results support the second hypothesis (H_2). Moreover, this study has utilized the TGARCH (1,1) model to further confirm the EGARCH asymmetric effects within PHO, PIO, FIW, and CGW water ETFs. The TGARCH (1,1) model results of the PHO, PIO, and FIW water ETFs returns exhibit strong volatility persistence and asymmetric (leverage) effects. However, volatility persistence does not spill over from the CGW water ETFs return. Based on the extensive knowledge gained from the GARCH, EGARCH, and TGARCH models results, it is clear that leverage effects exist in water ETFs monthly returns, except in the case of CGW.

The results of this study carry important implications for both individual and institutional investors looking to invest in the global private water sector, particularly in understanding the returns and volatility of this sector. However, solely examining volatility spillovers in water ETFs may not provide a comprehensive understanding of water investment globally. Hence, it is essential to consider other tools such as private water companies' stocks, water indices and water mutual funds to gain a more nuanced understanding of water investment worldwide. It is important to note that much more research is needed to fully comprehend the nature of the global private water sector. One limitation of this study is the lack of access to a longer-term data sample, as the data for PIO, FIW, and CGW water ETFs are not available prior to 2007. Additionally, there are several avenues for future research expansion. For instance, analyzing the returns and volatility of water ETFs in comparison to traditional ETFs, energy ETFs, ESG ETFs, green bond ETFs, and sustainable ETFs could provide insights into the relationships between these different types of ETFs.

REFERENCES

Aliyev, F., Ajayi, R., & Gasim, N. (2020). Modelling asymmetric market volatility with univariate GARCH models: Evidence from Nasdaq-100. *Journal of Economic Asymmetries*, 22, 1–10. 10.1016/j.jeca.2020.e00167

Alvarez, M., & Rodríguez, A. (2015). Water-related mutual funds: Investment performance and social role. *Social Responsibility Journal*, 11(3), 502–512. 10.1108/SRJ-08-2013-0104

Bollerslev, T. (1986). Generalized autoregressive conditional heteroskedasticity. *Journal of Econometrics*, 31(3), 307–327. 10.1016/0304-4076(86)90063-1

Buckland, R., Beecher, J., & Williams, J. (2015). Risk and regulation in water utilities: A cross-country comparison of evidence from the CAPM. *Journal of Regulatory Economics*, 47(2), 117–145. 10.1007/s11149-014-9261-z

Chevalliera, J., & Ielpo, F. (2013). Volatility spillovers in commodity markets. *Applied Economics Letters*, 20(13), 1211–1227. 10.1080/13504851.2013.799748

Chiu, C.-L., Chang, T.-H., Hsiao, I.-F., & Chiou, D.-S. (2024). The price continuity, return and volatility spillover effects of regular and after-hours trading. *PLoS One*, 19(3), 1–16. 10.1371/journal.pone.029920738466755

Díaz-Mendoza, A. C., & Pardo, A. (2023). Water and traditional asset classes. *Finance Research Letters*, 52, 1–8. 10.1016/j.frl.2022.103394

Engle, R. (2004). Risk and volatility: Econometric models and financial practice. *The American Economic Review*, 94(3), 405–420. 10.1257/0002828041464597

FAO. (2017). Water for sustainable food and agriculture. A report produced for the G20 Presidency of Germany. https://www.fao.org/3/i7959e/i7959e.pdf

Geman, H., & Kanyinda, A. (2007). Water as the next commodity. *Journal of Alternative Investments*, 10(2), 23–30. 10.3905/jai.2007.695264

Global Water and Development Report. (2020). Annual Report of Water Security, Sanitation, and Hygiene Activities. USAID.

Halkos, G., & Sepetis, A. (2007). Can capital markets respond to environmental policy of firms? Evidence from Greece. *Ecological Economics*, 63(2), 578–587. 10.1016/j.ecolecon.2006.12.015

Jiang, W., Ruan, Q., Li, J., & Li, Y. (2018). Modeling returns volatility: Realized GARCH incorporating realized risk measure. *Physica A*, 500, 249–25. 10.1016/j.physa.2018.02.018

Jin, Y., Li, B., Roca, E., & Wong, V. (2014). Investment returns in the water industry: A survey. *International Journal of Water*, 8(2), 183–199. 10.1504/IJW.2014.060965

Jin, Y., Li, B., Roca, E., & Wong, V. (2016). Water as an investment: Liquid yet illiquid. *Applied Economics*, 9(9), 731–745. 10.1080/00036846.2015.1085646

Jin, Y., Reza, R., Li, B., Roca, E., & Wong, V. (2019). Water as an investment and the impact of regulatory risk. *Financial Planning Research Journal*, 5(1), 55–81. 10.2478/fprj-2019-0003

Jin, Y., Roca, E., Li, B., Wong, V., & Cheung, A. (2015). Sprinkle your investment portfolio with water! *International Journal of Water*, 9(1), 43–59. 10.1504/IJW.2015.067445

Kalovwea, S. K., Mwanikia, J. I., & Simwa, R. O. (2021). On stock returns volatility and trading volume of the nairobi securities exchange index. *RMS: Research in Mathematics & Statistics*, 8(1), 1–10. 10.1080/27658449.2021.1889765

Ma, J., Feng, J., Chen, J., & Zhang, J. (2024). Volatility spillover from carbon prices to stock prices: Evidence from China's carbon emission trading markets. *Journal of Risk and Financial Management*, 17(3), 1–24. 10.3390/jrfm17030123

Naeem, M. A., Iqbal, N., Karim, S., & Lucey, B.M. (2023). From forests to faucets to fuel: Investigating the domino effect of extreme risk in timber, water, and energy markets. *Finance Research Letters,* 55, 1-8. 10.1016/j.frl.2023.104010

Naimy, V., Haddad, O., Ferna'ndez-Aviles, G., & Khoury, R. E. (2021). The predictive capacity of GARCH-type models in measuring the volatility of crypto and world currencies. *PLoS One*, 16(1), 1–17. 10.1371/journal.pone.024590433513150

Nelson, D. (1991). Conditional heteroskedasticity in asset returns: A New Approach. *Econometrica*, 59(2), 347–370. 10.2307/2938260

Peri, M., Vandone, D., & Baldi, L. (2017). Volatility spillover between water, energy and food. *Sustainability (Basel)*, 9(6), 1–16. 10.3390/su9061071

Piñeiro-Chousaa, J., López-Cabarcosb, M. A., & Ribeiro-Soriano, D. (2020). Does investor attention influence water companies' stock returns? *Technological Forecasting and Social Change*, 158, 1–10. 10.1016/j.techfore.2020.120115

Reza, R. (2017). *An investigation of water investment performance: Analysis of the global water industry* [PhD Thesis]. Griffith University. Retrieved from https://research-repository.griffith.edu.au/handle/10072/371256

Reza, R., & Sun, L. (2023). Impact of Gender Diversity on the Board of Directors on the Financial Performance of the Chinese Private Water Companies. In Kunjumuhammed, S. K., & Ramachandran, N. (Eds.), *Future Outlooks on Corporate Finance and Opportunities for Robust Economic Planning* (pp. 68–98). IGI Global. 10.4018/978-1-6684-5342-1.ch004

Reza, R., & Tularam, G. A. (2022). Financial investments in the global water market. In Rafay, A. (Ed.), *Finance for Sustainability in a Turbulent Economy* (pp. 1–25). IGI Global. 10.4018/978-1-6684-5580-7.ch001

Reza, R., Tularam, G. A., & Li, B. (2017). An investigation into the interdependence of global water indices: A VAR analysis. *Applied Economics*, 49(8), 769–796. 10.1080/00036846.2016.1205725

Reza, R., Tularam, G. A., & Li, B. (2018). Returns and volatility of water investments. *Cogent Economics & Finance*, 6(3), 1–33. 10.1080/23322039.2018.1438724

Reza, R., Tularam, G. A., & Li, B. (2021). A review of global research on private investment in the water sector. *Utilities Policy*, 72, 1–16. 10.1016/j.jup.2021.101283

Reza, R., Tularam, G. A., Li, B., & Li, B. (2022). Investments in the Asian water sector: An analysis based on the DCC-GARCH model. *Humanities & Social Sciences Communications*, 9(452), 1–9. 10.1057/s41599-022-01470-4

Roca, E., Tularam, G. A., & Reza, R. (2015). Fundamental signals of investment profitability in the global water industry. *International Journal of Water*, 9(4), 395–424. 10.1504/IJW.2015.072155

Roca, E. D., & Tularam, G. A. (2012). Which way does water flow? An econometric analysis of the global price integration of water stocks. *Applied Economics*, 44(23), 2935–2944. 10.1080/00036846.2011.568403

Rompotis, G. G. (2016). Evaluating a new hot trend: The case of water exchange-traded funds. *The Journal of Index Investing*, 6(4), 103–128. 10.3905/jii.2016.6.4.103

Sahooa, S., & Kumar, S. (2024). Volatility spillover among the sectors of emerging and developed markets: A hedging perspective. *Cogent Economics & Finance*, 12(1), 1–17. 10.1080/23322039.2024.2316048

Samitas, A., Papathanasiou, S., Koutsokostas, D., & Kampouris, E. (2022). Are timber and water investments safe-havens? A volatility spillover approach and portfolio hedging strategies for investors. *Finance Research Letters*, 47, 1–10. 10.1016/j.frl.2021.102657

Tiwari, A. K., Adewuyi, A. O., Adeleke, M. A., & Abakah, E. J. A. (2023). A time-varying Granger causality analysis between water stock and green stocks using novel approaches. *Energy Economics*, 126, 1–20. 10.1016/j.eneco.2023.107010

Tsuji, C. (2016). Does the fear gauge predict downside risk more accurately than econometric models? Evidence from the US stock market. *Cogent Economics & Finance*, 4(1), 1–42. 10.1080/23322039.2016.1220711

Tularam, A., Wong, V., & Roca, E. (2009). An analysis of Australian superannuation funds volatility using EGARCH approach. *Studies in Regional and Urban Planning*, 12, 143–160.

Tularam, G. A., & Marchisella, P. (2014). Water scarcity in Asia and its long-term water and border security implications for Australia. In Clark, R. M., & Hakim, S. (Eds.), *Securing Water and Wastewater Systems* (pp. 189–211). Springer. 10.1007/978-3-319-01092-2_9

Tularam, G. A., & Reza, R. (2016). Water exchange traded funds: A study on idiosyncratic risk using Markov switching analysis. *Cogent Economics & Finance*, 4(1), 1–12. 10.1080/23322039.2016.1139437

Vandone, D., Peri, M., Vandone, D., Baldi, L., & Tanda, A. (2018). The impact of energy and agriculture prices on the stock performance of the water industry. *Water Resources and Economics*, 23, 14–27. 10.1016/j.wre.2018.02.002

Vlady, A., Roca, E., & Tularam, G. A. (2008). The market value of Australian oil and gas industry and climate change: The VAR, ARCH, GARCH, approaches. *Studies in Regional and Urban Planning*, 11(1), 195–220.

Vo, D. H. (2023). Volatility spillovers across sectors and their magnitude: A sector-based analysis for Australia. *PLoS One*, 18(6), 1–18. 10.1371/journal.pone.028652837262027

Wang, Y., Xiang, Y., Lei, X., & Zhou, Y. (2022). Volatility analysis based on GARCH-type models: Evidence from the Chinese stock market. *Economic.Ekonomska Istrazivanja*, 35(1), 2530–2554. 10.1080/1331677X.2021.1967771

Yadav, M. P., Sharif, T., Ashok, S., Dhingra, D., & Abedin, M. Z. (2023). Investigating volatility spillover of energy commodities in the context of the Chinese and European stock markets. *Research in International Business and Finance*, 65, 1–16. 10.1016/j.ribaf.2023.101948

Zakoian, J. M. (1994). Threshold heteroskedastic models'. *Journal of Economic Dynamics & Control*, 18(5), 931–955. 10.1016/0165-1889(94)90039-6

ADDITIONAL READING

Buckland, R., & Fraser, P. (2001). Political and regulatory risk in water utilities: Beta sensitivity in the United Kingdom. *Journal of Business Finance & Accounting*, 28(7-8), 877–904. 10.1111/1468-5957.00397

Morana, C., & Sawkins, J. W. (2000). Regulatory uncertainty and share price volatility: The English and Welsh water industry's periodic price review. *Journal of Regulatory Economics*, 17(1), 87–100. 10.1023/A:1008105405621

Reza, R., & Tularam, G. A. (2017). An analysis of the relationships between ownership structure and capital structure of the global water industry. In *22nd International Congress on Modelling and Simulation,* Australia.

Reza, R., & Tularam, G. A. (2021). The determinants of capital structure: Evidence from the global water industry. In Marleau, K. (Ed.), *Advances in capital structure research* (pp. 1–31). Nova Science.

Tularam, G. A., & Reza, R. (2017). The critical importance of groundwater in coastal areas: Impact of climate change on Bangladesh Freshwater Resources. *Journal of Climate Change*, 3(1), 59–70. 10.3233/JCC-170006

ENDNOTES

1 https://www.un.org/en/global-issues/population
2 https://www.edisongroup.com/investment-themes/the-real-liquidity-crisis/
3 https://www.edisongroup.com/investment-themes/the-real-liquidity-crisis/
4 https://www.invesco.com/us/financial-products/etfs/product-detail?audienceType=investor&ticker=pho
5 https://www.invesco.com/us-rest/contentdetail?contentId=b6f8e01e98630410VgnVCM10000046f1bf0aRCRD&dnsName=us
6 https://www.invesco.com/us-rest/contentdetail?contentId=128b7c23dbd92610VgnVCM1000006e36b50aRCRD&dnsName=us
7 https://https://www.ftportfolios.com/retail/etf/etfsummary.aspx?Ticker=FIW

Chapter 5
An In-Depth Investigation Into Financial Literacy Levels in Indian Households

Anand Patil
https://orcid.org/0000-0003-4736-6571
Christ University, India

Niranjan L. R.
Christ University, India

Roopa Patavardhan
Christ University, India

Vibhor Jain
Christ University, India

ABSTRACT

In a complex financial world, lack of awareness complicates money management and savings. Emphasizing financial literacy is vital for informed decision-making. This study explores global financial illiteracy, advocating international initiatives. In India, it assesses disparities and government activities and reviews tax-saving and mobile banking. Gaps include limited studies on Indian households, necessitating gender-specific analyses and research on education's impact. The methodology outlines justification, operational definitions, and data collection techniques. With ANOVA and descriptive statistics on 285 respondents, the study reveals demographic analysis, indicating higher financial literacy with age and a gender gap. Education

DOI: 10.4018/979-8-3693-0863-9.ch005

positively correlates with financial literacy. Recommendations include interventions like financial seminars, collaboration with regulators, and destigmatizing money talks at home to enhance financial literacy and bridge gaps.

INTRODUCTION

In the realm of financial literacy, a pervasive challenge confronts nations globally, intricately weaving an individual's knowledge, skills, and attitude towards financial matters. In our contemporary world, marked by the complexities of financial products, the demand for financial literacy becomes not only essential but imperative. Recognizing this, nations like India, with burgeoning young populations, acknowledge the pivotal role of both government and private institutions in elevating financial literacy levels. Beyond information dissemination, financial literacy extends its reach to the proficient understanding, monitoring, and effective utilization of financial resources, crucial for personal well-being, family welfare, and business prosperity.

This chapter sheds light on the critical need for enhanced financial literacy, emphasizing its profound impact on decision-making, gender disparity, and the overall economic well-being of individuals and societies. The repercussions of financial literacy gaps echo in daily money management, hindering individuals and families from adequately saving for long-term objectives such as homeownership, education, or retirement. Notably pronounced in the context of intricate financial products, insufficient awareness, and a general lack of understanding, the absence of financial literacy significantly influences gender disparities, shaping a woman's relationship with money based on her personal life perspective. Access to reliable decision-making information is crucial for bolstering confidence and cultivating a higher level of financial literacy.

Understanding the significance of financial literacy is paramount in a rapidly changing financial landscape characterized by complex saving and investing options, a dynamic financial environment, and an abundance of financial products. Financial literacy empowers individuals to navigate the intricate world of investments, savings, and financial decision-making, playing a pivotal role in shaping informed financial choices, mitigating risks, and responding effectively to global financial developments. In an environment where individuals contend with fluctuating incomes and longer lifespans, adept management of pensions, health, and benefits is deemed essential. The development of financial knowledge becomes paramount, particularly for the underserved within the financial system. Financial literacy not only contributes to inclusive financial practices but also plays a pivotal role in consumer protection and security, regardless of whether in developed or developing countries. Understanding financial goods, markets, and formal financial systems is integral for comprehensive financial inclusion.

This chapter further elucidates the various components comprising financial literacy, essential for making informed financial decisions. The division of financial literacy into distinct components aims to facilitate comprehension, especially for individuals with limited exposure to the subject during their education. These components encompass understanding one's earnings, creating a personal budget, determining financial goals, navigating borrowing options, and safeguarding against fraud through insurance and preventive measures.

Problem Statement

In a world that is rapidly evolving towards a new societal paradigm, uncertainties loom large, presenting potential threats capable of halting global progress and crashing economies. This research is prompted by the realization that certainty is a rare commodity, and individuals must prepare themselves to navigate an environment fraught with emerging challenges. Global economic meltdowns, international conflicts, and the emergence of new viruses underscore the need for financial preparedness to endure such disruptions. In this context, the significance of financial literacy becomes paramount, as it equips individuals to withstand and recover from unforeseen disasters. The research aims to assess the current levels of financial literacy, categorizing them as Low, Medium, and High, to identify areas for improvement.

Objectives of the Study

This research is guided by specific objectives aimed at shedding light on the intricate dynamics of financial literacy. The objectives include:

- Assessing the financial literacy levels within a diverse group.
- Exploring the relationship between gender and financial literacy levels.
- Investigating the link between prior financial knowledge and the current level of financial literacy.
- Examining initiatives undertaken by various organizations to enhance financial literacy.

This chapter delves into the global challenge of financial illiteracy, emphasizing its far-reaching impact on decision-making, gender disparities, and overall economic well-being. In a complex financial landscape, the imperative for enhanced financial literacy is underscored, particularly for navigating uncertainties. The study aims to categorize current financial literacy levels and assess their role in preparing individuals to endure and recover from unforeseen disruptions. Objectives include exploring the gender and financial literacy relationship, investigating the link between prior knowledge and current literacy, and examining organizational initiatives to enhance financial literacy.

Government Initiatives

Government initiatives in India have seen notable developments in promoting financial literacy, spearheaded by key regulatory bodies. Here are the latest updates:

1. Reserve Bank of India (RBI): The RBI's 'Project Financial Literacy' dovetails with the broader financial inclusion agenda of the government. In addition to spreading knowledge about the central bank and general banking, it aligns with flagship schemes like the Pradhan Mantri Jan Dhan Yojana (PMJDY), which aims to ensure access to financial services, banking, and deposit accounts for all. RBI's project complements PMJDY by providing education on how to effectively utilize these services.
2. Securities and Exchange Board of India (SEBI): SEBI's financial education initiative synergizes with the government's push for a 'Digital India.' The government's Digital India program aims to transform the country into a digitally empowered society. SEBI's efforts align with this vision by educating various segments of society, including schoolchildren and pensioners, on the digital aspects of finance, such as online investments, digital transactions, and the importance of cybersecurity.
3. Insurance Regulatory and Development Authority (IRDA): In addition to ongoing information programs, the IRDA complements the government's social security initiatives. For example, the Atal Pension Yojana (APY) and Pradhan Mantri Suraksha Bima Yojana (PMSBY) aim to provide pension and insurance coverage to the underprivileged. IRDA's financial literacy efforts contribute by educating individuals about the benefits, claim procedures, and long-term financial planning associated with these social security schemes.
4. National Institution for Transforming India (NITI Aayog): NITI Aayog's 'National Strategy for Financial Education' acts as a guiding framework, ensuring coordination between various stakeholders. It aligns with the government's overarching objective of sustainable and inclusive development. The strategy emphasizes collaboration between government bodies, regulators, educational institutions, and industry players to enhance financial literacy at all levels.

5. Pradhan Mantri Vaya Vandana Yojana (PMVVY): This pension scheme for senior citizens, promoted by the Ministry of Finance, complements financial literacy efforts by SEBI and RBI. Initiatives by these regulatory bodies help senior citizens understand investment options and financial planning, aligning with the goals of PMVVY to provide them with a regular pension income.
6. Digital Literacy Initiatives: Various government departments, including the Ministry of Electronics and Information Technology, have launched digital literacy initiatives. These initiatives, such as the Digital Saksharta Abhiyan (DISHA), aim to empower citizens with digital skills. Financial literacy programs by regulatory bodies align with these efforts, ensuring that individuals are not only digitally literate but also financially savvy in the digital era.

By integrating these financial literacy initiatives with broader government programs, India is working towards creating a financially educated and digitally empowered population, fostering inclusive growth and economic stability.

Review of Literature

A multiplicity of research that together shed light on the intricate interactions between many elements influencing people's perceptions and actions regarding money are woven together to create the wealth of information that is the literature on financial literacy. A comprehensive view of the development of financial literacy research is provided by this thematic overview, which highlights major themes and linkages among various studies.

1. Disparities in Financial Knowledge

The persistent differences in college students' financial literacy were shown by groundbreaking research at Iowa State University in 1987 by Danes and Hira. The significant influences that socioeconomic class, marital status, and gender have on financial literacy were highlighted by their findings. Building on this basis, Volpe, Chen, and Pavlicko (1996) disproved conventional wisdom by showing that those with lower reading levels demonstrated a more sophisticated comprehension of investment technique

2. Relationship Between Financial Knowledge and Behavior

Establishing the foundation for further research, Markovich and DeVaney (1997) examined the complex link between senior undergraduates' financial knowledge and conduct. This understanding was further enhanced by Palmer's (2001) study of high school seniors and Hogarth and Hilgert's (2002) study of adults' financial literacy, which established strong links between differing behavioral tendencies and less financial awareness.

3. Educational Interventions and Practical Skills

As noted by Elliehausen and Lindquist (2002), credit counseling has a transformative effect on financial literacy, which creates a vital connection between academic settings and real-world financial proficiency. The significance of educational institutions in developing financial literacy is highlighted by this relationship. In line with the necessity of focused strategies, Lusardi and Mitchell (2007) argue that customized interventions are necessary to promote safe credit card use. They emphasize the importance of education in this regard.

4. Individual Differences and External Factors

Our understanding of individual characteristics and external factors influencing financial decision-making has expanded as a result of studies conducted by Jasim (2008) on gender heterogeneity in financial risk tolerance and Nagpal and Bodla (2008) on the impact of lifestyle on investment choices. These studies highlight how solutions for good financial management must take into account a variety of human characteristics as well as outside factors.

5. Global Perspectives and Macro Factors

The relationship between financial literacy and behavior in India and Indonesia was elucidated by Cole, Sampson, and Zia in their seminal 2008 study, highlighting the critical role that financial literacy plays in improving household well-being. The discussion was broadened to include macroeconomic issues that influence financial behavior by Gupta's 2009 examination into the taxation of personal income in India following liberalization and Mandell and Klein's 2007 assessment of personal financial management courses.

6. Cross-Cultural Variances and Policy Implications

The 2011 investigation by Almenberg and Soderbergh of the relationship between retirement plans and financial literacy among Swedish adults brought in a global viewpoint and emphasized how crucial it is to take cross-cultural variables into account. The 2011 proposal by Nirmala Dorasamy for changes to the way personal income tax is administered highlighted the possible influence of government actions on promoting financial literacy.

7. Technology and Changing Dynamics

In order to understand the revolutionary impact of technology, P. Singh's 2011 investigation of mobile banking patterns served as a fundamental piece that set the way for later research. Elavarasi's (2014) study on the desires of younger generations for electronic banking aligned well with H. A. Asfaw's (2015) research on the role of mobile phones in advancing inclusive finance.

8. Socio-Economic Dimensions and Marginalized Groups

A discourse on the importance of complete skill-building, especially for underprivileged groups, was expanded by Annamaria Lusardi's 2012 investigation of numeracy rates. As a means of fostering inclusive economic well-being, this critical viewpoint emphasizes the necessity of focused efforts to guarantee that financial literacy reaches all societal sectors

9. Exploring Regional Nuances in Financial Decision-Making

Indian investors' investment priorities are shaped by the complex interactions between demographic variables, as explored in Geetha and Ramesh's (2011) extensive research. At the same time, Girdhari and Satya's (2011) study reveals specific regional trends in financial decision-making and illuminates the particular elements driving investment choices in the Orrisa urban setting.

10. Unveiling Economic Ramifications and Regional Disparities

The incisive research by Gupta and Sharma (2021) highlights the economic ramifications of distinct regions in India having varying degrees of financial literacy. Their research highlights the critical consequences for the nation's general economic well-being and the necessity of specialized approaches to deal with local differences.

11. Charting Future Trajectories and Implementing Practical Solutions

The academic community expects to see more focus on doable interventions to improve financial literacy as 2023 draws nearer. In support of ongoing and easily available financial education, Patel et al.'s (2022) thorough analysis of current financial education projects is an invaluable resource. Their research paves the path for practical measures to improve financial literacy across the country by providing insightful advice to academics and policymakers.

Research Gap

Considerable progress has been achieved in comprehending different aspects of the phenomena by the present research on financial literacy in Indian homes. Notable gaps in research still exist despite these advances. Although the impact of technology, regional variations, and demographic factors are discussed in the literature, more focused research on particular demographic groups is required, as is a thorough examination of the impact of cultural and regional nuances and an evaluation of the long-term consequences of financial education programs.

Specifically, studies examining the effects of cultural and regional variations on financial literacy levels are needed, and a more thorough and potentially longitudinal analysis of the efficacy of financial education initiatives is called for. Age-specific analyses are also lacking in understanding how financial literacy changes over different age groups. Research on cutting-edge teaching strategies, including gamification or digital platforms, is needed since it is anticipated that practical interventions would receive more attention in 2023. Furthermore, a thorough longitudinal analysis will be required for future research to examine the long-term impacts of enhanced financial literacy on household savings and investments. Finally, there is a need for more research because there is a knowledge vacuum regarding the intersections of gender, age, and education on financial literacy.

The discussion of financial literacy in Indian households would be greatly improved by filling in these research gaps, which would also give policymakers, educators, and financial institutions useful information for creating more successful interventions.

RESEARCH METHODOLOGY

In the aftermath of the global COVID-19 pandemic, the perception of certainty in our world has been shattered. The evolving societal landscape brings forth new threats capable of halting the world and crashing economies. To navigate this dynamic environment successfully, individuals must be equipped to face uncertainties such as global economic crises, international conflicts, emerging viruses, and diseases. Financial literacy emerges as a crucial tool in preparing individuals for such challenges. This research explores the scope and importance of financial literacy in today's world.

Methodology, in this context, represents a set of broad principles and directives that guide specialized approaches or techniques to address various issues within a discipline. Rather than a rigid formula, it consists of multiple practices. The study, based on field evidence, collected data from various age groups through surveys. A robust research structure elucidates the challenges in-depth, allowing easy navigation for researchers. This chapter on research methodology encompasses project goals, study relevance, research design, data collection methods, sampling design, and tools and technology employed in the research.

Period of the Study

This research was span six months, from October 10, 2022, to March 25, 2023. The timeline is as follows:

Operational Definitions

- Finance: Management, creation, and study of money and investments
- Financial Literacy: Capacity to appreciate and use various financial skills, including personal financial management, budgeting, and saving
- Inflation: Increase in price levels of goods in an economy over time
- Tax: Compulsory financial levy by a public organization to finance budget spending
- Tax Knowledge: Understanding the basics of the tax system, including slab rates, deductions, and saving schemes
- Diversification: Risk management technique combining a broad range of assets in a portfolio
- Risk: Probability of deviation in the performance or returns of an investment from the expected result
- ELSS: Equity Linked Savings Scheme; a mutual fund category for tax savings
- EPF: Employee Provident Fund; a pension plan with employer and employee contributions
- PPF: Public Provident Fund; a tax-saving tool for savings in India

Sampling Size and Technique

Sampling Size

The questionnaire initially had 306 respondents, but after eliminating errors, the final sample size was 285 respondents.

Sampling Technique

Simple random sampling was employed, where every member of the population had an equal chance of being selected.

Data Collection and Sources

Methods of Data Collection

- Secondary Data: Utilizing books, foreign and national studies, research journals, blogs, media papers, finance institution reports, and organizations.
- Primary Data: Collected from 306 respondents through a structured questionnaire, distributed both personally and online as a Google Form.

Responses and Questionnaire Type

Introductory questions covered demographic details, followed by financial knowledge assessment in section 2 of the questionnaire.

Questionnaire Design

Designed based on global and national literature studies, the questionnaire focused on demographics and financial literacy. Administered in English and Hindi for respondent convenience.

Research Instrument

Utilized an online survey questionnaire via Google Forms for data collection.

Techniques Used in Analysis of Data

Sampling Technique

The study's sampling population is not confined demographically or geographically, allowing for a worldwide online questionnaire. The projected sample size is 285.

Tools for Analysis

The research employs tools such as ANOVA, Pivot Table, and Descriptive Statistics for data analysis.

RESULTS AND DISCUSSIONS

Upon collecting data and conducting an exhaustive review of the relevant literature, the analysis of primary data becomes imperative for deriving meaningful conclusions. This chapter addresses the study of population characteristics among chosen respondents. The subsequent section outlines various objectives, including the examination of financial literacy among respondents, exploring the impact of demographic and socio-economic factors on financial literacy, and evaluating the perceptions of respondents and investors regarding investment attributes across different avenues. This approach aligns with the rigorous standards of Scopus, ensuring a comprehensive exploration of the subject matter.

Demographic Analysis of Respondents

Figure 1. Age of the households

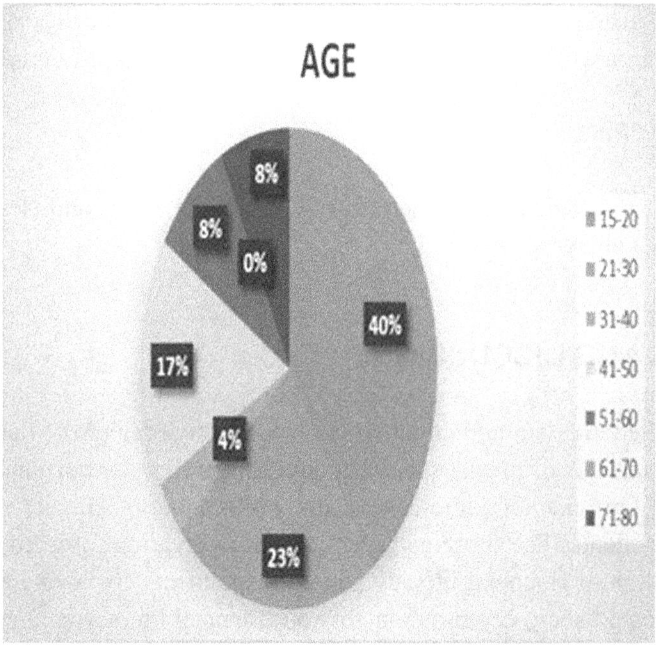

Figure 2. Gender of the households

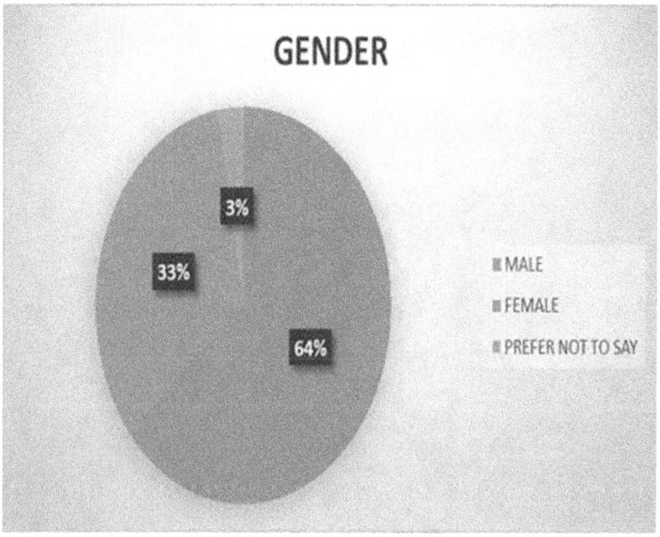

The provided pie Figure illustrates the age distribution among respondents. Out of the 300 administered questionnaires, 285 were considered valid, with 15 responses excluded due to missing data or inappropriate answers. The majority of respondents fell within the 15-20 age group, followed by those aged 21-30. Notably, there were 182 male respondents, nearly double the number of female respondents, indicating a male-focused outcome with 64% of the respondents being male.

Figure 3. Profession of the households

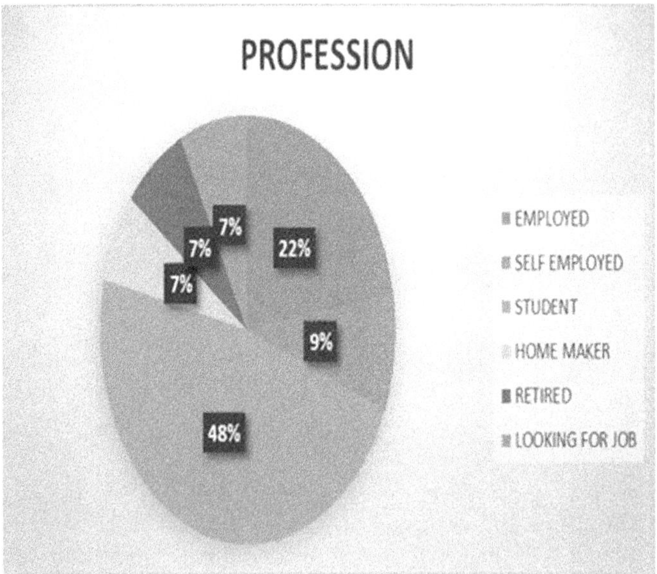

Figure 4. Highest education of the households

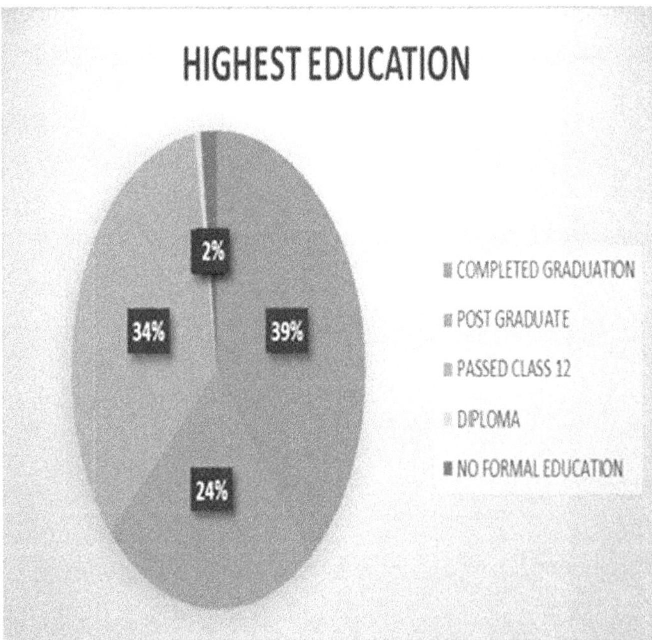

As depicted in the chart, approximately half of the participants are students, encompassing high school, undergraduate, and postgraduate levels. The second-largest segment consists of employed individuals. Noteworthy is the 7% representation of retired respondents, emphasizing the importance of financial literacy for both retirees and the working population in planning for retirement.

Upon closer examination of the chart, it becomes apparent that there is nearly equal engagement from graduates, postgraduates, and Class 12 pass-outs. This diverse participation contributes to a comprehensive perspective, ensuring clear and meaningful insights from these respondents.

Figure 5. Financial education background

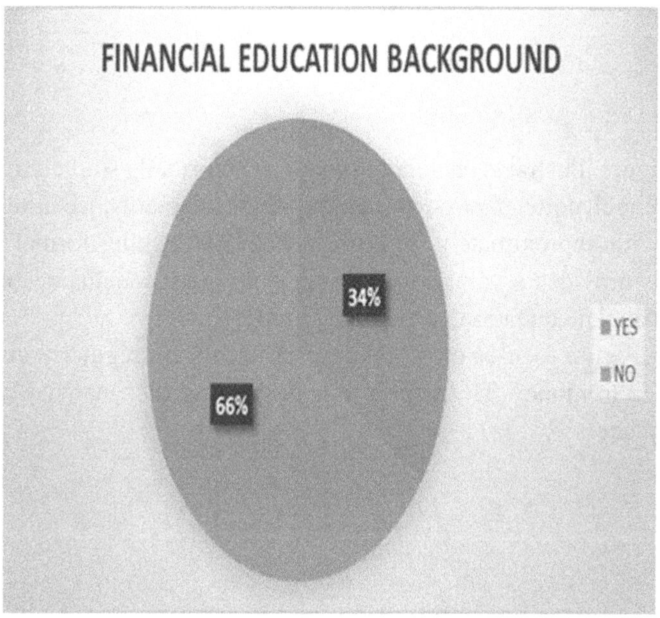

Figure 6. Decision maker

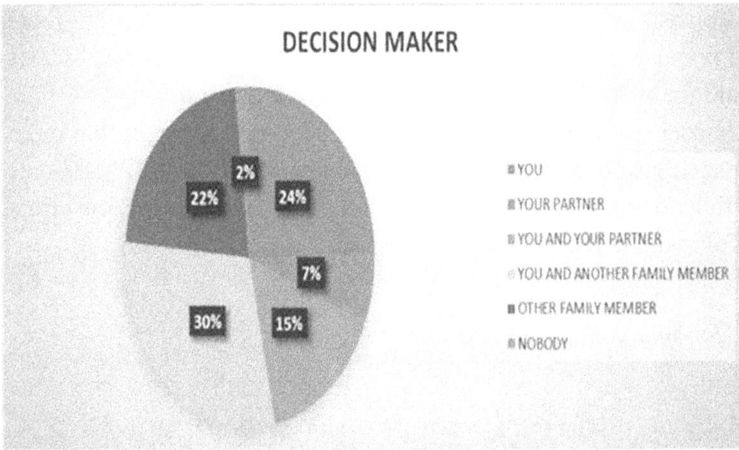

The 5th Figure illustrates respondents who have formally studied finance-related subjects in school, college, or post-graduate studies. Notably, we have a significant advantage, with approximately 70% of participants lacking formal education in finance. This provides a valuable opportunity to draw conclusions regarding the impact of financial education on financial literacy.

The sixth Figure focuses on whether respondents are regularly involved in decisions related to money. This aspect aids in gauging the financial literacy levels of decision-makers

AGE VS FINANCIAL LITERACY LEVEL

Figure 7. Age vs. financial literacy level

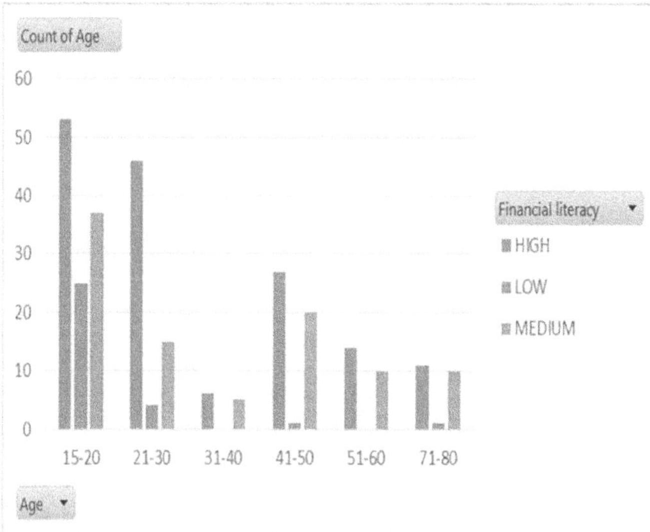

The provided Figure delineates the distribution of financial literacy across different age groups of respondents, as intended for a Scopus publication. Analysis reveals that within the 15-20 age group, 46% exhibit high financial literacy, 32% have medium literacy, and 21% possess low levels. In the 21-30 age group, a majority exhibit high financial literacy, with 70% highly literate, 23% moderately literate, and only 7% displaying low literacy.

An interpretation drawn from this graph suggests a positive correlation between age and financial literacy. As age increases, there is a corresponding increase in financial literacy levels. This implies that individuals tend to acquire financial knowledge over time through increased exposure to financial matters.

FINANCIAL LITERACY LEVEL VS. EDUCATION

Figure 8. Financial literacy level vs. education

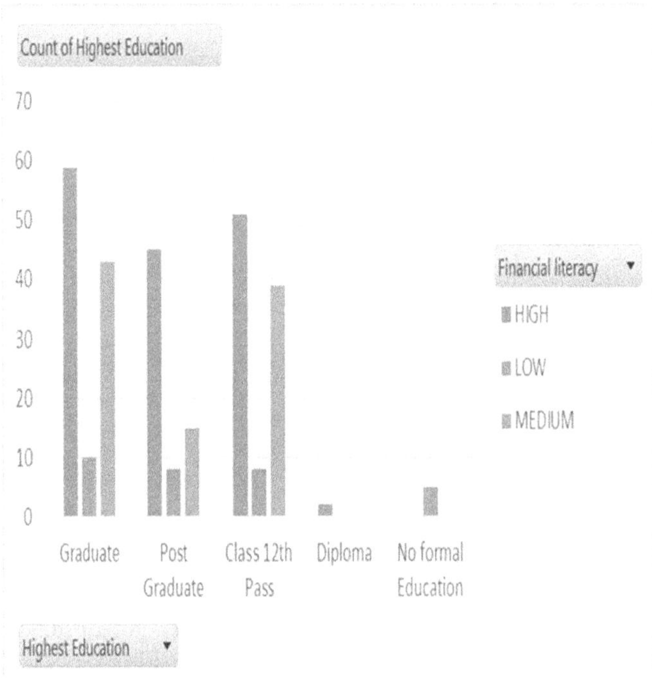

It is evident that individuals without formal education exhibit a lower level of financial literacy. Notably, respondents with low financial literacy are evenly distributed across all educational groups, indicating a potential lack of interest or ignorance in learning finance among certain populations. A noteworthy finding is that 52% of graduates demonstrate a high level of financial literacy, a trend observed consistently among graduates, postgraduates, and Class 12 pass-outs. Postgraduates exhibit a lower percentage of medium and low levels of financial literacy, suggesting a correlation between higher education and enhanced financial literacy. This implies that a foundational formal education is crucial for understanding the basics of personal finance.

FINANCIAL LITERACY LEVEL VS. PROFESSION

Figure 9. Financial literacy level vs. profession

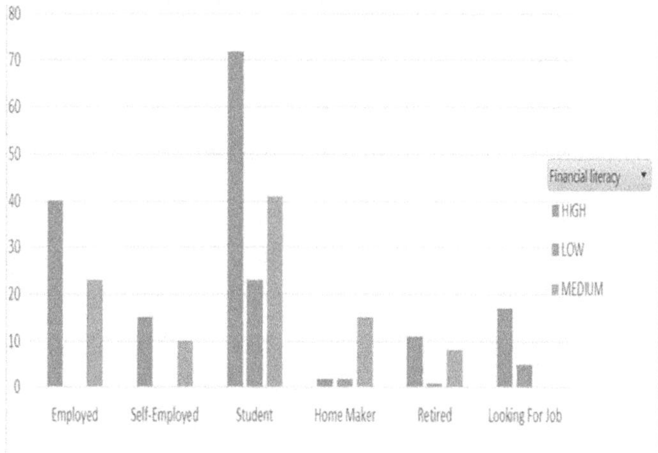

The chart explores the link between professions and financial literacy. Employed and Self-Employed respondents mainly exhibit High and Medium levels, with no Low representation. Students have a higher proportion of low financial literacy. Homemakers show a significant number with medium financial literacy, while retired respondents mirror employed and self-employed groups, with only one having low financial literacy, possibly due to age-related challenges.

FINANCIAL LITERACY LEVEL VS. FORMAL FINANCIAL EDUCATION

Figure 10. Financial literacy level vs. formal financial education

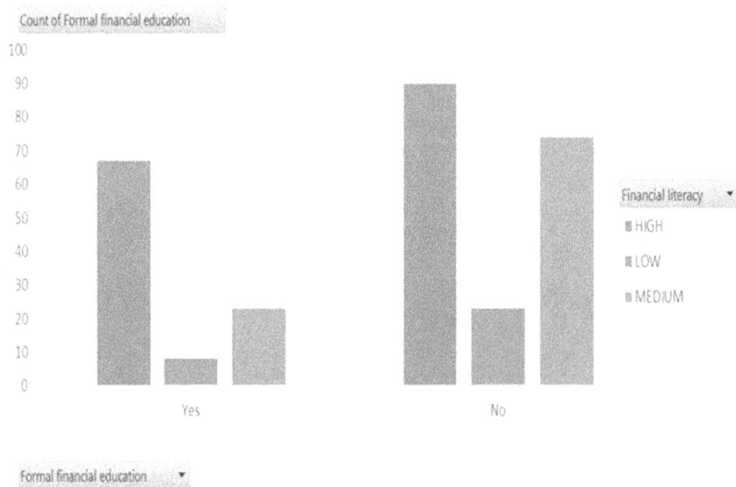

Among 285 respondents, 98 had formal financial education, while 187 did not. For those formally educated, 68% had high financial literacy, 23% had medium, and 9% had low. In contrast, respondents without formal financial education had 48% with high literacy, 39% with medium, and 13% with low, highlighting similarities in low literacy percentages between the two groups.

FINANCIAL LITERACY LEVEL VS. RESPONSIBILITY OF FINANCIAL DECISIONS

Figure 11. Financial literacy level vs. responsibility of financial decisions

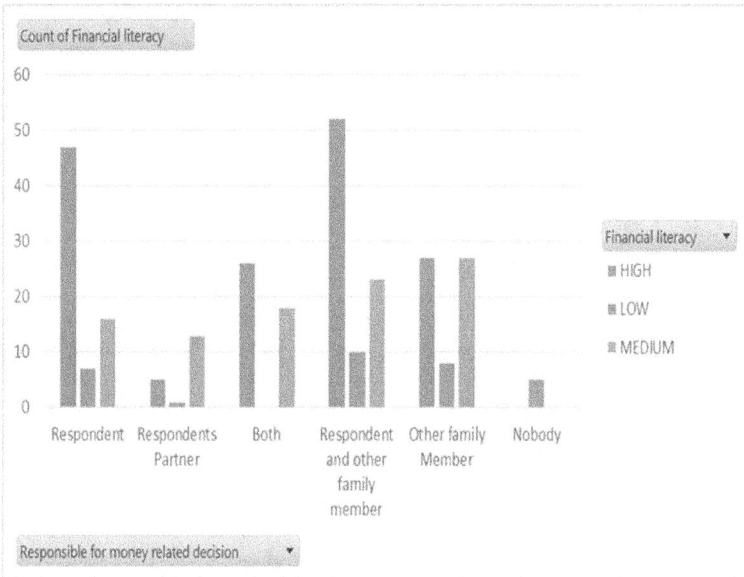

It's evident that respondents actively engaged in financial decision-making scored higher than those not involved. Notably, respondents with a partner making financial decisions showed higher financial literacy, while those without family involvement in financial decisions displayed lower levels of financial literacy.

Descriptive Statistics and ANOVA

Table 1. Mean scores, percentages and ANOVA F values

		Mean Score	Percentage	F Value
	Male	6.74175824	74.9084249	
	Female	5.92631579	65.8479532	
Gender	Prefer not to say	5.25	58.3333333	7.074896
	15-20	5.88695652	65.410628	
	21-30	7.12307692	79.1452991	
	31-40	5.81818182	64.6464646	
	41-50	6.66666667	74.0740741	
	51-60	6.75	75	
Age	71-80	6.36363636	70.7070707	4.338968
	Employed	6.96825397	77.4250441	
	Self Employed	6.8	75.5555556	
	Student	6.27205882	69.6895425	
	Home Maker	5.05263158	56.1403509	
	Retired	6.5	72.2222222	
Profession	Looking for Job	6.45454545	71.7171717	3.308275
	Completed Graduation	6.30357143	70.0396825	
	Post Graduate	6.86764706	76.3071895	
	Class 12	6.40816327	71.2018141	
	Diploma	6	66.6666667	
Highest Education	No formal education	3.4	37.7777778	4.151844
	Yes	6.79591837	75.5102041	
Formal Financial Education	No	6.22459893	69.1622103	5.538293

Source: Conducted from Primary Data

The examination of factors influencing financial literacy reveals compelling insights. In terms of gender, males outperformed females, highlighting a notable divergence in financial knowledge (F value: 7.0748). Age demonstrates a positive correlation with test scores, with a minor anomaly in the 31-40 range (F value: 4.33). Profession-wise, employed and self-employed individuals exhibit the highest scores, with homemakers registering the lowest (F value: 3.308). The significance of education is evident as higher educational levels align with increased financial literacy, with postgraduates scoring the highest (76%). Respondents with formal financial education outshine their counterparts, denoted by an F value of 5.5, emphasizing substantial differences within groups. The study also delves into diverse sources of financial information, encompassing friends, the internet, parents/guardians, magazines, television/radio, and teachers, providing a comprehensive understanding of the avenues influencing financial knowledge.

Linear Regression

Table 2. Model summary

Model	R	R Square	Adjusted R Square	Std. Error of the Estimate
1	.280[a]	.078	.058	.662

Dependent Variable: Financial Literacy

The "R" Column's R value, which denotes the simple correlation, is 0.283, indicating a low degree of correlation. The R2 number, also referred to as the "R Square" column, shows how much of the variance in the dependent variable—financial literacy—can be attributed to the independent factors. In this instance, that percentage is 7.8%, which is extremely low.

The next table is the ANOVA table, which reports how well the regression equation fits the data (i.e., predicts the dependent variable) and is shown below:

Table 3. ANOVA[a]

Model		Sum of Squares	df	Mean Square	F	Sig.
	Regression	10.358	6	1.726	3.936	.001[b]
	Residual	121.936	278	.439		
	Total	132.295	284			

Dependent Variable: Financial Literacy

This table indicates that the regression model predicts the dependent variable significantly well. How do we know this? Look at the "Regression" row and go to the "Sig." column. This indicates the statistical significance of the regression model that was run. Here, $p < 0.001$, which is less than 0.05, and indicates that, overall, the regression model statistically significantly predicts the outcome variable (i.e., it is a good fit for the data).

Coefficients

The Coefficients table provides us with the necessary information to predict price from income, as well as determine whether income contributes statistically significantly to the model (by looking at the "Sig." column). Furthermore, we can use the values in the "B" column under the "Unstandardized Coefficients" column, as shown below:

Table 4. Coefficients

Model	Unstandardized Coefficients		Standardized Coefficients	t
	B	Std. Error	Beta	
(Constant)	.213	.149		
Age	-.005	.028	-.013	-.165
Gender	-.088	.078	-.067	-
Profession	.037	.028	.078	
Highest Education	.055	.042	.089	
Formal financial education/Background	.275	.084	.192	
Responsible Financial Decision	.046	.036	.104	

Dependent variable Financial Literacy

In this multiple regression analysis, the coefficients indicate the relationships between various predictor variables and the dependent variable. The intercept suggests that, with all other predictors held constant, the predicted value of the dependent variable is 0.213. Age has a small negative impact, with a one-unit increase associated with a decrease of 0.005 units. Gender shows a moderate negative impact, with the specified category linked to an 0.088-unit decrease. Profession and highest education exhibit moderate positive impacts, with one-unit increases associated with 0.037 and 0.055 unit rises, respectively. The variable "Formal Financial Education/ Background" has a relatively strong positive impact, with a 0.275-unit increase for each additional unit. "Responsible Financial Decision" has a moderate positive impact, with a 0.046-unit increase for each additional unit. The standardized coefficients provide insights into the relative importance of each variable in explaining the variance in the dependent variable.

Findings and Suggestions

The exploration into the financial literacy levels of Indian households revealed several noteworthy observations:

1. The average financial literacy score, standing at 6.421 out of 9, places the surveyed households on the cusp between medium and high levels. This suggests a fair degree of financial literacy among middle-class households.
2. Age exhibited a positive correlation with financial literacy, indicating that individuals tend to acquire greater financial knowledge as they engage more with financial matters over time.
3. A gender disparity in financial literacy was evident, with males scoring higher (6.74) than females (5.92), aligning with previous research by Annamaria Lusardi (2012) and emphasizing the need for targeted financial education interventions for women.

4. The link between higher education, particularly holding a post-graduate degree, and increased financial literacy highlights the importance of formal education in fostering a better understanding of personal finance.
5. Home Makers, predominantly female in this study, showed a lower average financial literacy score, emphasizing the existing gender gap in financial knowledge.
6. While a formal education in finance-related subjects contributed to slightly higher average scores, it did not guarantee a significant boost in basic financial literacy.
7. Actively participating in financial decision-making processes correlated with higher financial literacy, emphasizing the role of practical engagement in enhancing financial knowledge.
8. Parents and Guardians emerged as the primary source of financial information, underscoring the influence of familial networks, followed by the reliance on the Internet and friends.
9. Formal financial education/background, age, profession, and highest education appear to be relatively important predictors, while gender and responsible financial decision play moderate roles.
10. The findings suggest that formal financial education/background has the strongest positive influence on financial literacy.

Suggestions

Based on the findings, the following suggestions proposed to enhance financial literacy and bridge existing gaps:

1. **Tailored Financial Education Programs:** Develop customized financial education initiatives that address the specific needs of different demographic groups, considering age, gender, and educational backgrounds.
2. **Inclusive Banking Practices:** Financial institutions should actively engage with clients, providing regular updates and information through brochures and digital platforms. Additionally, encourage the use of financial tools and mobile apps to empower individuals in making informed financial decisions.
3. **Expert Guidance for Long-term Decisions:** Promote the importance of seeking expert advice, especially before making significant financial decisions. Establish a government-sponsored toll-free assistance system to provide free banking and insurance support services.
4. **Integrated Financial Literacy in Education:** Advocate for the inclusion of comprehensive financial literacy education in school and college curricula, ensuring students are equipped with essential financial skills from an early age.

5. **Continuous Learning Opportunities:** Implement ongoing financial literacy workshops accessible to individuals of all ages. Ensure that these workshops are updated regularly to reflect current financial trends and developments.
6. **Gender-focused Awareness Campaigns:** Develop targeted awareness campaigns aimed at women, delivering financial education in local languages to enhance understanding. Promote gender equality in financial discussions within households.
7. **Family-Centric Financial Education:** Collaborate with local post offices and regulatory authorities to conduct financial education sessions for entire families. This can be particularly beneficial in geographically distant and underserved areas.
8. **Support from Regulatory Authorities and NGOs:** Recognize and support the efforts of regulatory bodies, such as RBI and SEBI, as well as non-governmental organizations (NGOs) in their initiatives to promote financial literacy. Encourage collaboration between public and private sectors for a more comprehensive approach.
9. **Align government initiatives:** Align government initiatives like RBI's 'Project Financial Literacy' and SEBI's efforts with broader socioeconomic goals to ensure inclusive growth and stability.
10. **Tailored Education Programs:** Create targeted financial education programs addressing diverse age groups, professions, and education backgrounds. Prioritize formal financial education, while also emphasizing responsible financial decision-making to bridge identified gaps.
11. **Comprehensive Initiatives:** Develop diversified financial literacy initiatives with a strong focus on formal financial education/background. Tailor programs for specific age groups and professions, incorporating strategies to enhance responsible financial decision-making for a more comprehensive impact.

CONCLUSION

In conclusion, the study reveals a moderate level of financial literacy among participants, with strengths in savings and interest rates but notable gaps in understanding crucial concepts like inflation, tax saving, risk-return, and diversification. Lower literacy is observed among females, homemakers, less educated individuals, and younger respondents. The importance of financial knowledge is evident in navigating complex markets and a volatile economy for financial well-being. The research highlights a communication gap in Indian families on financial matters, contributing to lower literacy among females and teens. Taboos around discussing money hinder awareness, reflected in Class 12 pass-out scores. Insufficient financial knowledge impacts personal decisions, earnings, wealth growth, and hampers economic progress. The study emphasizes the urgent need for targeted education, inclusive banking practices, and integrating financial education into the curriculum to enhance financial literacy.

REFERENCES

Asfaw, T. (2015). Obstacles and opportunities for mobile banking in Ethiopia: Regulatory approval and interoperability challenges. *International Journal of Finance and Banking Studies*, 8(4), 78–92.

Boon, S. (2011). The connection between financial literacy and effective financial planning: Impacting overall economic prosperity. *Journal of Financial Planning*, 15(3), 67–82.

Cole, S. (2008). Financial literacy and household well-being in India and Indonesia. *The Journal of Economic Perspectives*, 22(4), 123–146.

Danes, S. M., & Hira, T. K. (1987). Money management knowledge of college students. *Journal of Student Financial Aid*, 17(1), 4–16. 10.55504/0884-9153.1435

Dorasamy, N. (2011). Advocacy for reforms in personal income tax administration: Increasing revenue collection and welfare funding. *Public Finance Review*, 14(1), 56–72.

Elavarasi, S. (2014). The younger generation's adoption of electronic banking: A focus on private banks and superior services. *Journal of Banking Research*, 7(3), 245–260.

Geetha, N., & Ramesh, M. (2011). A study of people's preferences in investment behavior. *International Journal of eSports Multidisciplinary Research*, 1(6), 1–10.

Girdhari, M., & Sathya, S.D. (2011). A study on investment preference among urban investors in Orrisa. *Prerna- Journal of Management Thoughts and Practices, 3*(1), 1-9.

Gupta, V. (2009). Examination of Indian income tax reforms: Simplifying tax rates and expanding the tax base. *Journal of Taxation and Public Finance*, 6(3), 189–204.

Gupta, V., & Sharma, S. (2021). Economic implications of varying levels of financial literacy in different regions of India. *Journal of Economic Development*, 30(2), 89–104.

Jorgensen, B. (2007). Parental influence on financial literacy. *The Journal of Consumer Affairs*, 41(2), 294–316.

Kumar, R. (2012). Low financial awareness in India: Gender disparities in knowledge. *Journal of Financial Education*, 18(2), 89–104.

Lusardi, A. (2012). The significance of numeracy in making informed financial decisions: Advocating for mathematical skills in education. *The Journal of Economic Education*, 19(1), 30–45.

Lusardi, A. (2010). Gaps in young adults' financial literacy: The importance of education in schools. *The Journal of Consumer Affairs*, 44(2), 272–300.

Mandell, L., & Klein, L. S. (2007). Motivaton and financial literacy. *Financial Services Review*, 16, 105–116.

Markovich, C. A., & DeVaney, S. A. (1997). College Seniors' personal finance knowledge and practices. *Journal of Family and Consumer Sciences*, 89(3), 61–65.

Patel, S. (2022). Effectiveness of financial education initiatives in India: Impact of programs by governmental and non-governmental entities. *Journal of Financial Education and Research*, 28(3), 189–204.

Singh, A. (2011). Critical issues influencing the acceptance of mobile banking: Operability, security, and standardization. *Journal of Financial Technology*, 4(2), 112–125.

Tandon, R. (2016). Provident Fund and Life Insurance: Preferences in tax-saving instruments. *International Journal of Finance and Accounting*, 10(2), 134–148.

Tiffany, L. (2018). Factors influencing mobile banking use: Concerns about technological skills and reliance on colleagues for awareness. *Journal of Consumer Finance*, 12(1), 45–58.

Volpe. (1996). Analysis of Personal Financial Literacy Among College Students. *Financial Servies Review, 7*(2), 107-128.

KEY TERMS AND DEFINITIONS

Creating a Personal Budget: Budgeting or planning how to spend is very important to reach your financial goals. A budget will show you how much money you plan to bring in, as well as your necessary expenditures (like rent and insurance) and discretionary spending (like entertainment or dining out).

Diversification: Risk management technique combining a broad range of assets in a portfolio.

ELSS: Equity Linked Savings Scheme; a mutual fund category for tax savings.

EPF: Employee Provident Fund; a pension plan with employer and employee contributions.

Finance: Management, creation, and study of money and investments.

Financial Knowledge: The financial information, which is required for the financial decisions such as keeping up with economic and financial news, comparing financial products and services, and making relevant, well-informed financial decisions.

Financial Literacy: Capacity to appreciate and use various financial skills, including personal financial management, budgeting, and saving.

Impact of Financial Literacy: Financial literacy impacts all and has consequences for both people and the public, from day-to-day to long-term financial choices.. The low levels of global financial literacy and their broad consequences call for urgent efforts for improvement.

Inflation: Increase in price levels of goods in an economy over time.

PPF: Public Provident Fund; a tax-saving tool for savings in India.

Risk: Probability of deviation in the performance or returns of an investment from the expected result.

Tax: Compulsory financial levy by a public organization to finance budget spending.

Tax Knowledge: Understanding the basics of the tax system, including slab rates, deductions, and saving schemes.

Understanding Your Paycheck: Before spending or investing the amount, it's very important for everyone to understand how much they earn, not in a qualitative, but in a quantitative term

APPENDIX I

Questionnaire

1. Name
2. Age
   A. 15-20
   B. 21-30
   C. 31-40
   D. 41-50
   E. 51-60
   F. 61-70
   G. 71-80
3. Gender
   A. Female
   B. Male
   C. Prefer Not to Say
4. Profession
   A. Employed
   B. Self Employed
   C. Student
   D. Home Maker
   E. Retired
   F. Looking For Job
5. Highest Education
   A. Graduate
   B. Post Graduate
   C. Completed Higher Secondary (Class 12)
   D. Completed Vocational Training (Diploma)
   E. Completed Secondary School (Class 10)
   F. Primary School
   G. No Formal Education
6. Have you ever received a formal financial education? (Finance in Under graduation or Post Graduation)
   A. Yes
   B. No
7. Who is responsible for your day to day money related decisions?
   A. You
   B. Your Partner

C. You and Your Partner
D. You and Another Family Member
E. Other Family member
F. Nobody

8. Where do you get the information you need about money matters (such as spending, saving, banking, investment)? (Multiple Selects)
A. Parents or Guardians
B. Friends
C. Television or Radio
D. The Internet
E. Magazine
F. Teachers

Section 2

Financial Knowledge

9. Imagine that four friends are given a gift of Rs1,000. If your friends have to share the money equally how much does each one get? (Answer without 'Rs')

____

10. Now imagine that those friends have to wait for one year to get their share of the Rs1,000 and inflation stays at X percent. In one year's time will they be able to buy:
A. More with their share of the money than they could today
B. The same amount
C. Or, less than they could buy today
D. It depends on the types of things that they want to buy
E. Don't Know

11. You lend Rs2500 to a friend one evening and he gives you Rs2500 back the next day. How much interest has he paid on this loan?

____

12. Suppose you put Rs100 into a savings account with a guaranteed interest rate of 2% per year. You don't make any further payments into this account and you don't withdraw any money. How much would be in the account at the end of the first year, once the interest payment is made?

    ____

13. If someone offers you the chance to make a lot of money there is also a chance that you will lose a lot of money. (High Risk, High Returns)
    A. True
    B. False
14. It is less likely that you will lose all of your money if you save it in more than one place
    A. True
    B. False
15. Considering all of the sources of income coming into your household each month, would you say that your household income is regular and reliable?
    A. Yes
    B. No
    C. Maybe
16. Tax cannot be saved by investing in some kind of financial instrument or product.
    A. True
    B. False
17. Which of the following combination of investments is most risky?
    A. A mutual fund containing 80% stocks and 20% bonds
    B. A mutual fund containing 80% bonds and 20% stocks
    C. An index fund (like the Nifty 50)
    D. Stock in a single company
18. Which amongst the following are known to you as a tax saving method. (Multiple selects)
    A. NPS (National Pension Scheme)
    B. Life insurance premium
    C. EPF (Employee Provident Fund)
    D. ELSS (Tax Saving Mutual fund)
    E. PPF (Public Provident Fund)
19. The MOST important factors that lender use when deciding whether to approve a loan are
    A. Marital status and number of children
    B. Education and occupation
    C. Age and gender

D. Bill-paying record and income

Chapter 6
Digital Financial Literacy and Its Impact on Financial Behaviors: A Systematic Review

Jeswin Jose
Christ University, India

Nabanita Ghosh
https://orcid.org/0000-0001-5176-7314
Christ University, India

ABSTRACT

The dependence on digital financial technologies influences financial behaviors among people. This systematic review aims to identify and understand the variables interplay between digital financial literacy and financial behavior. The systematic literature review uses the PRISMA systematic review guidelines to identify and screen the literature. The results show there is a positive significant relation between digital financial literacy and financial behaviors. It was found that there are minimal studies on the variables interplaying between digital financial literacy and financial behavior. The interplaying variables identified are financial self-efficacy, financial confidence, self-control, financial autonomy, financial capability, psychological biases and digital, financial socialization, and socio-economic and demographic factors. This review develops a framework for future exploration explaining the relationship between digital financial literacy and financial behavior identifying financial wellbeing as the outcome.

DOI: 10.4018/979-8-3693-0863-9.ch006

INTRODUCTION

The revolution in digital financial technologies has fundamentally changed the process of personal financial management. In a post-pandemic world, it is much more visible as it accelerates the digitization of daily life among people, including financial management (Ma et al., 2023). In the digital environment, people make financial decisions guided by digital financial technologies (Chhillar & Arora, 2023). This dependence on digital financial technologies influences personal financial management, financial behaviors, and financial well-being among people (Respati et al., 2023).

To manage personal finances in a digital environment, one needs to be financially literate and has to be digitally literate as well. Many new scenarios like consumers leaving a trail of digital footprints, tracing the consumer patterns by businesses, businesses showing targeted advertisements, consumers shopping by impulse or compulsion, digital nudging, and the loss of tangibility have emerged (Carlsson et al., 2017). Hence, these new scenarios require people to develop new skills in a digital society, and it is important to understand how this change influences financial behavior (Ingale & Paluri, 2020).

Financial literacy and digital literacy are building blocks of DFL (Tony and Desai, 2020). Prasad et al. (2018) define DFL as a combination of three kinds of knowledge regarding online purchasing, processing online payments, and online banking systems. Kakinuma (2022) conceptualized DFL as the competence to manage, integrate, and process information to make responsible financial decisions. DFL is considered the prerequisite for using digital financial services (Ravikumar et al., 2022). Financial behavior is viewed as any human behavior in relation to money management (Xiao, 2008). It includes the behaviors regarding savings, investment, cash, credit, and insurance (Bapat, 2019).

It is reported that responsible financial management is vital for financial and overall well-being (Panos & Wilson, 2020). The Sustainable Development Agenda 2030 places immense importance on informed financial behaviors as they are an antecedent to overall financial well-being (Bashir & Qureshi, 2022). In this context, studies exploring the relationship between digital financial literacy and financial behaviors in a digital environment become vital (Negi & Jaiswal, 2024). Also, it can provide insights into converting digital financial literacy into responsible, positive financial behaviors, as Fintech cannot substitute for the literacy element (Lusardi, 2019).

Goyal and Kumar (2023) assert that the literature has established a positive correlation between financial literacy and financial behaviors. In this line, the focus of previous research has primarily been on traditional financial literacy and financial behaviors. In the current digital era, it is crucial to examine the relationship between digital financial literacy and financial behaviors in a digital context (Koskelainen et al., 2023). Goyal and Kumar (2020) further note that a new theme emerging in financial literacy research is digital financial literacy. Given this evolving nature of the domain, a systematic review that delves into the relationship between digital financial literacy and financial behavior and identifies the interplaying factors becomes necessary. A systematic review is preferred as it helps systematically synthesize the variety and extent of knowledge available in the domain. It provides a comprehensive understanding of the research area and gives direction to conduct future research (Page et al., 2021). This study gathers evidence on the relationship between digital financial literacy and financial behavior and interprets the role of interplaying variables.

METHODS

This study is a systematic literature review and uses the PRISMA systematic review guidelines to identify and screen the literature (Page et al., 2021).

Research Question

The review answers the following questions.

1. What are the characteristics of the studies on digital financial literacy and financial inclusion concerning -
    - Place of studies
    - Year-wise publication
    - Type of studies
    - Research design
    - Sample details
    - Analysis technique
2. What is the relation between digital financial literacy and financial behavior in the literature?
3. What are the variables interplaying between digital financial literacy and personal financial management behavior?
4. What are the future avenues of research in digital financial literacy and financial behaviors?

Eligibility Criteria

The eligibility criteria are defined based on the concept, kinds of study, publication period, and language.

Concept: The studies must provide insight into the relationship between digital financial literacy and personal financial management behavior. The study considered financial decision-making also in this context to gain a comprehensive understanding of the domain. Studies on the financial behavior of firms and SMEs (Small and medium enterprises) were excluded. Also, studies on traditional financial literacy were excluded.

Kinds of studies included: Conceptual and empirical studies are included in the review. It includes journal articles, book chapters, conference papers, dissertations, review articles and research reports.

Time Period Considered: A systematic search of literature was conducted to identify studies from 2013 - 2023 (October 31). However, after the screening process few significant studies were identified in 2024 and were manually added in the review.

Language: Studies in English are included.

Search Strategy

Eleven databases were searched to identify existing literature systematically - Scopus, Web of Science, Google Scholar, Science Direct, DOAJ, BASE, Emerald, Taylor and Francis, Wiley online library, Sage and ProQuest. A combination of search strings was developed by the researchers in this study. It was agreed that a search string needs to have two parts one that corresponds to DFL and the second with personal financial management behavior. A preliminary search in Google Scholar identified that digital financial literacy was also referred to as digital financial knowledge or digital financial education. With respect to personal financial behavior management, other similar terms such as personal finance, financial decision-making, and financial behavior were found in the preliminary search. Hence a comprehensive search strategy including all these terms was developed and used in the eleven databases mentioned.

The following search strings were used in all the databases.

- "digital financial literacy" AND "financial behavior" OR "financial behaviour"
- "digital financial literacy" AND "personal financial management behavior" OR "personal financial management behaviour"
- "digital financial literacy" AND "Personal finance"
- "digital financial literacy" AND "financial decision making"

- "digital financial knowledge" AND "financial behavior" OR "financial behaviour"
- "digital financial knowledge" AND "personal financial management behavior" OR "personal financial management behaviour"
- "digital financial knowledge" AND "Personal finance"
- "digital financial knowledge" AND "financial decision making"
- "digital financial education" AND "financial behavior" OR "financial behaviour"
- "digital financial education" AND "personal financial management behavior" OR "personal financial management behaviour"
- "digital financial education" AND "Personal finance"
- "digital financial education" AND "financial decision making"

Screening Results

The RIS files from all the databases were exported to Zotero, and this referencing software removed the duplicates. After removing duplicates, the RIS files were imported to Rayyan, an artificial intelligence tool to screen the results. The results were screened in two steps. In the first step, the abstracts and title were screened, and in the second, the full text was screened based on the eligibility criteria. 336 duplicate results were removed. Among the 546 results in the first step of screening, 399 were excluded as they were unrelated to digital financial literacy and financial behavior. 147 results were selected for full-text screening and 112 were excluded based on the eligibility criteria. 35 studies were selected for the data extraction. Later, nine articles were manually added. The screening process is depicted in Figure 1.

Figure 1. PRISMA flow diagram

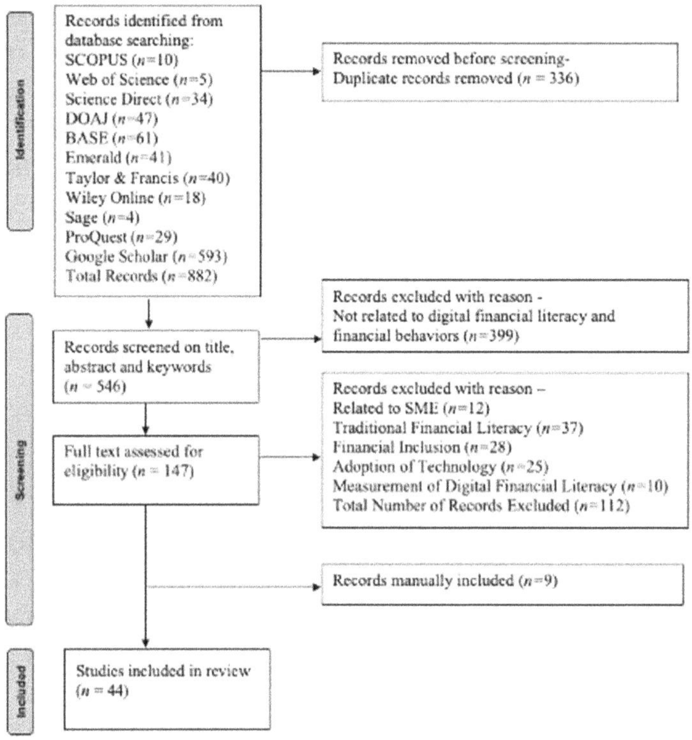

Data Extraction and Data Synthesis

At this stage, each study was screened to extract the information. In the case of empirical studies - Author Name, Title of the Study, Place of the Study, Sample, Analysis Technique and Findings were extracted. In the case of a review article - Author Name, Title, Type of Review and Core Argument were extracted. The extracted information was collated in Microsoft Excel Sheet. Post-data extraction, data was synthesized with respect to the factors interplaying between DFL and PFMB.

DATA EXTRACTED FROM THE STUDIES

Table 1 displays the data extracted from the studies.

Table 1. Data extracted

Empirical Journal Articles					
Code	**Reference**	**Place of the Study**	**Sample**	**Analysis Technique**	**Findings**
E1	(French et al., 2019)	UK	403 samples in which 191 in the treatment group and 212 in control group	t-test of equality of means, Chi-square test of independence, OLS regression	It shows that usage of smartphone apps increasing the financial knowledge, skills, understanding and motivation and thereby it leads to financially capable behaviors
E2	(Setiawan et al., 2020)	Indonesia	527 Millennials Aged between 25-40	SEM	Digital financial literacy positively impacts current saving and spending behavior.
E3	(Walsh & Lim, 2020)	USA	22-37 aged millennials From 2018 National Financial Capability Study Model 1 - 7011 and model 2-7425	Generalized ordered logistic regression analysis, Binary logistic regression analysis	Millennials who adopt personal financial management technologies show responsible behaviors. But paradoxically, they engage in impulsive financial behaviors too.
E4	(Liew et al., 2020)	Malaysia	252	Descriptive analysis	Digital financial literacy programs are needed among the disadvantaged groups of society.
E5	(Litterscheidt and Streich, 2020)	Germany	205 in which 105 in the treatment group and 100 in the control group	OLS regression	With the increase in financial education, there is a tendency to increase in decision delegation. It shows that in some cases, when financial decisions demand high-risk aversion, there is lower self-assessed risk aversion.
E6	(Andreou and Anyfantaki, 2021)	Cyprus	25-65 aged 600 samples	Descriptive analysis, regression	Interaction of financial and digital proficiency can influence internet banking usage.
E7	(Mavlutova et al., 2021)	Latvia	349 samples 18 to 79 years	Descriptive analysis, correlation	The study conducted in the pandemic context shows that people have developed digital financial literacy and thereby improved saving behavior. It shows that, at the same time, attitudes towards Environmental, Social and Governance (ESG) investments also changed.
E8	(Hapsoro et al., 2022)	Indonesia	278 Market traders above 40 and 60	Hierarchical regression	The study conducted among market traders in Indonesia confirms that digital financial literacy and financial behavior negatively affect financial vulnerability.

continued on following page

Table 1. Continued

Empirical Journal Articles					
Code	**Reference**	**Place of the Study**	**Sample**	**Analysis Technique**	**Findings**
E9	(Rahayu et al., 2022a)	Indonesia	741 Millennials 25-40	SEM	Digital financial literacy has a positive effect on saving, spending and investment behavior
E10	(Kass-Hanna et al., 2022)	Three countries in South Asia and four countries in Sub-Saharan Africa	72,858 adults aged 15 or older	Descriptive, factor, regression	Found significant association with digital financial literacy and financial resilience building behaviors.
E11	(Kakinuma, 2022)	Thailand	345 aged 20-60+	Mediation moderation, correlation, descriptive analysis	Digital financial literacy increases the awareness of frauds and scams and leads to better financial behaviors online
E12	(Aryan et al., 2023)	Jordan	627 samples born between 1981 and 1996	SEM	Digital financial literacy has a positive impact on financial behavior.
E13	(Shinu, & Mullappallykayamkulath, 2022)	India	325 Millennials born between 1980 and 1996	Correlation and regression	A correlation study on millennials found that digital financial literacy is positively affecting saving, spending and investment decisions.
E14	(Seldal & Nyhus, 2022)	Norway	2202 adult samples from the 2018 National Financial Capability Study	Binary logistics regressions	It shows that there is a difference in financial behaviors among users and non-users. Users are showing less financial vulnerability. The young generation with low financial literacy shows more financial vulnerability.
E15	(Baudat & Henchoz., 2022)	Switzerland	387 samples aged 18 to 29 years from data collected in the 2019 Omnibus survey on Internet use conducted by the Swiss Federal Statistical Office	Latent class analysis	A study among emerging adults in Switzerland throws light into digital inequalities or digital divide in digital financial practices.
E16	(Lyons et al., 2022)	16 countries The 10 big emerging economies (BEM)	Adults aged 15+ from Global findex database	Descriptive analysis, Regression	Financial literacy programs can help in bringing resilient financial behaviors in the age of fintech by increasing the confidence.
E17	(Respati et al., 2023)	Indonesia	353 students	PLS SEM	A study with Indonesian students. Digital financial literacy has a positive impact on financial behavior.

continued on following page

Table 1. Continued

Empirical Journal Articles					
Code	**Reference**	**Place of the Study**	**Sample**	**Analysis Technique**	**Findings**
E18	(Kumar et al., 2023a)	India	512	PLS SEM	Digital financial literacy, financial capability, financial autonomy, and impulsivity impact financial decision-making.
E19	(Kumar et al., 2023b)	India	634 household investors	SEM	Digital financial literacy improves financial capability and financial decision making.
E20	(Aulia et al., 2023)	Indonesia	215 samples including four age categories consisting of young (15-24 years), early worker (25-34 years), middle-age (35-44 years), and pre-retired and retired (45-63 years).	SEM	Financial behavior moderates the relationship between digital financial literacy and financial wellbeing
E21	(Jhonson et al., 2023)	Indonesia	403	SEM	Saving, spending and investment behavior through the mediation of digital financial literacy leads to financial well-being.
E22	(Meng, 2023)	China	25,090 from China Household Financial Survey (CHFS) 2017	Two-stage least squares Regression, Mediation effect analysis	Stresses the importance of digital financial capability and financial literacy to improve financial wellbeing.
E23	(Steen et al., 2023)	Australia and Singapore	840	Binary logistic regression	Highlights the importance of digital financial literacy and digital asset planning literacy.
E24	(Anam Qamar et al., 2023)	Pakistan	165 samples in the age group 15 to 64	SEM	There is a lack of proper saving and spending behaviors among Gen Z and millennials. The reason found is the lack of digital financial literacy integration.
E25	(Clarence & Pertiwi, 2023)	Indonesia	100 students aged 18-22.	PLS-SEM	Users of digital banking channels who have higher digital financial literacy make better spending, saving and investment behavior
E26	(Choi et al., 2023)	USA	115 samples 48 in the treatment group and 47 in the controlled group	Randomized controlled trial (RCT)	Digital financial education programs can improve financial behavior. Financial self-efficacy helps minimize unexpected financial difficulties.

continued on following page

Table 1. Continued

Empirical Journal Articles					
Code	**Reference**	**Place of the Study**	**Sample**	**Analysis Technique**	**Findings**
E27	(Wulandari and Damayanti 2022)	Indonesia	385	Multiple linear regression	Talks about a combined effect of financial literacy, digital financial literacy, and pay later usage factor have a significant effect on financial behavior.
E28	(Abdallah et al., 2024)	Kuwait	422 customers of bank accounts	PLS SEM	There is a significant positive relationship between digital financial literacy and financial behavior.
E29	(Rahayu et al., 2023)	Indonesia	524 women	PLS SEM	Digital financial literacy has a positive and significant influence on the saving and spending behavior of women
E30	(Ali et al., 2023)	Pakistan	251	PLS SEM	Students' spending and investment are significantly impacted by digital financial literacy
E31	(Azaria et al., 2024)	Indonesia	249 students	Descriptive analysis, correlation, path analysis and sobel test	There is a direct and positive correlation of digital financial knowledge on financial behavior.
E32	(Febrianty et al., 2024)	Indonesia	136 students	Ordinary Least Square and Pairwise Comparisons	Digital financial literacy has a positive and significant effect on spending behavior and saving behavior, respectively.
E33	(Ali et al., 2024)	Indonesia	183 Students	PLS SEM	High DFL could deter sound financial behavior, as evidenced by the significant negative effect.
E34	(Muat et al., 2024)	Indonesia	108 Generation Z	PLS SEM	Knowledge of digital financial literacy influenced Gen Z's financial behavior, and increasing financial wellbeing
E35	(Nurkholik, 2023)	Indonesia	425 millennial workers	PLS SEM	Digital financial literacy has a significantly positive effect on digital financial behavior
E36	(Dewmini et al., 2023)	Srilanka	370 undergraduate students	descriptive statistics, correlation analysis, and regression analysis	Digital financial awareness, digital financial skills and knowledge, and the digital financial usage significantly impact financial behavior.
Literature Review Studies					
Code	Reference	Type of Review			Summary

continued on following page

Table 1. Continued

Empirical Journal Articles					
Code	**Reference**	**Place of the Study**	**Sample**	**Analysis Technique**	**Findings**
L1	(Goyal & Kumar, 2020)	Systematic review and bibliometric analysis 175 studies			The review shows that in the domain of financial literacy, one of the emerging themes is digital financial education.
L2	(Koskelainen et al., 2023)	Integrative review 29 studies			The review finds prior studies have focused on the relationship between traditional financial literacy and financial behavior, and there is a need to explore the same relation in the context of digital financial literacy.
L3	(Ma et al., 2023)	Literature survey (No specific method reported)			It finds pandemic-driven digitalization impacts personal financial issues and behavior.
Book Chapter - Literature Review Studies					
L4	(Goyal & Kumar, 2023)	Review (No specific method reported) 210 articles			Reviews the construct of financial literacy and financial behaviors. It shows that digital financial literacy is a promising area for future exploration.
Research Report					
Code	Reference	Place of the Study	Sample	Analysis Technique	Findings
R1	(Lusardi et al., 2018)	USA	Millennials aged 18-34 from 8000-NCFS 2000- GFLEC	Multivariate OLS regressions	Shows that mobile payment users are not following good financial management practices.
Conference paper					
C1	(Gaol et al., 2023)	Indonesia	96 students aged 17-25	Descriptive analysis	There is a correlation between digital financial literacy and interest in capital market investments
C2	(Abdullah et al., 2023)	Malaysia	152 Malaysian university undergraduate students	Descriptive analysis, Regression	Digital financial literacy significantly impacts online buying behaviors during the pandemic.
C3	(Furinto et al., 2023)	Indonesia	116 individual investors aged less than 21 and above 55	SEM	Shows that digital financial literacy positively affects perceived socioeconomic status, which affects digital investment decisions.

CHARACTERISTICS OF THE STUDIES

44 studies were included in this review. The year-wise distribution of the studies is shown in Figure 2. The first study in DFL and financial behavior was published in 2018. The most number of studies (21) were published in 2023. The studies in the domain are increasing, indicating the relevance of studying the relationship between digital financial literacy and financial behaviors as in the first quarter of 2024 reported five studies.

Figure 2. Studies published year-wise

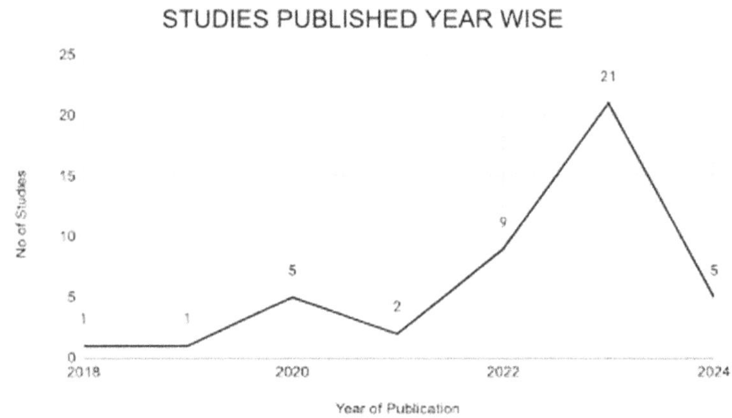

Figure 3 depicts the types of studies published in the domain. 86.4% (38 studies) of the studies are journal articles, 9.1% (4 studies) are conference papers, 2.3% (1 study) is a research report, and 2.3% (1 study) is a book chapter.

Figure 3. Types of studies

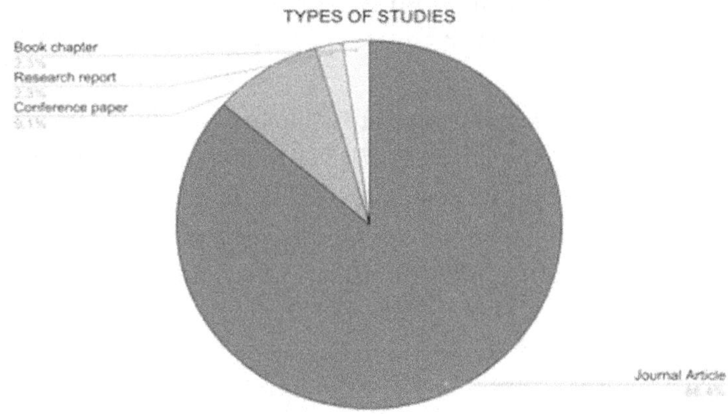

Figure 4 depicts the research designs adopted in the studies. 70.5% (31 studies) used a survey design, making it the predominant design in the domain. 13.6% (6 studies) used secondary data. 9.1% (4 studies) are literature review studies. The kinds of reviews present are systematic, bibliometric and integrative reviews. 6.8% (3 studies) are experimental studies.

Figure 4. Research designs used in the studies

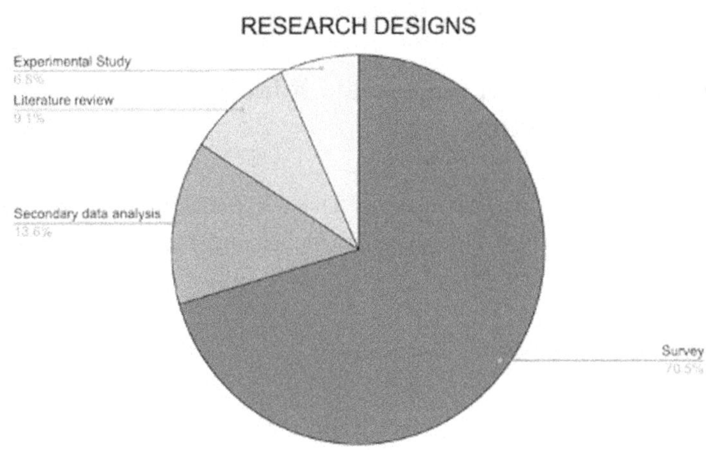

FINDINGS AND DISCUSSION

Relation Between Digital Financial Literacy and Financial Behavior

There is a positive and significant relationship between digital financial literacy and financial behaviors (Respati et al., 2023; Setiawan et al., 2020; Kumar et al., 2023a; Kumar et al., 2023b; Rahayu et al., 2022a; Jhonson et al., 2023; Shinu & Mullappallykayamkulath, 2022; Choi et al., 2023; Aryan et al., 2023 Abdallah et al., 2024; Rahayu et al., 2023; Ali et al., 2023; Azaria et al., 2024; Febrianty et al., 2024; Muat et al., 2024; Nurkholik, 2023; Dewmini et al., 2023). The positive relationship was found mainly in saving, spending and investing behaviors (Rahayu et al., 2022a; Jhonson et al., 2023; Shinu and Mullappallykayamkulath, 2022; Aryan et al., 2023). Some studies reported that it is seen among financial behaviors, specifically in saving and spending (Rahayu et al., 2023; Febrianty et al., 2024). Ali et al. (2023) reported it is seen in spending and investment behaviors. While considering financial behavior, it is crucial to understand the role of decision-making as it acts as a precedent to behavior (Ruggeri et al., 2019). In financial decision-making, the literature showed a positive significant relationship between digital financial literacy and financial behavior (Kumar et al., 2023a; Kumar et al., 2023b). It was found that digital financial literacy increased the interest in the capital market to make money out of money rather than keeping it idle. Gaol et al. (2023) provide evidence from the Romanian capital market, in the context of students, that it increased the interest in capital market investments. In contradiction to the findings, Ali et al. (2024) reported that high levels of DFL could deter sound financial behavior.

Measurement of Digital Financial Literacy and Financial Behavior

Although there are scales that have been used to measure the constructs, there is no consensus in the literature with respect to measuring individuals' digital financial literacy and financial behavior.

Digital Financial Literacy

The scales that measure digital financial literacy consider various dimensions, including Knowledge/awareness (of services, products, rights, risks, digital crimes), experience, behavior, practical skills, decision-making, attitude and social norms. Morgan and Trinh (2019) measured digital financial literacy as knowledge of digital financial services, awareness of the risk associated with digital financial services, knowledge of controlling digital financial risk, knowledge of consumer rights and issue redressal. Jhonson et al. (2023), Kumar et al. (2023a) and Ali et al. (2023) use the digital financial literacy scale from the study of Morgan and Trinh (2019). Lyons & Kass-Hanna (2021) measured digital financial literacy as basic knowledge and skill, awareness, practical know-how, decision making and self-protection. Respati et al. (2023) considered DFL as financial knowledge, digital knowledge, awareness of digital financial services, practical know-how of digital financial services, and decision-making in line with Lyons & Kass-Hanna (2021). Setiawan et al. (2020) considered the studies of Prasad and Meghwal (2017) and Morgan & Trinh (2019). They proposed four dimensions of DFL, including knowledge of digital financial products and services, experience in using digital financial products and services, awareness of digital financial risk, and skill in controlling and managing digital financial activities. Muat et al. (2024) used the scale by Setiawan et al. (2020) to measure DFL. Aulia et al. (2023) measure DFL using the understandings made by Setiawan et al. (2020), Prasad et al. (2018) and Morgan et al. (2019). Rahayu et al. (2022a) considered four criteria: knowledge of consumers and compensation maker rights, awareness of digital financial risks, and understanding of digital financial goods and services, to measure DFL. Clarence and Pertiwi (2023) used the scale Rahayu et al. (2022a) developed to measure digital financial literacy. Aryan et al. (2023) measured digital financial literacy by digital knowledge, digital experiences, digital awareness, and digital skills, in line with Liew et al. (2020). Azaria et al. (2024) consider DFL as digital financial knowledge (DFK) by using items related to trust in digital financial services, personal information risk, addiction risk, and digital crimes using the scale of Normawati et al. (2021). Nurkholik (2023) measured digital financial literacy by combining the understanding of Morgan et al. (2019), Prasad et al. (2018), and Setiawan et al. (2022). Dewmini et al. (2023) measured DFL by combining digital financial awareness developed by Azeez & Akhtar (2021), digital financial skills and knowledge developed by Lyons & Kass-Hanna (2021), digital financial attitude developed by Rajdev et al. (2020) and digital financial usage using the scale by Rajdev et al. (2020). Abdallah et al. (2024) considered digital financial literacy as financial knowledge, digital knowledge, practical know-how, awareness, decision making and self-protection. Ravikumar et al. (2022) measured DFL using digital knowledge, financial knowledge, knowledge of DFS, awareness of digital finance risk, digital finance risk control, knowledge of customer rights, product suitability, product quality, gendered social norm, practical application of knowledge and skill, self-determination to use the knowledge and skill and decision among Indian adults. Chhillar et al. (2024) measured DFL as digital financial risk and control, basic digital financial knowledge, advanced Digital Financial knowledge, digital financial attitude, and digital financial behavior.

Financial Behavior

There is no consensus in the literature with respect to measuring individuals' financial management behavior (Goyal et al., 2021). It is spread across savings, investment, credit, insurance and retirement domains. Along with that, in literature consumption, asset management, wealth accumulation, mortgage repayment, tax planning, estate planning, financial technologies and charitable giving. Most of the scales are not psychometric validated. However, Dew and Xiao's (2011) scale that measures selected financial behavior is psychometrically validated. In digital financial literacy, financial behaviors are measured using saving, spending, and investment behavior (Aryan et al., 2023; Rahayu et al., 2022a; Ali et al., 2023). Respati et al. (2023) considered financial behavior as Saving behavior, Shopping behavior, Long-term planning, and Short-term planning in line with Zulaihati & Widyastuti (2020). Jhonson et al. (2023) measured saving, spending and investing as financial behavior. Setiawan et al. (2020) considered saving behavior, spending behavior, future saving foresight, and future spending foresight as financial behaviors. Aulia et al. (2023) used Setiawan et al. (2020) scale for financial behavior. Clarence & Pertiwi (2023) measured using saving behavior, spending behavior, and investment behavior from Rahayu et al. (2022a). It can be seen that most financial behaviors are restricted to saving, spending and investing. Azaria et al. (2024) measured financial behavior (FB) using 15 items, including financial planning, future preparation, budgeting, investing and saving (Khawar & Sarwar, 2021). Muat et al. (2024) used Questions about the consistency with which certain financial behaviors are carried out, such as setting money aside for savings and retirement, having the plan to reach financial goals, having a weekly or monthly budget, and having cutting living expenses using Joo and Grable (2004) scale. Nurkholik (2023) measured Digital financial behavior measured by a combination from Alonso-García et al. (2017), Furnham (1999), Setiawan et al. (2022) and Watson (2003). Dewmini et al. (2023) measure financial behavior in line with the scale developed by Azeez and Akhtar (2021). Abdallah et al. (2024) measure financial behaviors such as saving behavior, shopping behavior, long-term planning, short-term planning.

Interplaying Variables

The literature establishes a positive and significant relationship between digital financial literacy and financial behaviors. Yadav and Banerji (2023) pointed out that the relationship between digital financial literacy and financial behavior needs to be examined in terms of moderating and mediating factors, exploring how the interplay of the variables empirically is vital. The study finds that the following variables can interplay between digital financial literacy and financial behaviors in this setting.

1. Financial self-efficacy
2. Financial confidence
3. Self-control
4. Financial autonomy
5. Financial capability
6. Psychological biases
7. Digital and financial socialization
8. Socio-economic and demographic factors

Also, an overview of variables that can interplay between digital financial literacy and financial behavior is discussed.

Financial self-efficacy is the perceived ability to complete financial activities (Lapp, 2010). It can minimize the negative effects of unforeseen financial difficulties. It was found that higher levels of self-efficacy led to lower levels of stress (Choi et al., 2023). Self-efficacy improves financial decision-making while interacting with technology (French et al., 2019). The findings point to the need to explore whether financial self-efficacy can translate digital financial literacy into responsible financial management behaviors related to conviction in one's ability.

Financial confidence is associated with self-assurance, which leads to making good financial decisions in personal finance (Palameta et al., 2016). In the context of digital financial literacy, both digital financial literacy and financial confidence have an effect on financial behavior (Respati et al., 2023). Lyons et al. (2022) supported that digital financial literacy can bring up financial resilience and improve financial confidence while engaging with fintech. As financial confidence improves, the usage of digital financial technologies increases. However, increased technology usage does not ensure responsible financial decision-making (Kass-Hanna et al., 2022). Given the importance of financial confidence in this context, exploring the mediating role of financial confidence becomes important.

Self-control is the ability to end bad habits, resist temptations, and deal effectively with impulses (Baumeister, 2002; Fujita et al., 2006). It has been found that self-control can contribute to responsible financial behavior as it helps control impulses (Younas et al., 2019; Rey-Ares et al., 2021). It becomes crucial in the context of millennials as there is evidence for impulsive behaviors. Lusardi et al. (2018) reported that millennials using mobile payment are not following responsible financial behaviors. Walsh & Lim (2020) report the same in the case of using personal financial management technologies. Also, self-control becomes crucial for people with high leisure who take risks optimistically in financial matters (Kakinuma, 2022). Lack of self-control can lead to risks due to decision delegation (Litterscheidt & Streich, 2020). Considering this context, exploring how self-control can help translate digital financial literacy into responsible financial behaviors is becoming relevant.

In contrast to classical theorists, the prospect theory founders Kahneman and Tversky (1979) argued that people can make suboptimal or irrational decisions by not adhering to the axioms of expected utility theory. Koskelainen et al. (2023) pointed out that consumers can make suboptimal decisions due to cognitive limitations, lack of knowledge, or psychological biases. Psychological biases can affect financial knowledge and financial behavior (Goyal & Kumar, 2020). As minimal research is done in this area, More research is needed to understand the role of psychological biases in digital financial literacy and financial behavior relationship (Goyal & Kumar, 2023).

In the current digital world of nudges and external influences, it is becoming difficult to make independent decisions (Puaschunder, 2022). This situation calls for financial autonomy. It is reported that advanced digital financial literacy provides greater autonomy in digital financial decisions (Kass-Hanna et al., 2022). Digital financial literacy and financial autonomy influence financial decision-making (Kumar et al., 2023a). Considering this evidence, exploring the role of financial autonomy in converting digital financial literacy and personal financial management behavior is required.

It is reported that financial capability can transform financial knowledge into positive and responsible financial behaviors (Xiao, 2016). Especially among digital consumers, it is essential to inculcate digital financial capability (Luo et al., 2021; Meng, 2023). financial capability is found to mediate the relationship between digital financial literacy and financial decision-making (Kumar et al., 2023a). The literature has not explored how financial capability can affect the relationship between digital financial literacy and personal financial management behaviors.

Previous research has shown that family financial socialization partially mediates the relationship between financial literacy and financial behavior (Khawar & Sarwar, 2021). In the case of the digital age, it is vital to consider digital socialization as well (Abdullah et al., 2023). It is also relevant to understand how childhood experiences can shape one's digital financial literacy (Sabri et al., 2023). So, when it comes to personal financial management behaviors, it is important to consider how digital and financial socialization can help translate digital financial literacy into positive financial management behaviors. Abdullah et al. (2023) confirm that digital financial literacy, including digital and financial socialization, significantly affects purchasing behaviors in the digital environment.

Zaimovic et al. (2023) pointed out that exploring demographic factors like gender and education in relation to financial literacy specific to digital environments is required. Also, socioeconomic aspects need to be considered in this context. Concerning the interaction of digital financial literacy and financial behaviors, there is evidence that socioeconomic and demographic factors play an important role. Furinto et al. (2023) show that digital financial literacy positively causes perceived socio-economic status, affecting investment decisions in the digital context. In contrast, Choi et al. (2023) argue that building financial literacy and financial self-efficacy is important among women. Moreover, it is reported that there is a difference between men and women in the effect of digital financial literacy on spending behavior and no difference in saving behavior (Febrianty et al., 2024). Concerning socio-economic factors, Liew et al. (2020) stressed the importance of digital financial literacy programs in the context of society's disadvantaged or marginalized sections. Also, digital inequalities or the digital divide in digital financial practices need to be taken care of (Baudat & Henchoz, 2022).

It is reported that financial literacy and financial behavior significantly influence financial well-being (Kumar et al., 2023). Financial behavior is considered the strongest predictor of financial well-being (Sehrawat & Vij, 2020; Rahman et al., 2021; Zulaihati & Widyastuti, 2020; Shim et al., 2009). Fundamentally. the idea behind the relationship between financial literacy and financial well-being is that those individuals with a good amount of financial literacy can have more access to financial services, practice positive financial behaviors, and, in turn, achieve financial well-being (Fan and Henager, 2022; Lee et al., 2020; Utkarsh et al., 2020). So, financial behavior mediates the relationship between financial literacy and financial well-being (Prakash et al., 2022; Sabri et al., 2022). By enhancing financial education and desirable financial behaviors, individuals can improve their financial well-being and community well-being and, thereby, the country's economic growth (Janjanam & Subba Lakshmi, 2024). Even though there are minimal studies in the context of digital financial literacy and financial behavior leading to financial well-being, existing literature reports that DFL shows a positive and significant association with financial-wellbeing (Kass-Hanna et al., 2022; Lyons & Fontes, 2021; Choung et al., 2023; Respati et al., 2023; Kamble et al., 2023; Rahayu et al., 2022b; Bushra & Mir, 2024). Aulia et al. (2023) argued that financial behavior strengthens the relationship between digital financial literacy and financial well-being. It is also reported that DFL influences financial well-being by the mediation of financial behavior, namely spending, saving, and investment (Jhonson et al., 2023; Rahayu et al., 2024). So, it is evident that financial well-being can be improved by gaining digital financial literacy and practicing responsible financial behaviors on digital platforms (Nurkholik, 2023). OECD (2018) reports that lower levels of digital financial literacy can have a negative impact on personal wellbeing. Also, the evidence shows that building financial knowledge and financial awareness is vital in reducing financial vulnerability (O'Connor et al., 2019). Hapsoro et al. (2022) found that digital financial literacy and financial behavior are negatively associated with financial vulnerability. It indicates that as the levels of digital financial literacy improve, financial behavior improves, and financial vulnerability will decrease.

At the same time, digital financial literacy also contributes to financial resilience (Kass-Hanna et al., 2022).

FUTURE RESEARCH AGENDA

There is a need for more studies to understand better the relationship between digital financial literacy and financial behaviors. The gaps in the literature are summarized below -

- There is a need for empirical advancements in the domain. The role of mediating variables such as financial self-efficacy, financial confidence, self-control, financial autonomy, financial capability, psychological biases, and digital and financial socialization in relation to digital financial literacy and financial behavior needs to be explored. Also, the moderating role of socioeconomic and demographic variables will help to understand the digital financial inequalities and divide. As an outcome variable, financial wellbeing also needs to be explored. This review identifies the interplaying variables between digital financial literacy and financial behaviors. In Figure 5, a conceptual framework that needs to be empirically explored is developed.

A conceptual model for future empirical exploration is presented in Figure 5.

Figure 5. Conceptual model

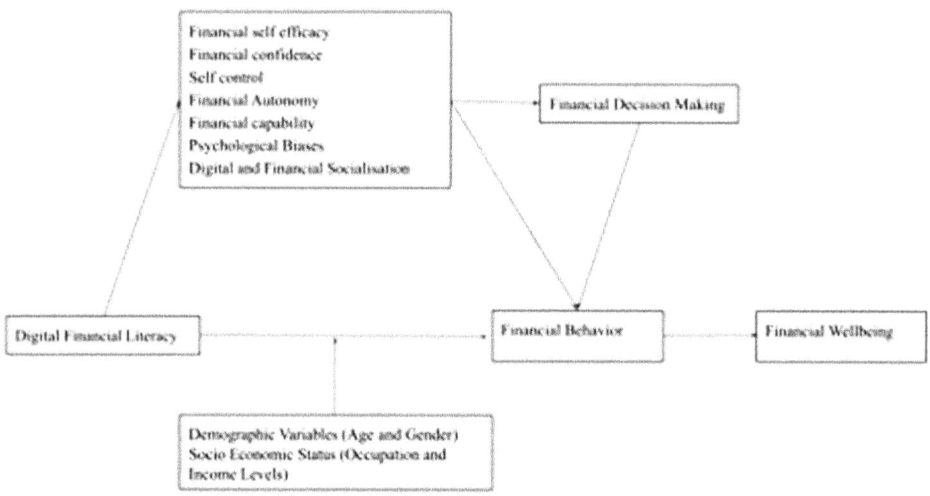

- There is a need for methodological advancements in the domain. More qualitative studies need to be conducted as they can provide an understanding of how financial experience contributes to financial behaviors.
- There is a need for conceptual advancements in the domain. Studies that establish a relationship between financial literacy and financial behaviors need to be replicated considering the context of digital technologies or fintech. Concerning personal financial management behavior, there is a need for studies comprehensively addressing the context, as the present literature focuses on very limited areas of financial behavior.

CONCLUSION

This systematic literature review explored the relationship between digital financial literacy and financial behavior and identified the mediating variables that can help translate the knowledge element into behavior. The review encompasses 44 studies published in the context of digital financial literacy and financial behavior through the PRISMA method. It shows a positive significant relation between digital financial literacy and financial behaviors. It is found that the interplaying factors such as financial self-efficacy, financial confidence, self-control, financial autonomy, financial capability, psychological biases, and digital and financial socialization are crucial in developing digital financial education programs for creating responsible financial behaviors. Also, it is found that this relationship is vital for achieving financial well-being. The study stresses the need to consider demographic and socio-economic factors while designing digital financial literacy programs. The review opens up the path for future empirical exploration of digital financial literacy, financial behavior, and financial well-being. The study has a few limitations. Firstly, the literature exploration is limited to eleven databases, and adding more databases may provide more insights into this context. Also, the present study considered only articles published in English, and adding studies in languages other than English may expand the understanding of the domain. Contextually, the study focuses on the financial behavior of individuals. Exploration into the financial behavior of small and medium enterprises and firms can provide more insights.

REFERENCES

Abdallah, W., Tfaily, F., & Harraf, A. (2024, March 25). The impact of digital financial literacy on financial behavior: Customers' perspective. *Competitiveness Review*. Advance online publication. 10.1108/CR-11-2023-0297

Abdullah, A. R., Che Musa, Z. K., Abdullah, S. S., Muhammad, M. Z., Muhamad, M., Ghazali, M. S., & Mat Yunoh, M. N. (2023). Effects of Digital Financial Literacy Towards Online Buying Behaviours Among Students During COVID-19 Pandemic. *Industry Forward and Technology Transformation in Business and Entrepreneurship*, 669–677. 10.1007/978-981-99-2337-3_57

Ali, M., Alamgir, M., & Nawaz, M. A. (2024). Emergence of the Digital Financial Literacy, and its Effect on the Financial Management Behavior among Students of Pakistan. *Pakistan Social Sciences Review*, 8(2), 141–155. 10.35484/pssr.2024(8-II)13

Ali, N., Mat Rahim, N., Adnan, M. F., Yanto, H., & Kiswanto, K. (2024, January 3). Determinants of Financial Behaviour: Does Digital Financial Literacy (DFL) Foster or Deter Sound Financial Behaviour? *Accounting and Finance Research*, 13(1), 6. 10.5430/afr.v13n1p6

Alonso-García, J., Bateman, H., Bonekamp, J., Van Soest, A., & Stevens, R. (2017). Saving preferences in retirement: the impact of pension policy design and health status. Available at: www.cepar.edu.au

Andreou, P. C., & Anyfantaki, S. (2021, October). Financial literacy and its influence on internet banking behavior. *European Management Journal*, 39(5), 658–674. 10.1016/j.emj.2020.12.001

Aryan, L. A., Alsharif, A., Alquqa, E. K., Ebbini, M. M. A., Alzboun, N., Alshurideh, M. H. T., & Al-Hawary, S. I. S. (2024). How digital financial literacy impacts financial behavior in Jordanian millennial generation. *International Journal of Data and Network Science*, 8(1), 117–124. 10.5267/j.ijdns.2023.10.011

Aulia, A., Rahayu, R., & Bahari, A. (2023, May 24). The Influence Of Digital Financial Literacy On Financial Well-Being With Financial Behavior As A Moderation Variable: Communities In West Sumatra. *Jurnal Akuntansi*, 13(2), 141–149. 10.33369/jakuntansi.13.2.141-149

Azaria, C., Susilaningsih, S., & Sudarno, S. (2024, March 9). An Integrated Perspective : The Impact of Digital Financial Knowledge and Self-Esteem on Financial Behavior in the Lives of College Students. *Jurnal Kependidikan: Jurnal Hasil Penelitian Dan Kajian Kepustakaan Di Bidang Pendidikan. Pengajaran Dan Pembelajaran*, 10(1), 48. 10.33394/jk.v10i1.10602

Azeez, N. P. A., & Akhtar, S. M. J. (2021, June 8). Digital Financial Literacy and Its Determinants: An Empirical Evidences from Rural India. *South Asian Journal of Social Studies and Economics*, 8–22. 10.9734/sajsse/2021/v11i230279

Bapat, D. (2019, June 1). Exploring Antecedents to Financial Management Behavior for Young Adults. *Financial Counseling and Planning*, 30(1), 44–55. 10.1891/1052-3073.30.1.44

Bashir, I., & Qureshi, I. H. (2022, June 29). A Systematic Literature Review on Personal Financial Well-Being: The Link to Key Sustainable Development Goals 2030. *FIIB Business Review*, 12(1), 31–48. 10.1177/23197145221106862

Baudat, S., & Henchoz, C. (2022, August 1). Money in one click: Inequalities in digital financial practices and digital Skills among emerging adults in Switzerland. *Journal of Family and Economic Issues*, 44(3), 602–618. 10.1007/s10834-022-09854-z

Baumeister, R. F. (2002, March). Yielding to Temptation: Self-Control Failure, Impulsive Purchasing, and Consumer Behavior. *The Journal of Consumer Research*, 28(4), 670–676. 10.1086/338209

Bushra, N., & Mir, M. A. (2024). Digital Financial Literacy and Financial Well-Being. In *Advances in finance, accounting, and economics book series* (pp. 57–73). 10.4018/979-8-3693-1750-1.ch003

Carlsson, H., Larsson, S., Svensson, L., & Åström, F. (2017). Consumer Credit Behavior in the Digital Context: A Bibliometric Analysis and Literature Review. *Financial Counseling and Planning*, 28(1), 76–94. 10.1891/1052-3073.28.1.76

Chhillar, N., & Arora, S. (2022, December). Personal Financial Management Behavior Using Digital Platforms and Its Domains. *Journal of Financial Management. Markets and Institutions*, 10(02), 2250009. Advance online publication. 10.1142/S2282717X22500098

Chhillar, N., Arora, S., & Chawla, P. (2024, January 8). *Measuring Digital Financial Literacy: Scale Development and Validation*. https://so05.tci-thaijo.org/index.php/TER/article/view/270077

Choi, A., Stoutland, D., & Blanco, L. (2023, April 21). An evaluation of a digital financial education program and the impact of COVID-19 on financial well-being among college students. *Journal of American College Health*, 1–13. 10.1080/07448481.2023.219114237084244

Choung, Y., Chatterjee, S., & Pak, T. Y. (2023). Digital financial literacy and financial well-being. *Finance Research Letters*, 58, 104438. 10.1016/j.frl.2023.104438

Clarence, J., & Pertiwi, D. (2023, August 13). Financial Management Behavior Among Students: The Influence of Digital Financial Literacy. [IJFIS]. *International Journal of Financial and Investment Studies*, 4(1), 9–16. 10.9744/ijfis.4.1.9-16

Dew, J., & Xiao, J. J. (2011). The Financial Management Behavior Scale: Development and validation. *Financial Counseling and Planning*, 22(1), 43–59.

Dewmini, E. A. T., Wijekumara, J. M. N., & Sugathadasa, D. D. K. (2023, December 31). Digital Financial Literacy on Financial Behaviour Among Management Undergraduates of State Universities in Sri Lanka. *Journal of Management Matters*, 10(2), 73–89. 10.4038/jmm.v10i2.56

Fan, L., & Henager, R. (2022). A structural determinants framework for financial well-being. *Journal of Family and Economic Issues*, 43(2), 415–428. 10.1007/s10834-021-09798-w34548774

Febrianty, F., Yuliansyah, Y., Hamzah, R. S., & Annisa, M. L. (2024, February 28). Gender Issues in Digital Financial Literacy and Financial Behavior among Millennials. *Journal of Economics*, 20(1), 79–94. 10.21831/economia.v20i1.56529

French, D., McKillop, D., & Stewart, E. (2019, July 14). The effectiveness of smartphone apps in improving financial capability. *European Journal of Finance*, 26(4–5), 302–318. 10.1080/1351847X.2019.1639526

Fujita, K., Trope, Y., Liberman, N., & Levin-Sagi, M. (2006). Construal levels and self-control. *Journal of Personality and Social Psychology*, 90(3), 351–367. 10.1037/0022-3514.90.3.35116594824

Furinto, A., Tamara, D., Yenni, & Rahman, N. J. (2023). Financial and digital literacy effects on digital investment decision mediated by perceived socio-economic status. *E3S Web of Conferences, 426*, 02076. 10.1051/e3sconf/202342602076

Furnham, A. (1999, December). The saving and spending habits of young people. *Journal of Economic Psychology*, 20(6), 677–697. 10.1016/S0167-4870(99)00030-6

Gaol, F. L., Dermawan, G., Rafif, M. R., Rubianto, R., & Matsuo, T. (2023). The Influence of Digital Financial Literacy on Interest in Investing in the Capital Market of Millennial Generation Students. *Inventive Computation and Information Technologies*, 189–206. 10.1007/978-981-19-7402-1_15

Goyal, K., & Kumar, S. (2020, August 4). Financial literacy: A systematic review and bibliometric analysis. *International Journal of Consumer Studies*, 45(1), 80–105. 10.1111/ijcs.12605

Goyal, K., & Kumar, S. (2023). *Financial literacy and financial behavior. A Research Agenda for Consumer Financial Behavior*. Edward Elgar Publishing.

Goyal, K., Kumar, S., & Xiao, J. J. (2021, June 1). Antecedents and consequences of Personal Financial Management Behavior: A systematic literature review and future research agenda. *International Journal of Bank Marketing*, 39(7), 1166–1207. 10.1108/IJBM-12-2020-0612

Hapsoro, D., Agung Saputro, J., Indraswono, C., Jauharia Hatta, A., & Sabandi, M. (2022, November 17). Effect of gender as a moderating variable on financial vulnerability using hierarchical regressions: Survey evidence from Indonesian traditional market traders. *Investment Management and Financial Innovations*, 19(4), 171–182. 10.21511/imfi.19(4).2022.14

Ingale, K. K., & Paluri, R. A. (2020, December 15). Financial literacy and financial behaviour: A bibliometric analysis. *Review of Behavioral Finance*, 14(1), 130–154. 10.1108/RBF-06-2020-0141

Janjanam, V. V. P., & SubbaLakshmi, A. (2024). Importance of Financial Literacy Education and Financial Behavior for Developing Nations in the World. In *CRC Press eBooks* (pp. 163–180). 10.1201/9781032667478-15

Jhonson, B., Andriani, R., Noviana, I., & Tamara, D. (2023, June 20). Influence Of Digital Financial Literacy on Financial Well-Being Through Spending, Saving, And Investment Behavior In Indonesia. *Journal of Business Studies and Mangement Review*, 6(2), 157–168. 10.22437/jbsmr.v6i2.24793

Joo, S. H., & Grable, J. E. (2004). An Exploratory Framework of the Determinants of Financial Satisfaction. *Journal of Family and Economic Issues*, 25(1), 25–50. 10.1023/B:JEEI.0000016722.37994.9f

Kahneman, D., & Tversky, A. (1979, March). Prospect Theory: An Analysis of Decision under Risk. *Econometrica*, 47(2), 263. 10.2307/1914185

Kakinuma, Y. (2022, June 27). Financial literacy and quality of life: A moderated mediation approach of fintech adoption and leisure. *International Journal of Social Economics*, 49(12), 1713–1726. 10.1108/IJSE-10-2021-0633

Kamble, P. A., Mehta, A., & Rani, N. (2023). Financial Inclusion and Digital Financial Literacy: Do they Matter for Financial Well-being? *Social Indicators Research*. Advance online publication. 10.1007/s11205-023-03264-w

Kass-Hanna, J., Lyons, A. C., & Liu, F. (2022, June). Building financial resilience through financial and digital literacy in South Asia and Sub-Saharan Africa. *Emerging Markets Review*, 51, 100846. 10.1016/j.ememar.2021.100846

Khawar, S., & Sarwar, A. (2021, July 18). Financial literacy and financial behavior with the mediating effect of family financial socialization in the financial institutions of Lahore, Pakistan. *Future Business Journal*, 7(1), 27. Advance online publication. 10.1186/s43093-021-00064-x

Koskelainen, T., Kalmi, P., Scornavacca, E., & Vartiainen, T. (2023, January). Financial literacy in the digital age—A research agenda. *The Journal of Consumer Affairs*, 57(1), 507–528. 10.1111/joca.12510

Kumar, J., Rani, V., Rani, G., & Sarker, T. (2023). Determinants of the financial wellbeing of individuals in an emerging economy: An empirical study. *International Journal of Bank Marketing*, 41(4), 860–881. 10.1108/IJBM-10-2022-0475

Kumar, P., Islam, M. A., Pillai, R., & Sharif, T. (2023, February). Analysing the behavioural, psychological, and demographic determinants of financial decision making of household investors. *Heliyon*, 9(2), e13085. 10.1016/j.heliyon.2023.e1308536793953

Lapp, W. M. (2010). Behavior models for prosperity: A statistical assessment of savings and behavioral change (EARN Research Brief). Retrieved from Earned Assets Resource Network website: https://files.eric.ed.gov/fulltext/EJ1048681.pdf

Lee, J. M., Lee, J., & Kim, K. T. (2020). Consumer financial well-being: Knowledge is not enough. *Journal of Family and Economic Issues*, 41(2), 218–228. 10.1007/s10834-019-09649-9

Liew, T., Lim, P., & Liu, Y. (2020). Digital financial literacy: a case study of farmers from rural areas in sarawak. *International Journal of Education and Pedagogy*, 2(4), 245-251. Retrieved from https://myjms.mohe.gov.my/index.php/ijeap/article/view/11612

Litterscheidt, R., & Streich, D. J. (2020, August). Financial education and digital asset management: What's in the black box? *Journal of Behavioral and Experimental Economics*, 87, 101573. 10.1016/j.socec.2020.101573

Luo, Y., Peng, Y., & Zeng, L. (2021, November). Digital financial capability and entrepreneurial performance. *International Review of Economics & Finance*, 76, 55–74. 10.1016/j.iref.2021.05.010

Lusardi, A. (2019, January 24). Financial literacy and the need for financial education: Evidence and implications. *Swiss Journal of Economics and Statistics*, 155(1), 1. Advance online publication. 10.1186/s41937-019-0027-5

Lusardi, A., de Bassa Scheresberg, C., & Avery, M. (2018). Millennial mobile payment users: a look into their personal finances and financial behaviors. GFLEC working paper.

Lyons, A. C., & Fontes, A. (2021). Impacts of financial and digital literacy and social media on the financial health of U.S. households.

Lyons, A. C., Kass-Hanna, J., & Fava, A. (2022, June). Fintech development and savings, borrowing, and remittances: A comparative study of emerging economies. *Emerging Markets Review*, 51, 100842. 10.1016/j.ememar.2021.100842

Ma, N., Siu, Y. W., Cheong, T. S., & Tung, B. (2022, December 13). Impact of COVID-19 on lifestyle and financial behaviour: The implications to research in financial vulnerability. *Frontiers in Psychology*, 13, 1073017. Advance online publication. 10.3389/fpsyg.2022.107301736582332

Mavlutova, I., Fomins, A., Spilbergs, A., Atstaja, D., & Brizga, J. (2021, December 29). Opportunities to Increase Financial Well-Being by Investing in Environmental, Social and Governance with Respect to Improving Financial Literacy under COVID-19: The Case of Latvia. *Sustainability (Basel)*, 14(1), 339. 10.3390/su14010339

Meng, D. (2023, January 16). Digital financial capability and household consumption: Evidence from China. *Applied Economics Letters*, 1–5. Advance online publication. 10.1080/13504851.2023.2167915

Morgan, P. J., Huang, B., & Trinh, L. Q. (2019). *The Need to Promote Digital Financial Literacy for the Digital Age*. Retrieved February 24, 2024, from https://t20japan.org/wp-content/uploads/2019/03/t20-japan-tf7-3-need-promote-digital-financial-literacy.pdf

Morris, T., Maillet, S., & Koffi, V. (2022, January 10). Financial knowledge, financial confidence and learning capacity on financial behavior: A Canadian study. *Cogent Social Sciences*, 8(1), 1996919. Advance online publication. 10.1080/23311886.2021.1996919

Muat, S., Fachrurrozi, F., & Sari, N. (2024, February 20). How do digital financial literacy, financial behavior, and skills affect financial well-being? An Exploratory Study on Gen Z. *Integrated Journal of Business and Economics*, 8(1), 728. 10.33019/ijbe.v8i1.851

Negi, P., & Jaiswal, A. (2024, May). Impact of financial literacy on consumer financial behavior: A systematic review and research agenda using TCCM framework. *International Journal of Consumer Studies*, 48(3), e13053. Advance online publication. 10.1111/ijcs.13053

Normawati, R., Rahayu, S., & Worokinasih, S. (2021). Financial Knowledge, Digital Financial Knowledge, Financial Attitude, Financial Behaviour and Financial Satisfaction on Millennials. *Proceedings of the 1st International Conference on Law, Social Science, Economics, and Education, ICLSSEE 2021*. 10.4108/eai.6-3-2021.2305967

Nurkholik, A. (2023, January 15). R Approach in Digital Financial Literacy Influence Subjective Financial Well-Being. *Revista Mexicana de Economía y Finanzas*, 19(1), 1–20. 10.21919/remef.v19i1.935

OECD. (2018), Financial Markets, Insurance and Private Pensions: Digitalisation and Finance. OECD. Retrieved From https://web-archive.oecd.org/2018-04-09/473485-financial-markets-insurance-and-pensions-2018.htm

Page, M. J., McKenzie, J., Bossuyt, P., Boutron, I., & Hoffmann, T. (2020). The PRISMA 2020 statement: an updated guideline for reporting systematic reviews. https://doi.org/10.31222/osf.io/v7gm2

Palameta, B., Nguyen, C., Hui, T. S., & Gyarmati, D. (2016), Link between financial confidence and financial outcomes among working-aged Canadians, Social Research and Demonstration Corporation, Retrieved from https://www.canada.ca/content/dam/canada/financial-consumer-agency/migration/eng/resources/researchsurveys/documents/link-confidence-outcomes.pdf

Panos, G. A., & Wilson, J. O. S. (2020, February 9). Financial literacy and responsible finance in the FinTech era: Capabilities and challenges. *European Journal of Finance*, 26(4–5), 297–301. 10.1080/1351847X.2020.1717569

Prakash, N., Alagarsamy, S., & Hawaldar, A. (2022). Demographic characteristics influencing financial wellbeing: A multigroup analysis. *Managerial Finance*, 48(9/10), 1334–1351. 10.1108/MF-09-2021-0466

Prasad, H., Meghwal, D., & Dayama, V. (2018, December 1). Digital Financial Literacy: A Study of Households of Udaipur. *Journal of Business and Management*, 5, 23–32. 10.3126/jbm.v5i0.27385

Puaschunder, J. (2022). *Advances in Behavioral Economics and Finance Leadership*. Contributions to Economics. 10.1007/978-3-031-15710-3

Qamar, A., Rasheed, N., Kamal, A., Rauf, S., & Nizam, K. (2023, July 30). Factors Affecting Financial Behavior of Millennial Gen Z: Mediating Role of Digital Financial Literacy Integration. *International Journal of Social Science & Entrepreneurship*, 3(3), 330–352. 10.58661/ijsse.v3i3.207

Rahayu, R., Ali, S., Aulia, A., & Hidayah, R. (2022a). The Current Digital Financial Literacy and Financial Behavior in Indonesian Millennial Generation. *Journal of Accounting and Investment*, 23(1), 78–94. 10.18196/jai.v23i1.13205

Rahayu, R., Juita, V., & Rahman, A. (2023). Digital Financial Literacy, Financial Behaviour, and Financial Well-being of Women's in Indonesia. *Proceedings of the International Conference on Entrepreneurship, Leadership and Business Innovation (ICELBI 2022)*, 550–563. https://doi.org/10.2991/978-94-6463-350-4_54

Rahayu, R., Juita, V., & Rahman, A. (2024, January). Digital Financial Literacy, Financial Behaviour, and Financial Well-being of Women's in Indonesia. In *International Conference on Entrepreneurship, Leadership and Business Innovation (ICELBI 2022)* (pp. 550-563). Atlantis Press

Rahayu, R., Juita, V., Rahman, A., Fitriamiranti, S., & Rafles, R. (2022b). The level of digital financial literacy and financial well-being of people in West Sumatra Indonesia. *Operations Management and Information System Studies*, 2(2), 66–76.

Rahman, M., Isa, C. R., Masud, M. M., Sarker, M., & Chowdhury, N. T. (2021). The role of financial behaviour, financial literacy, and financial stress in explaining the financial well-being of B40 group in Malaysia. *Future Business Journal*, 7(1), 52. Advance online publication. 10.1186/s43093-021-00099-0

Rajdev, A. A., Modhvadiya, T., & Sudra, P. (2020). An analysis of digital financial literacy among college students. *Pacific Business Review International*, 13(5), 32–40. Retrieved from www.pbr.co.in

Ravikumar, T., Suresha, B., Prakash, N., Vazirani, K., & Krishna, T. (2022, October 14). Digital financial literacy among adults in India: Measurement and validation. *Cogent Economics & Finance*, 10(1), 2132631. Advance online publication. 10.1080/23322039.2022.2132631

Respati, D. K., Widyastuti, U., Nuryati, T., Musyaffi, A. M., Handayani, B. D., & Ali, N. R. (2023, March 6). How do students' digital financial literacy and financial confidence influence their financial behavior and financial well-being? *Nurture*, 17(2), 40–50. 10.55951/nurture.v17i2.154

Rey-Ares, L., Fernández-López, S., Castro-González, S., & Rodeiro-Pazos, D. (2021, August). Does self-control constitute a driver of millennials' financial behaviors and attitudes? *Journal of Behavioral and Experimental Economics*, 93, 101702. 10.1016/j.socec.2021.101702

Ruggeri, K., Kunz, M., Berkessel, J., Kácha, O., Steinnes, K., Petrova, D., Caavassini, F., Naru, F., & Hardy, E. (2019). The science of behavior and decision-making. In Ruggeri, K. (Ed.), *Behavioral insights for public policy: Concepts and cases* (pp. 59–79). Routledge.

Sabri, M. F., Anthony, M., Law, S. H., Rahim, H. A., Burhan, N. A. S., & Ithnin, M. (2023, May 22). Impact of financial behaviour on financial well-being: Evidence among young adults in Malaysia. *Journal of Financial Services Marketing*. Advance online publication. 10.1057/s41264-023-00234-8

Sabri, M. F., Wahab, R., Mahdzan, N. S., Magli, A. S., & Rahim, H. A. (2022). Mediating Effect of Financial Behaviour on the Relationship Between Perceived Financial Wellbeing and Its Factors Among Low-Income Young Adults in Malaysia. *Frontiers in Psychology*, 13, 858630. Advance online publication. 10.3389/fpsyg.2022.85863035664172

Sehrawat, K., & Vij, M. (2020). Financial Wellbeing Among Public and Private Sector Employees: A Preliminary Study. *Indian Journal of Finance*, 14(1), 9. 10.17010/ijf/2020/v14i1/149855

Seldal, M. M. N., & Nyhus, E. K. (2022, March 7). Financial Vulnerability, Financial Literacy, and the Use of Digital Payment Technologies. *Journal of Consumer Policy*, 45(2), 281–306. 10.1007/s10603-022-09512-935283545

Setiawan, M., Effendi, N., Santoso, T., Dewi, V. I., & Sapulette, M. S. (2020, August 10). Digital financial literacy, current behavior of saving and spending and its future foresight. *Economics of Innovation and New Technology*, 31(4), 320–338. 10.1080/10438599.2020.1799142

Shim, S., Xiao, J. J., Barber, B. L., & Lyons, A. C. (2009, November). Pathways to life success: A conceptual model of financial well-being for young adults. *Journal of Applied Developmental Psychology*, 30(6), 708–723. 10.1016/j.appdev.2009.02.003

Shinu & Mullappallykayamkulath. (2022). Digital Financial Literacy and its Impact on the Financial Behaviour of Millennials: An Empirical Investigation. *International Journal of Financial Management, 12*(3), 10-16. http://publishingindia.com/downloads/7078.pdf

Steen, A., Graves, C., D'Alessandro, S., & Shi, H. X. (2023, February 28). Managing digital assets on death and disability: An examination of the determinants of digital asset planning literacy. *Australian Journal of Management*. Advance online publication. 10.1177/03128962231157005

Tokar Asaad, C. (2015, June 30). Financial literacy and financial behavior. *Financial Services Review*, 24(2), 101–117. 10.61190/fsr.v24i2.3236

Tony, N., & Desai, K. (2020). Impact of digital financial literacy on digital financial inclusion. *International Journal of Scientific and Technology Research*, 9(1), 1911–1915.

Utkarsh, N., Pandey, A., Ashta, A., Spiegelman, E., & Sutan, A. (2020). Catch them young: Impact of financial socialization, financial literacy and attitude towards money on financial well-being of young adults. *International Journal of Consumer Studies*, 44(6), 531–541. 10.1111/ijcs.12583

Walsh, B., & Lim, H. (2020, September). Millennials' adoption of personal financial management (PFM) technology and financial behavior. *Financial Planning Review*, 3(3), e1095. Advance online publication. 10.1002/cfp2.1095

Watson, J. J. (2003, December). The relationship of materialism to spending tendencies, saving, and debt. *Journal of Economic Psychology*, 24(6), 723–739. 10.1016/j.joep.2003.06.001

Wulandari, R. T., & Damayanti, S. M. (2022). The importance of digital financial literacy to anticipate impulsive buying behavior in buy-now-pay-later mode. *International Journal of Business and Economy*, 4(3), 170–182. https://myjms.mohe.gov.my/index.php/ijbec/article/view/19615

Xiao, J. J. (2008). Applying behavior theories to financial behavior. In *Handbook of consumer finance research* (pp. 69–81). Springer. 10.1007/978-0-387-75734-6_5

Xiao, J. J. (2016). Consumer Financial Capability and Wellbeing. In *Springer eBooks* (pp. 3–17). 10.1007/978-3-319-28887-1_1

Xiao, J. J., & Kumar, S. (2023, June 1). *A Research Agenda for Consumer Financial Behavior*. Edward Elgar Publishing.

Yadav, M., & Banerji, P. (2023, May 31). A bibliometric analysis of digital financial literacy. *American Journal of Business*, 38(3), 91–111. 10.1108/AJB-11-2022-0186

Younas, J., & Kalimuthu, F. (2019, January 30). Impact of Self-Control, Financial Literacy and Financial Behavior on Financial Well-Being. *The Journal of Social Sciences Research*, 51(51), 211–218. 10.32861/jssr.51.211.218

Zaimovic, A., Torlakovic, A., Arnaut-Berilo, A., Zaimovic, T., Dedovic, L., & Nuhic Meskovic, M. (2023, June 9). Mapping Financial Literacy: A Systematic Literature Review of Determinants and Recent Trends. *Sustainability (Basel)*, 15(12), 9358. 10.3390/su15129358

Zulaihati, S., & Widyastuti, U. (2020). Determinants of consumer financial behavior: Evidence from households in Indonesia. *Accounting*, 1193–1198. 10.5267/j.ac.2020.9.008

ADDITIONAL READING

Danes, S. M. (1994). Parental Perceptions of Children's Financial Socialization. *Financial Counseling and Planning*, 5, 127–146.

Gomber, P., Koch, J. A., & Siering, M. (2017). Digital Finance and FinTech: Current research and future research directions. *Journal of Business Economics*, 87(5), 537–580. 10.1007/s11573-017-0852-x

Smith, J., Hewitt, B., & Skrbiš, Z. (2015). Digital socialization: Young people's changing value orientations towards internet use between adolescence and early adulthood. *Information Communication and Society*, 18(9), 1022–1038. 10.1080/1369118X.2015.1007074

Vijaykumar, J. H. (2021). The Association of Financial Socialization with Financial Self-Efficacy and Autonomy: A Study of Young Students in India. *Journal of Family and Economic Issues*, 43(2), 397–414. 10.1007/s10834-021-09797-x

KEY TERMS AND DEFINITIONS

Digital Financial Literacy: Digital financial literacy is considered as knowledge of digital financial services, awareness of the risk associated with digital financial services, knowledge of controlling digital financial risk, knowledge of consumer rights and issue redressal (Morgan & Trinh, 2019).

Digital Socialization: It refers to the process by which young people learn to form value judgements about their use of digital media and the internet (Smith et al., 2015).

Financial Autonomy: It refers to the ability of individuals to freely decide on their financial affairs. The ability to manage their funds independently enables them to set and realize their financial goals (Vijaykumar, 2021).

Financial Behavior: Financial behavior is viewed as any human behavior in relation to money management (Xiao, 2008). It includes the behaviors regarding savings, investment, cash, credit, and insurance (Bapat, 2019).

Financial Confidence: It is associated with self-assurance, which leads to making good financial decisions in personal finance (Palameta et al., 2016).

Financial Self-Efficacy: It is the perceived ability to complete financial activities (Lapp, 2010).

Financial Socialization: It refers to acquiring and developing values, attitudes, standards, norms, knowledge, and behaviors that provide the context for one's financial practices (Danes, 1994).

Fintech: It describes the connection of modern and, mainly, Internet-related technologies with established business activities of the financial services industry (Gomber et al., 2017).

PRISMA: The Preferred Reporting Items for Systematic reviews and Meta-Analyses (PRISMA) Statement, published in 2009, was designed to help systematic reviewers transparently report why the review was done, what the authors did and what they found (Page et al., 2021).

Psychological Biases: These are systematic errors in judgment and thus, violate the principles of rational choice that prevents an individual to maximize one's utility (Kahneman & Riepe, 1998).

Self-Control: It refers to the ability to end bad habits, resist temptations, and deal effectively with impulses (Baumeister, 2002; Fujita et al., 2006).

Chapter 7
A Cross-Country Perspective on Initiatives and Strategies for Sustainable Green Finance in the UK and India

Dileep Kumar
Hensard University, Yenagoa, Nigeria

Lakshmi A. J.
TKMM College, Nangiarkulangara, India

Akhil M. P.
https://orcid.org/0000-0002-2409-0747
Narsee Monjee Institute of Management Studies, India

Abilash Unny
Price Waterhouse Coopers LLP, UK

Vinod Sharma
https://orcid.org/0000-0002-0815-8502
Symbiosis Centre for Management and Human Resource, Symbiosis International University (Deemed), Pune, India

ABSTRACT

Green finance is increasing its awareness and impact slowly but steadily across

DOI: 10.4018/979-8-3693-0863-9.ch007

the globe. As it is envisioned, green financing is a regulated, organized, and well-coordinated financial activity with fine-tuned products and services, viz., loans, debt mechanisms, and investments, that's been designed to guarantee a healthier environmental result. It is expected that the green bond market possibly will be worth \$2.36 trillion by 2023. To explore the receptivity of green financing and to understand its adoption among different countries, qualitative research was proposed with the support of interpretive philosophy. The green finance initiative scenarios from two countries were gathered through systematic literature review, case studies, and content analysis. Data extracted from the literature is analysed with proper coding and categorisation. The observations associated with two countries' analyses, viz., UK and India, clearly indicate that green financing is undeniably a vital approach that enables the shift to sustainable economic growth.

INTRODUCTION

Green finance is rapidly becoming a top focus for government policymakers. The sustainable finance concept depends on a two-dimensional spectrum that is interwoven with society and the environment. Society is confined to the environment to which it belongs for survival, and the environment itself has significant ramifications on human society (Coleton *et al.*, 2020). In both developed and developing economies, the burning issues concerning the environment are disproportionately affecting the people. Improvement of living standards of people and reduction of inequality among the people should be undertaken in a manner which is not create any kind of damage to the environment. Renewable energy, energy-efficient technology, sustainable natural resource management, green finance, and other possible sectors for economic and overall recovery have already been identified by prominent international organizations (Martinot *et al.*, 2002); (Taghizadeh-Hesary and Yoshino, 2020). Although there are major improvements in civic responsiveness and funding choices in India, high borrowing prices, false entitlements of ecological acquiescence, a multitude of green loan explanations, and maturity incongruities amongst long-term green venture and depositors' comparatively short-term interests might pose foremost issues (Freytag, 2020).

Several concepts associated with green like green bond marketplaces, enabling cross-border green bond ventures, information input on ecological perils, and refining overall green investment happenings are being identified by the Reserve Bank, in its Yearly Statement (2015-16). The central bank also shows its emphasis on issues such as the definition of green activities, intellectual property rights in progress and technology transfer from advanced nations, bank assessments of ecological risk, etc relating to sustainable finance that need to be addressed in the future. The

Reserve Bank of India underlined the risk of climate change on financial assets in its Report on 'Trend and Progress of Banking in India (2018-19)', as well as the need to expedite green finance for sustainable development of the environment. It recognizes the difficulties in the establishment of green finance initiatives, such as "greenwashing" or improper ecological acquiescence, the absence of a proper standard definition of green concepts, and maturity discrepancies of long-term and short-term green investment interests of the investors (Freytag, 2020). This calls for the creation of a proper framework and standardized policies that could promote India's green finance initiatives and green ecosystem through enhancing awareness among people.

The United Kingdom (UK) has already channeled its activities towards the reduction of emissions by 2030. In April 2021, the UK also announced a reduction of carbon emissions by 78% to be attained by the end of 2035. In tune with this target, the UK has extended its climate law in the areas of international aviation and shipping (IAS). Hence by 2050, the UK will be many ways forward towards the target to achieve net zero. Over 5 years from 2021 to 2025, the government of the UK has decided to enhance its international climate finance provision to £11.6 billion, which is a unique kind of gesture from a developed country. In addition to this, equipping developing countries capable of facing climate change challenges has also been initiated over the UK Affiliating for Accelerated Climate Transitions (UK PACT) program and the Prosperity Fund.

The UK is one of the leaders in the arena of green financing innovations. Green finance products like green bonds, Yieldcos, Green mortgages, ESG, ETF, etc. are the major contributors (Fender *et al.*, 2020). The UK is working with governments such as China, Brazil, and Mexico to create green finance markets. Considering these facts, a comprehensive evaluation of the dual-country perspective on green finance for sustainability is the need of the hour. Hence, a comparison of the green finance initiatives of a developing country, India, and a developed country, the United Kingdom (UK) is undertaken.

OBJECTIVES OF THE STUDY

The study aims to provide valuable insights into the current state of sustainable green finance in the UK and India, as well as opportunities for enhancing cooperation and driving collective action towards achieving global sustainability objectives. Thus, it undertakes the following objectives to attain:

1. To evaluate how India strategized its green initiatives and green finance initiatives as a developing nation

2. To evaluate how the United Kingdom strategized its green initiatives and green finance initiatives as a developed nation
3. To do a gap analysis on the green finance strategies of India and the UK

REVIEW OF LITERATURE

Energy consumption and greenhouse gas emissions have surged drastically in the previous two decades, posing a serious worldwide threat. Energy is considered one of the major requirements for the economic activities of both industry and households. Higher quantities of energy will inevitably be utilized as globalization advances, and carbon emissions will be the result (Shahbaz *et al.*, 2018). The advancements in the finance sector, although it was a good sign, on the other hand, contributed heavily to the deterioration of the environment (Haseeb *et al.*, 2018). Unquestionably, financial improvement is one of the guiding forces of monetary development of any economy (Borio and Disyatat, 2011); (Rajan and Zingales, 2003) and financial stableness is synonymous with economic stableness (Nasir *et al.*, 2014); (Borio and Disyatat, 2011); (Shahbaz *et al.*, 2018). Because of the recent focus on the United Nations' SDGs, the linkage between green finance and green economics is gaining popularity and attention globally. The main premise is that countries can thrive financially and economically while avoiding environmental deterioration.

The European Union's energy consumption causes greenhouse gas emissions which is approximately 8%. Following the United States' decision to quit from international climate agreement, ie Paris Agreement in 2017, the European Union has started increasing its efforts to combat climate change issues as well as addressing the issues concerning the environment (Weiland *et al.*, 2021). Green funding must be increased in the finance sector since the fact that conventional financing options may harm our ecological system (Maltais and Nykvist, 2020). Furthermore, as investors' improved awareness of the importance of green energy aspects that lead to environmental welfare, hence green finance initiatives are on the rise (Maltais and Nykvist, 2020);(Park and Kim, 2020);(Miralles-Quirós, Miralles-Quirós and Redondo-Hernández, 2019). Because sustainable company models have lower profit volatility, green financing reduces credit risk (Chen *et al.*, 2022). Borrowers with reduced credit risk entail fewer provisions regarding loan loss and requirement of capital for lenders, which aids in achieving environmental objectives (Umar *et al.*, 2021). According to research, green financial assets outperform non-green financial assets (Su *et al.*, 2022). The research has revealed that some factors restrain the investors who seek green alternatives, which requires attention to rectify (Chen *et al.*, 2022).

Alvarado and Toledo, (2017), have identified that there are three feasible routes between financial development aspects and the resulting environmental degradation. For starters, economic expansion can have an impact on environmental degradation. FDI is attracted by financial development, which promotes economic progress. Economic expansion leads to increased energy use, which causes environmental degradation (Alvarado and Toledo, 2017). In the Second route, ample credit options are available to people when there is a rising trend in the financial market which will ultimately increase purchasing power as well as increase the popularity of energy-consuming products. Consequently, if more of these things are purchased and used, pollution levels will rise (Niinimäki *et al.*, 2020). In the Third route, increased financial development leads to increased investment, which drives increased energy consumption, which contributes more to environmental degradation (Denisova, 2020); (Khan, Peng, and Li, 2019); (Adedoyin *et al.*, 2020). According to research, those countries that depend more on non-renewable energy sources experience comparatively slow-paced financial and economic progress (Panwar, Kaushik, and Kothari, 2010); (Umar *et al.*, 2021); (Taghizadeh-Hesary and Yoshino, 2020).

The Climate Conference held in Paris is a watershed moment in the global fight for environmental protection (Antal *et al.*, 2010). The popularisation of investment alternatives that promote sustainable business models will be a desirable consequence. To help achieve the aims of the Paris Climate Agreement, many experts advised integrating climate risks into portfolio management (Nüchter *et al.*, 2021); (Smit and Wandel, 2006); (Flórez Bossio, Ford and Labbé, 2019). Another important concern is the United Nations (UN) 17 Sustainable Development Goals, that are proclaimed in 2015 with a deadline of 2030 (Weiland *et al.*, 2021);(Morton, Pencheon and Squires, 2017). They address issues such as environmental conservation and poverty alleviation. As a result, the agenda of the United Nations has emphasized the necessity for developing green energy to reduce environmental pollution (Shoeibi, 2021). The COVID-19 epidemic has re-routed the SDG targets of the countries away from the planned objectives (Acuti Martellucci *et al.*, 2020); (He, Deng, and Li, 2020). As the globe struggles to bear the expenses of this catastrophe, pressure will mount to decrease environmental norms and prioritize economic growth. In this context, environmental degradation necessitates government intervention, driven by the UN's SDG and the Climate Agreement (Morton, Pencheon, and Squires, 2017).

METHODOLOGY

To explore the green initiatives and strategies of two countries, viz., the UK and India, the study followed qualitative research with an interpretive research philosophy. This paper intends to analyze the green finance initiatives and strategies of developed countries and developing countries. To fulfill this intention, two countries were chosen: the UK from the developed country category and India from the developing country category. The study follows a descriptive research method with a qualitative approach. Secondary information sources were extensively employed for undertaking the research. The published data from various sources such as websites, working papers, journals, study reports, etc. were taken and analyzed according to the study objectives.

THEORETICAL BACKGROUND

Green Finance Overview

Green finance can be described as the interlinkage of environmental, economic, and financial aspects. Green Finance is not an isolated concept. There are various related concepts such as Environmental, Social, and Governance (ESG), Sustainable development, Sustainable Finance, Climate change, Climate Finance, Responsible Investment (RI), etc.

Figure 1. Identified areas in which green finance initiatives

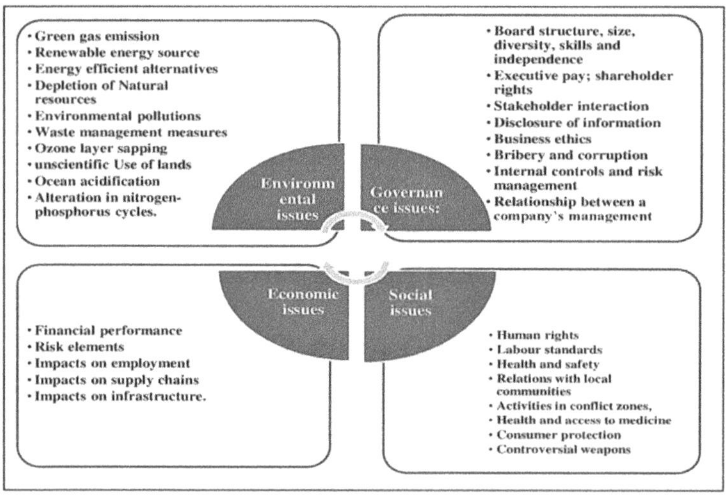

From the above figure, it is evident that the type of issues and their components that need to be addressed with prime importance. Among the same, Environmental issues such as green gas emissions, Renewable energy sources, Energy efficient alternatives, Depletion of natural resources, Environmental pollution, Waste management measures, Ozone layer sapping, unscientific use of lands, Ocean acidification, Alteration in nitrogen-phosphorus cycles, etc. are associated to the condition and operation of the environment and organic practices involving biodiversity cost.

Social issues like employment morals, healthiness, and care, relationships with resident societies, actions in conflict regions, well-being, and admittance to medication, buyer safety; contentious weaponry, etc. are related to moralities, comfort, and benefits of individuals and societies containing civil rights. The Economic issues are related to financial performance, risk elements, and impacts on employment, supply chains, and infrastructure. Here the performing zones involve immediate monetary operation and threat, and secondary effects such as out-of-work, supply chains, and providing infrastructure. The control and regulatory problems are the characteristics which are dealing with the management of investee entities. The issues related to the management include the panel structure, size, multiplicity, competencies, and freedom; managerial salary; stockholder rights; shareholder interface; revelation of data; commercial integrity; corruption; interior regulations and risk management; and, overall, matters dealing with the connection among a firm's administration, its board, its stockholders and its other stakeholders.

Figure 2. Different types of green products

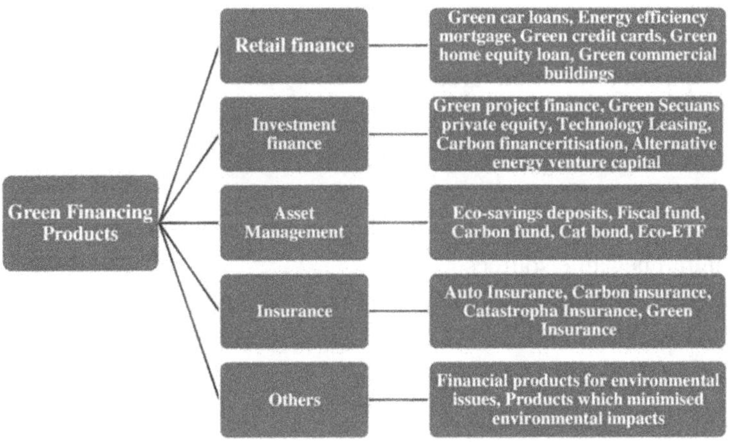

RESULTS AND DISCUSSION

Green Initiatives in India

Some of the green initiatives of India are stated as follows.

- In India, there have been several initiatives related to both fiscal and financial are in queue for implementation. The framed initiatives are in tune with the Paris Agreement and India's planned targets to reduce greenhouse gas emissions by the 2030 SDG deadline.
- The Government of India (GoI) is offering subsidized rates and incentives for the installation of rooftop solar panels to all stakeholders such as institutions, residents, and other social sectors. The rate of subsidy is 30% which might be up to 70% of the installation cost in some of the special category states. In addition, beneficiaries are eligible for a generation-based incentive of Rs.2 per unit of generation if annual generation surpasses 1100kWh1500kWh. Furthermore, if there is any excess generation of power occurs, the same could be sold at a specified rate prescribed by the government.
- In addition, between 2015 and 2019, the Government of India introduced a dual-phase Faster Adoption and Manufacturing of Hybrid and Electric Vehicles (FAME) initiative which improves the seamless flow of credit, lowers the preliminary purchase expenses of vehicles, as well as supports the development to promote green vehicle manufacturing and supply.
- In the field of renewable energy, the government implemented a Production Linked Incentive (PLI) Scheme to manufacture modules that generate high efficiency.
- In 2019, India announced that by 2030, it aims to generate 450 GW of energy through renewable sources.
- The Reserve Bank of India educates the stakeholder categories such as the general public, investors, and financial institutions on the importance, potential, and challenges of green finance. In May 2016, the Indian Renewable Energy Development Agency (IREDA), which is a government-aided organization established to boost renewable energy investments, is said to be considered the first Green Bank of India. The India Infrastructure Finance Corporation Limited (IIFCL) recently announced the creation of a special scheme for the enhancement of credit to eligible projects concerning infrastructure development with tenure ranges longer than five years.
- India pledged to achieve net-zero emissions by 2070 in the event of the COP26 brainstorming session that took place in Glasgow in 2021. In addition, India has an ambitious goal to develop 500 GW of energy from renew-

able sources by 2030 and cut carbon emissions to as low as 45 percent as part of the five-pronged "Panchamrit" pledge.

- Between 2021 and 2030, the country is intended to reduce anticipated carbon emissions by 1 billion tonnes.
- According to the Council on Energy, Environment, and Water (CEEW), achieving net zero by 2070 will necessitate investments of excess of $10 trillion. These investments would help to decarbonize different sectors in India such as industry, transportation, power, etc. According to the Council on Energy, Environment, and Water, India might be facing the challenge of investment shortage which is expected to be $3.5 trillion to achieve its net-zero goal.
- From 2018-2021, The government of India has utilized US$ 4.63 billion on hydroelectric projects for providing electricity to the rural areas of Jammu and Kashmir.
- For cleaner coal utilization, a US$ 238 million worth of 'National Mission on advanced ultra-supercritical technologies' was initiated by the Government.
- Indian Railways is also taking initiatives to attain sustainability. For this, sustainable energy-efficient steps have already been taken to reduce the emission level by 33% aimed for the year 2030.
- The Central Electricity Authority (CEA) and CEEW's Centre for Energy Finance (CEEW-CEF) in April 2021 join hands to introduce the 'India Renewables Dashboard' which gives guidelines on the status and operational information of Renewable Energy (RE) projects in the country.
- The Ministry of Power (MoP) released the draft of the National Electricity Policy (NEP) 2021 in April 2021 to invite valuable recommendations from all the stakeholders concerned to make the final NEP a sustainable-oriented one.
- Mission Innovation Clean Tech Exchange has launched at the Net-zero summit, which will establish an interconnected incubator network in all countries to boost clean energy motive.
- Indian Renewable Energy Development Agency Ltd. invited bids for the setup of solar manufacturing units under the Production Linked Incentive scheme worth US$ 616.76 million.
- To popularise the use of rooftop solar (RTS) in the country, the concerned Ministry has announced a 'Rooftop Solar Programme Phase II' in the rural areas of the country, with a planned capacity of 4,000 MW along with applicable subsidies.
- India's biggest solar park is proposed to be built at Rann of Kutch in Khavada, Gujarat with a capacity of 4750 MW. The park will be the wholly owned

subsidiary of NTPC Renewable Energy Ltd, which is the leading power generator in the country.

- In order to emphasize sustainability, the GoI has drafted new rules and regulations for the procurement and utilization of green energy. This step is to promote the extensive use of renewable sources of energy in all areas, particularly among industries and service sectors.
- In February 2022, the government of Nepal and the Government of India made a bilateral agreement to constitute a 'Joint Hydro Development Committee' to check the feasibility of hydroelectric power generation projects for mutual benefit.
- In the Union Budget 2022-23 also, the government shows it thrives towards sustainability by allocating US$ 132 million to the Solar Energy Corporation of India, which is the governing body of all the renewable energy sectors in the country. In addition, US$ 2.57 billion is allocated for the PLI scheme to manufacture more efficient solar modules in the country.

The banking sector of a country plays an important role in achieving financial and investment goals. Furthermore, banking is a sector that is directly affected by climate change, since the financial services industry is predicted to account for 72 percent of the entire potential financial effect of the change.

Financial institutions in an economy must give support to achieve the net-zero emission target of the country by enhancing their investment, particularly in green infrastructure projects (Chen *et al.*, 2022). Although it seems that banks and financial institutions may not have a crucial role in climate change directly, they do play a backend role as lenders to industries as financial institutions. Today, technology is playing an increasingly important role in the net-zero transition for a variety of industries, and it is a rapidly evolving (Volz, 2018). Electric transportation systems, energy efficient manufacturing, reduction of emissions from business sectors, provision of clean and green electricity, hydrogen fuel systems, renewable energy sources, carbon capture expansion, etc. are some of the areas that require more attention and huge financial backup to accelerate the achievement of net-zero emission target.

Green Finance Initiatives in India

India's emphasis on green finance begins in early 2007.

- Early in 2007, India started giving attention to green finance and sustainability.
- The Reserve Bank of India, in their notification in 2007 entitled "Corporate Social Responsibility, Sustainable Development, and Nonfinancial Reporting

- Role of Banks," highlighted how important are global warming and climate change issues when connected with the sustainable development concept.

- The National Action Plan on Climate Change (NAPCC) was established in 2008 with the broad objective of creating a comprehensive policy that minimizes the impact of climate change.
- The Climate Change Finance Unit (CCFU), formed in the year 2011 is an exclusive agency under the Ministry of Finance to coordinate and control various green finance institutions in the country.
- The introduction of sustainability disclosure requirements was one of the major strategic initiatives that happened in the year 2012. The Securities and Exchange Board of India (SEBI), the capital market regulator of the country, made it mandatory for the top hundred listed companies in the Bombay Stock Exchange and National Stock Exchange to submit their annual Corporate Responsibility Reports, which is updated from time to time.
- The Reserve Bank of India, being the central bank of the country has continuously promoted and supported green finance activities through their aggressive policy interventions and measures. In the year 2015, the central bank expanded its Priority Sector Lending scheme to include the renewable energy sector, which was a remarkable decision.
- SEBI established specific rules and regulations for the issue and disclosure requirements of green bonds in the year 2017.
- The Committee on Corporate Governance's Report from October 2017 recommended that there should be a director board meeting once every year to review the status and progress of strategies, budgeting, ESG compliance, risk management, performance evaluation, succession planning, etc of the company concerned.
- State Bank of India (SBI) is offering a 'Green Car Loans' scheme to purchase electric vehicles. The loan features a 20-basis point less rate of interest and a long-term repayment period compared to regular car loans.

The major products or schemes in India under the green finance category are identified as follows:

Table 1. Financial products-environmental basis

S. No	Green Products/ Schemes	Loans/ Mortgages provided
1	'Green' Savings	Vehicles converted to cleaner fuels
2	Mortgages focused on Energy efficiency	Individuals using Energy efficient strategies to cut short the cost.

continued on following page

Table 1. Continued

S. No	Green Products/ Schemes	Loans/ Mortgages provided
3	Vehicle Conversion Loans	For cleaner fuels
4	Green Technology Leasing	Leases options for implementing green technology
5	Conversion of Home to Office Loans	Creation of workspace at home
6	Loans for Community Housing	Communal housing facilities.
7	Eco-friendly Construction	Environment-friendly construction activities
8	Loans for Energy Efficiency	Improvements made with energy-efficient projects
9	Transport Finance Schemes	Packages for combined transport services, which is a cheaper mode than a private car
10	'Green' Investment	The money invested in 'Green' projects
11	'Green' Children Accounts	'Green' saving a/c for children.

Green Initiatives in the UK

Since signing the Kyoto Protocol in 1997 and the United Nations Framework Convention on Climate Change (UNFCCC) in 1992, the UK has been making efforts to combat climate change. The first major country to pass legislation promoting net-zero vision is the United Kingdom. The UK has, as part of the objective, reduced emissions by 43% since 1990, making it the G7 nation with the quickest progress in this area. The UK passed legislation enacting the Climate Change Act in 2008. The nation has also established a carbon budget to minimize emissions. The UK uses the following primary ways to gain from "greening of finance" and "financing of green":

- Bring forward the status of the UK as a worldwide center and leader intended for the green finance sector,
- Positioning the country in such a way at the forefront of financial innovations in sustainable finance and data analytics,
- Capacity building and skill development in green finance,
- Popularize the use and mainstreaming of products and services that come under green finance categories (Volz, 2018).

The UK's main goal is to develop and offer more cutting-edge financial services that propel environmental sustainability. It is a chance to catalyze the transition of the current economy to a cutting-edge green economy. To assure the accomplishment of long-term competitiveness, the nation has developed a green finance strategy that considers financial flows in the private sector as well and places an emphasis on clean, green, eco-friendly, sustainable growth. A "Green Finance Institute" has also been established, which will hasten the support, promotion, and application of the nation's green finance strategies. Another major objective was to mainstream green financing in the nation and the rest of the world.

- The UK stated in November 2020 that it will become the foremost main country to impose mandatory reporting of climate-related financial information across the economy by 2025, by the recommendations of the Task Force on Climate-related Financial Disclosures ("TCFD").
- At the G7 summit in 2021, the G7 leaders agreed to move toward requiring climate disclosures. This agreement was mediated by the UK.
- Over the Task Force on Nature-related Financial Disclosures (TNFD), the UK is likewise collaborating with international associates to support market-led accomplishments on enlightening nature-connected financial revelations.
- The UK will also put in place a green taxonomy that outlines which economic actions are ecologically maintainable to raise awareness of the ecological impact of firms' actions and investments. The Chancellor revealed the creation of the 18-member Green Technical Advisory Group (GTAG) in June 2021.
- The GTAG's work is anticipated to last for at least two years. In September 2021, it will present the government with its initial recommendations.

When brought all together, these actions will give investors a clear framework to help the government secure the low-carbon financing necessary for a net-zero economy by 2050.

Green Finance Initiatives in the UK

To boost the green finance initiatives in the UK, the government has taken major steps to implement the first Green Finance strategy published in July 2019, with three main objectives:

Strengthening the financial services industry's alignment with the UK's net-zero promise, the demand for climate change adaptation, and the UK's dedication to the recovery of flora and fauna.

- Supporting clean and robust growth by leveraging large-scale private investment.
- Assisting financial services in seizing the chance that the shift to a net-zero and environmentally friendly economy presents, solidifying the UK's leadership in green finance and ensuring that businesses stand to gain.
- The UK set forth a path for more extensive economy-wide Sustainable Disclosure Requirements and became the first G20 nation to mandate a task force on Climate-Related Financial Disclosures (TCFD) across the economy.

- The UK's green financing program will issue two sovereign green gilts for an aggregate of £16 billion, with the initial sale being the largest ever made by a sovereign.
- The world's first sovereign retail Green Savings Bond was launched by the UK.
- facilitating the creation of a framework for risk management and disclosure enabling organizations to report on risks associated with the environment. Increasing international climate finance from the UK by 50% to £11.6 billion between April 2021 and March 2026, including $3 billion for nature preservation and restoration.
- Foundation and the negotiation of the Leaders' Pledge for Nature (LPN), which includes undertakings to promote financial system incentives on a national and international level, to integrate financial flows with environmental commitments, and to take into consideration the importance of environmental protection and biodiversity.
- Collaborating on the Glasgow Leaders' Declaration on Forests and Land Use, which calls on signatories to match economic and financial flows with global targets to prevent and reverse deforestation and forest degradation by 2030.
- The new Green Finance Strategy will evaluate the country's environmental, energy security, and climate goals while also outlining how the UK can better ensure that the financial services sector is supporting those goals.
- The UK government released the Net Zero Strategy, outlining its plans to decarbonize the economy by 2050 while bolstering employment and raising living standards in the country (October 2021) After Russia's illegal invasion of Ukraine and the rise in energy prices, the UK government unveiled a new Energy Security Strategy to strengthen Britain's energy security and independence (April 2022) The UK government passed the groundbreaking Environment Act 2021, setting a statutory precedent for environmental aims like halting the loss of biodiversity (November 2021) as well as the National Adaptation Programme, which outlines the steps taken by the UK government, industry, and community to properly equip for the effects of climate change.

The UK Government Green Financing Framework

The "Green Financing Framework" developed by the UK Government is by the Green Bond Principles of ICMA in the year 2021. The four important components of the said framework are the Use of proceeds, evaluation & selection of projects, proceeds management, and the last element is Reporting. Apart from this, the HM Treasury tries to keep it in tune with the framework of the country's environmentally sustainable economic activities ("UK Taxonomy"). The main aim of the HM Treasury is to distribute whatever the proceeds raised from such as Green Gilt, Green Savings Bonds, or any other Green Finance Instruments which intend to finance or refinance the "Eligible Green Expenditures". Eligible green expenditures are those which meet the criteria of environmentally friendly that are specified in the framework. The snapshot of Eligible Green expenditure criteria is as follows:

- Eco-friendly transportation
- Renewable Energy sources
- Energy efficiency
- Prevention and control of environmental pollution
- Natural resources and living resources
- Adaptation to Climate change

As the United Kingdom's vision of a global financial system wherein the technologies need to be decarbonized that could fit to deliver a net-zero future, new sources of innovative financial models are the basic requirement for the expansion of green technologies. Undoubtedly, the fastest-growing sub-sector of low-carbon economies is the green finance sector. By tackling its international reputation and recognition as a world leader in the financial sector, the United Kingdom will stimulate the private sector for more investment in green projects and infrastructure for managing the ill effects of climate financial risks.

Table 2. Green finance products/schemes of the UK

S. No	Green Products/ Schemes	Description
1	Zero-Emission Vehicles	For providing reliable and cleaner transportation options for the households by Decarbonizing the bus fleet by the deployment of zero-emission buses
2	Renewable Heat incentives Schemes	Helps the households, businesses, the public sector, and non-profit organizations in offsetting the expenditure for the installation and running of renewable heat technologies, which include heat pumps and solar water heating.
3	Portfolio for Net-Zero Innovation	This portfolio of low-carbon technologies will decrease the costs of decarbonization and will contribute towards climate change
3	Schemes for Decarbonization of Public Sector	The main purpose of this scheme is carbon savings in public sector. In this initiative funding is given for energy effective measures and heat decarbonization measures in the public sector non-domestic buildings, that includes the NHS, Central Government Departments, Non-Departmental public bodies and the local authorities.

continued on following page

Table 2. Continued

S. No	Green Products/ Schemes	Description
4	Infrastructure for Carbon Capture, Usage and Storage (CCUS)	CCUS is the process of capturing the carbon dioxide emissions and reuse or store the same so that it will pollute the atmosphere which leads to maximizing the economic.
5	Countryside Program: Future Farming	Through this program environmentally sustainable farming is implemented to improve farm productivity and development. The schemes under these categories are the Local Nature Recovery Scheme, Sustainable Farming Incentive Scheme, and the Landscape Recovery Scheme.
6	Climate Fund Schemes	These are the schemes through which nature-based climate solutions are implemented by planting trees, restoration of Peatland etc.
7	Flood defense program	This program is developed to protect the issues due to the changing climatic conditions. Nature-based solution such as water storages which will also support the wildlife is initiated by building flood and coastal defenses.

Green Finance Initiatives in India vs. the UK

A comparison of the green initiatives taken by a developed country, the UK, and a developing country; India will give a clear snapshot of the current scenario. Hence, the products and schemes of both the countries were tabulated and the same has been linked with the UN's SDG with a planned target period of 2030 in Table 3. The broad areas like sustainable investment, Renewable Energy, Green-tec, Pollution Prevention, Climate change adoption, Green Transportation, and Natural resources & Living have been analyzed and the same is also depicted in Figure 3.

Table 3. Green finance initiatives in India vs. the UK

Sl No	Broad Areas	Green Products/ Schemes		Targets of SDG
		India	UK	
1	Sustainable investment	• Green children's accounts • Green bonds	• ESG Green funds • Green bonds	**9- Industry Innovation and Infrastructure** **12- Responsible consumption and production** # Channelize the investments towards sustainable infrastructure.

continued on following page

Table 3. Continued

Sl No	Broad Areas	Green Products/ Schemes		Targets of SDG
		India	UK	
2	Renewable Energy	• Energy-efficient mortgages & loans • Alternative fuel conversion	• The Renewable Heat Incentive Scheme • The Net Zero Innovation Portfolio	**7- Affordable clean energy** # Support the development of renewable energy through sources such as solar, hydrogen, and wind # Schemes specially for the use of renewable heat which includes processes like hydrogen heating, heat networks, and heat pumps. # Initiatives to support the energy storage systems. The means through which this process is implemented are through batteries, gravitational storage, and compressed air or liquid air. # For analyzing the commercial viability of using renewable energy technologies research and developmental activities are also initiated.
3	Green-tech	Environmental technology leasing	The Public Sector Decarbonization Scheme	**7- Affordable clean energy** **9- Industry Innovation and Infrastructure** # The schemes that support energy efficiency programmes in different sectors like the commercial, public, and industrial. # Residential energy efficiency programmes like heating, retrofit and insulation schemes are developed. # For the purpose of new energy efficient technologies, further research and development is implemented.
4	Pollution Prevention	Home office conversion loans	Carbon Capture, Usage and Storage (CCUS) Infrastructure	**12- Responsible consumption and production** # Reduction of carbon dioxide emissions and to control the greenhouse gas. # Energy/Emission-efficient waste management system must be developed so as to preserve the waste in such a way that waste reduction and waste recycling are made possible.

continued on following page

Table 3. Continued

Sl No	Broad Areas	Green Products/ Schemes		Targets of SDG
		India	UK	
5	Adoption of Climate change	Environmentally sound construction	• The Nature for Climate Fund • The flood defense programme	**13- Climate Action** # Protection of flood, resilience, and different risk mitigation programmes must be developed. # A solution of data driven climate monitoring initiative. # The activities in the area of engineering and technical consultancy should be developed in such a way that they should be dedicated to adaptation to climate change.
6	Green Transportation	Private transport finance packages	Zero-Emission Buses	**11- Sustainable cities and communities** # The transportation facilities should support low and zero-emission mobility, which includes vehicle conversion and other vehicle incentives. # Low zero-emission transportation technologies must be developed with the help of research and development.
7	Natural resources & Living	Organic farming	The Future Farming and Countryside Programme	**2- Zero Hunger** **15- Life on Land** **6- Clean water and sanitation** **14- Life below water** # Terrestrial and marine biodiversity, ecosystems, and natural capital should be protected and enhanced. # Incorporating environmentally sustainable agriculture so that land is used sustainably and the same can also be protected. # Activities such as clean water, water storage, and wastewater management initiatives that lead to environmental sustainability. # Initiatives to fund the environmental activities of public sector Arms-Length Bodies (ALBs)

Figure 3. SDG and its targets aimed

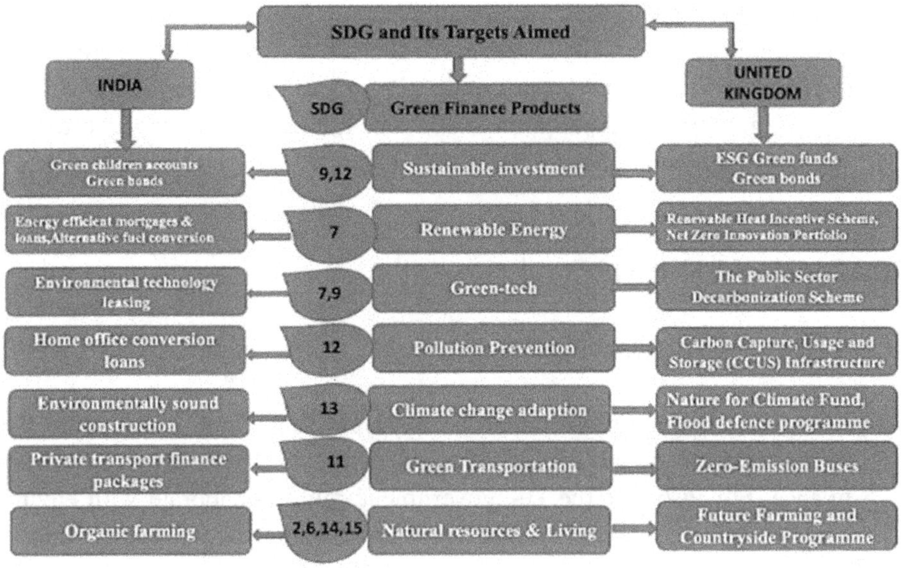

OBSERVATIONS AND FINDINGS

It is evident that the green finance initiatives in India when compared with the UK, India is far behind. The major reasons for the same are as follows:

- India faces an absence of proper rules and regulations in this regard when compared with the UK.
- As in the UK, there are no such green expenditure allocations in India
- Several green finance initiatives which are already been implemented in India are lacking proper follow-ups.
- Innovative green finance initiatives are not being addressed properly in India.
- India is lagging in taking initiatives towards attaining the targets of SDG 13-Climate Change.
- Even though the green finance initiatives in both countries are moving in the same direction, the structure and initiatives taken by the UK have a systematic and holistic approach.

- In the UK, there is a similar contribution by both governments as well as the private sector towards green finance initiatives and SDG target achievement. But in India, there exists a big gap in this regard.
- There is no proper clarity in the green finance policies and regulations. Due to this, investors are hesitant to invest in green finance avenues. Hence it is important to frame proper policies and regulations to attract the investors and smooth functioning of the scheme.

RECOMMENDATIONS

The study has come up with the following recommendations.

- **Awareness Campaigns:** Initiating awareness campaigns is essential to educate stakeholders and the public about sustainable development and green finance. For instance, the UK government could collaborate with environmental organizations to conduct workshops, webinars, and public seminars on topics such as the importance of sustainable investing, climate change mitigation, and the role of green finance in achieving environmental goals. Similarly, in India, government agencies could organize awareness drives in rural areas to educate farmers about sustainable agricultural practices and the benefits of adopting renewable energy solutions.
- **Promotion of Green Buildings:** The UK and Indian governments can incentivize the construction of green buildings through tax breaks and subsidies. For example, in the UK, local councils could offer reduced property tax rates for buildings that meet specific sustainability criteria, such as energy efficiency and use of renewable materials. Similarly, in India, municipal authorities could provide expedited approval processes and financial incentives for developers who incorporate green building practices, such as rainwater harvesting, solar panels, and efficient waste management systems, into their projects.
- **Government Participation in Green Initiatives:** Both governments can lead by example by implementing green initiatives in their operations. For instance, both the UK and Indian governments could commit to using renewable energy sources to power government buildings and vehicles, reducing carbon emissions and demonstrating their commitment to sustainability. Additionally, governments could conduct energy audits and implement energy-saving measures, such as installing LED lighting and improving insulation, to reduce energy consumption and operational costs.

- **Promotion of Renewable Energy:** Both governments can encourage the adoption of renewable energy sources by providing financial incentives and support to industries, businesses, and individuals involved in renewable energy activities. In the UK, the government could offer grants and subsidies to homeowners and businesses for installing solar panels, wind turbines, and other renewable energy systems. Similarly, in India, the government could provide low-interest loans and tax benefits to renewable energy companies and incentivize the use of clean energy technologies through feed-in tariffs and net metering schemes.
- **Promotion of Green Products:** Educational institutions can play a crucial role in nurturing sustainability consciousness among children. For example, schools in the UK could incorporate lessons on environmental conservation and sustainable living into their curriculum, teaching students about the importance of reducing waste, conserving energy, and supporting eco-friendly products. Similarly, in India, educational institutions could organize eco-awareness programs, tree-planting drives, and recycling initiatives to instill environmental values in students and encourage them to become responsible stewards of the planet.
- **Implementation of Green Initiatives:** It's essential to integrate green initiatives into administrative processes and policies at all levels of government. For instance, local councils in the UK could adopt sustainable procurement policies, prioritizing the purchase of eco-friendly products and services from suppliers with strong environmental credentials. Similarly, government agencies in India could incorporate green criteria into infrastructure projects, ensuring that environmental impact assessments are conducted, and sustainability standards are met during the planning and construction phases.

CONCLUSION

Green financing is unquestionably a crucial way to facilitate the transition to sustainable economic growth. Internalizing environmental externalities and lowering risk perceptions are the goals of green finance. To ensure transparency and long-term planning of investments flowing into environmental objectives lead to the fulfilment of SDGs, the same is promoted on a wide and economically viable scale. Achieving carbon neutrality depends heavily on using sustainable business practices. To ensure a better environmental outcome, the green finance initiatives in India and the UK have been analysed. From the analysis, it is found that both countries have taken adequate steps to bring more sustainable features and additions in the finance sector. In the initial stages, both countries have done a great job since the plans and policies are very concrete and futuristic. But when it comes to the implementation stage, India is far behind the UK due to a lack of systematic approach and proper follow-up mechanisms. The UK has a holistic approach to green financing in which the country tries for large-scale implementation of the initiatives in different sectors. However, in the case of India, this kind of sector-specific implementation is lacking. In this scenario, the successful ways and means taken by the developed countries for sustainability can be adopted and practiced by India like developing countries.

REFERENCES

Adedoyin, F., Abubakar, I., Bekun, F. V., & Sarkodie, S. A. (2020). Generation of energy and environmental-economic growth consequences: Is there any difference across transition economies? *Energy Reports*, 6, 1418–1427. 10.1016/j.egyr.2020.05.026

Alvarado, R., & Toledo, E. (2017). Environmental degradation and economic growth: Evidence for a developing country. *Environment, Development and Sustainability*, 19(4), 1205–1218. 10.1007/s10668-016-9790-y

Antal, M., & Janne, H. I. (2010). The art of the cognitive war to save the planet, *Ecological Economics, 69*(5), 937-943. Available at: https://econpapers.repec.org/RePEc:eee:ecolec:v:69:y:2010:i:5:p:937-943

Borio, C., & Disyatat, P. (2011). Global imbalances and the financial crisis: Link or no link? BIS Working Papers, 346, Bank for International Settlements. Available at: www.bis.org

Chen, J., Siddik, A. B., Zheng, G. W., Mohammad, M., & Bekhzod, S. (2022). Green Banking—Can Financial Institutions support green recovery? *Economic Analysis and Policy*, 75, 389–395. 10.1016/j.eap.2022.05.01735694019

Climate Change Committee (CCC). (2019). *Net Zero The UK's contribution to stopping global warming Committee on Climate Change*. Available at: www.theccc.org.uk/publications

Coleton, A., Brucart, M. F., Gutierrez, P., Tennier, F. L., & Moor, C. (2020). Sustainable Finance - Market Practices. EBA Staff Paper Series. https://www.eba.europa.eu/sites/default/documents/files/document_library/Sustainable%20finance%20Market%20practices.pdf

Denisova, V. (2020). Financial development and energy consumption: Evidence from Germany'. *International Journal of Energy Economics and Policy*, 10(2), 35–39. 10.32479/ijeep.8603

Fender, I., McMorrow, M., Sahakyan, V., & Zulaica, O. (2020). Reserve management and sustainability: the case for green bonds? Available at: www.bis.org

Flórez Bossio, C., Ford, J., & Labbé, D. (2019). Adaptive capacity in urban areas of developing countries'. *Climatic Change*, 157(2), 279–297. 10.1007/s10584-019-02534-2

Freytag, J. (2020). *Challenges for green finance in india. An Analysis of Deficiencies in India's Green Financial Market*. UMEA University.

Haseeb, M., Wattanapongphasuk, S., & Jermsittiparsert, K. (2019). Financial Development, Market Freedom, Political Stability, Economic Growth and CO2 Emissions: An Unexplored Nexus in ASEAN Countries. *Contemporary Economics, 13*(3), 363-375. 10.21203/rs.3.rs-843124/v1

He, F., Deng, Y., & Li, W. (2020). Coronavirus disease 2019: What we know? *Journal of Medical Virology*, 92(7), 719–725. 10.1002/jmv.2576632170865

Khan, S., Peng, Z., & Li, Y. (2019). Energy consumption, environmental degradation, economic growth and financial development in globe: Dynamic simultaneous equations panel analysis'. *Energy Reports*, 5, 1089–1102. 10.1016/j.egyr.2019.08.004

Maltais, A., & Nykvist, B. (2020). Understanding the role of green bonds in advancing sustainability'. *Journal of Sustainable Finance & Investment*, 11(3), 1–20. 10.1080/20430795.2020.1724864

Martellucci, A. C., Flaco, E. M., & Cappadona, R. (2020). SARS-CoV-2 pandemic: An overview'. *Advances in Biological Regulation*, 77, 100736. Advance online publication. 10.1016/j.jbior.2020.10073632773099

Martinot, E., Chaurey, A., Lew, D., Moreira, J. R., & Wamukonya, N. (2002). Renewable energy markets in developing countries'. *Annual Review of Energy and the Environment*, 27(1), 309–348. 10.1146/annurev.energy.27.122001.083444

Miralles-Quirós, M. M., Miralles-Quirós, J. L., & Redondo-Hernández, J. (2019). The impact of environmental, social, and governance performance on stock prices: Evidence from the banking industry'. *Corporate Social Responsibility and Environmental Management*, 26(6), 1446–1456. 10.1002/csr.1759

Morton, S., Pencheon, D., & Squires, N. (2017). Sustainable Development Goals (SDGs), and their implementation'. *British Medical Bulletin*, 124(1), 81–90. 10.1093/bmb/ldx03129069332

Nasir, N. S., Rosebery, A. S., Warren, B., & Lee, C. D. (2014). Learning as a cultural process: Achieving equity through diversity. *The Cambridge Handbook of the Learning Sciences, Second Edition*, 686–706. 10.1017/CBO9781139519526.041

Niinimäki, K., Peters, G., Dahlbo, H., Perry, P., Rissanen, T., & Gwilt, A. (2020). The environmental price of fast fashion. *Nature Reviews. Earth & Environment*, 1(4), 189–200. 10.1038/s43017-020-0039-9

Nüchter, V., Abson, D. J., von-Wehrden, H., & Engler, J.-O. (2021). The concept of resilience in recent sustainability research. *Sustainability (Basel)*, 13(5), 1–21. 10.3390/su13052735

Panwar, N. L., Kaushik, S. C., & Kothari, S. (2010). Role of renewable energy sources in environmental protection: A review. *Renewable & Sustainable Energy Reviews*, 15(3), 1513–1524. 10.1016/j.rser.2010.11.037

Park, H., & Kim, J. D. (2020). Transition towards green banking: role of financial regulators and financial institutions. *Asian Journal of Sustainability and Social Responsibility*, *5*(1), 1–25. 10.1186/s41180-020-00034-3

Rajan, R. G., & Zingales, L. (2003). The great reversals: The politics of financial development in the twentieth century. *Journal of Financial Economics*, 69(1), 5–50. 10.1016/S0304-405X(03)00125-9

Shahbaz, M., Nasir, A., & Roubaud, D. (2018). Environmental Degradation in France: The Effects of FDI, Financial Development, and Energy Innovations. *Energy Economics*, 74, 843–857. 10.1016/j.eneco.2018.07.020

Shoeibi, S. (2021). Use of clean energy and reduction of environmental pollution in developing countries. *Environmental Research, Engineering and Management*, 77(3). Advance online publication. 10.5755/j01.erem.77.3.29904

Smit, B., & Wandel, J. (2006). Adaptation, adaptive capacity and vulnerability. *Global Environmental Change*, 16(3), 282–292. 10.1016/j.gloenvcha.2006.03.008

Su, C.W., Chen, Y., Hu, J., Chang T., & Umar, M. (2022). Can the green bond market enter a new era under the fluctuation of oil price?, *Economic Research-Ekonomska Istraživanja*, 1–26. .10.1080/1331677X.2022.2077794

Taghizadeh-Hesary, F., & Yoshino, N. (2020). Sustainable solutions for green financing and investment in renewable energy projects. *Energies*, 13(4), 788. Advance online publication. 10.3390/en13040788

Umar, M., & Ji, X., & Mirza, N., & Rahat, B., (2021). The impact of resource curse on banking efficiency: Evidence from twelve oil producing countries, *Resources Policy, 72*(C). .10.1016/j.resourpol.2021.102080

Volz, U. (2018). *Fostering Green Finance For Sustainable Development In Asia.* Available at: www.adbi.org

Weiland, S., Hickmann, T., Lederer, M., Marquardt, J., & Schwindenhammer, S. (2021). The 2030 agenda for sustainable development: Transformative change through the sustainable development goals?'. *Politics and Governance*, 9(1), 90–95. 10.17645/pag.v9i1.4191

KEY TERMS AND DEFINITIONS

Climate Finance: Climate finance refers to financial flows directed toward projects, activities, and investments that support climate mitigation (reducing greenhouse gas emissions) and adaptation (building resilience to climate change impacts). It encompasses both public and private sector funding aimed at addressing climate-related challenges, such as transitioning to renewable energy sources, improving energy efficiency, implementing climate-resilient infrastructure, and supporting adaptation strategies in vulnerable communities. Climate finance plays a crucial role in facilitating the global transition to a low-carbon and climate-resilient economy, helping countries and organizations mitigate the effects of climate change and achieve sustainable development goals.

Environmental, Social, and Governance (ESG): Environmental, Social, and Governance (ESG) refers to a set of criteria used to evaluate a company's operations and performance in terms of sustainability and ethical impact. The Environmental aspect assesses how a company manages natural resources, its carbon footprint, and its initiatives for pollution control and environmental conservation. The Social component evaluates labor practices, diversity and inclusion, community engagement, and customer relations, emphasizing the company's impact on its workforce and the broader community. The Governance aspect examines corporate governance structures, ethical conduct, and transparency in reporting and decision-making. ESG criteria are increasingly used by investors to screen potential investments and by companies to measure and improve their sustainability and ethical practices.

Green Bond: A "Green Bond" is a type of fixed-income financial instrument specifically earmarked to raise funds for projects that have positive environmental benefits. The proceeds from green bonds are used to finance or refinance initiatives in areas such as renewable energy, energy efficiency, clean transportation, sustainable water management, biodiversity conservation, and climate change adaptation. Issuers of green bonds can include governments, municipalities, corporations, and financial institutions. These bonds provide investors with a way to support environmentally sustainable projects while receiving a return on their investment. Green bonds are typically certified by third-party organizations to ensure that the funds are used appropriately for green projects.

Green Children Accounts: "Green Children Accounts" are financial accounts specifically designed for children, with a focus on promoting environmentally sustainable practices and investments. These accounts may offer incentives for investing in eco-friendly initiatives, such as renewable energy projects, sustainable agriculture, and conservation efforts. The goal is to encourage young savers to learn about and support environmental sustainability from an early age. Features of green children accounts can include educational resources about environmental stewardship, investments in green bonds, and interest rates linked to sustainable financial products. By fostering an awareness of green finance, these accounts aim to instill values of environmental responsibility and financial literacy in children.

Green Financing Products: A "Green Financing Product" refers to any financial product or service designed to support environmentally sustainable projects and initiatives. These products aim to provide funding for activities that contribute to environmental conservation, energy efficiency, renewable energy development, pollution reduction, and sustainable resource management. Examples of green financing products include green bonds, green loans, green mortgages, and green investment funds. These products often come with specific criteria and certifications to ensure that the funds are used for environmentally beneficial purposes. By offering green financing products, financial institutions play a crucial role in promoting sustainable development and addressing climate change.

Green Investment: "Green Investment" refers to the allocation of capital into projects, companies, or financial instruments that are designed to generate environmental benefits alongside financial returns. This type of investment aims to support and promote sustainable practices, renewable energy, energy efficiency, pollution prevention, conservation, and other initiatives that contribute to the protection and improvement of the environment. Examples of green investments include funding for solar and wind energy projects, sustainable agriculture, green buildings, clean technology, and environmental conservation programs. By prioritizing sustainability, green investments seek to address climate change and other environmental challenges while delivering economic gains.

Green Savings: "Green Savings" refers to the financial benefits derived from adopting environmentally sustainable practices. These savings result from reducing resource consumption, enhancing energy efficiency, conserving water, minimizing waste, and utilizing renewable energy sources. By implementing such practices, individuals and organizations can lower utility bills, reduce operating costs, and achieve long-term economic and environmental sustainability.

Green Technology: "Green Technology" refers to the development and application of products, equipment, and systems used to conserve the natural environment and resources, which minimize and reduce the negative impact of human activities. This technology aims to mitigate the effects of pollution, conserve energy, promote the use of renewable energy sources, and enhance the sustainability of resources. Examples include solar panels, wind turbines, electric vehicles, energy-efficient appliances, and water purification systems. Green technology is integral to efforts in combating climate change, reducing carbon footprints, and promoting a sustainable future.

Responsible Investment: Responsible investment refers to an approach where environmental, social, and governance (ESG) factors are integrated into investment decisions, alongside financial considerations. This strategy aims to generate sustainable long-term returns while contributing to positive societal and environmental outcomes. Responsible investment involves assessing how investments impact issues such as climate change, human rights, labor standards, corporate ethics, and diversity. Investors practicing responsible investment may engage with companies to improve their ESG performance, advocate for transparency and accountability, and align their investment portfolios with their values and sustainability goals. Overall, responsible investment seeks to promote ethical practices, reduce risks, and support the transition to a more sustainable global economy.

Sustainable Development: Sustainable development refers to a development approach that meets the needs of the present without compromising the ability of future generations to meet their own needs. It involves integrating economic growth, social inclusion, and environmental protection in a balanced and holistic manner. Sustainable development aims to achieve long-term prosperity and well-being for all while preserving natural resources, biodiversity, and the ecosystems that support life on Earth. Key principles include ensuring equity and social justice, promoting environmental stewardship, and fostering economic resilience and innovation to address current challenges without compromising the future.

Sustainable Finance: Sustainable finance refers to financial services, products, and investments that integrate environmental, social, and governance (ESG) criteria into decision-making processes. This approach aims to support sustainable development goals by promoting responsible and ethical practices across economic sectors. Sustainable finance includes initiatives such as green bonds, social bonds, sustainability-linked loans, and impact investing, which channel capital toward projects and businesses that contribute positively to environmental protection, social well-being, and corporate governance standards. By aligning financial activities with sustainability principles, sustainable finance seeks to drive economic growth while addressing global challenges such as climate change, social inequality, and resource depletion.

Chapter 8
Financial Innovations in FinTech:
Unleashing the Power of Embedded Finance and AI in Firm Financing and Investment Strategies

Bhavna Taneja
https://orcid.org/0000-0002-5447-7758
Amity University, Ranchi, India

ABSTRACT

Financial technology (FinTech) has revolutionized the financial services industry, leading to the emergence of various financial innovations. Among these innovations, embedded finance has gained prominence as it integrates financial services into non-financial products and platforms. Additionally, the integration of artificial intelligence (AI) into financial processes has transformed how firms manage their financing and investment activities. This chapter provides an in-depth analysis of embedded finance and AI's impact on firm financing and investment strategies through case studies, highlighting the opportunities and challenges presented by these financial innovations.

INTRODUCTION

The financial services industry has undergone a remarkable transformation in recent years, largely driven by the rapid advancement of financial technology (Fin-Tech). FinTech encompasses a wide array of technological innovations that aim to

DOI: 10.4018/979-8-3693-0863-9.ch008

revolutionize and streamline traditional financial services. These innovations have not only disrupted the conventional banking and financial landscape but have also presented unprecedented opportunities for businesses and consumers alike.

The significance of financial innovations in reshaping traditional financial services cannot be overstated. They have addressed longstanding inefficiencies in legacy systems and brought agility to the financial sector. By harnessing cutting-edge technologies, FinTech companies have bridged gaps in financial access, especially in underserved and remote regions, empowering individuals who were previously excluded from formal financial systems.

Furthermore, financial innovations have also contributed to the rise of alternative financing mechanisms, disrupting traditional banking models. Crowdfunding platforms, digital wallets, and blockchain-based cryptocurrencies are among the key innovations that have democratized access to capital and wealth management services.

This research paper delves into two prominent financial innovations that have gained significant traction in the FinTech landscape: Embedded Finance and the integration of Artificial Intelligence (AI) technologies in financial decision-making processes. These innovations have the potential to reshape the way financial services are delivered, consumed, and utilized by individuals and businesses worldwide.

Definition and Concept of Embedded Finance

The integration of a financial service or product into the platform of a non-financial business, organization, or institution is known as embedded finance (EF) (Hensen and Kötting, 2022). In the field of financial technology (FinTech), where products that aren't related to finance smoothly merge with financial services, embedded finance is a ground-breaking idea (Kore Fusion, 2021). It is a paradigm shift that provides financial functionality directly to the user in their existing experiences, moving away from the old manner of providing financial services through stand-alone institutions. According to Smith and Wallraff (2021), embedded finance has the potential to drastically change the financial industry. Studies have shown that embedding financial services within existing ecosystems can significantly improve customer retention and engagement (Yermack, 2017). The research highlights how embedded finance facilitates greater financial inclusion, enhances customer experience, and creates new business opportunities for non-financial platforms.

The process of incorporating financial services and products into routine consumer and company operations is basically known as embedded finance (Ozil, 2023). For instance, e-commerce marketplaces, ride-hailing apps, and social media platforms now provide payment processing, lending, and insurance services directly to their users. This integration empowers businesses to offer tailored financial solutions, while consumers benefit from streamlined and convenient access to financial services without leaving the ecosystem they already engage with.

Embedded Finance represents a groundbreaking paradigm shift in the FinTech landscape. Traditionally, financial services were confined to standalone entities, such as banks or specialized financial institutions. Embedded Finance, on the other hand, integrates financial services seamlessly into non-financial products and platforms, offering customers financial functionalities within their existing experiences.

Embedded finance offers numerous benefits for both consumers and businesses. For consumers, it translates into greater convenience and a more streamlined experience, as they can conduct financial transactions within the same platform where they carry out their non-financial activities. This integrated approach also enhances financial inclusion by reaching individuals who may have limited access to traditional banking services but are actively engaged in digital ecosystems. For businesses, embedding financial services within their platforms opens new revenue streams and enhances customer engagement and loyalty. By providing value-added financial offerings, businesses can strengthen their user base and build deeper relationships with their customers. Additionally, this approach allows businesses to gather valuable financial data, enabling them to better understand their customers' financial behaviours and preferences.

While embedded finance presents exciting opportunities, it also brings forth several challenges and considerations. Regulatory compliance, data privacy, and security are critical concerns that must be addressed to ensure a trustworthy and secure environment for financial transactions. Moreover, the collaboration between non-financial and financial entities requires effective partnerships and interoperability to create a seamless and efficient user experience.

The concept of embedded finance is continuously evolving, and its applications are becoming increasingly diverse and sophisticated. As technology advances and market demand grows, more industries are likely to embrace embedded finance, leading to further innovation in the FinTech landscape. As such, understanding the dynamics and implications of embedded finance is crucial for policymakers, financial institutions, and businesses looking to capitalize on this transformative financial trend.

LITERATURE REVIEW

Research by Yang et al. (2020) provides an early exploration of the concept of embedded finance, defining it as the integration of financial services within non-financial platforms seamlessly. The authors emphasize how embedded finance blurs the lines between financial institutions and non-financial businesses, offering a more holistic customer experience. The potential of a non-financial company to integrate banking products into its platform will have a significant impact on traditional banking and the financial technology industry according to Kötting and Hensen, (2022). According to Torrance (2021), embedded finance makes it possible to include cutting-edge, reasonably priced financial services into fresh ideas and client interactions.

Ohnishi (2021) asserts that by offering convenience, embedded finance can increase non-financial enterprises' revenue, advance their primary line of business, and lead to high client retention.

Hoffman (2022) demonstrates that embedded finance can bring disparate financial and physical supply chains into alignment which will play a significant role in expanding the financing options available to trade-related small and medium-sized enterprises (SMEs) and could contribute to closing the global trade finance gap.

Advantages of Embedded Finance

Embedded finance has emerged as a powerful trend in the financial services industry, offering various advantages for consumers, businesses, and financial institutions. This literature review aims to explore the key advantages of embedded finance, highlighting its impact on customer experience, accessibility, and financial inclusion.

Enhanced Customer Experience: The integration of financial services into non-financial platforms through embedded finance has significantly improved the overall customer experience. Research by Chen (2021) found that consumers prefer streamlined and integrated financial services, and embedding financial functionalities within everyday activities aligns with their evolving preferences. For instance, mobile payment options embedded within e-commerce applications offer a seamless checkout experience, reducing friction and enhancing customer satisfaction. A study by Wagner et al. (2019) demonstrates how embedded finance simplifies payment processes within various digital platforms, making financial transactions more seamless and secure. Moreover, embedded finance provides personalized and contextually relevant financial solutions, tailored to individual user behaviors and needs. A study by Karjaluoto et al. (2021) demonstrated that embedding financial advice within budgeting and spending tracking applications resulted in increased user engagement and adherence to financial goals.

Increased Accessibility to Financial Services: Embedded finance has the potential to democratize access to financial services, making them more accessible to a broader segment of the population. Traditional banking services may be limited by physical branch locations and eligibility requirements, excluding many individuals from formal financial systems. Research by Werner et al. (2021) highlights how embedding financial services into mobile apps and digital platforms extends financial access to previously underserved and remote regions. Moreover, embedded finance enables businesses to offer financial products and services to their customers without the need for extensive financial infrastructure. This extends the reach of financial institutions and FinTech companies, allowing them to cater to previously untapped markets. Businesses can increase customer loyalty and generate new revenue streams by integrating financial services into their platforms (Chen, 2018). Embedded finance has the potential to revolutionize finance and generate US$ 7 trillion in market value by 2030, as demonstrated by Kore and Fusion (2021). They demonstrated how the move to e-commerce, the usage of APIs, and the adoption of banking as a service (BaaS) providers will propel the embedded financial revolution.

Improved Financial Inclusion: Financial inclusion is a crucial goal for policy-makers and financial institutions worldwide, and embedded finance plays a pivotal role in achieving it. The integration of financial services into digital ecosystems, particularly in emerging markets, has demonstrated positive effects on financial inclusion. A study by World Bank in 2019 shows that embedding mobile payment services in agriculture and retail platforms has enabled unbanked populations to participate in formal financial systems and access credit, insurance, and savings products. Embedded finance plays a crucial role in promoting financial inclusion by extending services to underserved populations (Buch and Goldberg, 2022). According to Torrance, (2021) embedded finance enables a company or merchant to incorporate affordable, cutting-edge financial services into client interactions by integrating banking and insurance features into the provision of non-financial services.

Additionally, embedded finance facilitates the provision of microloans and other financial products to small and medium-sized enterprises (SMEs) that were previously underserved by traditional banks. By analysing transactional data from embedded finance platforms, financial institutions gain insights into the creditworthiness of SMEs, enabling them to extend financing to these businesses says Cheng et al., (2020).

The literature on embedded finance underlines its advantages in enhancing customer experience, increasing accessibility to financial services, and promoting financial inclusion. Consumers benefit from seamless financial experiences within familiar digital platforms, while businesses gain new revenue streams and customer loyalty. Financial institutions can extend their reach and better serve underserved populations through embedded finance. Tebou et al. (2021) demonstrated that operationalizing embedded financial services will cost a lot for companies that wish to provide their clients with them. It also requires a high level of expertise to handle legal, regulatory, and compliance issues. Significant technological investment and specialized skills are also needed to operate the services at scale.

Existing Literature on the Impact of AI on Firm Financing and Investment Activities

The impact of AI on firm financing and investment activities has garnered significant attention in the academic and business communities. The existing literature reflects a growing body of research exploring the role of AI in revolutionizing financial decision-making processes.

AI in Credit Assessment and Risk Management: Advancements in artificial intelligence (AI) and machine learning have revolutionized the credit assessment and risk management processes within the financial services industry. This subsection explores the transformative impact of AI-powered algorithms on credit assessment, risk management, and default rate reduction.

- **Credit Assessment Process:** Traditionally, credit assessment relied on manual evaluations and historical data, making the process time-consuming and prone to human biases. With the integration of AI, financial institutions can now leverage vast amounts of data from multiple sources, including transactional data, social media activity, and alternative credit data. AI-powered algorithms can analyze this data in real-time, leading to more accurate and comprehensive credit evaluations. Research by Zhang et al. (2020) highlights how machine learning models can analyze vast datasets and historical credit data to make more accurate and efficient credit decisions.

AI-driven credit assessment models utilize machine learning algorithms to identify patterns and trends in the data, allowing for more precise credit risk predictions. Studies by Wang et al. (2022) demonstrate that AI-based credit scoring models outperform traditional credit scoring methods, enabling lenders to make data-driven and informed credit decisions.

- **Enhanced Risk Management**: AI's analytical capabilities enable financial institutions to improve risk management strategies significantly. By continuously monitoring and analyzing data, AI algorithms can detect early warning signals of potential credit defaults or financial distress. This proactive approach empowers lenders to take timely actions, such as adjusting credit terms or initiating debt recovery measures, to mitigate potential losses.

Furthermore, AI-driven risk management models can dynamically adapt to changing economic conditions and market trends. This adaptability allows financial institutions to respond swiftly to evolving risk landscapes, ensuring the maintenance of a robust risk management framework (Mahalakshmi et al., 2022).

- **Reducing Default Rates**: AI's ability to analyze large datasets and identify subtle patterns aids in reducing default rates in lending portfolios. . AI-driven credit scoring models have shown promise in reducing default rates and improving credit risk predictions (Cheng et al., 2021). By accurately assessing the creditworthiness of borrowers and predicting potential default risks, financial institutions can tailor credit terms and interest rates more effectively. This precision minimizes the likelihood of granting credit to high-risk borrowers, leading to lower default rates and improved loan portfolio performance (Yu et al., 2021).

Moreover, AI-powered algorithms facilitate the identification of previously overlooked creditworthy individuals, thus expanding access to credit for underserved populations. Research by Li et al. (2020) indicates that AI-based credit assessments promote financial inclusion by reaching individuals who were previously deemed too risky by conventional credit scoring methods.

AI-powered algorithms have revolutionized the credit assessment and risk management processes within the financial services industry. The integration of AI and machine learning has enabled financial institutions to make more accurate credit decisions, enhance risk management strategies, and reduce default rates. As technology continues to evolve, AI's role in credit assessment is expected to grow further, driving greater efficiency and inclusivity in the lending landscape.

AI-Driven Investment Decisions

The application of artificial intelligence (AI) in investment strategies has gained significant attention in the financial services industry. This literature review examines the utilization of AI in three key investment approaches: algorithmic trading, robo-advisors, and portfolio optimization techniques.

- **Algorithmic Trading**: Algorithmic trading, also known as algo-trading or automated trading, involves the execution of trading strategies based on predefined rules and algorithms. AI plays a crucial role in algo-trading, as machine learning models can analyze vast amounts of market data, identify patterns, and make real-time trading decisions. Research by Menkveld et al. (2019) explores how AI algorithms can analyze market data, identify patterns, and execute trades at high speeds, leading to improved market efficiency. Research by Zhang et al. (2018) demonstrates that AI-driven algorithmic trading outperforms human trading strategies in terms of speed, efficiency, and the ability to capitalize on short-term market movements. AI-powered algorithms can adapt to changing market conditions and adjust trading strategies accordingly. This adaptability allows algorithmic traders to respond swiftly to market trends, minimizing risks and capitalizing on opportunities. Studies by Cheng et al. (2023) highlight that AI-driven algorithms can significantly reduce trading errors and enhance overall portfolio performance. Studies have also examined the potential risks associated with algorithmic trading and the need for robust risk management measures (Biais et al., 2019).

- **Robo-Advisors:** Robo-advisors are digital platforms that use AI and machine learning algorithms to provide automated investment advice and portfolio management services to clients. Research by Ge et al. (2021) delves into the performance and suitability of robot-advisors for different investor profiles. These platforms consider factors such as risk tolerance, investment goals, and market conditions to construct and rebalance diversified investment portfolios. Research by Belanche et al., (2019) reveals that robo-advisors attract a broader customer base, including younger investors and those with lower investment amounts.

The use of AI in robo-advisors allows for more personalized and data-driven investment recommendations. This level of personalization enhances customer satisfaction and fosters long-term client relationships (Bhatt et al., 2022).

- **Portfolio Optimization Techniques:** AI-driven portfolio optimization techniques aim to maximize portfolio returns while minimizing risks. These techniques use complex mathematical models and machine learning algorithms to identify optimal asset allocations based on historical performance data and risk factors. Research by Leung et al. (2022) demonstrates that AI-based portfolio optimization outperforms traditional methods, achieving higher returns and lower volatility. AI-driven investment strategies have shown potential in optimizing portfolio allocations based on market trends, risk appetite, and investment goals (Zhou et al., 2020).

AI models consider multiple variables, including asset correlations, volatility, and macroeconomic indicators, to construct diversified and robust portfolios. This diversification helps investors mitigate concentration risks and achieve better risk-adjusted returns. Studies by Zhang et al. (2018) highlight that AI-based portfolio optimization leads to more stable and resilient investment strategies during market downturns.

- Sentiment Analysis and Market Sentiment: AI-driven sentiment analysis has been explored for its potential impact on financial markets. Research by Kaminski et al. (2021) examines the correlation between social media sentiment and stock market movements, suggesting that AI can offer insights into investor sentiment and market trends.

- AI and Corporate Finance Decisions: AI has also been studied in the context of corporate finance decisions, such as capital allocation, M&A, and investment planning. Research by Tang (2021) explores how AI can enhance strategic decision-making processes and improve financial performance. AI, including machine learning, natural language processing, and data analytics, has proven to be a game-changer in transforming how financial institutions manage their operations.

The use of AI in investment strategies, including algorithmic trading, robo-advisors, portfolio optimization techniques, and Corporate Finance Decisions has revolutionized the financial services industry. AI-driven approaches provide more efficient and personalized investment solutions, leading to improved portfolio performance, enhanced risk management, and better client outcomes.

Challenges and Risks of Embedded Finance

Embedded finance, while offering numerous advantages, also presents several challenges and risks that need to be carefully addressed to ensure its successful implementation. This literature review explores the key challenges and potential risks associated with embedded finance, focusing on data privacy concerns, regulatory compliance, and cybersecurity threats.

Data Privacy Concerns: One of the primary challenges of embedded finance revolves around data privacy and security. As financial services integrate into non-financial platforms, vast amounts of sensitive personal and financial data are collected and shared across different systems. Research by Zhang et al. (2020) explores the implications of data sharing in embedded finance ecosystems and emphasizes the importance of robust data protection measures. Research by Wang et al. (2021) indicates that consumers are increasingly concerned about the potential misuse of their data and the lack of transparency regarding data sharing practices in embedded finance applications.

To mitigate data privacy concerns, companies embedding financial services must implement robust data protection measures, comply with relevant data protection regulations such as GDPR or CCPA, and obtain explicit user consent for data sharing and usage. Clear and accessible privacy policies, along with user-friendly opt-out options, are crucial for building trust among consumers.

Regulatory Compliance: Embedded finance operates at the intersection of financial and non-financial sectors, making it subject to a complex web of regulatory frameworks. Ensuring regulatory compliance and maintaining transparency in embedded finance operations have been recognized as significant challenges says He et al. (2020). Ensuring compliance with multiple financial and data protection regulations is challenging for companies offering embedded finance solutions. Studies by Goel and Misra (2017) highlight the need for harmonization and standardization of regulatory guidelines to facilitate the adoption of embedded finance without compromising user protection. Studies have explored the impact on traditional banking models and the need for incumbents to adapt to the changing landscape (Kolbinger et al. 2022). Policymakers and regulatory authorities need to collaborate with industry participants to establish a balanced and comprehensive regulatory framework that fosters innovation while safeguarding consumer rights.

Cybersecurity Threats: The integration of financial services within digital ecosystems creates new opportunities for cybercriminals to exploit vulnerabilities. Embedded finance platforms become attractive targets for cyberattacks, with the potential to compromise user data, financial transactions, and system integrity. Research by Zhang et al. (2018) underscores the rising concern of cybersecurity threats in embedded finance applications.

To mitigate cybersecurity risks, businesses must implement robust security protocols, conduct regular security assessments, and invest in cybersecurity training for employees. Collaborative efforts among financial institutions, FinTech companies, and platform providers are essential to enhance cybersecurity resilience in the embedded finance ecosystem.

Embedded finance offers transformative opportunities for enhancing financial services accessibility and customer experience. However, it also poses significant challenges and risks, such as data privacy concerns, regulatory compliance, and cybersecurity threats. Addressing these challenges requires a collaborative approach involving policymakers, businesses, and technology experts.

Challenges of AI

Ethical and Regulatory Considerations

The adoption of artificial intelligence (AI) in financial decision-making processes has raised significant regulatory challenges and ethical implications. This literature review explores key concerns, including transparency, explainability, and potential bias, which have become focal points for regulators and stakeholders in the financial services industry says Ouyang et al. (2020). Regulatory bodies are increasingly focusing on the responsible use of AI in financial decision-making to prevent potential biases and discriminatory practices (Battiston 2021).

- Transparency:

Transparency is a critical regulatory consideration when deploying AI in financial decision-making. The black-box nature of certain AI models poses challenges in understanding how decisions are made, making it difficult for regulators, investors, and customers to grasp the rationale behind specific outcomes. Research by Brooks and Williams (2021) emphasizes the need for transparent AI models to build trust among stakeholders and ensure accountability.

Regulators are increasingly demanding more transparency from financial institutions regarding the use of AI algorithms. Proper documentation and reporting of AI models' functioning and data sources are vital to meet compliance requirements. Studies by Mei et al. (2023) underscore that transparent AI models enable regulators to conduct effective audits and ensure adherence to regulatory guidelines.

- Explainability:

Explainability refers to the ability to understand the reasoning behind AI-driven decisions. In financial services, explainability is crucial, as it enables customers and regulators to comprehend how AI models arrive at specific outcomes. Research by Lansiti, and Lakhani (2020) emphasizes the importance of explainable AI in the context of financial decision-making, especially when it involves sensitive matters like creditworthiness assessment or loan approvals.

Regulatory bodies are increasingly urging financial institutions to adopt explainable AI models. This approach ensures that decisions made by AI algorithms are justifiable and free from potential biases. Explainability also allows customers to challenge decisions and seek recourse in case of errors or discrepancies. However, striking a balance between model complexity and explainability remains a challenge (Rudin and Radin 2019), as more complex AI models might offer better performance but be less interpretable.

- Potential Bias:

AI algorithms are susceptible to biases present in training data, potentially leading to unfair or discriminatory outcomes. In financial decision-making, bias can affect credit assessments, loan approvals, and investment recommendations. Research by Xu et al. (2019) highlights the need for rigorous testing and monitoring of AI models to identify and address bias during the development phase.

Regulators are increasingly focusing on ensuring that AI models used in finance are free from bias and adhere to anti-discrimination laws. Financial institutions must adopt practices such as dataset diversification, bias-aware training, and ongoing model audits to mitigate potential biases (Obermeyer et al., 2019). Regulatory bodies are also encouraging the use of diverse and representative datasets to minimize bias in AI models' decision-making.

The adoption of AI in financial decision-making processes presents both regulatory challenges and ethical considerations. Transparency, explainability, and addressing potential biases are critical factors to ensure the responsible and fair use of AI in finance. Regulatory bodies are actively engaged in defining guidelines and standards to promote the ethical deployment of AI in financial services.

Financial institutions must prioritize the development of transparent and explainable AI models to build trust among stakeholders and ensure regulatory compliance. Additionally, they should continuously monitor and evaluate AI models for potential biases and take corrective actions to uphold fairness and inclusivity in financial decision-making processes. By striking the right balance between AI's transformative capabilities and regulatory and ethical requirements, the financial industry can leverage AI's potential to enhance decision-making while fostering trust and accountability among customers and investors.

The prospects of embedded finance and AI in the financial industry are bright, offering numerous opportunities for innovation and efficiency. Enhanced financial inclusion, personalized financial services, and improved risk management are just some of the benefits that these innovations bring to the financial ecosystem. However, to fully leverage these opportunities, financial institutions must overcome challenges related to data privacy, regulatory compliance, ethical AI use, and talent development. By addressing these challenges proactively, the financial industry can embrace the transformative power of embedded finance and AI to create a more inclusive, efficient, and customer-centric financial ecosystem.

Case Studies and Real-World Examples: This section presents case studies and real-world examples of firms that have successfully implemented embedded finance solutions and AI technologies in their financing and investment activities.

Case Studies of Embedded Finance

Square Inc.: Embedded Finance in Payment Solutions Square Inc., a financial technology company, has successfully implemented embedded finance in its payment solutions according to Paston and Harris (2019). Square's point-of-sale (POS) system allows small businesses to accept card payments seamlessly. By integrating financial services within its platform, Square provides merchants with access to real-time payment processing, inventory management, and analytics, all in one place. Through Square's embedded finance solutions, merchants can also access working capital loans based on their transaction history. The AI-driven credit assessment process considers transaction data and business performance, enabling Square to offer tailored financing options to small businesses that may have limited access to traditional bank loans.

PayPal and Shopify: PayPal, a leading digital payments platform, partnered with Shopify, a popular e-commerce platform, to offer embedded financial services to Shopify merchants. Byrum, (2022). Through this integration, Shopify merchants can seamlessly accept payments using PayPal, reducing checkout friction, and providing a more streamlined purchasing experience for customers. The embedded finance solution also includes access to working capital loans for eligible merchants, empowering them with additional financial resources to grow their businesses.

Uber and Uber Money: Ride-sharing giant Uber launched Uber Money, a suite of embedded financial services for its drivers and customers says Fava (2020). Through Uber Money, drivers can access real-time earnings, enabling them to instantly access their earnings after completing rides. Additionally, Uber offers cashback and rewards on purchases made through the Uber debit card, enhancing the financial experience for both drivers and riders within the Uber ecosystem.

Klarna and E-commerce Platforms: According to Casper, & Matthias, (2021), Klarna, a Swedish fintech company, has partnered with various e-commerce platforms, including Shopify, BigCommerce, and WooCommerce, to offer embedded “Buy Now, Pay Later” (BNPL) solutions. Klarna's BNPL service allows customers to split their purchases into instalments, enhancing affordability and encouraging higher order values for merchants. By embedding Klarna's financing options directly within the checkout process, e-commerce platforms can provide customers with a more flexible and convenient shopping experience.

Case Study of AI

JPMorgan Chase: AI in Credit Risk Management

JPMorgan Chase, one of the largest global banks, has implemented AI technologies to enhance credit risk management says Odinet, (2021). The bank employs AI-powered algorithms to assess creditworthiness and identify potential default risks in its loan portfolios. AI models analyze vast datasets, including transaction history, economic indicators, and market trends, to make accurate credit risk predictions. By leveraging AI in credit risk management, JPMorgan Chase has reduced default rates and improved the overall health of its lending portfolios. The use of AI enables the bank to respond swiftly to changing market conditions, ensuring proactive risk mitigation strategies.

Betterment - AI-Driven Robo-Advisors Betterment, a leading robo-advisor platform, utilizes AI-driven algorithms to offer personalized investment advice and portfolio management services say Ashok et al. (2022). The platform's AI models assess individual risk profiles, financial goals, and market conditions to construct and optimize diversified investment portfolios. Betterment's AI-based approach continuously monitors market trends and dynamically adjusts portfolio allocations to align with changing economic conditions. This ensures that investors receive timely and data-driven recommendations, leading to improved portfolio performance. Betterment's success in leveraging AI has attracted a broad customer base, including millennials and first-time investors.

Wealthfront - AI-Based Portfolio Optimization Wealthfront, an automated investment platform, uses AI-based portfolio optimization techniques to offer users diversified and personalized investment portfolios says Shanmuganathan, (2020). The platform considers various factors, including risk tolerance, investment goals, and tax implications, to construct portfolios tailored to each client's needs. Wealthfront's AI-driven approach has proven successful in delivering strong risk-adjusted returns to investors. The platform's dynamic rebalancing ensures that portfolios maintain their target allocations, optimizing performance over time.

These case studies and real-world examples highlight how firms have successfully implemented embedded finance solutions and AI technologies in their financing and investment activities. Embedded finance has enabled businesses to integrate financial services seamlessly within their platforms, enhancing customer experience, promote financial inclusion, and drive business growth. AI-driven solutions in investment strategies have led to more personalized, efficient, and data-driven decision-making, resulting in improved portfolio performance and risk management. These examples demonstrate the transformative impact of embedded finance and AI in reshaping the financial services industry and meeting evolving customer demands. As technology continues to advance, more firms are likely to adopt embedded finance and AI-driven solutions to further optimize financial processes and deliver innovative services to their customers.

Future and Opportunities of Embedded Finance and AI

The future of embedded finance and AI in the financial industry are promising, with numerous opportunities for innovation, efficiency, and enhanced customer experiences. As technology continues to advance, these innovations are expected to reshape the financial landscape in several ways.

Enhanced Financial Inclusion: Embedded finance and AI have the potential to drive greater financial inclusion by reaching underserved populations and remote regions. As digital platforms continue to proliferate, individuals who previously had limited access to formal financial services will gain opportunities to access banking, lending, and investment products seamlessly. The integration of financial services within non-financial ecosystems will bridge the financial gap, providing more individuals with the means to manage their finances and participate in the economy.

Personalized Financial Services: AI-powered algorithms enable financial institutions to offer highly personalized and tailored financial services. With access to vast amounts of customer data and real-time insights, businesses can understand their customers' preferences, risk tolerance, and financial goals more accurately. As a result, financial products and advice will be better suited to individual needs, leading to improved customer satisfaction and loyalty.

Enhanced Risk Management: AI's analytical capabilities will continue to play a vital role in risk management within the financial industry. By continuously monitoring data and market trends, financial institutions can detect and respond to potential risks swiftly. AI-driven risk models will become more sophisticated, enabling better identification of emerging risks and the implementation of proactive risk mitigation strategies. This, in turn, will enhance the resilience of financial systems and contribute to overall financial stability.

Algorithmic Trading and Investment Efficiency: The adoption of AI in algorithmic trading and robo-advisory services is expected to increase further. As AI models continue to evolve and learn from market data, their trading strategies will become more sophisticated and efficient. Algorithmic trading powered by AI will enable faster and more precise trade executions, reducing market inefficiencies and volatility. Robo-advisors, driven by AI algorithms, will offer increasingly customized investment solutions, making professional wealth management accessible to a broader audience.

CONCLUSION

This research paper delved into the transformative impact of embedded finance and AI on firm financing and investment activities within the financial services industry. Through the examination of existing literature, case studies, and real-world examples, several key findings have emerged.

Embedded finance, with its seamless integration of financial services into non-financial platforms, offers numerous advantages for consumers, businesses, and financial institutions. It enhances customer experience, increases accessibility to financial services, and promotes financial inclusion. By leveraging AI-powered algorithms, financial institutions can automate credit assessment, risk management, and investment strategies, leading to more efficient and personalized financial decision-making processes.

AI-powered technologies, such as algorithmic trading, robo-advisors, and portfolio optimization, have demonstrated their potential to improve investment outcomes, reduce risk, and enhance portfolio performance. Additionally, embedded finance and AI have opened up new opportunities for financial institutions to reach underserved populations and expand their customer base, fostering greater financial inclusion.

However, the adoption of embedded finance and AI also comes with challenges and ethical implications. Data privacy concerns, regulatory compliance, transparency, explainability, and potential biases require careful consideration. To fully leverage the benefits of embedded finance and AI, financial institutions must prioritize transparency, data protection, and ethical AI use.

As we look to the future, further research is needed to explore the long-term implications of embedded finance and AI adoption. Investigating the scalability and sustainability of these innovations, along with their effects on financial stability and systemic risk, will be crucial. Additionally, more research is needed on addressing potential biases and ethical concerns in AI-driven decision-making to ensure fairness and inclusivity in financial services.

In conclusion, embedded finance and AI are driving a paradigm shift in the financial industry, offering unprecedented opportunities for innovation and efficiency. Embracing these technologies responsibly and transparently will enable financial institutions to unlock their full potential and deliver transformative financial solutions that benefit both businesses and consumers. By addressing challenges, adhering to ethical principles, and prioritizing customer needs, the financial industry can usher in a new era of inclusive and data-driven financial services.

REFERENCES

Ashok, M., Madan, R., Joha, A., & Sivarajah, U. (2022). Ethical framework for Artificial Intelligence and Digital technologies. *International Journal of Information Management*, 62, 102433. 10.1016/j.ijinfomgt.2021.102433

Battiston, S., Dafermos, Y., & Monasterolo, I. (2021). Climate risks and financial stability. *Journal of Financial Stability*, 54, 100867. 10.1016/j.jfs.2021.100867

Belanche, D., Casaló, L. V., & Flavián, C. (2019). Artificial Intelligence in FinTech: Understanding robo-advisors adoption among customers. *Industrial Management & Data Systems*, 119(7), 1411–1430. 10.1108/IMDS-08-2018-0368

Bhatt, A., Joshipura, M., & Joshipura, N. (2022). Decoding the trinity of Fintech, digitalization and financial services: An integrated bibliometric analysis and thematic literature review approach. *Cogent Economics & Finance*, 10(1), 2114160. 10.1080/23322039.2022.2114160

Biais, B., Bisiere, C., Bouvard, M., & Casamatta, C. (2019). The blockchain folk theorem. *Review of Financial Studies*, 32(5), 1662–1715. 10.1093/rfs/hhy095

Brooks, C., & Williams, L. (2021). The impact of personality traits on attitude to financial risk. *Research in International Business and Finance*, 58, 101501. 10.1016/j.ribaf.2021.101501

Buch, C. M., & Goldberg, L. S. (2022). Complexity and riskiness of banking organizations: Evidence from the International Banking Research Network. *Journal of Banking & Finance*, 134, 106244. 10.1016/j.jbankfin.2021.106244

Byrum, J. (2022). The past, present, and future of the payment system as trusted broker and the implications for banking. *Innovative Technology at the Interface of Finance and Operations*, I, 101–151. 10.1007/978-3-030-75729-8_4

Casper, S., & Matthias, Y. (2021). *Orientation in a New World of Technology and Finance Integration*. Exploring the Concept of Embedded Lending.

Chen, Q. (2021). Stock movement prediction with financial news using contextualized embedding from bert. *arXiv preprint arXiv:2107.08721*.

Chen, Y., Wu, J., & Bu, H. (2018). Stock market embedding and prediction: A deep learning method. In *2018 15th International Conference on Service Systems and Service Management (ICSSSM)* (pp. 1-6). IEEE. 10.1109/ICSSSM.2018.8464968

Cheng, D., Yang, F., Wang, X., Zhang, Y., & Zhang, L. (2020). Knowledge graph-based event embedding framework for financial quantitative investments. In *Proceedings of the 43rd International ACM SIGIR Conference on Research and Development in Information Retrieval* (pp. 2221-2230). 10.1145/3397271.3401427

Cheng, X., Cohen, J., & Mou, J. (2023). AI-enabled technology innovation in e-commerce. *Journal of Electronic Commerce Research*, 24(1), 1–6.

Fava, D. (2022). How Embedded Finance Can Solve the Gig Economy's Retirement Planning Problem. *Journal of Financial Planning*, 35(7), 60–62.

Ge, R., Zheng, Z., Tian, X., & Liao, L. (2021). Human–robot interaction: When investors adjust the usage of robo-advisors in peer-to-peer lending. *Information Systems Research*, 32(3), 774–785. 10.1287/isre.2021.1009

Goel, P., & Misra, R. (2017). Sustainability reporting in India: Exploring sectoral differences and linkages with financial performance. *Vision (Basel)*, 21(2), 214–224. 10.1177/0972262917700996

He, X., Cui, L., & Meyer, K. E. (2020). How state and market logics influence firm strategy from within and outside? Evidence from Chinese financial intermediary firms. *Asia Pacific Journal of Management*, 1–28.

Hensen, J., & Kötting, B. (2022). From open banking to embedded finance: The essential factors for a successful digital transformation. *Journal of Digital Banking*, 6(4), 308–318. 10.69554/SRCL3482

Hoffman, C. (2022). Embedded finance: why banks are moving towards it and its impact on trade finance. *A Trade Finance Global Article*. Available at: https://Www.Tradefinanceglobal.Com/Posts/Embedded-Finance-Why-Banks-Are-Moving-Towards-It-And-Its-Impact-On-Trade-Finance/

Kamiński, M., Szymańska, C., & Nowak, J. K. (2021). Whose Tweets on COVID-19 gain the most attention: Celebrities, political, or scientific authorities? *Cyberpsychology, Behavior, and Social Networking*, 24(2), 123–128. 10.1089/cyber.2020.033632986469

Karjaluoto, H., Glavee-Geo, R., Ramdhony, D., Shaikh, A. A., & Hurpaul, A. (2021). Consumption values and mobile banking services: Understanding the urban–rural dichotomy in a developing economy. *International Journal of Bank Marketing*, 39(2), 272–293. 10.1108/IJBM-03-2020-0129

Kolbinger, F. R., Leger, S., Carstens, M., Rinner, F. M., Krell, S., Chernykh, A., . . . Speidel, S. (2022). Artificial Intelligence for context-aware surgical guidance in complex robot-assisted oncological procedures: an exploratory feasibility study. medRxiv, 2022-05. 10.1101/2022.05.02.22274561

Kore Fusion. (2021). Embedded finance: this decade's largest creator of value. *A Kore Fusion Report*. Available at: https://korefusion.com/embedded-finance-this-decades-largest-creator-of-valu/

Lansiti, M., & Lakhani, K. R. (2020). *Competing in the age of AI: Strategy and leadership when algorithms and networks run the world*. Harvard Business Press.

Leung, M. F., & Wang, J. (2022). Cardinality-constrained portfolio selection based on collaborative neurodynamic optimization. *Neural Networks*, 145, 68–79. 10.1016/j.neunet.2021.10.00734735892

Li, J., Wu, Y., & Xiao, J. J. (2020). The impact of digital finance on household consumption: Evidence from China. *Economic Modelling*, 86, 317–326. 10.1016/j.econmod.2019.09.027

Mahalakshmi, V., Kulkarni, N., Kumar, K. P., Kumar, K. S., Sree, D. N., & Durga, S. (2022). The Role of implementing Artificial Intelligence and Machine Learning Technologies in the financial services Industry for creating Competitive Intelligence. *Materials Today: Proceedings*, 56, 2252–2255. 10.1016/j.matpr.2021.11.577

Mei, A., Saxon, M., Chang, S., Lipton, Z. C., & Wang, W. Y. (2023). Users are the North Star for AI Transparency. *arXiv preprint arXiv:2303.05500*.

Menkveld, A. J., & Yueshen, B. Z. (2019). The Flash Crash: A cautionary tale about highly fragmented markets. *Management Science*, 65(10), 4470–4488. 10.1287/mnsc.2018.3040

Ni, H., Wang, S., & Cheng, P. (2021). A hybrid approach for stock trend prediction based on tweets embedding and historical prices. *World Wide Web (Bussum)*, 24(3), 849–868. 10.1007/s11280-021-00880-9

Obermeyer, Z., Powers, B., Vogeli, C., & Mullainathan, S. (2019). Dissecting racial bias in an algorithm used to manage the health of populations. *Science*, 366(6464), 447–453. 10.1126/science.aax234231649194

Odinet, C. K. (2021). Fintech Credit and the Financial Risk of AI. *Cambridge Handbook of AI and Law*.

Ohnishi, M. (2021). New Digital Financial Services Offer the Prospect of High Customer Retention–Expectations for The Growing Trend of "Embedded Finance". *A Mitsui & Co. Global Strategic Studies Institute Monthly Report.*

Ozili, P. K. (2022). Embedded finance: Assessing the benefits, use case, challenges and interest over time. *Journal of Internet and Digital Economics*, 2(2), 108–123. 10.1108/JIDE-05-2022-0014

Ozili, P. K. (2023). Assessing global interest in decentralized finance, embedded finance, open finance, ocean finance and sustainable finance. *Asian Journal of Economics and Banking*, 7(2), 197–216. 10.1108/AJEB-03-2022-0029

Ouyang, L., Zhang, Y., & Wang, Y. (2020, July). Unified graph embedding-based anomalous edge detection. In *2020 International Joint Conference on Neural Networks (IJCNN)* (pp. 1-8). IEEE.

Ozili, P. K. (2022). Embedded finance: Assessing the benefits, use case, challenges and interest over time. *Journal of Internet and Digital Economics*, 2(2), 108–123. 10.1108/JIDE-05-2022-0014

Paston, A., & Harris, M. (2019). FinTech 2.0: Software as the future of payments distribution. *Journal of Payments Strategy & Systems*, 13(3), 226–236. 10.69554/QAMX7766

Rudin, C., & Radin, J. (2019). Why are we using black box models in AI when we don't need to? A lesson from an explainable AI competition. *Harvard Data Science Review*, 1(2), 1–9. 10.1162/99608f92.5a8a3a3d

Shanmuganathan, M. (2020). Behavioural finance in an era of artificial intelligence: Longitudinal case study of robo-advisors in investment decisions. *Journal of Behavioral and Experimental Finance*, 27, 100297. 10.1016/j.jbef.2020.100297

Smith, J., & Wallraff, M. (2021). Embedded finance: this decade's largest creator of value. *Kore Fusion White Paper.*

Tang, Y. (2021). Corporate finance management in the age of ARTIFICIAL intelligence. *International Journal of Frontiers in Sociology.*

Teboul, L., & Angelos Anastasiou, A. (2021). The embedded finance journey: innovation that differentiates the customer experience. *A Goldman Sachs report on transaction banking, available at:*https://www. goldmansachs. com/what-we-do/transaction-banking/insights/baas. pdf

Torrance, S. (2021). Embedded finance: a $7 trillion game-changing opportunity for incumbents. *A Rainmaking Report, København.*

Zhao, W., Zhang, G., Yuan, G., Liu, J., Shan, H., & Zhang, S. (2020). The Study on the Text Classification for Financial News Based on Partial Information. *IEEE Access : Practical Innovations, Open Solutions*, 8, 100426–100437. 10.1109/ACCESS.2020.2997969

Wagner, T. D., Mahbub, K., Palomar, E., & Abdallah, A. E. (2019). Cyber threat intelligence sharing: Survey and research directions. *Computers & Security*, 87, 101589. 10.1016/j.cose.2019.101589

Wang, D., & Schøtt, T. (2022). Coupling between financing and innovation in a startup: Embedded in networks with investors and researchers. *The International Entrepreneurship and Management Journal*, 18(1), 327–347. 10.1007/s11365-020-00681-y

Wang, L., & Chen, J. (2021). Structure optimization of big data financial industry based on 5g network processor and embedded system. *Microprocessors and Microsystems*, 82, 103938. 10.1016/j.micpro.2021.103938

Werner, M., Wiese, M., & Maas, A. (2021). Embedding process mining into financial statement audits. *International Journal of Accounting Information Systems*, 41, 100514. 10.1016/j.accinf.2021.100514

Xu, F., Uszkoreit, H., Du, Y., Fan, W., Zhao, D., & Zhu, J. (2019). Explainable AI: A brief survey on history, research areas, approaches and challenges. *Natural Language Processing and Chinese Computing: 8th CCF International Conference, NLPCC 2019, Dunhuang, China, October 9–14, 2019Proceedings*, 8(Part II), 563–574.

Yang, R., Yu, L., Zhao, Y., Yu, H., Xu, G., Wu, Y., & Liu, Z. (2020). Big data analytics for financial Market volatility forecast based on support vector machine. *International Journal of Information Management*, 50, 452–462. 10.1016/j.ijinfomgt.2019.05.027

Yermack, D. (2017). Corporate governance and blockchains. *Review of Finance*, 21(1), 7–31.

Yu, C. H., Wu, X., Zhang, D., Chen, S., & Zhao, J. (2021). Demand for green finance: Resolving financing constraints on green innovation in China. *Energy Policy*, 153, 112255. 10.1016/j.enpol.2021.112255

Zhang, H., Zhao, Y., Wang, F., Zhang, A., Yang, P., & Shen, X. (2018, March). A new evolutionary algorithm based on MOEA/D for portfolio optimization. In *2018 Tenth International Conference on Advanced Computational Intelligence (ICACI)* (pp. 831-836). IEEE. 10.1109/ICACI.2018.8377569

Zhang, Y., Li, X., & Guo, S. (2018). Portfolio selection problems with Markowitz's mean–variance framework: A review of literature. *Fuzzy Optimization and Decision Making*, 17(2), 125–158. 10.1007/s10700-017-9266-z

Zhou, D., Hu, F., Zhu, Q., & Wang, Q. (2022). Regional allocation of renewable energy quota in China under the policy of renewable portfolio standards. *Resources, Conservation and Recycling*, 176, 105904. 10.1016/j.resconrec.2021.105904

KEY TERMS AND DEFINITIONS

Accessibility to Financial Services: Ensuring that all people and businesses, particularly marginalized communities, have fair access to basic financial services and products like credit, banking, insurance, and investing, is known as accessibility to financial services. Extending digital banking, mobile payments, microfinance, and community banking efforts are all part of improving accessibility. It tackles obstacles like cost, lack of financial understanding, and geographic restrictions. Enhanced accessibility promotes financial inclusion by enabling individuals to handle their money, save, invest, and reduce risks. Financial services may reach isolated and underprivileged regions by utilizing technology and creative business models, which will promote economic growth and decrease poverty.

AI: Artificial intelligence (AI) is the simulation of human intelligence processes by machines, especially computer systems. It includes a number of subfields, such as computer vision, robotics, natural language processing, and machine learning. AI gives systems the ability to do things like comprehend plain language, identify patterns, come to their own conclusions, and solve problems on their own. AI is used in a variety of applications, such as enhanced data analytics, driverless cars, and virtual assistants like Alexa and Siri. Artificial intelligence (AI) has the ability to completely transform industries by improving productivity, accuracy, and creativity, but it also brings up moral and societal issues including job displacement, bias, and privacy.

Credit Assessment Process: The process of assessing credit determines a borrower's capacity to repay a loan. It entails gathering and examining financial data, such as income, work status, credit history, and outstanding obligations. Creditworthiness is determined by lenders using credit ratings that are obtained from credit reports. The procedure also takes collateral, purpose, and loan amount into account. To evaluate risk, financial ratios like debt-to-income and loan-to-value are computed. Lenders can reduce default risk, set suitable interest rates, and make well-informed judgments with the support of a comprehensive credit evaluation. It guarantees ethical lending practices, safeguarding the borrower's financial stability as well as the interests of the lender.

Embedded Finance: The term "embedded finance" describes how financial services are incorporated into non-financial platforms or ecosystems, allowing loans, payments, insurance, banking, and other financial operations to be effortlessly integrated into daily activities. Through this integration, customers can directly access financial services while interacting with non-financial goods and services. Travel insurance on booking websites, buy-now-pay-later options in e-commerce, and in-app payments in ride-sharing apps are a few examples. By making financial services more widely available, embedded finance increases accessibility, boosts convenience, and broadens financial inclusion. It also creates new revenue streams for businesses and fosters deeper customer engagement. But it also presents challenges including complicated integration, data security issues, and regulatory compliance. Embedded finance is positioned to grow as customer expectations and technology both continue to progress.

Enhanced Risk Management: Using cutting-edge techniques and tools to better detect, evaluate, and reduce risks is known as enhanced risk management. This includes anticipating and monitoring potential threats through the use of machine learning, artificial intelligence, and data analytics. To speed up decision-making and response times, enhanced risk management frameworks incorporate automated controls, scenario analysis, and real-time data. Proactive contingency planning, strong compliance controls, and thorough risk assessments are also prioritized by organizations. Through the utilization of these innovations, enterprises can enhance asset safeguarding, guarantee regulatory adherence, and preserve operational robustness, ultimately cultivating a more secure and steady atmosphere for expansion and prosperity.

Financial Inclusion: Financial inclusion refers to ensuring that people and businesses have access to suitable and reasonably priced financial services and products, such as payment systems, credit, savings, and insurance. It seeks to improve livelihoods, foster economic growth, and give people more economic power Achieving financial inclusion involves reducing barriers such as geographical constraints, high costs, and lack of documentation. To reach marginalized groups, initiatives such as microfinance, mobile banking, fintech technologies, and regulatory reforms are being undertaken. Financial inclusion enhances resilience against financial shocks, promotes inclusive economic development, and helps to reduce poverty by increasing access to formal financial systems.

Financial Innovations: Financial innovations include the development and uptake of new financial services, technologies, business models, and products to increase the effectiveness and accessibility of financial systems. Peer-to-peer lending, cryptocurrencies, blockchain technology, digital payments, and robo-advisors are some of the major advances. PayPal and mobile banking/wallets are examples of digital payment platforms that improve transaction speed and convenience. Cryptocurrencies like Bitcoin are based on blockchain technology, which provides safe and decentralized transaction processes. Peer-to-peer lending websites, such as LendingClub, facilitate alternative financing by putting borrowers and lenders in direct contact. Algorithms are used by robo-advisors to provide individualized investment advice at a reduced cost. By giving underserved groups access to banking and financial services, these innovations advance financial inclusion. They also promote competition within the banking industry, increase efficiency, and lower transaction costs. However, Financial innovations present challenges, like the need to comply with regulations, cybersecurity threats, and the possibility of disrupting the market. In order to promote sustainable and equitable growth in the financial industry, it is necessary to address these difficulties with flexible regulatory frameworks and strong security measures.

Financial Services: Financial services comprise a broad spectrum of economic services offered by the finance sector, such as wealth management, banking, insurance, and investing. Deposit taking, loan issuance, payment processing, asset management, and risk management are important services. These services are made available to people, enterprises, and governments by organizations like banks, credit unions, insurance providers, and investment firms. Financial services facilitate money movement, investment, and wealth generation, all of which are critical for economic progress. They also assist with financial planning and risk management. Financial services are becoming more digitalized as a result of technological advancements, providing more accessibility, convenience, and efficiency through developments like mobile payments, fintech solutions, and online banking.

FinTech: FinTech, or financial technology, refers to the innovative use of technology to provide financial services more efficiently and effectively. Peer-to-peer lending, robo-advisors, digital payments, mobile banking, and blockchain-based cryptocurrencies are just a few of the many applications it covers. By increasing accessibility, cutting costs, and enhancing user experience, fintech companies are upending traditional financial services through the use of technologies like blockchain, big data, artificial intelligence, and cloud computing. Key examples of FinTech innovations include Peer-to-peer lending platforms like LendingClub, robo-advisors like Betterment, and mobile payment systems like PayPal and Venmo. Blockchain technology has revolutionized digital currency and transaction procedures, giving rise to cryptocurrencies like Ethereum and Bitcoin. FinTech encourages financial inclusion by boosting competition, promoting innovation, and offering services to underbanked and unbanked communities. However, it also poses challenges in regulatory compliance, cybersecurity, and data privacy, necessitating robust frameworks to ensure safe and equitable growth.

Chapter 9
Sustainable Impacts of Micro Fintech in Indonesia

Abubakar Jamilu Baita
https://orcid.org/0000-0002-4923-9763
Universitas Islam Internasional Indonesia, Indonesia

Shellvy Lukito
https://orcid.org/0009-0000-5666-5798
Universitas Islam Internasional Indonesia, Indonesia

Suhail Suhail
Universitas Islam Internasional Indonesia, Indonesia

Mamadou Salieu Jallow
Universitas Islam Internasional Indonesia, Indonesia

ABSTRACT

The chapter aims to investigate the sustainable and social impacts of micro Fintech in Indonesia. To achieve the research goal, the chapter utilized the case of Amartha Micro Fintech firm based in Indonesia. Data were collected from the annual Amartha's social accountability/sustainability reports between 2016 and 2022. The chapter employed both descriptive and SWOT analyses to evaluate the sustainable impacts of Fintech in terms of social services, financial models, empowerment of women entrepreneurs, environmental awareness campaign, as well collaboration with external partners. The results of findings revealed substantial sustainable impacts of Amartha Fintech, particularly in providing social impact services such as health and education and the empowerment of women micro entrepreneurs. In addition, it

DOI: 10.4018/979-8-3693-0863-9.ch009

has pushed its frontier in collaborating with external partners and donors in both domestic and international spheres. However, the SWOT analysis showed that the firm needs to integrate a green digital innovation framework into its business model.

1. INTRODUCTION

Generally, financial technology (Fintech) is transforming the financial landscape and stretching to the realm of sustainable development. It was observed that Fintech is less expensive, easier to use, and more transparent. This is because it increases small investors' financial access and can identify their unmet financial needs, improving financial inclusiveness (Cen & He, 2018). Likewise, financial technology firms could serve as viable options for promoting sustainable development goals (Hoang et al. 2022). More so, more businesses are becoming conscious of the need to address the rising environmental and social concerns. In fact, it is demonstrated that business decisions, that solely emphasize economic benefit without its repercussions on the local environment, frequently leave out social and environmental factors as well (Varga, 2018). Furthermore, financial technology firms are orienting businesses into environmentally responsible, as society becomes increasingly receptive to the new financial services. Therefore, new businesses (e.g. sharing economy) supported by Fintech are becoming socially and ecologically beneficial (Cen & He, 2018). They provide social impacts such as health services, education, job creation, and poverty reduction services. Despite promoting sustainable development, their environmental benefits are uncertain (Hoang et al. 2022).

Indonesia, being the largest economy in Southeast Asia, encounters a multitude of obstacles in its pursuit of sustainable development. These challenges encompass the need for greater financial inclusivity, improved access to funding for small and medium-sized businesses, and a focus on environmental sustainability. Fintech has become a formidable tool in tackling these challenges and generating positive outcomes in the nation. In 2022, the Indonesian economy is projected to reach IDR 19,588.4 trillion in terms of Gross Domestic Product (GDP) at current prices. Additionally, the GDP per capita is expected to reach IDR 71.0 million or US$4,783.9. In 2022, the Indonesian economy is projected to experience a growth rate of 5.31 percent, surpassing the 3.70 percent growth achieved in 2021 (Badan Pusat Statistik, 2023). As well, Indonesia is a rapidly developing nation with a significant population and a diverse economy. In 2022, Indonesia's population reached a staggering 275 million (Badan Pusat Statistik, 2023).

Over the past decade, there has been a significant rise in the number of Fintech companies in Indonesia. As of October 9, 2023, there are currently 101 companies licensed by the OJK in the field of Fintech peer-to-peer lending or Fintech lending

(The Financial Services Authority, 2023). This growth has been driven by the emergence of wealth-tech, Fintech-focused SaaS providers, and insurance activities, which have brought fresh and dynamic energy to the industry. By the end of 2020, the payment sector had a staggering number of over 60 million active users. Experts predict that this sector will continue to experience significant growth, with an annual growth rate of 26% expected between 2020 and 2025. Meanwhile, in the lending space, there are over 30 million active borrower accounts in the peer-to-peer (P2P) sector. In addition, the wealth segment is experiencing significant growth, with more than 9 million retail investors. There has been a significant increase in the adoption of Fintech SaaS, with a staggering six million SMEs currently utilizing SaaS platforms. This represents a 26 times increase compared to the previous three years. The growth of transaction values is quite impressive, with over US$20 billion of e-wallet transactions recorded between 2017 and 2021, showing a remarkable 123% compound annual growth rate. Between 2017 and 2022, over US$17 billion loans were disbursed, while there was a significant net asset value of over US$20 billion in wealth tech and digital trading in 2021 (Kumar et al. 2023).

Indonesia has experienced a notable increase in the adoption of Fintech and its subsequent effects on various sectors. The integration of the financial industry and financial technology (Fintech) is crucial in expanding financial services access and inclusion for the significant unbanked population in Indonesia (Setiawan et al. 2021). Indonesia's lack of specific regulations hinders the establishment of a strong legal foundation for progress in the financial industry (Sudirman & Disemadi, 2022). The Fintech industry in Indonesia has a promising potential for growth, and it is crucial to establish a strong legal framework through Indonesian Law to support its development. When it comes to Fintech, Indonesia currently lacks a dedicated law addressing this area (Kharisma, 2021). More so, business organisations push beyond the frontiers of maximizing profits and economic value creation by promoting social impact and supporting a sustainable environment. That is why Care et al. (2023) suggested developing an Impact-based Fintech model, which integrates social and environmental impacts in serving the communities. Varga (2018) noted that two parameters are crucial in assessing Fintech's social impact: 1) depth scaling by addressing environmental and social challenges, thus creating more adaptive financial products; 2) breadth scaling by broadening financial inclusiveness as well as building partnerships. In a schematic framework, Mhlanga (2022) demonstrated the link between Fintech expansion and sustainability via a reduction in climate emissions in the Fourth Industrial Era. From the foregoing discussion, the goal of the study is to assess the impact of Fintech on sustainable development, focusing on the case study of Amartha Micro Fintech in Indonesia. Thus, the chapter poses the following research questions to guide in achieving the research goal:

1. Do Amartha activities align with sustainable impacts?
2. To what extent does Amartha Fintech empower women micro entrepreneurs?
3. How sustainable are Amartha's financial business practices?
4. Does Amartha Fintech promote green digital innovation?

The outline of the chapter comprises six parts. Following the "Introduction", the other sections include "Fintech Industry in Indonesia", "Literature Review", "Methodology", "Assessment of Sustainable Impacts" and "Conclusion".

2. FINTECH INDUSTRY IN INDONESIA

The expansion of Indonesia's digital economy is linked to recent advancements in financial technology. The AFTECH AMS Report for the year of 2022/2023 provides insights into the state of the Fintech industry in Indonesia up until the third quarter of 2022. Approximately 33% of the overall capital allocated to Fintech businesses in Southeast. Singapore, the second largest recipient of money, received 43% of the total funding. Moreover, it is worth noting that the Indonesian Fintech industry continues to exhibit significant growth potential. The objective of enhancing financial inclusion. According to the World Bank assessment, up until the present day, Indonesia currently harbors a substantial population of 97.74 million adult inhabitants who have not yet attained a certain status or condition. The ability to avail oneself of banking and financial services (Asosiasi FinTech Indonesia, 2023). The ongoing technological disruptions has led to substantial expansion of digital economy in Indonesia. A group research revealed that Indonesia's digital economy reached US$77 billion in 2022, equivalent to around 5.8% of its GDP in the same year (SEA e-Conomy 2022, Google, Temasek, & Bain & Company). The projected growth is anticipated to persist until it reaches the estimated range of US$220-360 billion by the year 2030, which would represent around 9-15% of GDP in the same year. The digital economy is expected to not only see absolute growth, but also exhibit a relative gain in comparison to other sectors (Fintech Indonesia, 2022; 2023).

The expansion of the digital economy has coincided with the ongoing progression of the Fintech Industry in Indonesia. The number of registered Fintech firms has witnessed an upward trend. As a member of AFTECH, it was documented that the number of members rose to 366 in 2022, compared to 352 in 2021 and 302 by the conclusion of 2020 (Fintech Indonesia, 2022; 2023). Conversely, the internet catalyzes Indonesia towards the adoption and advancement of Digital Finance. The level of Internet penetration in Indonesia has witnessed a notable rise (Indonesia Internet Service Provider, 2023). It rose from 64.8% in 2018 to 78.20% in 2022-2023 period, representing 13.4 percentage growth.

Figure 1. Internet penetration in Indonesia

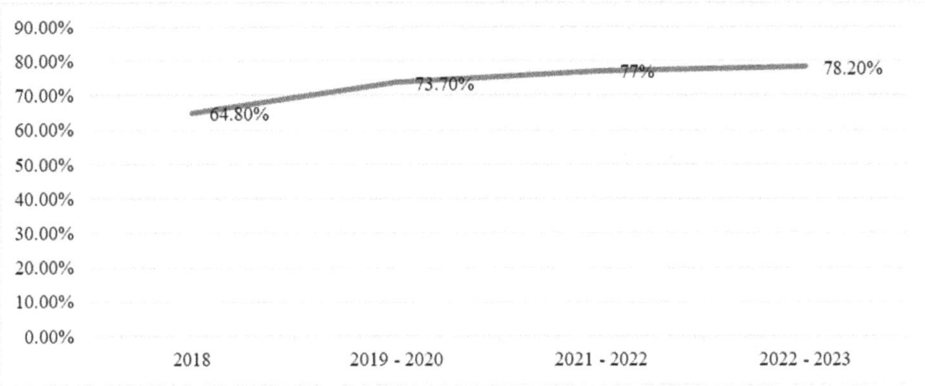

The Indonesia's Fintech industry has witnessed tremendous growth in the beginning from 2018. According to Indonesia's Fintech Lending Report, the number of borrower accounts have increased from 86 million in July 2022 to 117 million in July 2023 representing 36% growth rate. Whereas the lender accounts rose from 928,000 to 1,133,210 within the same period. The industry showed resilience in 2023 by recording 96.5% success in providing lending services to consumers within 90 days or less, while the lenders' default rate was marginally 3.5%.

In 2016, Bank Indonesia established Fintech Office in response to the emerging growth of the Fintech industry. The purpose of this platform is to serve as a forum for the examination and evaluation of risk reduction in the context of Fintech services. In order to ensure the advancement of Fintech as a disruptive force in the financial services industry, the Bank of Indonesia and the Financial Services Authority (OJK) introduced the Fintech regulatory sandbox in 2017 and 2018, respectively. The regulatory sandbox is a testing tool that allows entrepreneurs to evaluate the reliability of their products, services, and business models within a specified timeframe (Fintech Indonesia, 2022; 2023).

Figure 2. Fintech regulatory sandbox

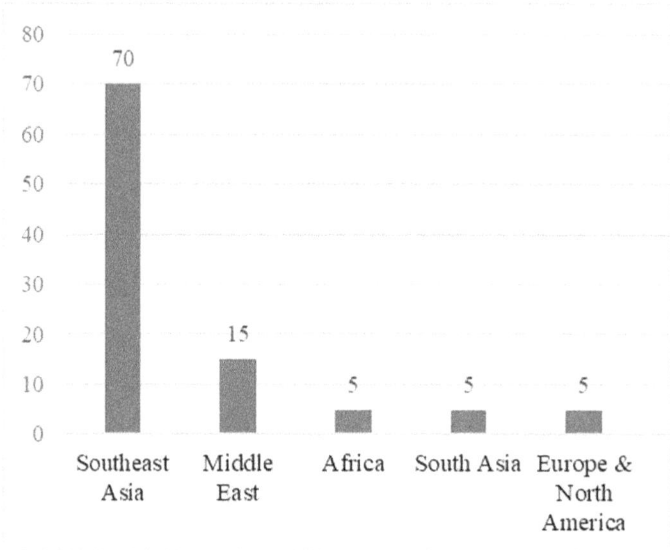

The business model cluster of Fintech firms reveals that the three dominant business models among AFTECH members are online loans, with 102 members accounting for 30.0% of the total, followed by IKD with 88 members (25.9%), and digital payments with 40 members (11.8%).

Figure 3. Business model cluster

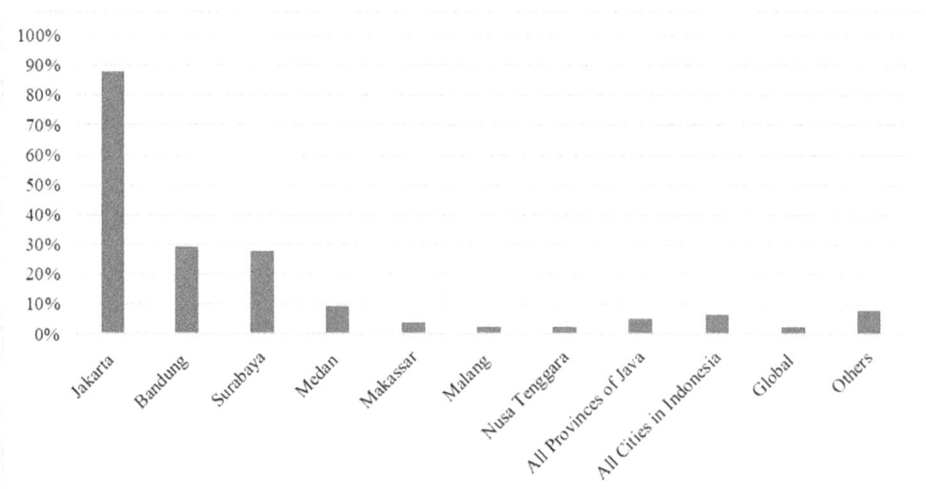

The majority of Fintech companies in Indonesia continue to focus their operations primarily on the island of Java. According to the AMS 2022/2023 report, the Fintech firms with the highest market shares are Jakarta (88.0%), Bandung (29.3%), and Surabaya (28.0%). A notable proportion of Fintech entities, namely up to 5.3%, are actively operating in various markets across the island of Java (Fintech Indonesia, 2022; 2023)

3. LITERATURE REVIEW

3.1 Theory of Triple Bottom Line (TBL) and Sustainable Financial Business Practices

Elkington (1998) introduces the concept of the triple bottom line (TBL) in business evaluation. It emphasizes that businesses should be accountable not only for financial performance but also for their social and environmental impacts. The TBL framework encompasses economic, social, and environmental dimensions, urging businesses to consider long-term sustainability, social responsibility, and ecological footprint. Elkington's work has a significant impact on sustainability discussions in business and it is widely embraced worldwide. It advocates for a balanced approach, recognizing that success is no longer solely measured by financial gains. Instead, businesses should strive for a harmonious blend of economic, social, and environmental considerations in their operations.

Elkington (2013)'s paper revolutionized corporate sustainability discourse. The TBL framework advocates for businesses to measure success not only in financial terms but also in social and environmental dimensions. Elkington argues that to be truly successful, a company must balance profits with a commitment to people and the planet. The TBL framework assesses a company's performance based on three pillars: economic, social, and environmental, providing a holistic perspective on organizational impact. Besides, Govindan (2013) underscored the significance of measuring and managing supplier sustainability performance. The fuzzy multi-criteria approach based on the TBL framework offers organizations a valuable tool for making informed decisions and promoting sustainable supply chain practices. Similarly, Vergara and Agudo (2021) explored the relationship between Fintech and sustainability by emphasizing the importance of regulation and consumer protection in the Fintech industry. It uncovered its potential in enabling sustainable financial business practices. Intuitively, the impact of Fintech from a TBL viewpoint might be much more significant from an economic and social standpoint. They have effectively broadened the provision of financial services where conventional banks fail by maintaining frequent interactions with their customers in order to discover the true needs of locales and produce customized alternatives. As a result, they may use this opportunity to strengthen their capacity for social interaction, while continually adapting to the social needs of the local community (Varga, 2018). Gimenez, et al. (2012) explored the impact of sustainable operations on the TBL framework. The authors argued that integrating sustainability into operations management practices could lead to improved overall performance and contribute to the achievement of sustainable development goals.

Accordingly, Varga (2018) proposes a TBL Impact Analysis Framework for Fintech Companies and highlights the importance of partnerships and stakeholder management. The research also focused on the Bottom of the Pyramid (BoP) social group, which faces critical economic, social, and environmental issues with limited access to financial services. The author analysed over a hundred Fintech companies that impact the BoP and grouped them into domains based on the Fintech business model categories. Existing frameworks for assessing the TBL of financial institutions were found to have limitations, as they were designed for large financial institutions and did not consider factors such as social scaling and financial inclusion. These frameworks also often excluded indirect factors like dynamic capabilities, innovation, and human resources. Overall, the research emphasized the need for a lightweight TBL Impact Analysis Framework for Fintech. Such a framework would allow operating ventures to assess their current business practices, guide companies in integrating TBL perspectives into their operations, and provide a basis for structured reporting and investment decisions.

Hamidi and Worthington (2021) introduced a novel extension to the conventional triple bottom line framework, which encompasses Prosperity, People, and Planet (commonly referred to as the 3Ps), by incorporating a fourth dimension, Prophet. This addition is aimed at aligning banking practices with Islamic principles, thus forming the 4Ps model. The study involves a comprehensive survey of 504 stakeholders within Islamic banks across six provinces in Indonesia. Through regression analysis, the applicability of the 4Ps framework is evaluated. Additionally, the research delved into its implementation within two prominent Islamic banks located in Indonesia and Malaysia. The findings of demonstrated the significance of the models, effectively capturing a broad spectrum of stakeholder perspectives on bank performance. Among the four elements, Prosperity emerges as the highest priority according to stakeholders, followed by Prophet and then Planet. From a practical standpoint, this quadruple bottom line framework offered valuable utility for practitioners in evaluating organizational performance.

3.2 Empirical Literature Review

3.2.1 Fintech and Sustainable Impacts

Recent empirical evidences document the role of financial technology in facilitating sustainable impacts. Care et al. (2023) examined the effect of Fintech in driving sustainable social and environmental development using multiple case studies. The researchers showed that Fintech firms contribute to sustainable development by upscaling social and environmental impacts. Specifically, they support education, track sustainable impact metrics and promote partnership to expand the social benefits to the underserved communities. Hoang et al. (2022) explored the potential of Fintech in achieving the Sustainable Development Goals (SDGs). It discusses the role of digital finance, mobile technology, blockchain, big data, and artificial intelligence in promoting inclusive and sustainable growth. The review also highlights the challenges and risks associated with these technologies and provides references to relevant studies in the field.

Jamil and Abu Seman (2019) examined the talent shortage in the Islamic Fintech industry in Malaysia and proposed strategies to address it. The study suggested educational interventions, incubators and extra-curricular events, and government and policy interventions as potential solutions. It emphasized the need for collaboration between stakeholders to improve Islamic Fintech education and talent in Malaysia. The paper concluded by highlighting the opportunities for improvement within the country's Fintech ecosystem. Shin and Choi (2019) examined the feasibility of Fintech as a platform for sustainable economic growth in Korea. The study analyses the economic performance of Fintech using various methodologies and finds that it has a strong effect on production inducement and industry linkage. However, the industry faces regulatory challenges in Korea. The study concludes by suggesting the need for regulatory reforms to promote innovation and inclusive economic growth. Deng et al. (2019) examined the connection between Fintech and sustainable development in China, and found nonlinear relationship with initial positive effect, but turning negative beyond certain level.

Furthermore, Fintech firms are critical enablers of financial inclusion for the poor. As Nuryitamawan (2023) observes, Islamic Fintech minimises transaction cost, mitigates information inequality, facilitates access to e-commerce platform for the rural households and ensures the poor are financially included. Besides, Islamic Fintech requires a better regulatory framework to enable Fintech companies operate in a conducive and secure business environment to ensure a sustainable socioeconomic development in Indonesia. Mhlanga (2022) explained that Fintech facilitates access to microcredit, engender saving habit and provide insurance to the clients, thereby making clean energy resources affordable. This helps in improving the environmental quality and abating pollution. The author further proposed promoting programs, which expand customers' ability to use resource-efficient manufacturing and consumption. Varga (2017) explained the potential of Fintech companies in promoting sustainable development. The author discussed the role of Fintech in filling the financial needs of underserved populations, particularly those at the bottom of the pyramid. The research highlighted the use of human-centred design in driving innovation in the financial sector. It also emphasized the potential positive effects of Fintech on individuals who lacked access to financial services. The paper concluded by highlighting the significant impact of Fintech on financial inclusion. A related study by Fersi et al. (2023) analysed the effect of digitalised microfinance institutions (MFIs) in achieving sustainable development and financial inclusion. The study covered 387 MFIs (including 80 Micro Fintech) in 69 countries between 2005 and 2019. The findings indicated that, Micro Fintech have advantage in terms of social efficiency compare to MFIs. However, they are weak in terms of operational efficiency when compared to MFIs that do not provide Fintech services. The authors argued that, MFIs being better in terms of social efficiency denotes that they are socially oriented especially in ensuring financial inclusion of the poor to enhance wellbeing and sustainable development.

In similar vein, Ozili (2020) analysed how digital financial services facilitate the participation of the poor people into the financial sector. He explained the influence of technological firms in convincing governments to discourage large physical cash transactions. As a result, the government imposed charges on people who make bulk cash withdrawals to encourage the adoption of digital platforms including Fintech services. In order to improve financial inclusion, the author suggested that governments should encourage private sectors to use Fintech services when paying the salaries of their employees. However, Ozili (2020) highlighted that poor people were not so interested in digital technology, as they struggled to provide meals to feed their families. Therefore, the development of Fintech as well as its affordability to the poor was a good improvement, although, there was no hope that the poor would be willing to use it. Among the challenges preventing the poor from adopting Fintech services were lack of internet connectivity, economical barriers, digital illiteracy, trust issues and transfer of risk to customers (Gupta & Kiran, 2023; Ozili, 2020).

3.2.2 Fintech and Women Financial Empowerment

Fintech can serve as an institution for women financial empowerment. Wahbi et al. (2023) investigated whether female choice of adopting digital Fintech products and conventional loans varies from that of men in Madagascar. The study highlighted that, digital finance through mobile banking help to accelerating financial inclusion especially the financially excluded rural women. Again, the study indicated that, microfinance institutions focused more on granting loans to women due to their trustworthiness and efficiency in repaying the loan as well as its positive spillover societal impact when women were granted loans. Thus, the results of the study revealed that, women were more preferred for both conventional and digital Fintech products and services than male in Madagascar. In addition, the preference for digital loan and conventional features differed but the variations were indeed low in the aspect of repayment condition. Likewise, Rani and Kumar (2023) compared women and men behavioural intention in the usage of Fintech in Haryana, India. The study highlighted that; the development of the technology has given a new dimension in the operational activities of the financial sector. Hence, resulted in development of the Fintech services, which enhanced operational activities of the financial sector as well as improved financial inclusion through mobile banking, P2P lending and quick response code (QR). The results found that perceived usefulness and ease of use have significantly affected attitude and behavioural intention of men and women toward using digital financial services. In addition, the results indicated that perceived value immensely drive behavioural intention towards the adaptation of Fintech services, whereas, perceive risk did the opposite. Besides, the results showed that attitude and behavioural intention have a significant impact in adopting Fintech for both men and women.

Similarly, Pal et al. (2021) revealed that women that take part in financial decision-making processes at household level were more financially inclusive. The researchers noted that female recipients of social welfare programs have high financial inclusion, as they need bank account to access their funds. Thus, the authors suggested that financial inclusion enhanced women empowerment. Again, Hasan et al. (2022) found that digital financial literacy was crucial driver for women's financial inclusion and financial empowerment. Furthermore, Moghadam and Karami (2023) examined the impact of financial inclusion through Fintech on women financial empowerment. They found that Fintech financial inclusion significantly enhanced women financial empowerment in countries with low gender discrimination. They observed that Fintech improved women access to finance through mobile banking and web-based services and support growth and development in countries with low gender discrimination. On the other hand, the study revealed that financial inclusion through Fintech has no significant effect on women financial empowerment for countries that have high gender discrimination. Thus, the authors argued that gender disparity was a hindrance to women financial independence. Moreover, Hasan et al. (2022) acknowledged that introduction of digital financial services has helped poor and rural households access financial services as well as enhance financial inclusion.

3.2.3 Fintech and Green Digital Innovation

There is intersection between digital solution and sustainable innovation (Mhlanga, 2022). Indrawati et al. (2023) surveyed 225 Indonesian food-based rural SMEs to determine the effects of drivers of green innovation adoption. The findings established that organisational factors has the highest significant positive explanatory power in predicting green innovation adoption. Organisation factors composed of sustainable human capital, management support and environmental literacy. These factors collectively make substantially contribution in promoting the adoption of green innovation. Besides, technology and environment are critical factors that push forward green innovation by SMEs. The authors highlighted the need for exploring consumers' behaviour in promoting the adoption of green innovation. Again, Ashta (2023) stated that the literature on green Fintech is still limited, but research has started to explore the potential of using blockchain technology. Some studies suggest that Fintech firms can improve sustainability performance by increasing green financing and investments. However, more research is needed to understand the actions Fintech firms take to promote environmental sustainability. Xu and Liu (2023) examined Chinese listed companies between 2001 and 2021, and found significant positive connection between digital transformation and green innovation.

Likewise, Pawlowska et al. (2022) revealed that Fintech platforms help to accelerate green finance by offering green bonds which help to reduce environmental degradation, and address climate change. The authors further highlighted that Fintech reduce operational cost compare to traditional banks and provide access to finance to wider group of people at a larger coverage, which makes it possible for the less privilege people to have access to finance at a lower cost, as a result it ensures countries attain sustainable economic growth. However, the authors noted that, Fintech also has a negative effect on the environment and this mainly due to the development of technologies that are harmful and causing pollution to the environment but they stressed that the advantage of using Fintech for sustainable development outweigh the negative effects it causes in the environment. Farahani et al. (2022) provided insights into the role of Fintech and AI in achieving sustainable development goals and mitigating the negative effects of COVID-19. It explores the impact of Fintech and Artificial Intelligence (AI) on COVID-19 and Sustainable Development Goals (SDGs). It highlights the potential of Fintech and AI in achieving SDGs and mitigating the negative effects of COVID-19, discuss topics such as digitalization, green finance, climate change, and the role of AI in sustainable development. They emphasize the need for a comprehensive approach that combines Fintech, AI, and green finance for sustainable development. Cen and He (2018) explored the potential of Fintech in supporting green finance and promoting sustainable development by reducing costs, addressing information asymmetry, and encouraging practical sustainable lifestyles. They cited case of example of Ant Forest Fintech that promotes tree planting and environmental awareness. Overall, the authors emphasized the need to develop Fintech and green finance together to address climate change and achieve sustainable development.

4. METHODOLOGY

The researchers utilised case study method to achieve the goals of the research. The chapter adopted Amartha Micro Fintech as the case study. In order to analyse the sustainable impacts of Amartha, the study collected annual reports on Social Accountability/Sustainability reports between 2016 and 2022. Descriptive statistics and data visualisations were employed to analyses the trend and extent of sustainable economic, environmental and social activities. More so, the study conducted interview with Amartha's Head of Impact Reporting and Sustainability Unit. The information gathered focused mainly on the sustainable digital activities. As such, the responses were summarised and presented in tabular form under section 5.3 "Sustainable Digital Innovation". Besides, the research adopted strength, weakness, opportunities, and threats (SWOT) analysis to assess the core areas where the Fintech should focus to improve their financial and sustainable services. SWOT analysis is a well-established tool and utilized for strategic planning (Puyt et al., 2023; Phadermrod et al. 2019). Albert Humphrey at Stanford Research Institute developed the concept in the 1960s (Madsen, 2016) by analysing Fortune 500 companies in order to create a fresh approach to change management and control. To address the challenges arising within a company, there was a need for thorough research by developing efficient and effective strategies, which could solve these issues. Several factors need to be taken into account when making decisions, (David & Fred as cited in Munandar, 2014):

1. Strengths (S)

Strengths refer to the resources, skills, or advantages that a company possesses in relation to its competitors and the market needs it can fulfill. Strength is a unique competition that gives the company a competitive edge in the market.

2. Weakness (W)

Weaknesses refer to limitations or shortcomings in resources, power, skills, and capabilities that can hinder company performance. These limitations, such as inadequate facilities, limited resources, financial constraints, weak management abilities, and insufficient marketing skills, can pose challenges for a company.

3. Opportunities (O)

Opportunities are valuable and advantageous situations in the Company environment. Key trends to consider include the potential for technological advancements and improvements, as well as the dynamics between companies and their buyers or suppliers. It is also important to have a comprehensive understanding of the various opportunities available to the company.

4. Threat (T)

An important unfavourable situation in a company environment is a threat. Challenges pose significant obstacles to the company's current or desired position. The presence of new or updated government regulations can pose a potential challenge to a company's success, as it introduces a unique form of competition that can potentially give the company an advantage in the market.

In order to conduct a more thorough analysis of the SWOT, it is crucial to consider both external and internal factors as integral components of the analysis. The SWOT matrix provides a comprehensive analysis of the company's internal strengths and weaknesses, as well as the external opportunities and threats it faces. The SWOT matrix will greatly facilitate the formulation of different strategies. In order to achieve success, it is crucial to focus on utilizing strengths, addressing weaknesses, capitalizing on opportunities, and overcoming threats. By analysing the SWOT matrix, you can identify four distinct groups of alternative strategies: SO strategies, ST strategies, WO strategies, and WT strategies (Rangkuti, 2004). The SWOT matrix provides a clear illustration of how the company can align its strengths and weaknesses with external opportunities and threats. Kearns (1992) developed SWOT matrix as a method for analysing strengths, weaknesses, opportunities, and threats. This matrix provides a concise summary of the key factors to consider when evaluating a business as presented in Table 1.

Table 1. Analytical framework for SWOT analysis

IFAS EFAS	Strengths (S) Lists all strengths possessed	Weakness (W) List all weaknesses
Opportunities (O) List all identifiable opportunities	SO Strategy: A strategy that uses strengths to exploit opportunities	WO Strategy: A strategy that minimizes weaknesses to take advantage of opportunities
Threats (T) Lists all identifiable threats	ST Strategy: A strategy that uses force to overcome threats	WT Strategy: A strategy that minimizes weaknesses to avoid threats

Source: Kearns (1992)

IFAS (internal strategic factory analysis summary) is required for the project. Put simply, a company's internal strategic factors are organised to create internal factors within the framework of strengths and weakness. Meanwhile, EFAS (external strategic factory analysis summary) in other words, the external strategic factors of a company are compiled to formulate external factors in the framework of opportunities and threats

After obtaining the results from the IFAS and EFAS matrices, the subsequent task involves identifying the strategic position within the SWOT quadrant. Here are the different quadrants in the SWOT analysis:

Figure 4. Results from IFAS and EFAS matrices

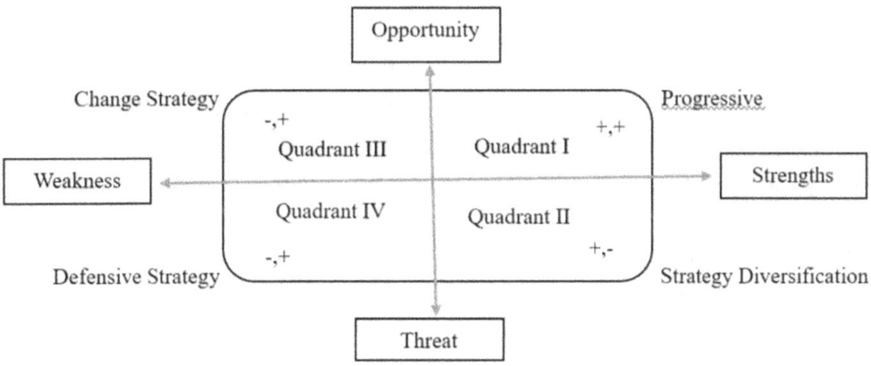

Quadrant 1: *This is an extremely lucrative scenario. The company capitalises on its current strengths and opportunities. In this condition, strategies are favourable for implementing aggressive growth policies (Growth Oriented Strategy).*

Quadrant 2: *Despite encountering numerous challenges, the company continues to demonstrate resilience and internal fortitude. Hence, it leverages strengths to capitalise on future prospects through a well-planned diversification strategy (product/market).*

Quadrant 3: *The company has significant market opportunity ahead, but it encounters various internal obstacles and weaknesses. The primary objective of this approach is to address the company's internal issues effectively, enabling it to capitalise on favourable market conditions.*

Quadrant 4: *This is a highly challenging situation as the company confronts numerous internal challenges and vulnerabilities.*

4.1 Overview of Amartha Micro Fintech

Amartha, established in 2010 as a microfinance, converted to a financial technology firm in 2016. The company allocates 70% of its financing to women microentrepreneurs in rural areas outside the Java Province and other underserved regions. It provides financial services across multiple sectors including trade, agriculture, water and sanitation, health, education, and housing. As a condition for membership, a woman entrepreneur must have a minimum of Rp. 1.5 million to be a member of a group. Each group consists of 15 to 20 persons before they could access loans. In the event of a member's default, the group members are collectively responsible for the loan repayment. In respect of new group, the initial loan is channelled to finance family education, provision of healthcare or improving the household. However, the subsequent loans would finance business working capital.

Currently, Amartha is expanding its reach as a technology company, aiming to create a comprehensive microfinance ecosystem that seamlessly integrates with the fast-growing digital economy. This includes providing capital, investment, and payment services. Amartha contributes to the growth of the lower pyramid economy by enhancing the competitiveness of micro and small entrepreneurship. By adopting this approach, we are able to support a greater number of women MSMEs, generate employment opportunities, and foster a more inclusive form of economic growth. With its mission of promoting fair and inclusive economic growth through the development of digital financial infrastructure for the grassroots economy. As we investigated the company's website, we found that micro, small and medium enterprises (MSMEs) by providing four types of loans services. These include Group Loans, Paylater, Working Capital Loans and Multipurpose Loan (Amartha, 2023). In Group Loan, the members must be between 15 and 20 individuals before they could access the loan. Paylater finances clients' daily transactions up to a maximum of Rp. 500,000. Working Capital Loan provides financing for business capital needs without recourse to collateral. Finally, Multipurpose Loan is an individual loan scheme, which caters for individual multiple needs.

Amartha, also, has a collaborative partnership with various international organisations such the International Finance Corporation (IFC), the World Bank, and the Australian Department of Foreign Affairs and Trade in order to promote the company's sustainable development activities in Indonesia. Amartha published a Sustainability Report starting from 2016 when it transformed into Micro Fintech. Therefore, the chapter gathers, arranges, and synthesizes data from the Sustainability Reports to draw insights on the impact of the case study firm in driving sustainable development in Indonesia. This will ensure the quality and reliability of the documents as the reports are externally audited and certified, which is in line with the existing Financial Regulations in Indonesia.

5. ASSESSMENT OF SUSTAINABLE IMPACTS

5.1 Evaluating Amartha Sustainable Impact Activities

In its bid to provide environmental, social and governance (ESG) impact, the firm initiated Amartha Lestari, Amartha Madani and Amartha Bestari. The goal of the initiatives was to empower the vulnerable individuals, particularly women and the underserved communities. Some of the impact projects under ESG initiative include "Mangrove Planting", "Light the Village", "Amartha Cendekia Scholarship", "Digital Village", and "Public Service Donation". Firstly, "Mangrove Planting" in 2022 where Amartha, in collaboration with Blueforest planted 4,000 mangrove trees covering 2 hectares in South Sulawesi. It plans to expand the environmental conservation project by covering 70 hectares of land in the year 2026. Secondly, "Light the Village" provided green solar energy in Sumatra. It contributed 500 solar-powered lamps and 35 extra street lamps to 2 remote villages in South Sumatra (https://amartha.com/en/impact/).

Thirdly, under "Local Heroes Award" program, Amartha selects and awards resilient and innovative women entrepreneurs in the rural areas. The awards consist of monetary awards and household electronics. Fourthly, "Amartha Cendekia Scholarship" aims to eliminate educational inequality among the underprivileged youth, with sole focus on women. In 2022, Amartha has successfully awarded 30 scholarship to high school female students. The program is continued in 2023 though the number of beneficiaries is yet to be readily. Fifthly, "Digital Village" provides rural dwellers with free WiFi access points to improve business efficiency and facilitate digital learning activities for the rural children. Three villages (Balaesang, Donggala, and Central Sulawesi) have benefitted from the program. Sixthly, it initiated "Public Service Donation" to assist rural communities by providing social assistance such as free gas stove, milk packages, and other essential services.

Furthermore, Amartha Fintech employs field staff who engaged in providing training on financial literacy, loan disbursement, weekly engagements with small business owners, mentoring borrower on capacity development and business professionalism. This is in order to streamline its financial operation and engage its members. In 2016, the borrowers' income increased by 41% in 2015-2016 period. During the period, the average income level was Rp. 2.53 million. The members' usage of clean energy rose by 8% and more than 40% have used tile instead of mud floor in the residential houses. Similarly, it collaborated with four institutions to provide health services to more 500 members and provided free eye care examination to 1000 citizens in Bogor and distributed 513 medical eyeglasses to people with eye impairments. As regards educational services, it provided training on best practices for managing business to 112 members. To foster savings habit, it leverages its personal contribution and the members' savings to subsidize the price of essential commodities (such as oil, rice and sugar) by about one-half during the Eid festival.

In 2015, 94% of the members were below poverty line. However, the members' poverty rate was 53%, dropping to 41% in 2017. Again, borrowers' monthly income rose from Rp. 1.44 million in 2015 to Rp. 3.47 million in 2017. The number of borrowers earning above Rp. 5 million monthly income more than doubled as they experienced 34% improvement in 2017 compared to 16% in 2016. Housing renovation increased from 10% in 2016 to 31% in 2017. Clean energy utilization rose to 97% in 2017 from 91% in 2016; this corresponds with 6 percentage point decline in firewood utilization. Access to clean water source slightly increased by 2% in 2017. Nearly 90% of the borrowers were able to spend at least Rp. 500,000 to consume food with sufficient nutrients. The business trained 70 borrowers in financial skills to enhance financial literacy and business productivity. Before the program, only 9.5% could record income and expenses. Consequent to the training, more than 40% of the members were able to routinely record income and expenditure. As well, about 85% of the members were capable of making substantial financial savings to improve their business activities and raise their social welfare. There was health seminar and free medical check-up to 70 members in Bogor. As part of CSR, it raised Rp. 69 million and donated 1,115 kilometres praying mats to mosques in four towns across West Java and East Java. The business collaborated with Avrist, Melbourne Microfinance Initiative, 2.5 NVG Essilor, Oxford Microfinance Initiative, Aflatoun International, Kitabisa.com, Republika Online.

In the year 2018, Amartha received Frontier Innovator Award from the Australian Department of Foreign Affairs and Trade. Specifically, it received AUD 100,000 grant to finance SDG-related programs, which covered health, environment and entrepreneurship. The total SDG-related programs benefitted 168,284 people during the year (through grant and non-grant funding). More than 18,000 person access to free medical service and 7,039 collected free eyeglasses to 7,039. The major borrowers' occupation (69%) was trade, 20% of borrowers have bank account and 42.3% of borrowers owned mobile phone. In terms of the borrowers' family income, 70% earned more than Rp. 5 million monthly income, while only 2% earned less than Rp. 1.5million. As well, the family income of the remaining 28% lies between Rp. 1.5million and Rp. 5million.

Table 2. Social impact projects

Activity	Period	Number of Beneficiaries
Financial training	2016-2021	550,461
Entrepreneurship training	2019-2020	49,256

continued on following page

Table 2. Continued

Activity	Period	Number of Beneficiaries
Health intervention	2016-2019	22,733
Free medical glasses	2016-2020	11923

Source: Amartha Social Accountability / Sustainability Reports (2016-2021)

In Table 2, Amartha has achieved a lot in the providing social impacts to its members as well as the communities. Between 2016 and 2021, it provided several trainings to more than half million persons (550,461) on financial literacy in order to assist them improve their financial well-beings. In-between 2019 and 2020, nearly 50,000 people benefitted from entrepreneurship training programs. As part of community development initiatives, 22,733 were provided free medical check-up within four years (2016-2019), about 12,000 members of the community accessed free medical glasses.

5.2 Amartha and Women Empowerment

To facilitate women empowerment through financial inclusion, Amartha initiated digital apps that were easy to use by rural women micro entrepreneurs. The goal was to transport rural into a digital society who embrace contactless and cashless transactions. Due to gap in digital literacy and access between urban and rural areas, Amartha integrated financial literacy training with digital literacy to empower women-led small businesses. Among the important milestones in 2022 resulting from digital skills interventions, which include:

i. To promote cashless transactions, we help our borrowers open a bank account with our banking partners. Hence, 50.96% of the borrowers have bank accounts.
ii. 831,556 borrowers use Amarthafin app. Additionally, 54% of these borrowers start using the Amarthafin app for their daily financial needs, such as purchase of phone credit, pay the electricity bills, and national insurance fee.
iii. Nearly 564,540 borrowers, representing 67.89%, save their money with non-bank financial institutions, such as cooperative, religious groups, at home, and through arisan (regular social gathering).
iv. Among the borrowers, Amartha has trained 20,482 persons as AmarthaOne agents. Their task was to enable cash in cash out service in rural areas across Amartha area (Java, Sumatera, and Sulawesi) (Amartha Internal Document, 2023).

During 2017, Amartha provided enabling environment for more than 15,000 married women to start new businesses. Besides, women borrowers were able to provide employment opportunities as shown in Figure 5. They employed 87,000 persons in 2019. The jobs rose to 210,637 and 271,722 in 2020 and 2021 respectively. The year 2021 recoded lower job creation (156,298) compared to previous two consecutive years. This may be attributed to the impact of COVID-19 were business were severely affected by the lock-down regulations.

Figure 5. Jobs creation

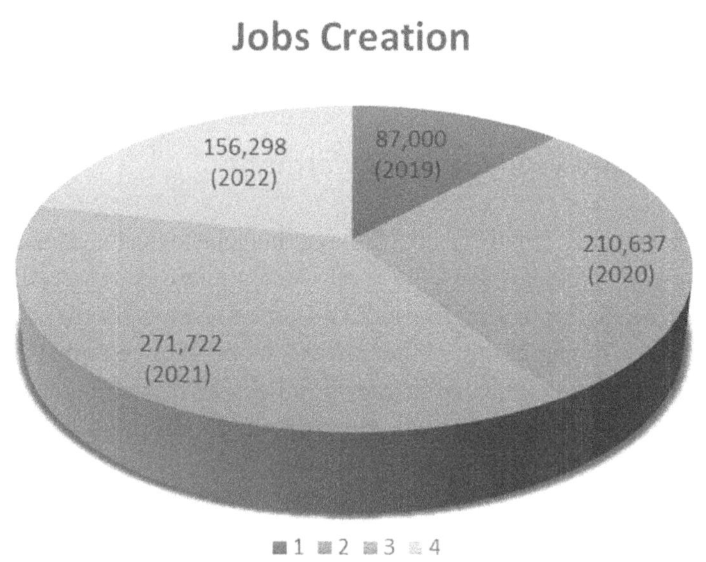

5.3 Analysis of Sustainable Financial Business Practices

For a sustainable business model, Fintech firms diversify their financing sources, expand the market share (i.e. engage more clients), empower their customers, and increase the staff capacity for quality service delivery. In this respect, this sub-section presents data on the population of lenders and borrowers, growth in clients' employment generation, expansion in the size of lending, and staff capacity alongside business outreach. Figure 6 depicts steady growth in both the size of lenders and borrowers.

Figure 6. Number of lenders and borrowers

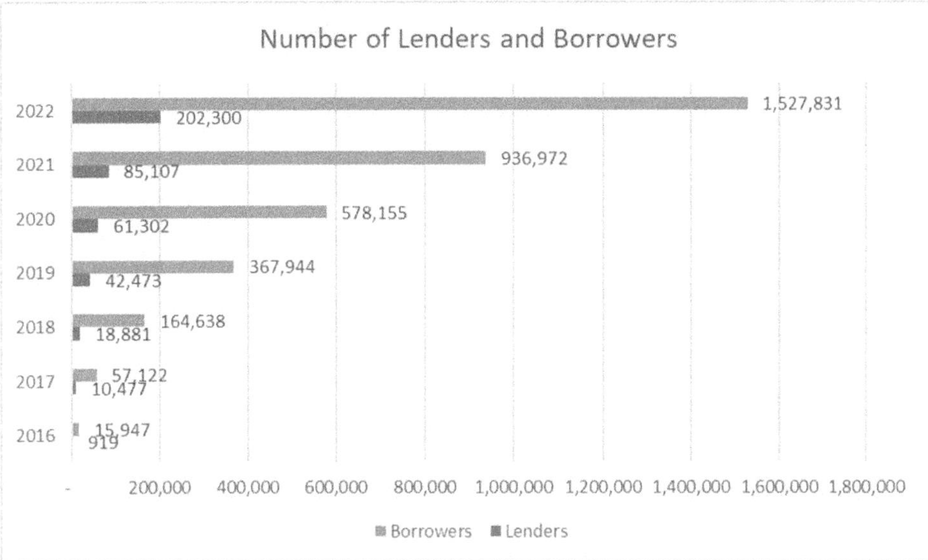

From Figure 6, Amartha had 919 unique lenders and 15,947 borrowers in 2016. The number of lenders and borrowers rose to 10,477 and 57,122 in 2017, representing 10 times and 250 percent growth in the size of lenders and borrowers respectively. Between 2018 and 2019, unique lenders grew by 125 percent, while borrowers increased by 123 percent. Between 2021 and 2022, the number of unique lenders grew by 137 percent reaching 202,300 in 2020. Similarly, there was more than 1.5 million borrowers in 2022 compared to 936,972 in 2021, constituting 63 percent growth in borrowers. Figure 7 depicts the trend in the company's total loan disbursement to women entrepreneurs in order to empower the members and reduce poverty.

Figure 7. Total loans disbursed (Rp. billion)

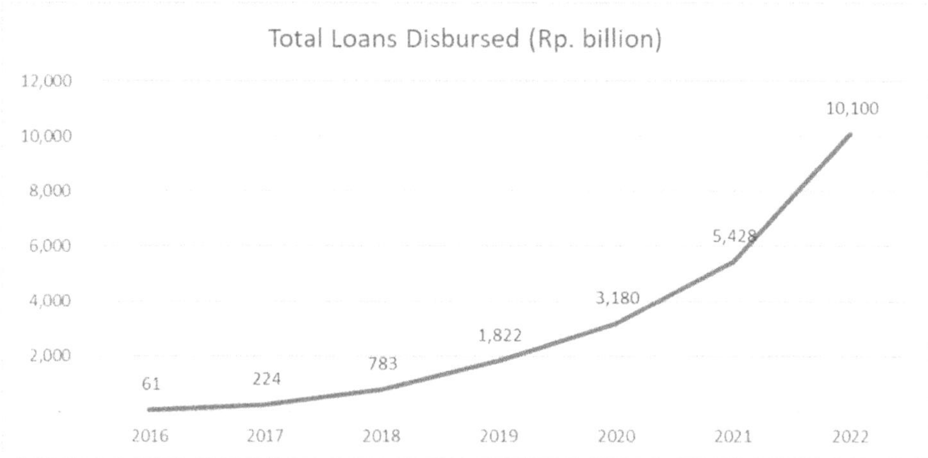

As shown in Figure 7, the initial loan disbursement was Rp. 61 billion in 2016. It was in 2016 that Amartha registered as a micro Fintech. The trend analysis showed that subsequent loans disbursement rose steadily and exceeded Rp. 10 trillion in 2022. Between 2016 and 2017, total loans increased by 267 percent. Between 2021 and 2022, total loans disbursed nearly doubled by Rp. 5 trillion. The average annual loan disbursement was Rp. 3.085 trillion during the 7-year period.

Figure 8. Staff capacity and outreach

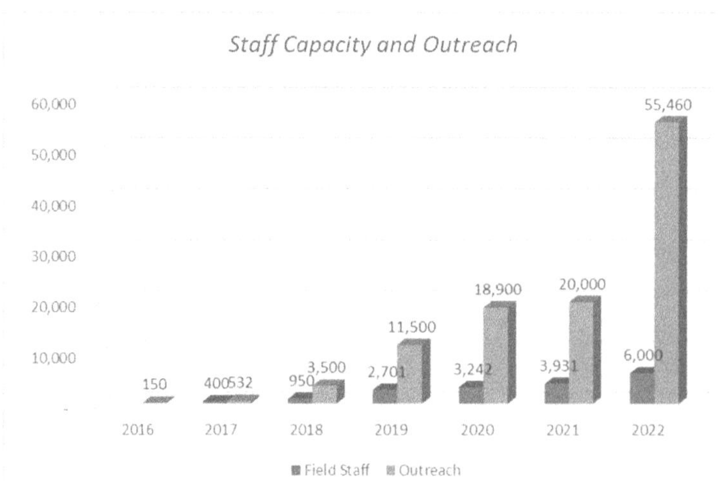

In Figure 8, the outreach of Amartha in 2016 comprised of 150 villages cutting across Bandung, Bogor and Subang in Java. Its outreach expanded to 3,500 in 2018 and exceeded 10,000 in 2019 (reaching 11,500 villages). The outreach was precisely 20,000 villages in 2021 and rose astronomically to 55000+ in 2022. On the other hand, its field staff capacity kept improving from 400 staff in 2017 to more than 6,000 field workers in 2022.

5.4 Green Digital Innovation

To explore the extent of green digital innovation, the study interviewed Amartha's Head of Impact Reporting and Sustainability. The questions revolved around four themes, which comprise of energy use, sustainable environment, digital innovation and green initiatives. Table 3 analysed the components of sustainable digital innovations grouped under four themes.

Table 3. Thematic Analysis of Sustainable Digital Innovation

Theme: Sub Items	Information
Energy use: Source	Electricity constitutes 90% of energy source for daily business operations. These include daily activities such as lighting, cooling and operating information technology.
Energy use: Optimisation	It installed monitoring devices to track daily power usage for its data centres. This step ensures reduction in consumption electricity.
Sustainable environment: Emission	1. It generates 7,546 metric tons of CO2 from electricity, transportation, operations and other activities. 2. It targets 50% emission reduction 2025 in line with sustainability goals.
Sustainable environment: Efficiency	1. It applies energy efficiency device, which automatically switch off light while not in use. The measure reduces electricity consumption without fall in productivity. 2. It has Go Green Program, which encourages employees to apply energy-saving behaviour. This program awards employee(s) with best rating in energy saving records. 3. Solarisation Program has installed solar panels in the Amartha data centre. The program aims to upscale green electricity by 20%.
Digital innovation: Sustainable	Its websites provide information about environmental sustainability. The beneficiary-members, employees and public users can access information. It has integrated a donation site in its application for funding "green environment". The site enables users to donate for sustainable environmental projects like reforestation, management waste and water conservation.

continued on following page

Table 3. Continued

Theme: Sub Items	Information
Digital innovation: Financial	1. Launched *Afin* apps for borrowers, to familiarise rural MSMEs with digital platform. 2. Launched *AmarthaOne* agent network, to enable cash-in cash-out (CICO) points in rural villages. 3. Initiated cashless disbursement, digital bill payment, including national insurance (*BPJS*), and phone credits, embedded into Afin apps among rural people.
Green initiatives	1. Amartha provides training to trader micro about sustainable business practice including energy efficiency practice. 2. Environment Education Programme to micro traders about circular waste management such as sorting of waste and reducing plastic use, and use of environment-friendly products made from natural ingredients. 3. Assistance Programme donates micro traders with solar panels and other equipment to promote energy saving.

Source: Interview Responses from Amartha Staff

5.5 SWOT Analysis of Sustainable Impacts of Amartha Fintech

This chapter examined the sustainable impact activities of Amartha Fintech. The authors explored the social impacts of Amartha in terms of women's economic empowerment, social development (including financial literacy and provision of medical services), entrepreneurship development, poverty reduction through improving members' income, and campaigns towards environmental awareness. In light of the foregoing discussions, Table 4 summarises the strengths, weaknesses, opportunities, and threats surrounding the sustainability motive of Amartha Fintech.

Table 4. Results of SWOT framework

STRENGTHS	WEAKNESSES
1. Digital inclusion of un-bankable women entrepreneurs. 2. Application of an in-house credit-scoring algorithm to assess and track members' creditworthiness. 3. Extensive financial training programs for both members and non-members. 4. Tailor-made entrepreneurship training to existing members on sustainable business practices. 5. Enhancing social capital by engaging membership as a single entity. 6. Intensive business training to the new members before giving out loans. 7. Proper concern for poverty alleviation. 8. Enables more convenient capital acquisition for women micro entrepreneurs, hence stimulating employment generation. 9. Contribute to a more transparent and efficient financial system. 10. It facilitates enhanced financial access for micro entrepreneurs.	1. The company does not assess the quality of jobs created by the beneficiaries. It focuses mainly on the quantity of employment growth. 2. High emission due to reliance on fossil-fuelled electricity and energy sources. 3. Inadequate emphasis on environmental awareness among members. 4. No available records of strategic planning for financing research & development (R&D). 5. Underinvestment in consumer psychology 6. The dynamic nature of Fintech regulations can pose hurdles, which could impede capacity for innovation. 7. Data security and privacy problems are raised by the acquisition and utilization of personal and financial data by companies. 8. Fintech platforms are vulnerable to cyber attacks, potentially eroding faith in the financial system and disrupt services. 9. Low target for solarisation of the data centre.
OPPORTUNITIES	**THREATS**
1. Competitive advantage in technological innovation. 2. Collaboration with national and international partners. 3. Expanding outreach 4. Investing in sustainable finance 5. Pool of skilled workers in digital finance and artificial intelligence. 6. Promoting digital financial inclusion of the small business owners. 7. Creation of reliable and transferable digital identity solutions, which are essential for gaining access to financial services. 8. Promoting environmental sustainability awareness through Amartha app.	1. Proliferation of competing Fintech companies. 2. Lack of financial buffer for financing short-term excessive demand for Funds (borrowers). 3. Policy uncertainty from the government regulators. 4. Vulnerability to cyber assaults, fraud and other financial crimes, which can compromise confidential financial and personal information. 5. Concerns for data privacy and consumer protection. 6. High costs of installing green electricity. 7. Emergence of green micro Fintech model.

Source: Authors' own.

6. CONCLUSION

The chapter investigated the sustainable impacts and sustainable business practices of Indonesian Fintech by focusing on Amartha Micro Fintech. Besides, the research explored the role of Fintech in empowering micro entrepreneurs as well as its ability to promote green digital initiatives. After examining Amartha's Sustainability Reports for 7 years ranging from 2016 to 2022, the chapter found that Amartha has achieved significant strides in empowering women entrepreneurs through income enhancement, job creation and provision of loanable funds to its members. As at 2022, more than 1.5 million women have access to Amartha Fintech loans, hence generating 156,000 additional jobs despite the adverse effects of COVID-19. Amartha Fintech has kept in touch with the community members through social impact projects in education, financial training and medical services. It has consistently raised loan financing from Rp. 61 billion in 2016 to Rp. 10.1 trillion in 2022, suggesting lenders' confidence in its financial operations. Our investigation showed that, despite these remarkable achievements, the Fintech has some weaknesses in its quest for adopting a sustainable business model. Though it recognises the importance of green sustainable digital framework, it has no comprehensive framework for integrating green digital innovation. However, integrated sustainable digital framework is critical for achieving a comprehensive sustainable business model. In addition, the firm succeeded in empowering its women to create additional employment, thus facilitating poverty reduction. However, it should to appraise the quality of new jobs created. Its social impact could be more effective when new jobs generate income beyond poverty line. Therefore, sustainable impact oriented Fintech models should emulate Amartha's impact programmes in order to achieve sustainable business model.

REFERENCES

Amartha. (2023). Heading towards sustainability. Retrieved December 15, 2023, from https://amartha.com/en/

Ashta, A. (2023). How Can Fintech Companies Get Involved in the Environment? *Sustainability (Basel)*, 15(13), 10675. 10.3390/su151310675

Asosiasi FinTech Indonesia (AFTECH). (2023). *AFTECH Annual Members Survey 2022/2023, Industri Fintech Indonesia Semakin Mantap Melangkah Menuju Arah Keberlanjutan dan Inklusi.* AFTECH.

Badan Pusat Statistik. (2023). *Statistical Yearly Book of Indonesia.* BPS - Statistics of Indonesia.

Cen, T., & He, R. (2018). Fintech, Green Finance and Sustainable Development. *Advances in Social Science, Education and Humanities Research*, 291, 222–225.

Deng, X., Huang, Z., & Cheng, X. (2019). FinTech and Sustainable Development: Evidence from China Based on P2P Data. *Sustainability (Basel)*, 11(22), 6434. 10.3390/su11226434

Dinard Standard. (2021). *State of The Global Islamic Economy Report.* Dinard Standard. Retrieved September 01, 2023, from https://www.icricinternational.org/state-of-the-global-islamic-economy-2020-21-report-is-published/

Elkington, J. (1998). Partnerships from cannibals with forks: The triple bottom line of 21st-century business. *Environmental Quality Management, 8*(1), 37-51. 10.1002/tqem.3310080106

Elkington, J. (2013). Enter the triple bottom line. *The Triple Bottom Line: Does it All Add Up*, 1-16. 10.4324/9781849773348

Farahani, M. S., Esfahani, A., Moghaddam, M. N. F., & Ramezani, A. (2022). The Impact of Fintech and Artificial Intelligence on COVID-19 and Sustainable Development Goals. *International Journal of Innovation in Management Economics and Social Sciences*, 2(3), 14–31.

Fersi, M., Boujelbena, M., & Arous, F. (2023). Microfinance's digital transformation for sustainable inclusion. *European Journal of Management and Business Economics*, 32(5), 525–559. 10.1108/EJMBE-10-2022-0332

Fintech Indonesia. (2022/2023). *Annual Member Surveys.* Jakarta: Asosiasi Fintech Indonesia (AFTECH).

Gimenez, C. (2012). Sustainable operations: Their impact on the triple bottom line. *International Journal of Production Economics, 140*(1), 149-159. 10.1016/j.ijpe.2012.01.035

Govindan, K. (2013). A fuzzy multi criteria approach for measuring sustainability performance of a supplier based on triple bottom line approach. *Journal of Cleaner Production, 47*, 345-354. 10.1016/j.jclepro.2012.04.014

Gupta, M., & Kiran, R. (2023). Digital exclusion of women: A systematic review. *Global Knowledge, Memory and Communication*. https://doi.org/10.1108/GKMC-12-2022-0301

Hamidi, M. L., & Worthington, A. C. (2021). Beyond the triple bottom line: Prosperity, People, Planet, and Prophet in Islamic banking. *Journal of Islamic Marketing*, 14(2), 394–409. 10.1108/JIMA-02-2021-0036

Hasan, R., Ashfaq, M., Parveen, T., & Gunardi, A. (2022). Financial inclusion – does digital financial literacy matter for women entrepreneurs? *International Journal of Social Economics*, •••, 1085–1104. 10.1108/IJSE-04-2022-0277

Hoang, T. G., Nguyen, G. N. T., & Le, D. A. (2022). *Developments in Financial Technologies for Achieving the Sustainable Development Goals (SDGs). Handbook of Research on Sustainable International Business and the Sustainable Development Goals*. IGI Global.

Indonesia Internet Service Provider (APJII). (2023). *Survey Penetrasi dan Perilaku Konsumen*. APJII.

Indonesia.go.id. (2021, May 17). *Portal Informasi Indonesia*. Retrieved September 01, 2023, from https://indonesia.go.id/kategori/feature/2794/indonesia-berpeluang-memimpin-industri-halal-dunia

Indrawati, H., Caska, C., Hemita, N., Sumarno, S., & Syahza, A. (2023). Green innovation adoption of SMEs in Indonesia: What factors determine it? *International Journal of Innovation Science*. Advance online publication. 10.1108/IJIS-02-2023-0047

Jamil, N. N., & Abu Seman, J. (2019). The Impact of Fintech on the Sustainability of Islamic Accounting and Finance Education in Malaysia. *Journal of Islamic, SocialEconomics and Development*, 4(17), 74–88.

Kearns, K. P. (1992). *From comparative advantage to damage control: Clarifying strategic issues using swot analysis.* 10.1002/nml.4130030103

Kharisma, D. B. (2021). Urgency of financial technology (Fintech) laws in Indonesia. *International Journal of Law and Management*, 63(3), 320–331. Advance online publication. 10.1108/IJLMA-08-2020-0233

Kumar, S., Li, A., Wong, H., Chauhan, H., Shubhankar, S., & Oetama, I. (2023). *Indonesia's Fintech Industry is Ready to Rise*. Boston Consulting Group and AC Ventures.

Madsen, D. Ø. (2016). Swot analysis: A management fashion perspective. *International Journal of Business Research*, 16(1), 39–56. Advance online publication. 10.18374/IJBR-16-1.3

Mhlanga, D. (2022). The role of financial inclusion and FinTech in addressing climate-related challenges in the industry 4.0: Lessons for sustainable development goals. *Frontiers in Climate*, 4, 949178. 10.3389/fclim.2022.949178

Moghadam, H. E., & Karami, A. (2023). Financial inclusion through FinTech and women's financial empowerment. *International Journal of Social Economics*, 50(8), 1038–1069. 10.1108/IJSE-04-2022-0246

Munandar, H. (2014). *Manajemen Strategis Berdasarkan Konsep Fred R. David.*

Nuryitmawan, T. R. (2023). The Impact of Islamic Fintech on Poverty Alleviation in Indonesia: A Socio-Economic Implications. *Airlangga Journal of Innovation Management*, 4(2), 136–146. 10.20473/ajim.v4i2.49478

Ozili, P. K. (2020). Contesting digital finance for the poor. *Digital Policy. Regulation & Governance*, 22(2), 135–151. https://doi.org/10.1108/DPRG-12-2019-0104

Pal, M., Gupta, H., & Joshi, Y. C. (2021). Social and economic empowerment of women through financial inclusion: Empirical evidence from India. *Equality, Diversity and Inclusion*, 41(2), 294–305. 10.1108/EDI-04-2021-0113

Pawłowska, M., Staniszewska, A., & Grzelak, M. (2022). Impact of FinTech on Sustainable Development. *Financial Sciences*, 27(2), 50–66. 10.15611/fins.2022.2.05

Phadermrod, B., Crowder, R. M., & Wills, G. B. (2019). Importance-Performance Analysis based SWOT analysis. *International Journal of Information Management*, 44, 194–203. Advance online publication. 10.1016/j.ijinfomgt.2016.03.009

Puyt, R. W., Lie, F. B., & Wilderom, C. P. M. (2023). The origins of SWOT analysis. *Long Range Planning*, 56(3), 102304. Advance online publication. 10.1016/j.lrp.2023.102304

Rangkuti, F. (2004). *Analisis SWOT Teknik Membedah Kasus Bisnis*. Gramedia Pustaka Utama.

Rani, V., & Kumar, J. (2023). Gender differences in FinTech adoption: What do we know, and what do we need to know? *Journal of Modelling in Management*. Advance online publication. 10.1108/JM2-06-2023-0121

Setiawan, B., Nugraha, D. P., Irawan, A., Nathan, R. J., & Zoltan, Z. (2021). User innovativeness and fintech adoption in indonesia. *Journal of Open Innovation*, 7(3), 188. Advance online publication. 10.3390/joitmc7030188

Shin, Y. J., & Choi, Y. (2019). Feasibility of the Fintech Industry as an Innovation Platform for Sustainable Economic Growth in Korea. *Sustainability (Basel)*, 11(19), 5351. 10.3390/su11195351

Sudirman, L., & Disemadi, H. S. (2022). Titik Lemah Industri Keuangan Fintech di Indonesia: Kajian Perbandingan Hukum. *Jurnal Pembangunan Hukum Indonesia*, 4(3), 471–493. Advance online publication. 10.14710/jphi.v4i3.471-493

The Financial Services Authority (OJK). (2023). *Penyelenggara Fintech Lending Berizin di OJK per 9 Oktober 2023*. Retrieved November 02, 2023, from https://www.ojk.go.id/id/kanal/iknb/financial-technology/Pages/Penyelenggara-Fintech-Lending-Berizin-di-OJK-per-9-Oktober-2023.aspx

Varga, D. (2017). *Fintech: Supporting Sustainable Development by Disrupting Finance*. Corvinus University Budapest.

Varga, D. (2018). Triple-Bottom-Line Impact Analysis Framework of Fintech Companies. *Budapest Management Review*, 49(11), 3. 10.14267/VEZTUD.2018.11.03

Vergara, C., & Agudo, F. L. (2021). Fintech and Sustainability: Do They Affect Each Other? *Sustainability (Basel)*, 13(13), 7012. 10.3390/su13137012

Wahbi, A., Sarfo, Y., & Musshoff, O. (2023). Female smallholder farmers' preferences for digital and conventional credit attributes: Evidence from Madagascar. *Agricultural Finance Review*, 83(4/5), 549–571. 10.1108/AFR-01-2023-0008

Xu, X., & Liu, Y. (2023). The association between managerial short-termism and green innovation: The moderating role of firms' digital transformation. *Asia Pacific Journal of Innovation and Entrepreneurship*, 17(3/4), 195–214. 10.1108/APJIE-07-2023-0147

KEY TERMS AND DEFINITIONS

Fintech: This refers to financial technology company, which provides peer to peer lending to micro and small businesses.

Green Digital Innovation: This involves expanding business' digital capability and outreach alongside low carbon emission and clients' sustainable business and green practices.

P2P Lending: Peer-to-peer lending is a digital innovation, which connects lenders and borrowers.

Sustainable Impacts: Business initiatives that focus on providing lasting impacts on businesses, society and the environment.

SWOT Analysis: It is analytical framework for identify and evaluating the company's strengths, weaknesses, opportunities and threats.

Triple Bottom Line (TBL): TBL aims to provide a business framework that is growth-oriented and compatible with social impacts and environmental protection.

Compilation of References

Abd Samad, K., Mohd Daud, S. N., & Mohd Dali, N. R. S. (2020). Determinants of household debt in emerging economies: A macro panel analysis. *Cogent Business & Management*, 7(1), 1831765. 10.1080/23311975.2020.1831765

Abdallah, W., Tfaily, F., & Harraf, A. (2024, March 25). The impact of digital financial literacy on financial behavior: Customers' perspective. *Competitiveness Review*. Advance online publication. 10.1108/CR-11-2023-0297

Abdullah, A. R., Che Musa, Z. K., Abdullah, S. S., Muhammad, M. Z., Muhamad, M., Ghazali, M. S., & Mat Yunoh, M. N. (2023). Effects of Digital Financial Literacy Towards Online Buying Behaviours Among Students During COVID-19 Pandemic. *Industry Forward and Technology Transformation in Business and Entrepreneurship*, 669–677. 10.1007/978-981-99-2337-3_57

Adams, C. A. (2017). Conceptualising the contemporary corporate value creation process. *Accounting, Auditing & Accountability Journal*, 30(4), 906–931. 10.1108/AAAJ-04-2016-2529

Adams, C. A., Heijltjes, M. G., Jack, G., Marjoribanks, T., & Powell, M. (2011). The development of leaders able to respond to climate change and sustainability challenges: The role of business schools. *Sustainability Accounting. Management and Policy Journal*, 2(1), 165–171. 10.1108/20408021111162191

Adedoyin, F., Abubakar, I., Bekun, F. V., & Sarkodie, S. A. (2020). Generation of energy and environmental-economic growth consequences: Is there any difference across transition economies? *Energy Reports*, 6, 1418–1427. 10.1016/j.egyr.2020.05.026

Aizawa, M., & Yang, C. (2010). Green credit, green stimulus, green revolution? China's mobilization of banks for environmental cleanup. *Journal of Environment & Development*, 19, 119–144.

Albuquerque, R., Koskinen, Y., & Zhang, C. (2019). Corporate social responsibility and firm risk: Theory and empirical evidence. *Management Science*, 65(10), 4451–4469. 10.1287/mnsc.2018.3043

Alhenawi, Y., & Yazdanparast, A. (2022). Households' intentions under financial vulnerability conditions: Is it likely for the COVID-19 pandemic to leave a permanent scar? *International Journal of Bank Marketing*, 40(3), 425–457. 10.1108/IJBM-05-2021-0200

Ali, L., Khan, M. K. N., & Ahmad, H. (2020). Education of the Head and Financial Vulnerability of Households: Evidence from a Household's Survey Data in Pakistan. *Social Indicators Research*, 147(2), 439–463. 10.1007/s11205-019-02164-2

Ali, M., Alamgir, M., & Nawaz, M. A. (2024). Emergence of the Digital Financial Literacy, and its Effect on the Financial Management Behavior among Students of Pakistan. *Pakistan Social Sciences Review*, 8(2), 141–155. 10.35484/pssr.2024(8-II)13

Ali, N., Mat Rahim, N., Adnan, M. F., Yanto, H., & Kiswanto, K. (2024, January 3). Determinants of Financial Behaviour: Does Digital Financial Literacy (DFL) Foster or Deter Sound Financial Behaviour? *Accounting and Finance Research*, 13(1), 6. 10.5430/afr.v13n1p6

Aliyev, F., Ajayi, R., & Gasim, N. (2020). Modelling asymmetric market volatility with univariate GARCH models: Evidence from Nasdaq-100. *Journal of Economic Asymmetries*, 22, 1–10. 10.1016/j.jeca.2020.e00167

Allen, F., & Gale, D. (1999). *Comparing Financial Systems*. MIT Press.

Allen, F., & Oura, H. (2004). Sustained Economic Growth and the Financial System. *Monetary and Economic Studies*, 22, 95–119.

Alonso-García, J., Bateman, H., Bonekamp, J., Van Soest, A., & Stevens, R. (2017). Saving preferences in retirement: the impact of pension policy design and health status. Available at: www.cepar.edu.au

Alp, E., & Seven, Ü. (2019). The dynamics of household final consumption: The role of wealth channel. *Central Bank Review*, 19(1), 21–32. 10.1016/j.cbrev.2019.03.002

Al-Qudah, A. A., Al-Okaily, M., & Alqudah, H. (2021). The relationship between social entrepreneurship and sustainable development from economic growth perspective: 15 'RCEP' countries. *Journal of Sustainable Finance & Investment*, 1(1), 1–18.

Aluko, O. A., & Obalade, A. A. (2020). Financial development and environmental quality in sub-Saharan Africa: Is there a technology effect? *The Science of the Total Environment*, 747, 141515.32795805

Alvarado, R., & Toledo, E. (2017). Environmental degradation and economic growth: Evidence for a developing country. *Environment, Development and Sustainability*, 19(4), 1205–1218. 10.1007/s10668-016-9790-y

Alvarez, M., & Rodríguez, A. (2015). Water-related mutual funds: Investment performance and social role. *Social Responsibility Journal*, 11(3), 502–512. 10.1108/SRJ-08-2013-0104

Amartha. (2023). Heading towards sustainability. Retrieved December 15, 2023, from https://amartha.com/en/

Ampudia, M., van Vlokhoven, H., & Żochowski, D. (2016). Financial fragility of euro area households. *Journal of Financial Stability*, 27, 250–262. 10.1016/j.jfs.2016.02.003

Anderloni, L., Bacchiocchi, E., & Vandone, D. (2012). Household financial vulnerability: An empirical analysis. *Research in Economics*, 66(3), 284–296. 10.1016/j.rie.2012.03.001

Ando, A., & Modigliani, F. (1963). The "Life Cycle" Hypothesis of Saving: Aggregate Implications and Tests. *The American Economic Review*, 53(1), 55–84.

Andreou, P. C., & Anyfantaki, S. (2021, October). Financial literacy and its influence on internet banking behavior. *European Management Journal*, 39(5), 658–674. 10.1016/j.emj.2020.12.001

Ansah, I. G. K., Gardebroek, C., & Ihle, R. (2021). Shock interactions, coping strategy choices and household food security. *Climate and Development*, 13(5), 414–426. 10.1080/17565529.2020.1785832

Antal, M., & Janne, H. I. (2010). The art of the cognitive war to save the planet, *Ecological Economics, 69*(5), 937-943. Available at: https://econpapers.repec.org/RePEc:eee:ecolec:v:69:y:2010:i:5:p:937-943

Anthony, M., Sabri, M. F., Wijekoon, R., Abdul Rahim, H., & Abdullah, H., Othman, M. A., & Md. Yusoff, I. S. (2021). The Influence of Financial Socialization, Financial Behavior, Locus of Control and Financial Stress on Young Adults' Financial Vulnerability. *International Journal of Academic Research in Business & Social Sciences*, 11(19). Advance online publication. 10.6007/IJARBSS/v11-i19/11738

Aras, G., Tezcan, N., & Furtuna, O. K. (2018). Multidimensional comprehensive corporate sustainability performance evaluation model: Evidence from an emerging market banking sector. *Journal of Cleaner Production*, 185, 600–609.

Arize, A., Kalu, E. U., & Nkwor, N. N. (2018). Banks versus markets: Do they compete, complement or co-evolve in the Nigerian financial system? An ARDL approach. *Research in International Business and Finance*, 45, 427–434.

Aryan, L. A., Alsharif, A., Alquqa, E. K., Ebbini, M. M. A., Alzboun, N., Alshurideh, M. H. T., & Al-Hawary, S. I. S. (2024). How digital financial literacy impacts financial behavior in Jordanian millennial generation. *International Journal of Data and Network Science*, 8(1), 117–124. 10.5267/j.ijdns.2023.10.011

Asfaw, T. (2015). Obstacles and opportunities for mobile banking in Ethiopia: Regulatory approval and interoperability challenges. *International Journal of Finance and Banking Studies*, 8(4), 78–92.

Asheim, G. B. (1994). Sustainability: Ethical foundations and economic properties. *Policy Research Working Paper Series, 1302*. The World Bank. https://documents1.worldbank.org/curated/en/605011468739497097/pdf/multi0page.pdf

Ashok, M., Madan, R., Joha, A., & Sivarajah, U. (2022). Ethical framework for Artificial Intelligence and Digital technologies. *International Journal of Information Management*, 62, 102433. 10.1016/j.ijinfomgt.2021.102433

Ashta, A. (2023). How Can Fintech Companies Get Involved in the Environment? *Sustainability (Basel)*, 15(13), 10675. 10.3390/su151310675

Aşıcı, A. A. (2013). Economic growth and its impact on environment: A panel data analysis. *Ecological Indicators*, 24, 324–333.

Asosiasi FinTech Indonesia (AFTECH). (2023). *AFTECH Annual Members Survey 2022/2023, Industri Fintech Indonesia Semakin Mantap Melangkah Menuju Arah Keberlanjutan dan Inklusi.* AFTECH.

Aulia, A., Rahayu, R., & Bahari, A. (2023, May 24). The Influence Of Digital Financial Literacy On Financial Well-Being With Financial Behavior As A Moderation Variable: Communities In West Sumatra. *Jurnal Akuntansi*, 13(2), 141–149. 10.33369/jakuntansi.13.2.141-149

Azaria, C., Susilaningsih, S., & Sudarno, S. (2024, March 9). An Integrated Perspective : The Impact of Digital Financial Knowledge and Self-Esteem on Financial Behavior in the Lives of College Students. *Jurnal Kependidikan: Jurnal Hasil Penelitian Dan Kajian Kepustakaan Di Bidang Pendidikan. Pengajaran Dan Pembelajaran*, 10(1), 48. 10.33394/jk.v10i1.10602

Azeez, N. P. A., & Akhtar, S. M. J. (2021, June 8). Digital Financial Literacy and Its Determinants: An Empirical Evidences from Rural India. *South Asian Journal of Social Studies and Economics*, 8–22. 10.9734/sajsse/2021/v11i230279

Azzopardi, D., Fareed, F., Lenain, P., & Sutherland, D. (2019). Assessing Household Financial Vulnerability: Empirical evidence from the U.S. using machine learning. In *OECD Economic Survey of the United States: Key Research Findings* (pp. 121–142). OECD.

Babiarz, P., & Robb, C. A. (2014). Financial Literacy and Emergency Saving. *Journal of Family and Economic Issues*, 35(1), 40–50. 10.1007/s10834-013-9369-9

Badan Pusat Statistik. (2023). *Statistical Yearly Book of Indonesia*. BPS - Statistics of Indonesia.

Baek, E., & Hong, G.-S. (2004). Effects of Family Life-Cycle Stages on Consumer Debts. *Journal of Family and Economic Issues*, 25(3), 359–385. 10.1023/B:JEEI.0000039946.59422.5f

Bahaddin, B., Weinberg, S., Luna-Reyes, L. F., & Andersen, D. (2019). Building a bridge to behavioral economics: Countervailing cognitive biases in lifetime saving decisions. *System Dynamics Review*, 35(3), 187–207. 10.1002/sdr.1631

Bapat, D. (2019, June 1). Exploring Antecedents to Financial Management Behavior for Young Adults. *Financial Counseling and Planning*, 30(1), 44–55. 10.1891/1052-3073.30.1.44

Barkemeyer, R., Holt, D., Preuss, L., & Tsang, S. (2011). What happened to the 'development' in sustainable development? Business guidelines two decades after Brundtland. *Sustainable Development*, 22, 15–32.

Barkemeyer, R., Holt, D., Preuss, L., & Tsang, S. (2014). What happened to the development in 'sustainable development'? Business Guidelines Two Decades After Brundtland. *Sustainable Development (Bradford)*, 22(1), 15–32. 10.1002/sd.521

Bashir, I., & Qureshi, I. H. (2022, June 29). A Systematic Literature Review on Personal Financial Well-Being: The Link to Key Sustainable Development Goals 2030. *FIIB Business Review*, 12(1), 31–48. 10.1177/23197145221106862

Bassen, A., & Kovacs, A. M. M. (2008). Environmental, social and governance key performance indicators from a capital market perspective. *Zeitschrift für Wirtschafts- und Unternehmensethik*, 9(2), 182–192. 10.5771/1439-880X-2008-2-182

Battiston, S., Dafermos, Y., & Monasterolo, I. (2021). Climate risks and financial stability. *Journal of Financial Stability*, 54, 100867. 10.1016/j.jfs.2021.100867

Baudat, S., & Henchoz, C. (2022, August 1). Money in one click: Inequalities in digital financial practices and digital Skills among emerging adults in Switzerland. *Journal of Family and Economic Issues*, 44(3), 602–618. 10.1007/s10834-022-09854-z

Baumeister, R. F. (2002, March). Yielding to Temptation: Self-Control Failure, Impulsive Purchasing, and Consumer Behavior. *The Journal of Consumer Research*, 28(4), 670–676. 10.1086/338209

Bayer, C., Luetticke, R., Pham-Dao, L., & Tjaden, V. (2019). Precautionary Savings, Illiquid Assets, and the Aggregate Consequences of Shocks to Household Income Risk. *Econometrica*, 87(1), 255–290. 10.3982/ECTA13601

BBC. (2020, February 9). *Indigenous man and girl handcuffed for opening bank account*. BBC.

Bebbington, J., & Larrinaga, C. (2014). Accounting and sustainable development: An exploration. *Accounting, Organizations and Society*, 39(6), 395–413. 10.1016/j.aos.2014.01.003

Beck, T., & Levine, R. (2002). Industry growth and capital allocation: Does having a market-or bank- based system matter? *Journal of Financial Economics*, 64, 147–180.

Belanche, D., Casaló, L. V., & Flavián, C. (2019). Artificial Intelligence in FinTech: Understanding robo-advisors adoption among customers. *Industrial Management & Data Systems*, 119(7), 1411–1430. 10.1108/IMDS-08-2018-0368

Berk, J. B., & Green, R. C. (2004). Mutual Fund Flows and Performance in Rational Markets. *Journal of Political Economy*, 112, 1269–1295.

Berry, H. L., & Welsh, J. A. (2010). Social capital and health in Australia: An overview from the household, income and labour dynamics in Australia survey. *Social Science & Medicine*, 70(4), 588–596. 10.1016/j.socscimed.2009.10.01219931236

Bhatt, A., Joshipura, M., & Joshipura, N. (2022). Decoding the trinity of Fintech, digitalization and financial services: An integrated bibliometric analysis and thematic literature review approach. *Cogent Economics & Finance*, 10(1), 2114160. 10.1080/23322039.2022.2114160

Biais, B., Bisiere, C., Bouvard, M., & Casamatta, C. (2019). The blockchain folk theorem. *Review of Financial Studies*, 32(5), 1662–1715. 10.1093/rfs/hhy095

Biju, D. S., & Tantia, V. (2023). Social capital in the form of self-help groups in India: A powerful resilient solution to reduce household financial vulnerability. *Social Work with Groups*, 1–14. 10.1080/01609513.2023.2257754

Bollerslev, T. (1986). Generalized autoregressive conditional heteroskedasticity. *Journal of Econometrics*, 31(3), 307–327. 10.1016/0304-4076(86)90063-1

Bonekamp, J., & van Soest, A. (2022). Evidence of behavioural life-cycle features in spending patterns after retirement. *The Journal of the Economics of Ageing*, 23, 100408. 10.1016/j.jeoa.2022.100408

Boon, S. (2011). The connection between financial literacy and effective financial planning: Impacting overall economic prosperity. *Journal of Financial Planning*, 15(3), 67–82.

Boot, A. W., Greenbaum, S. I., & Thakor, A. V. (1993). Reputation and discretion in financial contracting. *The American Economic Review*, 83, 1165–1183.

Borio, C., & Disyatat, P. (2011). Global imbalances and the financial crisis: Link or no link? BIS Working Papers, 346, Bank for International Settlements. Available at: www.bis.org

Bragdon, J., & Marlin, J. (1972). Is Pollution Profitable? *Risk Management*, 19, 9–18.

Breitung, J. (2000). The local power of some unit root tests for panel data. *Advances in Econometrics*, 15, 161–178.

Broadstock, D. C., Chan, K., Cheng, L. T. W., & Wang, X. (2020). The role of ESG performance during times of financial crisis: Evidence from COVID-19 in China. *Finance Research Letters*, 38(1), 101716.32837385

Brooks, C., & Williams, L. (2021). The impact of personality traits on attitude to financial risk. *Research in International Business and Finance*, 58, 101501. 10.1016/j.ribaf.2021.101501

Brounen, D., Koedijk, K. G., & Pownall, R. A. J. (2016). Household financial planning and savings behavior. *Journal of International Money and Finance*, 69, 95–107. 10.1016/j.jimonfin.2016.06.011

Buch, C. M., & Goldberg, L. S. (2022). Complexity and riskiness of banking organizations: Evidence from the International Banking Research Network. *Journal of Banking & Finance*, 134, 106244. 10.1016/j.jbankfin.2021.106244

Buckland, J., & Spotton Visano, B. (2022). *Financial Vulnerability in Canada*. Springer International Publishing. 10.1007/978-3-030-92581-9

Buckland, R., Beecher, J., & Williams, J. (2015). Risk and regulation in water utilities: A cross-country comparison of evidence from the CAPM. *Journal of Regulatory Economics*, 47(2), 117–145. 10.1007/s11149-014-9261-z

Bushra, N., & Mir, M. A. (2024). Digital Financial Literacy and Financial Well-Being. In *Advances in finance, accounting, and economics book series* (pp. 57–73). 10.4018/979-8-3693-1750-1.ch003

Byrum, J. (2022). The past, present, and future of the payment system as trusted broker and the implications for banking. *Innovative Technology at the Interface of Finance and Operations*, I, 101–151. 10.1007/978-3-030-75729-8_4

Camilleri, M. A. (2017). Socially Responsible and Sustainable Investing. In *Corporate Sustainability, Social Responsibility and Environmental Management* (pp. 61–77). Springer International Publishing. 10.1007/978-3-319-46849-5_4

Carlsson, H., Larsson, S., Svensson, L., & Åström, F. (2017). Consumer Credit Behavior in the Digital Context: A Bibliometric Analysis and Literature Review. *Financial Counseling and Planning*, 28(1), 76–94. 10.1891/1052-3073.28.1.76

Casper, S., & Matthias, Y. (2021). *Orientation in a New World of Technology and Finance Integration.* Exploring the Concept of Embedded Lending.

Cen, T., & He, R. (2018). Fintech, Green Finance and Sustainable Development. *Advances in Social Science, Education and Humanities Research*, 291, 222–225.

Chang, K., Zeng, Y., Wang, W., & Wu, X. (2019). The effects of credit policy and financial constraints on tangible and research and development investment: Firm-level evidence from China's renewable energy industry. *Energy Policy*, 130, 438–447.

Chang, S. C. (2015). Effects of financial developments and income on energy consumption. *International Review of Economics & Finance*, 35, 28–44.

Chatzitheodorou, K., Tsalis, A. T., Tsagarakis, K. P., Grigoroudis, E., & Nikolaou, I. (2021). A new practical methodology for the banking sector to assess corporate sustainability risks with an application in the energy sector. *Sustainable Production and Consumption*, 27, 1473–1487.

Chen, Q. (2021). Stock movement prediction with financial news using contextualized embedding from bert. *arXiv preprint arXiv:2107.08721.*

Chen, Y., Wu, J., & Bu, H. (2018). Stock market embedding and prediction: A deep learning method. In *2018 15th International Conference on Service Systems and Service Management (ICSSSM)* (pp. 1-6). IEEE. 10.1109/ICSSSM.2018.8464968

Cheng, D., Yang, F., Wang, X., Zhang, Y., & Zhang, L. (2020). Knowledge graph-based event embedding framework for financial quantitative investments. In *Proceedings of the 43rd International ACM SIGIR Conference on Research and Development in Information Retrieval* (pp. 2221-2230). 10.1145/3397271.3401427

Cheng, X., Cohen, J., & Mou, J. (2023). AI-enabled technology innovation in e-commerce. *Journal of Electronic Commerce Research*, 24(1), 1–6.

Chen, J., Siddik, A. B., Zheng, G. W., Mohammad, M., & Bekhzod, S. (2022). Green Banking—Can Financial Institutions support green recovery? *Economic Analysis and Policy*, 75, 389–395. 10.1016/j.eap.2022.05.01735694019

Chevalliera, J., & Ielpo, F. (2013). Volatility spillovers in commodity markets. *Applied Economics Letters*, 20(13), 1211–1227. 10.1080/13504851.2013.799748

Chhillar, N., Arora, S., & Chawla, P. (2024, January 8). *Measuring Digital Financial Literacy: Scale Development and Validation*. https://so05.tci-thaijo.org/index.php/TER/article/view/270077

Chhillar, N., & Arora, S. (2022, December). Personal Financial Management Behavior Using Digital Platforms and Its Domains. *Journal of Financial Management. Markets and Institutions*, 10(02), 2250009. Advance online publication. 10.1142/S2282717X22500098

Chiu, C.-L., Chang, T.-H., Hsiao, I.-F., & Chiou, D.-S. (2024). The price continuity, return and volatility spillover effects of regular and after-hours trading. *PLoS One*, 19(3), 1–16. 10.1371/journal.pone.029920738466755

Cho, C. H., Michelon, G., Patten, D. M., & Roberts, R. W. (2015). CSR disclosure: The more things change…? *Accounting, Auditing & Accountability Journal*, 28(1), 14–35. 10.1108/AAAJ-12-2013-1549

Choi, A., Stoutland, D., & Blanco, L. (2023, April 21). An evaluation of a digital financial education program and the impact of COVID-19 on financial well-being among college students. *Journal of American College Health*, 1–13. 10.1080/07448481.2023.219114237084244

Choi, S., & Shin, J. (2023). Household indebtedness and the macroeconomic effects of tax changes. *Journal of Economic Behavior & Organization*, 209, 22–52. 10.1016/j.jebo.2023.02.022

Choung, Y., Chatterjee, S., & Pak, T. Y. (2023). Digital financial literacy and financial well-being. *Finance Research Letters*, 58, 104438. 10.1016/j.frl.2023.104438

Christen, M., & Morgan, R. M. (2005). Keeping Up With the Joneses: Analyzing the Effect of Income Inequality on Consumer Borrowing. *Quantitative Marketing and Economics*, 3(2), 145–173. 10.1007/s11129-005-0351-1

Churchill, A. S., Trinh, T.-A., & Danquah, M. (2023). *Temperature, climate change, and household financial behaviour*. Academic Press.

Churchill, S. A., Inekwe, J., Smyth, R., & Zhang, X. (2019). R&D intensity and carbon emissions in the G7: 1870–2014. *Energy Economics*, 80, 30–37.

Cifuentes, R., Margaretic, P., & Saavedra, T. (2020). Measuring households' financial vulnerabilities from consumer debt: Evidence from Chile. *Emerging Markets Review*, 43, 100677. 10.1016/j.ememar.2020.100677

Clarence, J., & Pertiwi, D. (2023, August 13). Financial Management Behavior Among Students: The Influence of Digital Financial Literacy. [IJFIS]. *International Journal of Financial and Investment Studies*, 4(1), 9–16. 10.9744/ijfis.4.1.9-16

Clarkson, M. B. E. (1995). A Stakeholder Framework for Analyzing and Evaluating Corporate Social Performance. *Academy of Management Review*, 20(1), 92–117. 10.2307/258888

Clarkson, P. M., Li, Y., Richardson, G. D., & Vasvari, F. P. (2008). Revisiting the relation between environmental performance and environmental disclosure: An empirical analysis. *Accounting, Organizations and Society*, 33, 303–327.

Climate Change Committee (CCC). (2019). *Net Zero The UK's contribution to stopping global warming Committee on Climate Change*. Available at: www.theccc.org.uk/publications

Coleman, J. S. (1988). Social Capital in the Creation of Human Capital. *American Journal of Sociology*, 94, S95–S120. 10.1086/228943

Cole, S. (2008). Financial literacy and household well-being in India and Indonesia. *The Journal of Economic Perspectives*, 22(4), 123–146.

Coleton, A., Brucart, M. F., Gutierrez, P., Tennier, F. L., & Moor, C. (2020). Sustainable Finance - Market Practices. EBA Staff Paper Series. https://www.eba.europa.eu/sites/default/documents/files/document_library/Sustainable%20finance%20Market%20practices.pdf

Copur, Z., Gutter, M. S., & Erkal, S. (2014). Behavioral Approach to Financial Distress and Health. In *Globalization of Financial Institutions* (pp. 217–233). Springer International Publishing. 10.1007/978-3-319-01125-7_16

Cordero, J. M., Gil-Izquierdo, M., & Pedraja-Chaparro, F. (2022). Financial education and student financial literacy: A cross-country analysis using PISA 2012 data. *The Social Science Journal*, 59(1), 15–33. 10.1016/j.soscij.2019.07.011

Costanza, R., Hart, M., Posner, S., & Talberth, J. (2009). Beyond GDP: The need for new measures of progress. *Pardee Papers*, 39(0109), 970401.

Cunha, M. R., Lambrecht, B. M., & Pawlina, G. (2011). Household Liquidity and Incremental Financing Decisions: Theory and Evidence. *Journal of Business Finance & Accounting*, 38(7–8), 1016–1052. 10.1111/j.1468-5957.2011.02248.x

Cutillo, A., & Centra, M. (2017). Gender-Based Occupational Choices and Family Responsibilities: The Gender Wage Gap in Italy. *Feminist Economics*, 23(4), 1–31. 10.1080/13545701.2017.1285041

Danes, S. M., & Hira, T. K. (1987). Money management knowledge of college students. *Journal of Student Financial Aid*, 17(1), 4–16. 10.55504/0884-9153.1435

Daud, S. N. M., Marzuki, A., Ahmad, N., & Kefeli, Z. (2019). Financial Vulnerability and Its Determinants: Survey Evidence from Malaysian Households. *Emerging Markets Finance & Trade*, 55(9), 1991–2003. 10.1080/1540496X.2018.1511421

De Micco, P., Rinaldi, L., Vitale, G., Cupertino, S., & Maraghini, M. P. (2021). The challenges of sustainability reporting and their management: The case of Estra. *Meditari Accountancy Research*, 29(3), 430–448. 10.1108/MEDAR-09-2019-0555

DeBondt, W., Forbes, W., Hamalainen, P., & Gulnur Muradoglu, Y. (2010). What can behavioural finance teach us about finance? *Qualitative Research in Financial Markets*, 2(1), 29–36. 10.1108/17554171011042371

Deloitte. (2021), Climate & sustainability. Retrieved from https://www2.deloitte.com/us/en/insights/focus/climate-and-sustainability.html

Deng, X., Huang, Z., & Cheng, X. (2019). FinTech and Sustainable Development: Evidence from China Based on P2P Data. *Sustainability (Basel)*, 11(22), 6434. 10.3390/su11226434

Denisova, V. (2020). Financial development and energy consumption: Evidence from Germany'. *International Journal of Energy Economics and Policy*, 10(2), 35–39. 10.32479/ijeep.8603

Dennis, O. (2020). Ethics of Posterity for Environmental Development of the Niger Delta. *GNOSI: An Interdisciplinary Journal of Human Theory and Praxis*, 3(3), 83–96.

Dew, J., & Xiao, J. J. (2011). The Financial Management Behavior Scale: Development and validation. *Financial Counseling and Planning*, 22(1), 43–59.

Dewmini, E. A. T., Wijekumara, J. M. N., & Sugathadasa, D. D. K. (2023, December 31). Digital Financial Literacy on Financial Behaviour Among Management Undergraduates of State Universities in Sri Lanka. *Journal of Management Matters*, 10(2), 73–89. 10.4038/jmm.v10i2.56

Díaz-Mendoza, A. C., & Pardo, A. (2023). Water and traditional asset classes. *Finance Research Letters*, 52, 1–8. 10.1016/j.frl.2022.103394

Dinard Standard. (2021). *State of The Global Islamic Economy Report.* Dinard Standard. Retrieved September 01, 2023, from https://www.icricinternational.org/state-of-the-global-islamic-economy-2020-21-report-is-published/

Din, S. M. U., Mehmood, S. K., Shahzad, A., Ahmad, I., Davidyants, A., & Abu-Rumman, A. (2021). The Impact of Behavioral Biases on Herding Behavior of Investors in Islamic Financial Products. *Frontiers in Psychology*, 11, 600570. Advance online publication. 10.3389/fpsyg.2020.60057033613358

Dolan, P., Elliott, A., Metcalfe, R., & Vlaev, I. (2012). Influencing Financial Behavior: From Changing Minds to Changing Contexts. *Journal of Behavioral Finance*, 13(2), 126–142. 10.1080/15427560.2012.680995

Dong, Y., Ma, S., Zhang, B., Wang, W., & Pacheco, J. (2021). Financial incentives to poor countries promote net emissions reductions in multilateral climate agreements. *One Earth*, 4, 1141–1149.

Dorasamy, N. (2011). Advocacy for reforms in personal income tax administration: Increasing revenue collection and welfare funding. *Public Finance Review*, 14(1), 56–72.

Drever, A., Odders-White, E., Kalish, C. W., Else-Quest, N. M., Hoagland, E. M., & Nelms, E. N. (2015). Foundations of Financial Well-Being: Insights into the Role of Executive Function, Financial Socialization, and Experience-Based Learning in Childhood and Youth. *The Journal of Consumer Affairs*, 49(1), 13–38. 10.1111/joca.12068

Eccles, R. G., & Krzus, M. (2010). *One Report: Integrated Reporting for a Sustainable Strategy.* John Wiley & Sons.

Eika, L., Mogstad, M., & Vestad, O. L. (2020). What can we learn about household consumption expenditure from data on income and assets? *Journal of Public Economics*, 189, 104163. 10.1016/j.jpubeco.2020.104163

Eisenhauer, J. G., & Ventura, L. (2006). The prevalence of hyperbolic discounting: Some European evidence. *Applied Economics*, 38(11), 1223–1234. 10.1080/00036840500392391

Elavarasi, S. (2014). The younger generation's adoption of electronic banking: A focus on private banks and superior services. *Journal of Banking Research*, 7(3), 245–260.

Elkington, J. (1998). Partnerships from cannibals with forks: The triple bottom line of 21st-century business. *Environmental Quality Management, 8*(1), 37-51. 10.1002/tqem.3310080106

Elkington, J. (2013). Enter the triple bottom line. *The Triple Bottom Line: Does it All Add Up*, 1-16. 10.4324/9781849773348

Engle, R. (2004). Risk and volatility: Econometric models and financial practice. *The American Economic Review*, 94(3), 405–420. 10.1257/0002828041464597

Erner, C., Goedde-Menke, M., & Oberste, M. (2016). Financial literacy of high school students: Evidence from Germany. *The Journal of Economic Education*, 47(2), 95–105. 10.1080/00220485.2016.1146102

Faiella, I., Lavecchia, L., Michelangeli, V., & Mistretta, A. (2022). A climate stress test on the financial vulnerability of Italian households and firms. *Journal of Policy Modeling*, 44(2), 396–417. 10.1016/j.jpolmod.2021.11.001

Falcone, P. M. (2018). Green investment strategies and bank-firm relationship: A firm-level analysis. *Economic Bulletin*, 38, 2225–2239.

Fan, L., & Henager, R. (2022). A structural determinants framework for financial well-being. *Journal of Family and Economic Issues*, 43(2), 415–428. 10.1007/s10834-021-09798-w34548774

FAO. (2017). Water for sustainable food and agriculture. A report produced for the G20 Presidency of Germany. https://www.fao.org/3/i7959e/i7959e.pdf

Farahani, M. S., Esfahani, A., Moghaddam, M. N. F., & Ramezani, A. (2022). The Impact of Fintech and Artificial Intelligence on COVID-19 and Sustainable Development Goals. *International Journal of Innovation in Management Economics and Social Sciences*, 2(3), 14–31.

Farrall, S. (2021). *Where Have All the People Gone? Theories of Structuration.* Practice and Agency. 10.1007/978-3-030-74830-2_6

Fatihudin, D., & Mochklas, M. (2018). How measuring financial performance. *International Journal of Civil Engineering and Technology*, 6(9), 553–557.

Fava, D. (2022). How Embedded Finance Can Solve the Gig Economy's Retirement Planning Problem. *Journal of Financial Planning*, 35(7), 60–62.

Febrianty, F., Yuliansyah, Y., Hamzah, R. S., & Annisa, M. L. (2024, February 28). Gender Issues in Digital Financial Literacy and Financial Behavior among Millennials. *Journal of Economics*, 20(1), 79–94. 10.21831/economia.v20i1.56529

Feiveson, L., & Sabelhaus, J. (2019). Lifecycle Patterns of Saving and Wealth Accumulation. *Finance and Economics Discussion Series, 2019*(10). 10.17016/FEDS.2019.010

Fender, I., McMorrow, M., Sahakyan, V., & Zulaica, O. (2020). Reserve management and sustainability: the case for green bonds? Available at: www.bis.org

Fernández-López, S., Álvarez-Espiño, M., Castro-González, S., & Rey-Ares, L. (2023). Financial capability and households' financial vulnerability: Evidence for the Spanish case. *Managerial Finance*, 49(4), 679–702. 10.1108/MF-02-2022-0086

Fernando, J. L. (2003). *Rethinking Sustainable Development*. SAGE Publications.

Fersi, M., Boujelbena, M., & Arous, F. (2023). Microfinance's digital transformation for sustainable inclusion. *European Journal of Management and Business Economics*, 32(5), 525–559. 10.1108/EJMBE-10-2022-0332

Field, J. (2016). *Social Capital*. Routledge. 10.4324/9780203794623

Fintech Indonesia. (2022/2023). *Annual Member Surveys*. Jakarta: Asosiasi Fintech Indonesia (AFTECH).

Flórez Bossio, C., Ford, J., & Labbé, D. (2019). Adaptive capacity in urban areas of developing countries'. *Climatic Change*, 157(2), 279–297. 10.1007/s10584-019-02534-2

Freeman, R. E. (1984). *Strategic management: A stakeholder approach*. Pitman.

French, D., & McKillop, D. (2016). Financial literacy and over-indebtedness in low-income households. *International Review of Financial Analysis*, 48, 1–11. 10.1016/j.irfa.2016.08.004

French, D., McKillop, D., & Stewart, E. (2019, July 14). The effectiveness of smartphone apps in improving financial capability. *European Journal of Finance*, 26(4–5), 302–318. 10.1080/1351847X.2019.1639526

Freytag, J. (2020). *Challenges for green finance in india. An Analysis of Deficiencies in India's Green Financial Market*. UMEA University.

Fujita, K., Trope, Y., Liberman, N., & Levin-Sagi, M. (2006). Construal levels and self-control. *Journal of Personality and Social Psychology*, 90(3), 351–367. 10.1037/0022-3514.90.3.35116594824

Furinto, A., Tamara, D., Yenni, & Rahman, N. J. (2023). Financial and digital literacy effects on digital investment decision mediated by perceived socio-economic status. *E3S Web of Conferences, 426*, 02076. 10.1051/e3sconf/202342602076

Furnham, A. (1999, December). The saving and spending habits of young people. *Journal of Economic Psychology*, 20(6), 677–697. 10.1016/S0167-4870(99)00030-6

Gamble, A., Gärling, T., & Michaelsen, P. (2019). Young Adults' Consumption Desires, Feelings of Financial Scarcity and Borrowing. In *Indebtedness in Early Adulthood* (pp. 89–108). Springer International Publishing. 10.1007/978-3-030-13996-4_5

Gangi, F., Meles, A., D'Angelo, E., & Daniele, L. M. (2019). Sustainable development and corporate governance in the financial system: Are environmentally friendly banks less risky? *Corporate Social Responsibility and Environmental Management*, 26, 529–547.

Gaol, F. L., Dermawan, G., Rafif, M. R., Rubianto, R., & Matsuo, T. (2023). The Influence of Digital Financial Literacy on Interest in Investing in the Capital Market of Millennial Generation Students. *Inventive Computation and Information Technologies*, 189–206. 10.1007/978-981-19-7402-1_15

Gaspara, J. S., Marquesb, A. C., & Fuinhas, J. A. (2017). The traditional energy-growth nexus: A comparison between sustainable development and economic growth approaches. *Ecological Indicators*, 75, 286–296.

Geczy, C., Stambaugh, R., & Levin, D. (2003). *Investing in Socially Responsible Mutual Funds*. Working Paper, University of Pennsylvania.

Geetha, N., & Ramesh, M. (2011). A study of people's preferences in investment behavior. *International Journal of eSports Multidisciplinary Research*, 1(6), 1–10.

Geman, H., & Kanyinda, A. (2007). Water as the next commodity. *Journal of Alternative Investments*, 10(2), 23–30. 10.3905/jai.2007.695264

George, N. L., & Krishnan, M. R. (2022). Pain of Paying and Different Payment Paradigms. In *New Innovations in Economics, Business and Management Vol. 4* (pp. 161–167). Book Publisher International (a part of SCIENCEDOMAIN International). 10.9734/bpi/niebm/v4/15522D

Ge, R., Zheng, Z., Tian, X., & Liao, L. (2021). Human–robot interaction: When investors adjust the usage of robo-advisors in peer-to-peer lending. *Information Systems Research*, 32(3), 774–785. 10.1287/isre.2021.1009

Ge, Y., Chen, H., Zou, L., & Zhou, Z. (2021). Political Background and Household Financial Asset Allocation in China. *Emerging Markets Finance & Trade*, 57(4), 1232–1246. 10.1080/1540496X.2020.1865147

Ghosh, T., Sahu, S., & Chattopadhyay, S. (2021). Inflation expectations of households in India: Role of oil prices, economic policy uncertainty, and spillover of global financial uncertainty. *Bulletin of Economic Research*, 73(2), 230–251. 10.1111/boer.12244

Gimenez, C. (2012). Sustainable operations: Their impact on the triple bottom line. *International Journal of Production Economics, 140*(1), 149-159. 10.1016/j.ijpe.2012.01.035

Girdhari, M., & Sathya, S.D. (2011). A study on investment preference among urban investors in Orrisa. *Prerna- Journal of Management Thoughts and Practices, 3*(1), 1-9.

Giustozzi, C. (2023). Unemployment and Social Integration: Analysing the Impact of Financial Strain, Social Roles, and Identity. *KZfSS Kölner Zeitschrift Für Soziologie Und Sozialpsychologie*. 10.1007/s11577-023-00893-4

Global Reporting Initiative (GRI). (2016). GRI Standards: The World's Most Widely Used Sustainability Reporting Standards. Retrieved from https://www.globalreporting.org/standards/

Global Reporting Initiative (GRI). (2021). GRI Universal Standards. Retrieved from https://www.globalreporting.org/media/zauil2g3/public-faqs-universal-standards.pdf

Global Water and Development Report. (2020). Annual Report of Water Security, Sanitation, and Hygiene Activities. USAID.

Goel, P., & Misra, R. (2017). Sustainability reporting in India: Exploring sectoral differences and linkages with financial performance. *Vision (Basel)*, 21(2), 214–224. 10.1177/0972262917700996

Goldsmith, R. W. (1969). *Financial structure and development*. Yale University Press.

Goldstein, D. (2001). Financial sector reform and sustainable development: The case of Costa Rica. *Ecological Economics*, 37, 199–215.

Govindan, K. (2013). A fuzzy multi criteria approach for measuring sustainability performance of a supplier based on triple bottom line approach. *Journal of Cleaner Production, 47*, 345-354. 10.1016/j.jclepro.2012.04.014

Goyal, K., & Kumar, S. (2020, August 4). Financial literacy: A systematic review and bibliometric analysis. *International Journal of Consumer Studies*, 45(1), 80–105. 10.1111/ijcs.12605

Goyal, K., & Kumar, S. (2023). *Financial literacy and financial behavior. A Research Agenda for Consumer Financial Behavior*. Edward Elgar Publishing.

Goyal, K., Kumar, S., & Xiao, J. J. (2021, June 1). Antecedents and consequences of Personal Financial Management Behavior: A systematic literature review and future research agenda. *International Journal of Bank Marketing*, 39(7), 1166–1207. 10.1108/IJBM-12-2020-0612

Greenacre, M., Groenen, P. J. F., Hastie, T., D'Enza, A. I., Markos, A., & Tuzhilina, E. (2022). Principal component analysis. *Nature Reviews. Methods Primers*, 2(1), 100. 10.1038/s43586-022-00184-w

Greenwood, J., & Jovanovic, B. (1990). Financial Development, Growth, and the Distribution of Income. *Journal of Political Economy*, 98, 1076–1107.

Gupta, M., & Kiran, R. (2023). Digital exclusion of women: A systematic review. *Global Knowledge, Memory and Communication*. https://doi.org/10.1108/GKMC-12-2022-0301

Gupta, J. (2015). Role of Green Banking in Environment Sustainability- A study of selected Commercial Banks in Himachal Pradesh. *International Journal of Multidisciplinary Research and Development*, 2, 349–353.

Gupta, V. (2009). Examination of Indian income tax reforms: Simplifying tax rates and expanding the tax base. *Journal of Taxation and Public Finance*, 6(3), 189–204.

Gupta, V., & Sharma, S. (2021). Economic implications of varying levels of financial literacy in different regions of India. *Journal of Economic Development*, 30(2), 89–104.

Hadri, K. (2000). Testing for stationarity in heterogeneous panel data. *Econometrics Journal. Revue Economique et Sociale*, 3, 148–161.

Halkos, G., & Sepetis, A. (2007). Can capital markets respond to environmental policy of firms? Evidence from Greece. *Ecological Economics*, 63(2), 578–587. 10.1016/j.ecolecon.2006.12.015

Hamidi, M. L., & Worthington, A. C. (2021). Beyond the triple bottom line: Prosperity, People, Planet, and Prophet in Islamic banking. *Journal of Islamic Marketing*, 14(2), 394–409. 10.1108/JIMA-02-2021-0036

Hamilton, R. W., Mittal, C., Shah, A., Thompson, D. V., & Griskevicius, V. (2019). How Financial Constraints Influence Consumer Behavior: An Integrative Framework. *Journal of Consumer Psychology*, 29(2), 285–305. 10.1002/jcpy.1074

Hapsoro, D., Agung Saputro, J., Indraswono, C., Jauharia Hatta, A., & Sabandi, M. (2022, November 17). Effect of gender as a moderating variable on financial vulnerability using hierarchical regressions: Survey evidence from Indonesian traditional market traders. *Investment Management and Financial Innovations*, 19(4), 171–182. 10.21511/imfi.19(4).2022.14

Hasan, R., Ashfaq, M., Parveen, T., & Gunardi, A. (2022). Financial inclusion – does digital financial literacy matter for women entrepreneurs? *International Journal of Social Economics*, •••, 1085–1104. 10.1108/IJSE-04-2022-0277

Haseeb, M., Wattanapongphasuk, S., & Jermsittiparsert, K. (2019). Financial Development, Market Freedom, Political Stability, Economic Growth and CO2 Emissions: An Unexplored Nexus in ASEAN Countries. *Contemporary Economics, 13*(3), 363-375. 10.21203/rs.3.rs-843124/v1

Ha, X. S., Le, T. H., Phan, T. T., Nguyen, H. H. D., Vo, H. K., & Duong-Trung, N. (2021). *Scrutinizing Trust and Transparency in Cash on Delivery Systems*. 10.1007/978-3-030-68851-6_15

Heckman, S. J., & Hanna, S. D. (2015). Individual and Institutional Factors Related to Low-Income Household Saving Behavior. *Financial Counseling and Planning*, 26(2), 187–199. 10.1891/1052-3073.26.2.187

He, F., Deng, Y., & Li, W. (2020). Coronavirus disease 2019: What we know? *Journal of Medical Virology*, 92(7), 719–725. 10.1002/jmv.2576632170865

Hellemans, J., Willems, K., & Brengman, M. (2023). Covid-19 and mobile payment in Belgium: Closing the digital divide or just for the young, social, and impulsive? *Electronic Commerce Research*, 23(3), 1539–1564. 10.1007/s10660-022-09655-4

Hensen, J., & Kötting, B. (2022). From open banking to embedded finance: The essential factors for a successful digital transformation. *Journal of Digital Banking*, 6(4), 308–318. 10.69554/SRCL3482

Herzig, C., & Schaltegger, S. (2006). Corporate Sustainability Reporting. An Overview. In Schaltegger, S., Bennett, M., & Burritt, R. (Eds.), *Sustainability Accounting and Reporting* (Vol. 21). Springer. 10.1007/978-1-4020-4974-3_13

He, X., Cui, L., & Meyer, K. E. (2020). How state and market logics influence firm strategy from within and outside? Evidence from Chinese financial intermediary firms. *Asia Pacific Journal of Management*, 1–28.

Higgins, C., & Coffey, B. (2016). Improving how sustainability reports drive change: A critical discourse analysis. *Journal of Cleaner Production*, 136, 18–29. 10.1016/j.jclepro.2016.01.101

Hoang, T. G., Nguyen, G. N. T., & Le, D. A. (2022). *Developments in Financial Technologies for Achieving the Sustainable Development Goals (SDGs). Handbook of Research on Sustainable International Business and the Sustainable Development Goals*. IGI Global.

Hoffman, C. (2022). Embedded finance: why banks are moving towards it and its impact on trade finance. *A Trade Finance Global Article*. Available at: https://Www.Tradefinanceglobal.Com/Posts/Embedded-Finance-Why-Banks-Are-Moving-Towards-It-And-Its-Impact-On-Trade-Finance/

Hoffmann, A. O. I., & McNair, S. J. (2019). How Does Consumers' Financial Vulnerability Relate to Positive and Negative Financial Outcomes? The Mediating Role of Individual Psychological Characteristics. *The Journal of Consumer Affairs*, 53(4), 1630–1673. 10.1111/joca.12233

Hong, H., & Kacperczyk, M. (2009). The Price of Sin: The Effects of Social Norms on Markets. *Journal of Financial Economics*, 93, 15–36.

Iacoviello, M. (2008). Household Debt and Income Inequality, 1963–2003. *Journal of Money, Credit and Banking*, 40(5), 929–965. 10.1111/j.1538-4616.2008.00142.x

IKEA. (2021). Sustainability Report FY21. Retrieved from https://about.ikea.com/en/newsroom/2022/01/17/sustainability-report-fy21-and-climate-report

Im, K. S., Pesaran, M. H., & Shin, Y. (2003). Testing for unit roots in heterogeneous panels. *Journal of Econometrics*, 115, 53–74.

Indonesia Internet Service Provider (APJII). (2023). *Survey Penetrasi dan Perilaku Konsumen*. APJII.

Indonesia.go.id. (2021, May 17). *Portal Informasi Indonesia*. Retrieved September 01, 2023, from https://indonesia.go.id/kategori/feature/2794/indonesia-berpeluang-memimpin-industri-halal-dunia

Indrawati, H., Caska, C., Hemita, N., Sumarno, S., & Syahza, A. (2023). Green innovation adoption of SMEs in Indonesia: What factors determine it? *International Journal of Innovation Science*. Advance online publication. 10.1108/IJIS-02-2023-0047

Ingale, K. K., & Paluri, R. A. (2020, December 15). Financial literacy and financial behaviour: A bibliometric analysis. *Review of Behavioral Finance*, 14(1), 130–154. 10.1108/RBF-06-2020-0141

International Financial Reporting (IFRS) Foundation. (2021a). Integrated Reporting Framework. Retrieved from https://www.integratedreporting.org/resource/international-ir-framework/

International Financial Reporting Standards (IFRS) Foundation. (2021b). Sustainability-related Reporting. Retrieved from https://www.ifrs.org/projects/completed-projects/2021/sustainability-reporting/

Jacobs, M. (1999). Sustainable development as a contested concept. In Dobson, A. (Ed.), *Fairness and Futurity* (pp. 21–45). Routledge. 10.1093/0198294891.003.0002

Jalal, M., Khan, M. A., Hossain, M. E., Yedla, S., & Alam, G. M. M. (2021). Does climate change stimulate household vulnerability and income diversity? Evidence from southern coastal region of Bangladesh. *Heliyon*, 7(9), e07990. 10.1016/j.heliyon.2021.e0799034585010

Jamil, N. N., & Abu Seman, J. (2019). The Impact of Fintech on the Sustainability of Islamic Accounting and Finance Education in Malaysia. *Journal of Islamic, SocialEconomics and Development*, 4(17), 74–88.

Janjanam, V. V. P., & SubbaLakshmi, A. (2024). Importance of Financial Literacy Education and Financial Behavior for Developing Nations in the World. In *CRC Press eBooks* (pp. 163–180). 10.1201/9781032667478-15

Janssens, W., Pradhan, M., de Groot, R., Sidze, E., Donfouet, H. P. P., & Abajobir, A. (2021). The short-term economic effects of COVID-19 on low-income households in rural Kenya: An analysis using weekly financial household data. *World Development*, 138, 105280. 10.1016/j.worlddev.2020.105280

Jhonson, B., Andriani, R., Noviana, I., & Tamara, D. (2023, June 20). Influence Of Digital Financial Literacy on Financial Well-Being Through Spending, Saving, And Investment Behavior In Indonesia. *Journal of Business Studies and Mangement Review*, 6(2), 157–168. 10.22437/jbsmr.v6i2.24793

Jiang, M., Sun, R., & Zhang, B. (2022). Social networks and household financial decisions: Evidence from China. *Journal of Applied Econometrics*, 25(1), 58–92. 10.1080/15140326.2021.2007725

Jiang, W., Ruan, Q., Li, J., & Li, Y. (2018). Modeling returns volatility: Realized GARCH incorporating realized risk measure. *Physica A*, 500, 249–25. 10.1016/j.physa.2018.02.018

Jin, Y., Li, B., Roca, E., & Wong, V. (2014). Investment returns in the water industry: A survey. *International Journal of Water*, 8(2), 183–199. 10.1504/IJW.2014.060965

Jin, Y., Li, B., Roca, E., & Wong, V. (2016). Water as an investment: Liquid yet illiquid. *Applied Economics*, 9(9), 731–745. 10.1080/00036846.2015.1085646

Jin, Y., Reza, R., Li, B., Roca, E., & Wong, V. (2019). Water as an investment and the impact of regulatory risk. *Financial Planning Research Journal*, 5(1), 55–81. 10.2478/fprj-2019-0003

Jin, Y., Roca, E., Li, B., Wong, V., & Cheung, A. (2015). Sprinkle your investment portfolio with water! *International Journal of Water*, 9(1), 43–59. 10.1504/IJW.2015.067445

Johnson, K. W., & Li, G. (2010). The Debt-Payment-to-Income Ratio as an Indicator of Borrowing Constraints: Evidence from Two Household Surveys. *Journal of Money, Credit and Banking*, 42(7), 1373–1390. 10.1111/j.1538-4616.2010.00345.x

Johnson, L. (2016). *What Is Social Capital?*10.1007/978-3-319-33264-2_4

Jones, P., Hillier, D., & Comfort, D. (2017). The sustainable development goals and the financial services industry. *Athens Journal of Business and Economics*, 3, 37–50.

Joo, S. H., & Grable, J. E. (2004). An Exploratory Framework of the Determinants of Financial Satisfaction. *Journal of Family and Economic Issues*, 25(1), 25–50. 10.1023/B:-JEEI.0000016722.37994.9f

Jorgensen, B. (2007). Parental influence on financial literacy. *The Journal of Consumer Affairs*, 41(2), 294–316.

Kahneman, D., & Tversky, A. (1979, March). Prospect Theory: An Analysis of Decision under Risk. *Econometrica*, 47(2), 263. 10.2307/1914185

Kakinuma, Y. (2022, June 27). Financial literacy and quality of life: A moderated mediation approach of fintech adoption and leisure. *International Journal of Social Economics*, 49(12), 1713–1726. 10.1108/IJSE-10-2021-0633

Kalovwea, S. K., Mwanikia, J. I., & Simwa, R. O. (2021). On stock returns volatility and trading volume of the nairobi securities exchange index. *RMS: Research in Mathematics & Statistics*, 8(1), 1–10. 10.1080/27658449.2021.1889765

Kamble, P. A., Mehta, A., & Rani, N. (2023). Financial Inclusion and Digital Financial Literacy: Do they Matter for Financial Well-being? *Social Indicators Research*. Advance online publication. 10.1007/s11205-023-03264-w

Kamiński, M., Szymańska, C., & Nowak, J. K. (2021). Whose Tweets on COVID-19 gain the most attention: Celebrities, political, or scientific authorities? *Cyberpsychology, Behavior, and Social Networking*, 24(2), 123–128. 10.1089/cyber.2020.033632986469

Kaplan, G., & Schulhofer-Wohl, S. (2017). Inflation at the household level. *Journal of Monetary Economics*, 91, 19–38. 10.1016/j.jmoneco.2017.08.002

Karjaluoto, H., Glavee-Geo, R., Ramdhony, D., Shaikh, A. A., & Hurpaul, A. (2021). Consumption values and mobile banking services: Understanding the urban–rural dichotomy in a developing economy. *International Journal of Bank Marketing*, 39(2), 272–293. 10.1108/IJBM-03-2020-0129

Kass-Hanna, J., Lyons, A. C., & Liu, F. (2022, June). Building financial resilience through financial and digital literacy in South Asia and Sub-Saharan Africa. *Emerging Markets Review*, 51, 100846. 10.1016/j.ememar.2021.100846

Kaur, A., & Lodhia, S. (2018). Stakeholder engagement in sustainability accounting and reporting: A study of Australian local councils. *Accounting, Auditing & Accountability Journal*, 31(1), 338–368. 10.1108/AAAJ-12-2014-1901

Kearns, K. P. (1992). *From comparative advantage to damage control: Clarifying strategic issues using swot analysis.* 10.1002/nml.4130030103

Khando, K., Islam, M. S., & Gao, S. (2022). The Emerging Technologies of Digital Payments and Associated Challenges: A Systematic Literature Review. *Future Internet*, 15(1), 21. 10.3390/fi15010021

Khan, S., Peng, Z., & Li, Y. (2019). Energy consumption, environmental degradation, economic growth and financial development in globe: Dynamic simultaneous equations panel analysis'. *Energy Reports*, 5, 1089–1102. 10.1016/j.egyr.2019.08.004

Kharas, H. (2010). *The Emerging Middle Class in Developing Countries.* Academic Press.

Kharisma, D. B. (2021). Urgency of financial technology (Fintech) laws in Indonesia. *International Journal of Law and Management*, 63(3), 320–331. Advance online publication. 10.1108/IJLMA-08-2020-0233

Khawar, S., & Sarwar, A. (2021, July 18). Financial literacy and financial behavior with the mediating effect of family financial socialization in the financial institutions of Lahore, Pakistan. *Future Business Journal*, 7(1), 27. Advance online publication. 10.1186/s43093-021-00064-x

Kim, J., & Chatterjee, S. (2021). Financial Debt and Mental Health of Young Adults. *Journal of Financial Counseling and Planning*. 10.1891/JFCP-18-00048

Kim, K. T., Wilmarth, M. J., & Henager, R. (2017). Poverty Levels and Debt Indicators Among Low-Income Households Before and After the Great Recession. *Financial Counseling and Planning*, 28(2), 196–212. 10.1891/1052-3073.28.2.196

King, R., & Levine, R. (1993). Finance, Entrepreneurship and Economic Development. *Journal of Monetary Economics*, 32, 513–542.

Kolbinger, F. R., Leger, S., Carstens, M., Rinner, F. M., Krell, S., Chernykh, A., . . . Speidel, S. (2022). Artificial Intelligence for context-aware surgical guidance in complex robot-assisted oncological procedures: an exploratory feasibility study. medRxiv, 2022-05. 10.1101/2022.05.02.22274561

Kore Fusion. (2021). Embedded finance: this decade's largest creator of value. *A Kore Fusion Report.* Available at: https://korefusion.com/embedded-finance-this-decades-largest-creator-of-valu/

Koskelainen, T., Kalmi, P., Scornavacca, E., & Vartiainen, T. (2023, January). Financial literacy in the digital age—A research agenda. *The Journal of Consumer Affairs*, 57(1), 507–528. 10.1111/joca.12510

KPMG. (2020), The sustainable infrastructure opportunity. Retrieved from: https://kpmg.com/xx/en/home/insights/2020/06/covid-19-recovery.html

Kukk, M. (2016). How did household indebtedness hamper consumption during the recession? Evidence from micro data. *Journal of Comparative Economics*, 44(3), 764–786. 10.1016/j.jce.2015.07.004

Kumar, J., Rani, V., Rani, G., & Sarker, T. (2023). Determinants of the financial wellbeing of individuals in an emerging economy: An empirical study. *International Journal of Bank Marketing*, 41(4), 860–881. 10.1108/IJBM-10-2022-0475

Kumar, P., Islam, M. A., Pillai, R., & Sharif, T. (2023, February). Analysing the behavioural, psychological, and demographic determinants of financial decision making of household investors. *Heliyon*, 9(2), e13085. 10.1016/j.heliyon.2023.e1308536793953

Kumar, R. (2012). Low financial awareness in India: Gender disparities in knowledge. *Journal of Financial Education*, 18(2), 89–104.

Kumar, S., Li, A., Wong, H., Chauhan, H., Shubhankar, S., & Oetama, I. (2023). *Indonesia's Fintech Industry is Ready to Rise*. Boston Consulting Group and AC Ventures.

Kuo, Y. C., Huang, Y. H., Sun, L., Small, G., & Lin, S. J. (2023). Identifying key factors of sustainability practice in financial institutions based on decision-making trial and evaluation laboratory method. *Asian Review of Accounting*, 31, 661–679.

Kureishi, W., Paule-Paludkiewicz, H., Tsujiyama, H., & Wakabayashi, M. (2021). Time preferences over the life cycle and household saving puzzles. *Journal of Monetary Economics*, 124, 123–139. 10.1016/j.jmoneco.2021.10.004

La Torre, M., Sabelfeld, S., Blomkvist, M., Tarquinio, L., & Dumay, J. (2018). Harmonising non-financial reporting regulation in Europe: Practical forces and projections for future research. *Meditari Accountancy Research*, 26(4), 598–621. 10.1108/MEDAR-02-2018-0290

Labatt, S., & White, R. (2007). *Carbon Finance: The Financial Implications of Climate Change*. John Wiley.

Lai, A., & Stacchezzini, R. (2021). Organisational and professional challenges amid the evolution of sustainability reporting: A theoretical framework and an agenda for future research. *Meditari Accountancy Research*, 29(3), 405–429. 10.1108/MEDAR-02-2021-1199

Laine, M., Tregidga, H., & Unerman, J. (2021). *Sustainability Accounting and Accountability*. Routledge. 10.4324/9781003185611

Lansiti, M., & Lakhani, K. R. (2020). *Competing in the age of AI: Strategy and leadership when algorithms and networks run the world*. Harvard Business Press.

Lapp, W. M. (2010). Behavior models for prosperity: A statistical assessment of savings and behavioral change (EARN Research Brief). Retrieved from Earned Assets Resource Network website: https://files.eric.ed.gov/fulltext/EJ1048681.pdf

LeBaron, A. B., Hill, E. J., Rosa, C. M., & Marks, L. D. (2018). Whats and Hows of Family Financial Socialization: Retrospective Reports of Emerging Adults, Parents, and Grandparents. *Family Relations*, 67(4), 497–509. 10.1111/fare.12335

Leclaire, J. (2023). Does Household Debt Matter to Financial Fragility? *Review of Political Economy*, 35(2), 434–453. 10.1080/09538259.2021.1945192

Lee, J. M., Lee, J., & Kim, K. T. (2020). Consumer financial well-being: Knowledge is not enough. *Journal of Family and Economic Issues*, 41(2), 218–228. 10.1007/s10834-019-09649-9

Leung, M. F., & Wang, J. (2022). Cardinality-constrained portfolio selection based on collaborative neurodynamic optimization. *Neural Networks*, 145, 68–79. 10.1016/j.neunet.2021.10.00734735892

Levine, R. (2002). Bank-based or market-based financial systems: Which is better? *Journal of Financial Intermediation*, 11, 398–428.

Liew, T., Lim, P., & Liu, Y. (2020). Digital financial literacy: a case study of farmers from rural areas in sarawak. *International Journal of Education and Pedagogy*, 2(4), 245-251. Retrieved from https://myjms.mohe.gov.my/index.php/ijeap/article/view/11612

Li, G., & Fang, C. (2014). Global mapping and estimation of ecosystem services values and gross domestic product: A spatially explicit integration of national green GDP accounting. *Ecological Indicators*, 46, 293–314.

Li, J., Wu, Y., & Xiao, J. J. (2020). The impact of digital finance on household consumption: Evidence from China. *Economic Modelling*, 86, 317–326. 10.1016/j.econmod.2019.09.027

Litterscheidt, R., & Streich, D. J. (2020, August). Financial education and digital asset management: What's in the black box? *Journal of Behavioral and Experimental Economics*, 87, 101573. 10.1016/j.socec.2020.101573

Loibl, C. (2017). Living in Poverty: Understanding the Financial Behaviour of Vulnerable Groups. In *Economic Psychology* (pp. 421–434). Wiley. 10.1002/9781118926352.ch26

Long, M. G. (2018). Pushed into the Red? Female-headed Households and the Pre-crisis Credit Expansion. *The Forum for Social Economics*, 47(2), 224–236. 10.1080/07360932.2018.1451762

Lourenço, I., Branco, M., Curto, J., & Eugénio, T. (2012). How does the market value corporate sustainability performance? *Journal of Business Ethics*, 108(4), 417–428. 10.1007/s10551-011-1102-8

Luo, Y., Peng, Y., & Zeng, L. (2021, November). Digital financial capability and entrepreneurial performance. *International Review of Economics & Finance*, 76, 55–74. 10.1016/j.iref.2021.05.010

Lusardi, A., de Bassa Scheresberg, C., & Avery, M. (2018). Millennial mobile payment users: a look into their personal finances and financial behaviors. GFLEC working paper.

Lusardi, A. (2010). Gaps in young adults' financial literacy: The importance of education in schools. *The Journal of Consumer Affairs*, 44(2), 272–300.

Lusardi, A. (2012). The significance of numeracy in making informed financial decisions: Advocating for mathematical skills in education. *The Journal of Economic Education*, 19(1), 30–45.

Lusardi, A. (2019, January 24). Financial literacy and the need for financial education: Evidence and implications. *Swiss Journal of Economics and Statistics*, 155(1), 1. Advance online publication. 10.1186/s41937-019-0027-5

Lusardi, A., Mitchell, O. S., & Oggero, N. (2018). The Changing Face of Debt and Financial Fragility at Older Ages. *AEA Papers and Proceedings. American Economic Association*, 108, 407–411. 10.1257/pandp.20181117

Lusardi, A., Mitchell, O. S., Sconti, A., & Sticha, A. (2023). *Understanding Financial Vulnerability Among Asians*. Blacks, and Hispanics in the United States.

Lyons, A. C., & Fontes, A. (2021). Impacts of financial and digital literacy and social media on the financial health of U.S. households.

Lyons, A. C., Kass-Hanna, J., & Fava, A. (2022, June). Fintech development and savings, borrowing, and remittances: A comparative study of emerging economies. *Emerging Markets Review*, 51, 100842. 10.1016/j.ememar.2021.100842

Madsen, D. Ø. (2016). Swot analysis: A management fashion perspective. *International Journal of Business Research*, 16(1), 39–56. Advance online publication. 10.18374/IJBR-16-1.3

Mahalakshmi, V., Kulkarni, N., Kumar, K. P., Kumar, K. S., Sree, D. N., & Durga, S. (2022). The Role of implementing Artificial Intelligence and Machine Learning Technologies in the financial services Industry for creating Competitive Intelligence. *Materials Today: Proceedings*, 56, 2252–2255. 10.1016/j.matpr.2021.11.577

Ma, J., Feng, J., Chen, J., & Zhang, J. (2024). Volatility spillover from carbon prices to stock prices: Evidence from China's carbon emission trading markets. *Journal of Risk and Financial Management*, 17(3), 1–24. 10.3390/jrfm17030123

Malik, A. N. A., & Annuar, S. N. S. (2021). *The Effect of Perceived Usefulness, Perceived Ease of Use, Reward, and Perceived Risk toward E-Wallet Usage Intention*. 10.1007/978-3-030-65147-3_8

Maltais, A., & Nykvist, B. (2020). Understanding the role of green bonds in advancing sustainability'. *Journal of Sustainable Finance & Investment*, 11(3), 1–20. 10.1080/20430795.2020.1724864

Ma, N., Siu, Y. W., Cheong, T. S., & Tung, B. (2022, December 13). Impact of COVID-19 on lifestyle and financial behaviour: The implications to research in financial vulnerability. *Frontiers in Psychology*, 13, 1073017. Advance online publication. 10.3389/fpsyg.2022.107301736582332

Mandell, L., & Klein, L. S. (2007). Motivaton and financial literacy. *Financial Services Review*, 16, 105–116.

Manes-Rossi, F., Tiron-Tudor, A., Nicolò, G., & Zanellato, G. (2018). Ensuring More Sustainable Reporting in Europe Using Non-Financial Disclosure—De Facto and De Jure Evidence. *Sustainability (Basel)*, 10(4), 1162. 10.3390/su10041162

Markovich, C. A., & DeVaney, S. A. (1997). College Seniors' personal finance knowledge and practices. *Journal of Family and Consumer Sciences*, 89(3), 61–65.

Martellucci, A. C., Flaco, E. M., & Cappadona, R. (2020). SARS-CoV-2 pandemic: An overview'. *Advances in Biological Regulation*, 77, 100736. Advance online publication. 10.1016/j.jbior.2020.10073632773099

Martinot, E., Chaurey, A., Lew, D., Moreira, J. R., & Wamukonya, N. (2002). Renewable energy markets in developing countries'. *Annual Review of Energy and the Environment*, 27(1), 309–348. 10.1146/annurev.energy.27.122001.083444

Massenot, B., & Pettinicchi, Y. (2019). Can households see into the future? Survey evidence from the Netherlands. *Journal of Economic Behavior & Organization*, 164, 77–90. 10.1016/j.jebo.2019.05.021

Matthews, R. (2021). 10 Reasons Why Patagonia Is the World's Most Responsible Company. https://changeoracle.com/2021/09/10/10-reasons-why-patagonia-is-worlds-most/

Mavlutova, I., Fomins, A., Spilbergs, A., Atstaja, D., & Brizga, J. (2021, December 29). Opportunities to Increase Financial Well-Being by Investing in Environmental, Social and Governance with Respect to Improving Financial Literacy under COVID-19: The Case of Latvia. *Sustainability (Basel)*, 14(1), 339. 10.3390/su14010339

Mazumder, B., & Miller, S. (2016). The Effects of the Massachusetts Health Reform on Household Financial Distress. *American Economic Journal. Economic Policy*, 8(3), 284–313. 10.1257/pol.20150045

Mead, G., & Neves, B. B. (2018). Recursive approaches to technology adoption, families, and the life course: actor network theory and strong structuration theory. In *Connecting Families?* (pp. 41–58). Policy Press. 10.2307/j.ctv2867xm.9

Mei, A., Saxon, M., Chang, S., Lipton, Z. C., & Wang, W. Y. (2023). Users are the North Star for AI Transparency. *arXiv preprint arXiv:2303.05500.*

Meltzer, R., & Ghorbani, P. (2017). Does gentrification increase employment opportunities in low-income neighborhoods? *Regional Science and Urban Economics*, 66, 52–73. 10.1016/j.regsciurbeco.2017.06.002

Meng, D. (2023, January 16). Digital financial capability and household consumption: Evidence from China. *Applied Economics Letters*, 1–5. Advance online publication. 10.1080/13504851.2023.2167915

Menkveld, A. J., & Yueshen, B. Z. (2019). The Flash Crash: A cautionary tale about highly fragmented markets. *Management Science*, 65(10), 4470–4488. 10.1287/mnsc.2018.3040

Mhlanga, D. (2022). The role of financial inclusion and FinTech in addressing climate-related challenges in the industry 4.0: Lessons for sustainable development goals. *Frontiers in Climate*, 4, 949178. 10.3389/fclim.2022.949178

Microsoft. (2023). Microsoft Carbon Removal Observations from our third year, Observations from our third year. https://query.prod.cms.rt.microsoft.com/cms/api/am/binary/RW16V26

Milne, M. J., & Gray, R. (2007). Future prospects for corporate sustainability reporting. *Sustainability Accounting. Management and Policy Journal*, 1, 184–207.

Miralles-Quirós, M. M., Miralles-Quirós, J. L., & Redondo-Hernández, J. (2019). The impact of environmental, social, and governance performance on stock prices: Evidence from the banking industry'. *Corporate Social Responsibility and Environmental Management*, 26(6), 1446–1456. 10.1002/csr.1759

Moghadam, H. E., & Karami, A. (2023). Financial inclusion through FinTech and women's financial empowerment. *International Journal of Social Economics*, 50(8), 1038–1069. 10.1108/IJSE-04-2022-0246

Morgan, P. J., Huang, B., & Trinh, L. Q. (2019). *The Need to Promote Digital Financial Literacy for the Digital Age*. Retrieved February 24, 2024, from https://t20japan.org/wp-content/uploads/2019/03/t20-japan-tf7-3-need-promote-digital-financial-literacy.pdf

Morgan, P. J., & Long, T. Q. (2020). Financial literacy, financial inclusion, and savings behavior in Laos. *Journal of Asian Economics*, 68, 101197. 10.1016/j.asieco.2020.101197

Morris, T., Maillet, S., & Koffi, V. (2022). Financial knowledge, financial confidence and learning capacity on financial behavior: A Canadian study. *Cogent Social Sciences*, 8(1), 1996919. Advance online publication. 10.1080/23311886.2021.1996919

Morton, S., Pencheon, D., & Squires, N. (2017). Sustainable Development Goals (SDGs), and their implementation'. *British Medical Bulletin*, 124(1), 81–90. 10.1093/bmb/ldx03129069332

Moskowitz, M. (1972). Choosing Socially Responsible Stocks. *Business and Society Review*, 1, 71–75.

Muat, S., Fachrurrozi, F., & Sari, N. (2024, February 20). How do digital financial literacy, financial behavior, and skills affect financial well-being? An Exploratory Study on Gen Z. *Integrated Journal of Business and Economics*, 8(1), 728. 10.33019/ijbe.v8i1.851

Munandar, H. (2014). *Manajemen Strategis Berdasarkan Konsep Fred R. David.*

Muradoglu, G., & Harvey, N. (2012). Behavioural finance: The role of psychological factors in financial decisions. *Review of Behavioral Finance*, 4(2), 68–80. 10.1108/19405971211284862

Mützel, S. (2021). Unlocking the payment experience: Future imaginaries in the case of digital payments. *New Media & Society*, 23(2), 284–301. 10.1177/1461444820929317

Naeem, M. A., Iqbal, N., Karim, S., & Lucey, B.M. (2023). From forests to faucets to fuel: Investigating the domino effect of extreme risk in timber, water, and energy markets. *Finance Research Letters,* 55, 1-8. 10.1016/j.frl.2023.104010

Naimy, V., Haddad, O., Ferna'ndez-Aviles, G., & Khoury, R. E. (2021). The predictive capacity of GARCH-type models in measuring the volatility of crypto and world currencies. *PLoS One*, 16(1), 1–17. 10.1371/journal.pone.024590433513150

Nasir, N. S., Rosebery, A. S., Warren, B., & Lee, C. D. (2014). Learning as a cultural process: Achieving equity through diversity. *The Cambridge Handbook of the Learning Sciences, Second Edition*, 686–706. 10.1017/CBO9781139519526.041

Natura &Co. (2021). Natura &Co gives first annual update on Commitment to Life 2030 Sustainability Vision. https://naturaeco.com/press-release/natura-co-gives-first-annual-update-on-commitment-to-life-2030-sustainability-vision/

Negi, P., & Jaiswal, A. (2024, May). Impact of financial literacy on consumer financial behavior: A systematic review and research agenda using TCCM framework. *International Journal of Consumer Studies*, 48(3), e13053. Advance online publication. 10.1111/ijcs.13053

Nelson, D. (1991). Conditional heteroskedasticity in asset returns: A New Approach. *Econometrica*, 59(2), 347–370. 10.2307/2938260

Ni, H., Wang, S., & Cheng, P. (2021). A hybrid approach for stock trend prediction based on tweets embedding and historical prices. *World Wide Web (Bussum)*, 24(3), 849–868. 10.1007/s11280-021-00880-9

Niinimäki, K., Peters, G., Dahlbo, H., Perry, P., Rissanen, T., & Gwilt, A. (2020). The environmental price of fast fashion. *Nature Reviews. Earth & Environment*, 1(4), 189–200. 10.1038/s43017-020-0039-9

Noerhidajati, S., Purwoko, A. B., Werdaningtyas, H., Kamil, A. I., & Dartanto, T. (2021). Household financial vulnerability in Indonesia: Measurement and determinants. *Economic Modelling*, 96, 433–444. 10.1016/j.econmod.2020.03.02832836621

Nofsinger, J. R. (2012). Household behavior and boom/bust cycles. *Journal of Financial Stability*, 8(3), 161–173. 10.1016/j.jfs.2011.05.004

Normawati, R., Rahayu, S., & Worokinasih, S. (2021). Financial Knowledge, Digital Financial Knowledge, Financial Attitude, Financial Behaviour and Financial Satisfaction on Millennials. *Proceedings of the 1st International Conference on Law, Social Science, Economics, and Education, ICLSSEE 2021*. 10.4108/eai.6-3-2021.2305967

Nüchter, V., Abson, D. J., von-Wehrden, H., & Engler, J.-O. (2021). The concept of resilience in recent sustainability research. *Sustainability (Basel)*, 13(5), 1–21. 10.3390/su13052735

Nurkholik, A. (2023, January 15). R Approach in Digital Financial Literacy Influence Subjective Financial Well-Being. *Revista Mexicana de Economía y Finanzas*, 19(1), 1–20. 10.21919/remef.v19i1.935

Nuryitmawan, T. R. (2023). The Impact of Islamic Fintech on Poverty Alleviation in Indonesia: A Socio-Economic Implications. *Airlangga Journal of Innovation Management*, 4(2), 136–146. 10.20473/ajim.v4i2.49478

Obermeyer, Z., Powers, B., Vogeli, C., & Mullainathan, S. (2019). Dissecting racial bias in an algorithm used to manage the health of populations. *Science*, 366(6464), 447–453. 10.1126/science.aax234231649194

Odinet, C. K. (2021). Fintech Credit and the Financial Risk of AI. *Cambridge Handbook of AI and Law*.

OECD. (2018), Financial Markets, Insurance and Private Pensions: Digitalisation and Finance. OECD. Retrieved From https://web-archive.oecd.org/2018-04-09/473485-financial-markets-insurance-and-pensions-2018.htm

Ofer, Z. (1996). *The pain of paying*. Carnegie Mellon University.

Ohnishi, M. (2021). New Digital Financial Services Offer the Prospect of High Customer Retention–Expectations for The Growing Trend of "Embedded Finance". *A Mitsui & Co. Global Strategic Studies Institute Monthly Report*.

Ouyang, L., Zhang, Y., & Wang, Y. (2020, July). Unified graph embedding-based anomalous edge detection. In *2020 International Joint Conference on Neural Networks (IJCNN)* (pp. 1-8). IEEE.

Ozili, P. K. (2020). Contesting digital finance for the poor. *Digital Policy. Regulation & Governance*, 22(2), 135–151. https://doi.org/10.1108/DPRG-12-2019-0104

Ozili, P. K. (2022). Embedded finance: Assessing the benefits, use case, challenges and interest over time. *Journal of Internet and Digital Economics*, 2(2), 108–123. 10.1108/JIDE-05-2022-0014

Ozili, P. K. (2023). Assessing global interest in decentralized finance, embedded finance, open finance, ocean finance and sustainable finance. *Asian Journal of Economics and Banking*, 7(2), 197–216. 10.1108/AJEB-03-2022-0029

Page, M. J., McKenzie, J., Bossuyt, P., Boutron, I., & Hoffmann, T. (2020). The PRISMA 2020 statement: an updated guideline for reporting systematic reviews. https://doi.org/10.31222/osf.io/v7gm2

Palameta, B., Nguyen, C., Hui, T. S., & Gyarmati, D. (2016), Link between financial confidence and financial outcomes among working-aged Canadians, Social Research and Demonstration Corporation, Retrieved from https://www.canada.ca/content/dam/canada/financial-consumer-agency/migration/eng/resources/researchsurveys/documents/link-confidence-outcomes.pdf

Pal, M., Gupta, H., & Joshi, Y. C. (2021). Social and economic empowerment of women through financial inclusion: Empirical evidence from India. *Equality, Diversity and Inclusion*, 41(2), 294–305. 10.1108/EDI-04-2021-0113

Panos, G. A., & Wilson, J. O. S. (2020, February 9). Financial literacy and responsible finance in the FinTech era: Capabilities and challenges. *European Journal of Finance*, 26(4–5), 297–301. 10.1080/1351847X.2020.1717569

Pantagonia. (2015). Environmental & Social Initiatives 2015. https://www.patagonia.com/on/demandware.static/Sites-patagonia-us-Site/Library-Sites-PatagoniaShared/en_US/PDF-US/patagonia-enviro-initiatives-2015.pdf

Panwar, N. L., Kaushik, S. C., & Kothari, S. (2010). Role of renewable energy sources in environmental protection: A review. *Renewable & Sustainable Energy Reviews*, 15(3), 1513–1524. 10.1016/j.rser.2010.11.037

Park, H., & Kim, J. D. (2020). Transition towards green banking: role of financial regulators and financial institutions. *Asian Journal of Sustainability and Social Responsibility*, *5*(1), 1–25. 10.1186/s41180-020-00034-3

Paston, A., & Harris, M. (2019). FinTech 2.0: Software as the future of payments distribution. *Journal of Payments Strategy & Systems*, 13(3), 226–236. 10.69554/QAMX7766

Patel, S. (2022). Effectiveness of financial education initiatives in India: Impact of programs by governmental and non-governmental entities. *Journal of Financial Education and Research*, 28(3), 189–204.

Patten, D. M., & Zhao, N. (2014). Standalone CSR reporting by U.S. retail companies. *Accounting Forum*, 38(2), 132–144. 10.1016/j.accfor.2014.01.002

Patten, M. D., Ren, Y., & Zhao, N. (2015). Standalone corporate social responsibility reporting in China: An exploratory analysis of its relation to legitimation. *Social and Environmental Accountability Journal*, 35(1), 17–31. 10.1080/0969160X.2015.1007467

Pawłowska, M., Staniszewska, A., & Grzelak, M. (2022). Impact of FinTech on Sustainable Development. *Financial Sciences*, 27(2), 50–66. 10.15611/fins.2022.2.05

Peri, M., Vandone, D., & Baldi, L. (2017). Volatility spillover between water, energy and food. *Sustainability (Basel)*, 9(6), 1–16. 10.3390/su9061071

Pesaran, M. H., Shin, Y., & Smith, R. (1999). Pooled mean group estimation of dynamic heterogeneous panels. *Journal of the American Statistical Association*, 94, 621–634.

Pesaran, M. H., & Smith, R. (1995). Estimating long-run relationships from dynamic heterogeneous panels. *Journal of Econometrics*, 68, 79–113.

Phadermrod, B., Crowder, R. M., & Wills, G. B. (2019). Importance-Performance Analysis based SWOT analysis. *International Journal of Information Management*, 44, 194–203. Advance online publication. 10.1016/j.ijinfomgt.2016.03.009

Piñeiro-Chousaa, J., López-Cabarcosb, M. A., & Ribeiro-Soriano, D. (2020). Does investor attention influence water companies' stock returns? *Technological Forecasting and Social Change*, 158, 1–10. 10.1016/j.techfore.2020.120115

Pissarides, C. A. (2013). Unemployment in the Great Recession. *Economica*, 80(319), 385–403. 10.1111/ecca.12026

Platt, H., & Platt, M. (2008). Financial Distress Comparison Across Three Global Regions. *Journal of Risk and Financial Management*, 1(1), 129–162. 10.3390/jrfm1010129

Pollin, R. (1988). The growth of U.S. household debt: Demand-side influences. *Journal of Macroeconomics*, 10(2), 231–248. 10.1016/0164-0704(88)90060-2

Portugal. (2023). *IMF Staff Country Reports, 2023*(219), 1. 10.5089/9798400246104.002

Prakash, N., Alagarsamy, S., & Hawaldar, A. (2022). Demographic characteristics influencing financial wellbeing: A multigroup analysis. *Managerial Finance*, 48(9/10), 1334–1351. 10.1108/MF-09-2021-0466

Prasad, H., Meghwal, D., & Dayama, V. (2018, December 1). Digital Financial Literacy: A Study of Households of Udaipur. *Journal of Business and Management*, 5, 23–32. 10.3126/jbm.v5i0.27385

Puaschunder, J. (2022). *Advances in Behavioral Economics and Finance Leadership*. Contributions to Economics. 10.1007/978-3-031-15710-3

Puyt, R. W., Lie, F. B., & Wilderom, C. P. M. (2023). The origins of SWOT analysis. *Long Range Planning*, 56(3), 102304. Advance online publication. 10.1016/j.lrp.2023.102304

Qamar, A., Rasheed, N., Kamal, A., Rauf, S., & Nizam, K. (2023, July 30). Factors Affecting Financial Behavior of Millennial Gen Z: Mediating Role of Digital Financial Literacy Integration. *International Journal of Social Science & Entrepreneurship*, 3(3), 330–352. 10.58661/ijsse.v3i3.207

Radin, T. J. (2007). Stakeholders and Sustainability: An Argument for Responsible Corporate Decision-Making. *William and Mary Environmental Law and Policy Review*, 31, 363. https://scholarship.law.wm.edu/wmelpr/vol31/iss2/4

Rahayu, R., Ali, S., Aulia, A., & Hidayah, R. (2022a). The Current Digital Financial Literacy and Financial Behavior in Indonesian Millennial Generation. *Journal of Accounting and Investment*, 23(1), 78–94. 10.18196/jai.v23i1.13205

Rahayu, R., Juita, V., & Rahman, A. (2023). Digital Financial Literacy, Financial Behaviour, and Financial Well-being of Women's in Indonesia. *Proceedings of the International Conference on Entrepreneurship, Leadership and Business Innovation (ICELBI 2022)*, 550–563. https://doi.org/10.2991/978-94-6463-350-4_54

Rahayu, R., Juita, V., & Rahman, A. (2024, January). Digital Financial Literacy, Financial Behaviour, and Financial Well-being of Women's in Indonesia. In *International Conference on Entrepreneurship, Leadership and Business Innovation (ICELBI 2022)* (pp. 550-563). Atlantis Press

Rahayu, R., Juita, V., Rahman, A., Fitriamiranti, S., & Rafles, R. (2022b). The level of digital financial literacy and financial well-being of people in West Sumatra Indonesia. *Operations Management and Information System Studies*, 2(2), 66–76.

Rahman, M., Isa, C. R., Masud, M. M., Sarker, M., & Chowdhury, N. T. (2021). The role of financial behaviour, financial literacy, and financial stress in explaining the financial well-being of B40 group in Malaysia. *Future Business Journal*, 7(1), 52. Advance online publication. 10.1186/s43093-021-00099-0

Rajan, R. G., & Zingales, L. (2003). The great reversals: The politics of financial development in the twentieth century. *Journal of Financial Economics*, 69(1), 5–50. 10.1016/S0304-405X(03)00125-9

Rajdev, A. A., Modhvadiya, T., & Sudra, P. (2020). An analysis of digital financial literacy among college students. *Pacific Business Review International*, 13(5), 32–40. Retrieved from www.pbr.co.in

Ramachandran, N. (2000). *Monitoring Sustainability: Indices and Techniques of Analysis*. Concept Publishing Company.

Rangkuti, F. (2004). *Analisis SWOT Teknik Membedah Kasus Bisnis*. Gramedia Pustaka Utama.

Rani, A., Quddoos, A., Yaseen, M. R., Tabassum, S., & Asif, A. (2021). The Impact of Social Capital on Household Well-being in Pakistan. *Social Indicators Research*, 158(3), 927–946. 10.1007/s11205-021-02717-434456449

Rani, V., & Kumar, J. (2023). Gender differences in FinTech adoption: What do we know, and what do we need to know? *Journal of Modelling in Management*. Advance online publication. 10.1108/JM2-06-2023-0121

Ravikumar, T., Suresha, B., Prakash, N., Vazirani, K., & Krishna, T. (2022, October 14). Digital financial literacy among adults in India: Measurement and validation. *Cogent Economics & Finance*, 10(1), 2132631. Advance online publication. 10.1080/23322039.2022.2132631

Rebai, S., Azaiez, M. N., & Saidane, D. (2016). A multi-attribute utility model for generating a sustainability index in the banking sector. *Journal of Cleaner Production*, 113, 835–849.

Rehman, A., Ma, H., Ahmad, M., Irfan, M., Traore, O., & Chandio, A. A. (2021). Towards environmental Sustainability: Devolving the influence of carbon dioxide emission to population growth, climate change, Forestry, livestock and crops production in Pakistan. *Ecological Indicators*, 125, 107460.

Respati, D. K., Widyastuti, U., Nuryati, T., Musyaffi, A. M., Handayani, B. D., & Ali, N. R. (2023, March 6). How do students' digital financial literacy and financial confidence influence their financial behavior and financial well-being? *Nurture*, 17(2), 40–50. 10.55951/nurture.v17i2.154

Rey-Ares, L., Fernández-López, S., Castro-González, S., & Rodeiro-Pazos, D. (2021, August). Does self-control constitute a driver of millennials' financial behaviors and attitudes? *Journal of Behavioral and Experimental Economics*, 93, 101702. 10.1016/j.socec.2021.101702

Reza, R. (2017). *An investigation of water investment performance: Analysis of the global water industry* [PhD Thesis]. Griffith University. Retrieved from https://research-repository.griffith.edu.au/handle/10072/371256

Reza, R., & Sun, L. (2023). Impact of Gender Diversity on the Board of Directors on the Financial Performance of the Chinese Private Water Companies. In Kunjumuhammed, S. K., & Ramachandran, N. (Eds.), *Future Outlooks on Corporate Finance and Opportunities for Robust Economic Planning* (pp. 68–98). IGI Global. 10.4018/978-1-6684-5342-1.ch004

Reza, R., & Tularam, G. A. (2022). Financial investments in the global water market. In Rafay, A. (Ed.), *Finance for Sustainability in a Turbulent Economy* (pp. 1–25). IGI Global. 10.4018/978-1-6684-5580-7.ch001

Reza, R., Tularam, G. A., & Li, B. (2017). An investigation into the interdependence of global water indices: A VAR analysis. *Applied Economics*, 49(8), 769–796. 10.1080/00036846.2016.1205725

Reza, R., Tularam, G. A., & Li, B. (2018). Returns and volatility of water investments. *Cogent Economics & Finance*, 6(3), 1–33. 10.1080/23322039.2018.1438724

Reza, R., Tularam, G. A., & Li, B. (2021). A review of global research on private investment in the water sector. *Utilities Policy*, 72, 1–16. 10.1016/j.jup.2021.101283

Reza, R., Tularam, G. A., Li, B., & Li, B. (2022). Investments in the Asian water sector: An analysis based on the DCC-GARCH model. *Humanities & Social Sciences Communications*, 9(452), 1–9. 10.1057/s41599-022-01470-4

Richardson, B. (2009). Climate finance and its governance: Moving to a low carbon economy through socially responsible financing? *The International and Comparative Law Quarterly*, 58, 597–626.

Richardson, T., Elliott, P., Roberts, R., & Jansen, M. (2017). A Longitudinal Study of Financial Difficulties and Mental Health in a National Sample of British Undergraduate Students. *Community Mental Health Journal*, 53(3), 344–352. 10.1007/s10597-016-0052-027473685

Roberts, R. W. (1992). Determinants of Corporate Social Responsibility Disclosure. *Accounting, Organizations and Society*, 17, 595–612.

Roca, E. D., & Tularam, G. A. (2012). Which way does water flow? An econometric analysis of the global price integration of water stocks. *Applied Economics*, 44(23), 2935–2944. 10.1080/00036846.2011.568403

Roca, E., Tularam, G. A., & Reza, R. (2015). Fundamental signals of investment profitability in the global water industry. *International Journal of Water*, 9(4), 395–424. 10.1504/IJW.2015.072155

Rompotis, G. G. (2016). Evaluating a new hot trend: The case of water exchange-traded funds. *The Journal of Index Investing*, 6(4), 103–128. 10.3905/jii.2016.6.4.103

Rudin, C., & Radin, J. (2019). Why are we using black box models in AI when we don't need to? A lesson from an explainable AI competition. *Harvard Data Science Review*, 1(2), 1–9. 10.1162/99608f92.5a8a3a3d

Ruggeri, K., Kunz, M., Berkessel, J., Kácha, O., Steinnes, K., Petrova, D., Caavassini, F., Naru, F., & Hardy, E. (2019). The science of behavior and decision-making. In Ruggeri, K. (Ed.), *Behavioral insights for public policy: Concepts and cases* (pp. 59–79). Routledge.

Sabri, M. F., Abd Rahim, H., Wijekoon, R., Zakaria, N. F., Magli, A. S., & Reza, T. S. (2020). The Mediating Effect of Money Attitude on Association Between Financial Literacy, Financial Behaviour, and Financial Vulnerability. *International Journal of Academic Research in Business & Social Sciences*, 10(15). Advance online publication. 10.6007/IJARBSS/v10-i15/8254

Sabri, M. F., Anthony, M., Law, S. H., Rahim, H. A., Burhan, N. A. S., & Ithnin, M. (2023, May 22). Impact of financial behaviour on financial well-being: Evidence among young adults in Malaysia. *Journal of Financial Services Marketing*. Advance online publication. 10.1057/s41264-023-00234-8

Sabri, M. F., Wahab, R., Mahdzan, N. S., Magli, A. S., & Rahim, H. A. (2022). Mediating Effect of Financial Behaviour on the Relationship Between Perceived Financial Wellbeing and Its Factors Among Low-Income Young Adults in Malaysia. *Frontiers in Psychology*, 13, 858630. Advance online publication. 10.3389/fpsyg.2022.85863035664172

Sahooa, S., & Kumar, S. (2024). Volatility spillover among the sectors of emerging and developed markets: A hedging perspective. *Cogent Economics & Finance*, 12(1), 1–17. 10.1080/23322039.2024.2316048

Salisbury, L. C., Nenkov, G. Y., Blanchard, S. J., Hill, R. P., Brown, A. L., & Martin, K. D. (2023). Beyond Income: Dynamic Consumer Financial Vulnerability. *Journal of Marketing*, 87(5), 657–678. 10.1177/00222429221150910

Samitas, A., Papathanasiou, S., Koutsokostas, D., & Kampouris, E. (2022). Are timber and water investments safe-havens? A volatility spillover approach and portfolio hedging strategies for investors. *Finance Research Letters*, 47, 1–10. 10.1016/j.frl.2021.102657

Sardianoua, E., Stauropouloub, A., Evangelinosc, K., & Nikolaou, I. (2021). A materiality analysis framework to assess sustainable development goals of banking sector through sustainability reports. *Sustainable Production and Consumption*, 27, 1775–1793.

Scholtens, B. (2006). Finance as a driver of corporate social responsibility. *Journal of Business Ethics*, 68, 19–33.

Schumpeter, J. (1934). *Theorie der Wirtschaftlichen Entwicklung (The Theory of Economic Development)* (Opie, R., Trans.). Harvard University Press.

Sconti, A. (2022). Having Trouble Making Ends Meet? Financial Literacy Makes the Difference. *Italian Economic Journal*. 10.1007/s40797-022-00212-4

Sehrawat, K., & Vij, M. (2020). Financial Wellbeing Among Public and Private Sector Employees: A Preliminary Study. *Indian Journal of Finance*, 14(1), 9. 10.17010/ijf/2020/v14i1/149855

Seldal, M. M. N., & Nyhus, E. K. (2022, March 7). Financial Vulnerability, Financial Literacy, and the Use of Digital Payment Technologies. *Journal of Consumer Policy*, 45(2), 281–306. 10.1007/s10603-022-09512-935283545

Selvaraj, J. J., Guerrero, D., Cifuentes-Ossa, M. A., & Guzmán Alvis, Á. I. (2022). The economic vulnerability of fishing households to climate change in the south Pacific region of Colombia. *Heliyon*, 8(5), e09425. 10.1016/j.heliyon.2022.e0942535620620

Setiawan, B., Nugraha, D. P., Irawan, A., Nathan, R. J., & Zoltan, Z. (2021). User innovativeness and fintech adoption in indonesia. *Journal of Open Innovation*, 7(3), 188. Advance online publication. 10.3390/joitmc7030188

Setiawan, M., Effendi, N., Santoso, T., Dewi, V. I., & Sapulette, M. S. (2020, August 10). Digital financial literacy, current behavior of saving and spending and its future foresight. *Economics of Innovation and New Technology*, 31(4), 320–338. 10.1080/10438599.2020.1799142

Seymour, G., & Peterman, A. (2018). Context and measurement: An analysis of the relationship between intrahousehold decision making and autonomy. *World Development*, 111, 97–112. 10.1016/j.worlddev.2018.06.027

Shahbaz, M., Hye, Q. M. A., Tiwari, A. K., & Leitao, N. C. (2013). Economic growth, energy consumption, financial development, international trade and CO_2 emissions in Indonesia. *Renewable & Sustainable Energy Reviews*, 25, 109–121.

Shahbaz, M., Nasir, A., & Roubaud, D. (2018). Environmental Degradation in France: The Effects of FDI, Financial Development, and Energy Innovations. *Energy Economics*, 74, 843–857. 10.1016/j.eneco.2018.07.020

Shanmuganathan, M. (2020). Behavioural finance in an era of artificial intelligence: Longitudinal case study of robo-advisors in investment decisions. *Journal of Behavioral and Experimental Finance*, 27, 100297. 10.1016/j.jbef.2020.100297

Sheehy, B. (2005). Scrooge-The Reluctant Stakeholder: Theoretical Problems in the Shareholder-Stakeholder Debate. *University of Miami Business Law Review, 14*, 193. Retrieved from https://repository.law.miami.edu/umblr/vol14/iss1/6

Shefrin, H. M., & Thaler, R. H. (1988). The Behavioral Life-Cycle Hypothesis. *Economic Inquiry*, 26(4), 609–643. 10.1111/j.1465-7295.1988.tb01520.x

Sherraden, M. S., & Ansong, D. (2016). Financial Literacy to Financial Capability: Building Financial Stability and Security. In *International Handbook of Financial Literacy* (pp. 83–96). Springer Singapore. 10.1007/978-981-10-0360-8_7

Sherraden, M. (2013). Building Blocks of Financial Capability. In *Financial Capability and Asset Development* (pp. 3–43). Oxford University Press. 10.1093/acprof:oso/9780199755950.003.0012

Shim, S., Xiao, J. J., Barber, B. L., & Lyons, A. C. (2009, November). Pathways to life success: A conceptual model of financial well-being for young adults. *Journal of Applied Developmental Psychology*, 30(6), 708–723. 10.1016/j.appdev.2009.02.003

Shinu & Mullappallykayamkulath. (2022). Digital Financial Literacy and its Impact on the Financial Behaviour of Millennials: An Empirical Investigation. *International Journal of Financial Management, 12*(3), 10-16. http://publishingindia.com/downloads/7078.pdf

Shin, Y. J., & Choi, Y. (2019). Feasibility of the Fintech Industry as an Innovation Platform for Sustainable Economic Growth in Korea. *Sustainability (Basel)*, 11(19), 5351. 10.3390/su11195351

Shoeibi, S. (2021). Use of clean energy and reduction of environmental pollution in developing countries. *Environmental Research, Engineering and Management*, 77(3). Advance online publication. 10.5755/j01.erem.77.3.29904

Singh, A. (2011). Critical issues influencing the acceptance of mobile banking: Operability, security, and standardization. *Journal of Financial Technology*, 4(2), 112–125.

Singh, K. N., & Malik, S. (2022). An empirical analysis on household financial vulnerability in India: Exploring the role of financial knowledge, impulsivity and money management skills. *Managerial Finance*, 48(9/10), 1391–1412. 10.1108/MF-08-2021-0386

Singh, V. (2022). Dynamics of affordability and immigration in the Canadian housing market. *International Journal of Housing Markets and Analysis*, 15(3), 709–732. 10.1108/IJHMA-04-2021-0037

Smit, B., & Wandel, J. (2006). Adaptation, adaptive capacity and vulnerability. *Global Environmental Change*, 16(3), 282–292. 10.1016/j.gloenvcha.2006.03.008

Smith, J., & Wallraff, M. (2021). Embedded finance: this decade's largest creator of value. *Kore Fusion White Paper.*

Sohn, S., Joo, S., Grable, J. E., Lee, S., & Kim, M. (2012). Adolescents' financial literacy: The role of financial socialization agents, financial experiences, and money attitudes in shaping financial literacy among South Korean youth. *Journal of Adolescence*, 35(4), 969–980. 10.1016/j.adolescence.2012.02.00222418452

Son, J., & Feng, Q. (2019). In Social Capital We Trust? *Social Indicators Research*, 144(1), 167–189. 10.1007/s11205-018-2026-9

Steen, A., Graves, C., D'Alessandro, S., & Shi, H. X. (2023, February 28). Managing digital assets on death and disability: An examination of the determinants of digital asset planning literacy. *Australian Journal of Management*. Advance online publication. 10.1177/03128962231157005

Stiglitz, J. E. (1985). Credit markets and the control of capital. *Journal of Money, Credit and Banking*, 17, 133–152.

Stiglitz, J., & Weiss, A. (1981). Credit rationing in markets with imperfect information. *The American Economic Review*, 71, 393–410.

Stones, R. (2005). *Structuration Theory*. Macmillan Education UK. 10.1007/978-0-230-21364-7

Stulz, R. M. (2000). Financial structure, corporate finance and economic growth. *International Review of Finance*, 1, 11–38.

Su, C.W., Chen, Y., Hu, J., Chang T., & Umar, M. (2022). Can the green bond market enter a new era under the fluctuation of oil price?, *Economic Research-Ekonomska Istraživanja*, 1–26. .10.1080/1331677X.2022.2077794

Sudirman, L., & Disemadi, H. S. (2022). Titik Lemah Industri Keuangan Fintech di Indonesia: Kajian Perbandingan Hukum. *Jurnal Pembangunan Hukum Indonesia*, 4(3), 471–493. Advance online publication. 10.14710/jphi.v4i3.471-493

Sullivan, L., & Meschede, T. (2016). Race, Gender, and Senior Economic Well-Being: How Financial Vulnerability Over the Life Course Shapes Retirement for Older Women of Color. *The Public Policy and Aging Report*, 26(2), 58–62. 10.1093/ppar/prw001

Sultana, S., Zulkifli, N., & Zainal, D. (2018). Environmental, social and governance (ESG) and investment decision in Bangladesh. *Sustainability (Basel)*, 10(6), 1831. 10.3390/su10061831

Sun, L., & Small, G. (2021). Has sustainable investing made an impact in the period of COVID-19?: Evidence from Australian exchange traded funds. *Journal of Sustainable Finance & Investment*, 12, 251–273.

Sun, L., Small, G., Huang, Y.-H., & Ger, T.-B. (2022). Financial Shocks, Financial Stress and Financial Resilience of Australian Households during COVID-19. *Sustainability (Basel)*, 14(7), 3736. 10.3390/su14073736

Sun, S., Chen, Y.-C., Ansong, D., Huang, J., & Sherraden, M. S. (2022). Household Financial Capability and Economic Hardship: An Empirical Examination of the Financial Capability Framework. *Journal of Family and Economic Issues*, 43(4), 716–729. 10.1007/s10834-022-09816-535095251

Sussman, A. B., & O'Brien, R. L. (2016). Knowing When to Spend: Unintended Financial Consequences of Earmarking to Encourage Savings. *JMR, Journal of Marketing Research*, 53(5), 790–803. 10.1509/jmr.14.0455

Swamy, V. (2018). Financial Inclusion And The Resilience Of Poor Households. *Journal of Developing Areas*, 53(4). Advance online publication. 10.1353/jda.2018.0079

Taghizadeh-Hesary, F., & Yoshino, N. (2020). Sustainable solutions for green financing and investment in renewable energy projects. *Energies*, 13(4), 788. Advance online publication. 10.3390/en13040788

Tai, F.-M., & Chuang, S.-H. (2014). Corporate Social Responsibility. *iBusiness, 6*(3), 13-19. 10.4236/ib.2014.63013

Tandon, R. (2016). Provident Fund and Life Insurance: Preferences in tax-saving instruments. *International Journal of Finance and Accounting*, 10(2), 134–148.

Tang, Y. (2021). Corporate finance management in the age of ARTIFICIAL intelligence. *International Journal of Frontiers in Sociology.*

Tarmuji, I., Maelah, R., & Tarmuji, N. H. (2016). The impact of environmental, social and governance practices (ESG) on economic performance: Evidence from ESG score. *International Journal of Trade. Economics and Finance*, 7(3), 67–74.

Teboul, L., & Angelos Anastasiou, A. (2021). The embedded finance journey: innovation that differentiates the customer experience. *A Goldman Sachs report on transaction banking, available at:*https://www. goldmansachs. com/what-we-do/transaction-banking/insights/baas. pdf

The Financial Services Authority (OJK). (2023). *Penyelenggara Fintech Lending Berizin di OJK per 9 Oktober 2023.* Retrieved November 02, 2023, from https://www.ojk.go.id/id/kanal/iknb/financial-technology/Pages/Penyelenggara-Fintech-Lending-Berizin-di-OJK-per-9-Oktober-2023.aspx

Tiffany, L. (2018). Factors influencing mobile banking use: Concerns about technological skills and reliance on colleagues for awareness. *Journal of Consumer Finance*, 12(1), 45–58.

Tiwari, A. K., Adewuyi, A. O., Adeleke, M. A., & Abakah, E. J. A. (2023). A time-varying Granger causality analysis between water stock and green stocks using novel approaches. *Energy Economics*, 126, 1–20. 10.1016/j.eneco.2023.107010

Tokar Asaad, C. (2015, June 30). Financial literacy and financial behavior. *Financial Services Review*, 24(2), 101–117. 10.61190/fsr.v24i2.3236

Tony, N., & Desai, K. (2020). Impact of digital financial literacy on digital financial inclusion. *International Journal of Scientific and Technology Research*, 9(1), 1911–1915.

Torrance, S. (2021). Embedded finance: a $7 trillion game-changing opportunity for incumbents. *A Rainmaking Report, København.*

Tsuji, C. (2016). Does the fear gauge predict downside risk more accurately than econometric models? Evidence from the US stock market. *Cogent Economics & Finance*, 4(1), 1–42. 10.1080/23322039.2016.1220711

Tularam, A., Wong, V., & Roca, E. (2009). An analysis of Australian superannuation funds volatility using EGARCH approach. *Studies in Regional and Urban Planning*, 12, 143–160.

Tularam, G. A., & Marchisella, P. (2014). Water scarcity in Asia and its long-term water and border security implications for Australia. In Clark, R. M., & Hakim, S. (Eds.), *Securing Water and Wastewater Systems* (pp. 189–211). Springer. 10.1007/978-3-319-01092-2_9

Tularam, G. A., & Reza, R. (2016). Water exchange traded funds: A study on idiosyncratic risk using Markov switching analysis. *Cogent Economics & Finance*, 4(1), 1–12. 10.1080/23322039.2016.1139437

Ugurlu-Yildirim, E., & Ordu-Akkaya, B. M. (2022). Does the impact of geopolitical risk reduce with the financial structure of an economy? A perspective from market vs. bank-based emerging economies. *Eurasian Economic Review*, 12, 681–703.

Ulucak, R., & Danish, K. Y. (2020). An assessment of the environmental sustainability corridor: Investigating the non-linear effects of environmental taxation on CO_2 emissions. *Sustainable Development*, 28, 1010–1018.

Umar, M., & Ji, X., & Mirza, N., & Rahat, B., (2021). The impact of resource curse on banking efficiency: Evidence from twelve oil producing countries, *Resources Policy, 72*(C). .10.1016/j.resourpol.2021.102080

Uniliver. (2021). Unilever Sustainable Living Plan 2010 to 2020 Summary of 10 years' progress. https://www.unilever.com/files/92ui5egz/production/16cb778e4d31b81509dc5937001559f1f5c863ab.pdf

United Nations Global Compact. (2018). Integrating the Sustainable Development Goals into Corporate Reporting: A Practical Guide. Retrieved from https://unglobalcompact.org/library/5628

United Nations. (2004). The Global Compact Leaders Summit. Author.

United Nations. (2021). Climate Change Conference (COP26) Glasgow: Mobilise finance. Available at https://ukcop26.org/cop26-goals/finance/

Utkarsh, N., Pandey, A., Ashta, A., Spiegelman, E., & Sutan, A. (2020). Catch them young: Impact of financial socialization, financial literacy and attitude towards money on financial well-being of young adults. *International Journal of Consumer Studies*, 44(6), 531–541. 10.1111/ijcs.12583

Uzunkaya, M. (2012). Economic performance in bank-based and market-based financial systems: Do non-financial institutions matter? *Journal of Applied Finance and Banking*, 2, 159–176.

Van Aelst, K., & Holvoet, N. (2018). Climate change adaptation in the Morogoro Region of Tanzania: Women's decision-making participation in small-scale farm households. *Climate and Development*, 10(6), 495–508. 10.1080/17565529.2017.1318745

Van Nguyen, H., Ha, G. H., Nguyen, D. N., Doan, A. H., & Phan, H. T. (2022). Understanding financial literacy and associated factors among adult population in a low-middle income country. *Heliyon*, 8(6), e09638. 10.1016/j.heliyon.2022.e0963835677404

Vandone, D., Peri, M., Vandone, D., Baldi, L., & Tanda, A. (2018). The impact of energy and agriculture prices on the stock performance of the water industry. *Water Resources and Economics*, 23, 14–27. 10.1016/j.wre.2018.02.002

Varga, D. (2017). *Fintech: Supporting Sustainable Development by Disrupting Finance*. Corvinus University Budapest.

Varga, D. (2018). Triple-Bottom-Line Impact Analysis Framework of Fintech Companies. *Budapest Management Review*, 49(11), 3. 10.14267/VEZTUD.2018.11.03

Vergara, C., & Agudo, F. L. (2021). Fintech and Sustainability: Do They Affect Each Other? *Sustainability (Basel)*, 13(13), 7012. 10.3390/su13137012

Vifell, Å. C., & Soneryd, L. (2012). Organizing matters: How 'the social dimension' gets lost in sustainability projects. *Sustainable Development (Bradford)*, 20(1), 18–27. 10.1002/sd.461

Vlady, A., Roca, E., & Tularam, G. A. (2008). The market value of Australian oil and gas industry and climate change: The VAR, ARCH, GARCH, approaches. *Studies in Regional and Urban Planning*, 11(1), 195–220.

Vo, D. H. (2023). Volatility spillovers across sectors and their magnitude: A sector-based analysis for Australia. *PLoS One*, 18(6), 1–18. 10.1371/journal.pone.028652837262027

Volpe. (1996). Analysis of Personal Financial Literacy Among College Students. *Financial Servies Review, 7*(2), 107-128.

Volz, U. (2018). *Fostering Green Finance For Sustainable Development In Asia*. Available at: www.adbi.org

Wagner, T. D., Mahbub, K., Palomar, E., & Abdallah, A. E. (2019). Cyber threat intelligence sharing: Survey and research directions. *Computers & Security*, 87, 101589. 10.1016/j.cose.2019.101589

Wahbi, A., Sarfo, Y., & Musshoff, O. (2023). Female smallholder farmers' preferences for digital and conventional credit attributes: Evidence from Madagascar. *Agricultural Finance Review*, 83(4/5), 549–571. 10.1108/AFR-01-2023-0008

Walsh, B., & Lim, H. (2020, September). Millennials' adoption of personal financial management (PFM) technology and financial behavior. *Financial Planning Review*, 3(3), e1095. Advance online publication. 10.1002/cfp2.1095

Wang, D., & Schøtt, T. (2022). Coupling between financing and innovation in a startup: Embedded in networks with investors and researchers. *The International Entrepreneurship and Management Journal*, 18(1), 327–347. 10.1007/s11365-020-00681-y

Wang, L., & Chen, J. (2021). Structure optimization of big data financial industry based on 5g network processor and embedded system. *Microprocessors and Microsystems*, 82, 103938. 10.1016/j.micpro.2021.103938

Wang, Y., Xiang, Y., Lei, X., & Zhou, Y. (2022). Volatility analysis based on GARCH-type models: Evidence from the Chinese stock market. *Economic.Ekonomska Istrazivanja*, 35(1), 2530–2554. 10.1080/1331677X.2021.1967771

Warmath, D., Piehlmaier, D., & Robb, C. (2019). The impact of shared financial decision making on overconfidence for married adults. *Financial Planning Review*, 2(1), e1032. Advance online publication. 10.1002/cfp2.1032

Watson, J. J. (2003, December). The relationship of materialism to spending tendencies, saving, and debt. *Journal of Economic Psychology*, 24(6), 723–739. 10.1016/j.joep.2003.06.001

WCED. (Ed.). (1987). *Our Common Future: The World Commission on Environment and Development*. Oxford University Press.

Weiland, S., Hickmann, T., Lederer, M., Marquardt, J., & Schwindenhammer, S. (2021). The 2030 agenda for sustainable development: Transformative change through the sustainable development goals?'. *Politics and Governance*, 9(1), 90–95. 10.17645/pag.v9i1.4191

Werner, M., Wiese, M., & Maas, A. (2021). Embedding process mining into financial statement audits. *International Journal of Accounting Information Systems*, 41, 100514. 10.1016/j.accinf.2021.100514

Winkler, S. (2017). Housing, Finance, Policy and the Wider Economy. *Journal of Management and Sustainability*, 7(2), 45. 10.5539/jms.v7n2p45

World Commission on Environment and Development. (1987). Our Common Future (The Brundtland Report). In *Medicine and War (Vol. 4)*. 10.1080/07488008808408783

World Economic Outlook (WEO) Database. (2023). International Monetary Fund. Groups and Aggregates Information. https://www.imf.org/en/Publications/WEO/weo-database/2023/April/groups-and-aggregates

Worthington, A. C. (2006). Debt as a source of financial stress in Australian households. *International Journal of Consumer Studies*, 30(1), 2–15. 10.1111/j.1470-6431.2005.00420.x

Wu, H.-S. (2022). Constructing Indices and Scales. In *CFDR Workshop Series*. Bowling Green State University.

Wulandari, R. T., & Damayanti, S. M. (2022). The importance of digital financial literacy to anticipate impulsive buying behavior in buy-now-pay-later mode. *International Journal of Business and Economy*, 4(3), 170–182. https://myjms.mohe.gov.my/index.php/ijbec/article/view/19615

Xiao, J. J. (2016). Consumer Financial Capability and Wellbeing. In *Springer eBooks* (pp. 3–17). 10.1007/978-3-319-28887-1_1

Xiao, J. J., & Kumar, S. (2023, June 1). *A Research Agenda for Consumer Financial Behavior*. Edward Elgar Publishing.

Xiao, J. J. (2008). Applying behavior theories to financial behavior. In *Handbook of consumer finance research* (pp. 69–81). Springer. 10.1007/978-0-387-75734-6_5

Xiao, J. J., Huang, J., Goyal, K., & Kumar, S. (2022). Financial capability: A systematic conceptual review, extension and synthesis. *International Journal of Bank Marketing*, 40(7), 1680–1717. 10.1108/IJBM-05-2022-0185

Xie, J., Nozawa, W., Yagi, M., Fujii, H., & Managi, S. (2019). Do environmental, social, and governance activities improve corporate financial performance? *Business Strategy and the Environment*, 28(2), 286–300. 10.1002/bse.2224

Xu, D., Sheraz, M., Hassan, A., Sinha, A., & Ullah, S. (2022). Financial development, renewable energy and CO_2 emission in G7 countries: New evidence from non-linear and asymmetric analysis. *Energy Economics*, 109, 105994.

Xu, F., Uszkoreit, H., Du, Y., Fan, W., Zhao, D., & Zhu, J. (2019). Explainable AI: A brief survey on history, research areas, approaches and challenges. *Natural Language Processing and Chinese Computing: 8th CCF International Conference, NLPCC 2019, Dunhuang, China, October 9–14, 2019Proceedings*, 8(Part II), 563–574.

Xu, X., & Liu, Y. (2023). The association between managerial short-termism and green innovation: The moderating role of firms' digital transformation. *Asia Pacific Journal of Innovation and Entrepreneurship*, 17(3/4), 195–214. 10.1108/APJIE-07-2023-0147

Yadav, M. P., Sharif, T., Ashok, S., Dhingra, D., & Abedin, M. Z. (2023). Investigating volatility spillover of energy commodities in the context of the Chinese and European stock markets. *Research in International Business and Finance*, 65, 1–16. 10.1016/j.ribaf.2023.101948

Yadav, M., & Banerji, P. (2023, May 31). A bibliometric analysis of digital financial literacy. *American Journal of Business*, 38(3), 91–111. 10.1108/AJB-11-2022-0186

Yang, R., Yu, L., Zhao, Y., Yu, H., Xu, G., Wu, Y., & Liu, Z. (2020). Big data analytics for financial Market volatility forecast based on support vector machine. *International Journal of Information Management*, 50, 452–462. 10.1016/j.ijinfomgt.2019.05.027

Yang, S., Zou, K., Lei, T., Ni, Z., & Yang, J. (2022). Climate Change and Farmers' Household Financial Vulnerability: Evidence From China. *Frontiers in Environmental Science*, 10, 908428. Advance online publication. 10.3389/fenvs.2022.908428

Yang, X., & Tang, X. (2021). Does financial structure affect CO_2 emissions? Evidence from G20 countries. *Finance Research Letters*, 41, 101791.

Yazdanparast, A., & Alhenawi, Y. (2022). Impact of COVID-19 pandemic on household financial decisions: A consumer vulnerability perspective. *Journal of Consumer Behaviour*, 21(4), 806–827. 10.1002/cb.203837519436

Yermack, D. (2017). Corporate governance and blockchains. *Review of Finance*, 21(1), 7–31.

Yilmazer, T., Babiarz, P., & Liu, F. (2015). The impact of diminished housing wealth on health in the United States: Evidence from the Great Recession. *Social Science & Medicine*, 130, 234–241. 10.1016/j.socscimed.2015.02.02825728483

Yoon, B., Lee, J. H., & Byun, R. (2018). Does ESG performance enhance firm value? Evidence from Korea. *Sustainability (Basel)*, 10(10), 3635. Advance online publication. 10.3390/su10103635

Younas, J., & Kalimuthu, F. (2019, January 30). Impact of Self-Control, Financial Literacy and Financial Behavior on Financial Well-Being. *The Journal of Social Sciences Research*, 51(51), 211–218. 10.32861/jssr.51.211.218

Yuan, R., Liao, H., & Wang, J. (2022). A nexus study of carbon emissions and financial development in China using the decoupling analysis. *Environmental Science and Pollution Research International*, 29, 88224–88239.35831650

Yu, C. H., Wu, X., Zhang, D., Chen, S., & Zhao, J. (2021). Demand for green finance: Resolving financing constraints on green innovation in China. *Energy Policy*, 153, 112255. 10.1016/j.enpol.2021.112255

Yu, C., Jia, N., Li, W., & Wu, R. (2022). Digital inclusive finance and rural consumption structure – evidence from Peking University digital inclusive financial index and China household finance survey. *China Agricultural Economic Review*, 14(1), 165–183. 10.1108/CAER-10-2020-0255

Yu, H.-C., Hsi, K.-H., & Kuo, P.-J. (2002). Electronic payment systems: An analysis and comparison of types. *Technology in Society*, 24(3), 331–347. 10.1016/S0160-791X(02)00012-X

Zaimovic, A., Torlakovic, A., Arnaut-Berilo, A., Zaimovic, T., Dedovic, L., & Nuhic Meskovic, M. (2023, June 9). Mapping Financial Literacy: A Systematic Literature Review of Determinants and Recent Trends. *Sustainability (Basel)*, 15(12), 9358. 10.3390/su15129358

Zakoian, J. M. (1994). Threshold heteroskedastic models'. *Journal of Economic Dynamics & Control*, 18(5), 931–955. 10.1016/0165-1889(94)90039-6

Zhang, H., Zhao, Y., Wang, F., Zhang, A., Yang, P., & Shen, X. (2018, March). A new evolutionary algorithm based on MOEA/D for portfolio optimization. In *2018 Tenth International Conference on Advanced Computational Intelligence (ICACI)* (pp. 831-836). IEEE. 10.1109/ICACI.2018.8377569

Zhang, Y., Li, X., & Guo, S. (2018). Portfolio selection problems with Markowitz's mean–variance framework: A review of literature. *Fuzzy Optimization and Decision Making*, 17(2), 125–158. 10.1007/s10700-017-9266-z

Zhao, H., & Zhang, L. (2020). Talking money at home: The value of family financial socialization. *International Journal of Bank Marketing*, 38(7), 1617–1634. 10.1108/IJBM-04-2020-0174

Zhao, W., Zhang, G., Yuan, G., Liu, J., Shan, H., & Zhang, S. (2020). The Study on the Text Classification for Financial News Based on Partial Information. *IEEE Access : Practical Innovations, Open Solutions*, 8, 100426–100437. 10.1109/ACCESS.2020.2997969

Zhou, D., Hu, F., Zhu, Q., & Wang, Q. (2022). Regional allocation of renewable energy quota in China under the policy of renewable portfolio standards. *Resources, Conservation and Recycling*, 176, 105904. 10.1016/j.resconrec.2021.105904

Zulaihati, S., & Widyastuti, U. (2020). Determinants of consumer financial behavior: Evidence from households in Indonesia. *Accounting*, 1193–1198. 10.5267/j.ac.2020.9.008

About the Contributors

Lan Sun holds a Ph.D. from Curtin University and Master of Applied Finance and MBA from the University of Newcastle, Australia. She is a Member of CPA Australia and Member of Accounting and Finance Association of Australia and New Zealand. She has above twenty years teaching experience across universities, currently she works in Central Queensland University, and previously she was a Senior Lecturer in University of New England, also worked in the University of Newcastle, Curtin University, and New York University (NYU) Sydney Campus. Her teaching focuses on undergraduate and postgraduate finance, business finance, corporate finance, international finance, accounting and financial management, financial accounting, international accounting and auditing. Her research interests cover asset pricing, market efficiency, fair value, financial reporting quality, earnings management, corporate governance, executive compensation, sustainable finance and investing, financial wellbeing etc. Dr Sun has a track record of over 50 publications including journal articles, book and book chapters, and conference proceedings. She has published high quality research papers in Scopus indexed and SCImago Q1 ranked journals including Journal of Sustainable Finance and Investment, International Journal of Accounting and Information Management, Sustainability, Asian Review of Accounting, Pacific Accounting Review, Australasian Accounting Business and Finance Journal, etc.

* * *

Abubakar Jamilu Baita obtained both degree and masters from the Department of Economics, Bayero University Kano. He currently undergoes a PhD programme in the Faculty of Economics and Business, Universitas Islam Internasional Indonesia. He is also a permanent staff in the Department of Economics, Yusuf Maitama Sule University Kano - Nigeria. He has presented papers in national and international conferences, and published research articles in refereed journals. His research interests include green/climate economics, Islamic finance and financial development.

Diya Biju is a research scholar investigating household financial vulnerability for a more sustainable and inclusive society.

Nabanita Ghosh is an Assistant Professor in the Department of Commerce at CHRIST University, India. She has a doctoral degree from CMR University. She is a member of Institute of Cost Accountants of India. Her interest areas include quality management, cost accounting, artificial intelligence and automation in banking industry.

Laksitha M. Herath earned her Master of Science in Accounting degree at New York University's Stern School of Business and works at Pricewaterhouse Coopers (PwC). Prior to her current endeavor, she gained valuable experience as a program accountant at Enstar Group Limited, a well-known global insurance company, and at Deloitte, a Big Four accounting firm, in Atlanta and New York. Laksitha holds a Bachelor of Arts degree in Accounting from Clark Atlanta University, where she held executive positions in its Toastmasters Club and she and a team of selected classmates won the Deloitte Regional Case Study Competition. She also published two book chapters and an article in a reputable journal. In her leisure time, she enjoys photography, cooking, and quality time with her family and friends.

Siriyama Kanthi Herath is an Associate Professor of Accounting at Clark Atlanta University's School of Business (CAU) and was a Renwick Faculty Fellow at New York University's Stern School of Business in 2022. She earned a Bachelor of Commerce Honors and an MBA from the University of Colombo in Sri Lanka, as well as a Ph.D. and a Master of Commerce Honors in Accounting from the University of Wollongong in Australia. She worked at the University of Lynchburg, Georgia State University and Georgia Institute of Technology before joining CAU. Prior to relocating to the United States, Dr. Herath worked in Australia at the University of Wollongong and Western Sydney University and in Sri Lanka at the University of Ruhuna and the University of Colombo. She holds positions on the editorial boards of multiple academic journals and has contributed over 70 publications to a diverse range of journals. She has published 12 book chapters. Her research areas include Accounting Education, Management Control and Outsourcing, Cost Management, Corporate Governance, Data Analytics, and Sustainability Accounting. She is a Distinguished Toastmaster and served as the President and Treasurer of the Georgia Institute of Technology Toastmasters International Club from 2019 to 2020, the Treasurer of the Emory University Toastmasters International Club from 2019 to 2020, and as an Area Director from 2020 to 2021 in Georgia, United States. Additionally, she possesses the TESOL Professional Certificate from Arizona State University and the Professional Certificate in Google Data Analytics. In her leisure time, she enjoys traveling and gardening.

Lakshmi J. is a dedicated academic professional serving as an Assistant Professor in the Department of Commerce at a prestigious college affiliated with the University of Kerala, India. With a strong background in commerce, she has emerged as a notable figure in the field, particularly focusing on Social enterprises, Cooperatives, Governance and sustainability. Dr. Lakshmi's academic journey includes an extensive research endeavour culminating in her doctoral work, where she delved into the intricate dynamics of the regulatory framework and its impact on the governance of credit cooperatives. Her commitment to advancing knowledge in this domain is reflected in her published patent titled "Indian Cooperative Trade Platform: A grounded model," showcasing her innovative contributions to the field. A seasoned presenter and author, Dr. Lakshmi has actively participated in various international conferences and workshops. She has presented and authored five papers, demonstrating her expertise and engagement in cooperative research. Notable events in her conference portfolio include the ICA Asia Pacific Research Conference in New Castle, Australia, the 10th EURICSE Workshop on Cooperative and Responsible Finance for Development in Trento, Italy, the 33rd World Cooperative Congress and Legal Forum Conference in Seoul, South Korea, and the 16th ICA AP Research Conference in Indonesia. Dr. Lakshmi has also contributed to the 54th UKSCS Conference in Lincoln, UK, and is slated to participate in the ICA Global and European Conference 2023 in Leuven, Belgium. Through her multifaceted involvement in academia, research, and international conferences.

Mamadou Salieu Jallow currently pursues an MA degree in Economics at the Indonesian International Islamic University. He holds a Higher Teachers' Certificate (HTC) from the Gambia College and a BSc degree in Economics from the University of the Gambia in 2016 and 2021 respectively. Previously, Mr. Jallow taught Economics for five years in different schools in the Gambia. He published a research article titled "The impact of macroeconomics variables and bank internal factors on Islamic Banking performance during covid-19 in Indonesia".

Jeswin Jose is a doctoral scholar at CHRIST University, India. He has a Masters degree in Commerce from University of Calicut. His research interest includes digital financial literacy and financial behavior.

About the Contributors

Shellvy Lukito is a junior researcher with a strong inclination for delving into the realm of study. Following the successful completion of her undergraduate studies in Sharia Economics at the SEBI School of Islamic Economics, Indonesia, she decided to pursue further academic endeavours within the realm of research. At present, Shellvy is a recipient of a scholarship as a master's student from the Ministry of Religion of the Republic of Indonesia, pursuing studies at the Faculty of Economics and Business, Indonesia International Islamic University. Shellvy is actively engaged in various writing endeavours, including composing multiple opinion articles for various online mass media platforms in Indonesia. In recent years, she has dedicated herself to pursuing more education with the aim of becoming a researcher, aligning with her personal philosophy encapsulated by the phrase, "If you can't stand the fatigue of study, you will feel poignant of stupidity".

Anand Patil, with 23 years of teaching experience at both graduate and postgraduate levels, as well as three years of industry experience, is a highly accomplished Associate Professor at the School of Business and Management at Christ University in Bangalore. His expertise is in the areas of Accounting, Taxation, and Finance, and he holds an M.Com, an M.Phil., and a Ph.D. in Commerce from Shivaji University, Kolhapur. Dr. Patil is a passionate researcher, having presented papers at national and international conferences and published articles in respected journals and books. He has also chaired numerous national and international conferences and acted as a resource person for the Board of Studies, Board of Examinations, and Consultancy projects for universities and government institutions. He serves as a guiding figure for graduate, postgraduate, and Ph.D. scholars and has supervised and mentored many students in finance and management. In addition to his academic pursuits, Dr. Patil is an active participant in various administrative committees, serving as the Head of the Curriculum Development Committee, Coordinator of IQAC, and External Ph.D. Evaluator. His extensive administrative and industry experience makes him a valuable asset to the academic community.

Rajibur Reza received a PhD in Finance from the Department of Accounting, Finance, and Economics at Griffith University, Australia. His research experience spans over ten years at Griffith University. His primary research interests are in the areas of Banking, corporate governance, financial wellbeing and literacy, housing finance and investment, international finance, and water finance and investment.

Vinod Sharma's 23 years of experience in academics and business, at various managerial levels in India and overseas, have equipped him to be a successful researcher and teacher. His areas of expertise are consumer behaviour, marketing strategy, and marketing research and analytics. He has completed three international projects on business strategy and climate change, and he has authored 6 books and published over 85 articles in journals of international repute. He has conducted numerous research workshops, participated in consulting research projects, and led training sessions on a range of management-related topics in collaboration with FIEO and MSME.

Suhail obtained a Bachelor of Economics from Universitas Pendidikan Indonesia, Bandung, and a Master of Science in Islamic Economics from Universitas Indonesia. Presently, he is enrolled in MA Economics at Universitas Islam Internasional Indonesia. He received an Outstanding Student Award at the Islamic Economics Study Program in 2018. He attended several national and international conferences and published journal articles in highly refereed journals.

Bhavna Taneja has a doctorate in Management and an MBA specializing in marketing and finance. She has over 18 years of teaching experience In premium institutes like Xiss, Xaviers College Ranchi, Birsa Agricultural University, etc. Presently she is associated with Amity University Jharkhand. She has several publications to her name. Dr. Taneja is an active Rotarian and is presently on the board of directors of the Rotary Club of Ranchi. She is a Pranic healer.

Veerta Tantia is an Associate Professor in the Department of Commerce, Christ University, whose expertise lies in the area of finance.

Gurudeo Anand Tularam is a Senior Adjunct Research Fellow At the Griffith University. His research expertise in time series and stochastic calculus methods in business and finance applications.

Index

A

B

C

D

E

F

www.ingramcontent.com/pod-product-compliance
Lightning Source LLC
LaVergne TN
LVHW080639011026
849160LV00014B/1264

* 9 7 9 8 3 6 9 3 4 5 5 0 4 *